The Sacraments

Source of Our Life in Christ

The Didache Series

SEMESTER EDITION

The Didache

[DID-uh-kay]

The *Didache* is the first known Christian catechesis. Written in the first century, the *Didache* is the earliest known Christian writing outside of Scripture. The name of the work, "*Didache*," is indeed appropriate for such a catechesis because it comes from the Greek word for "teaching," and indicates that this writing contains the teaching of the Apostles.

The *Didache* is a catechetical summary of Christian Sacraments, practices, and morality. Though written in the first century, its teaching is timeless. The *Didache* was probably written by the disciples of the Twelve Apostles, and it presents the Apostolic Faith as taught by those closest to Jesus Christ. This series of books takes the name of this early catechesis because it shares in the Church's mission of passing on that same Faith, in its rich entirety, to new generations.

Below is an excerpt from the *Didache* in which we see a clear example of its lasting message, a message that speaks to Christians of today as much as it did to the first generations of the Church. The world is different, but the struggle for holiness is the same. In the *Didache*, we are instructed to embrace virtue, to avoid sin, and to live the Beatitudes of our Lord.

> My child, flee from everything that is evil and everything that is like it. Do not be wrathful, for wrath leads to murder, nor jealous nor contentious nor quarrelsome, for from all these murder ensues.
>
> My child, do not be lustful, for lust leads to fornication, nor a filthy-talker nor a lewd-looker, for from all these adulteries ensue.
>
> My child, do not be an interpreter of omens, since it leads to idolatry, nor an enchanter nor an astrologer nor a magical purifier, nor wish to see them, for from all these idolatry arises.
>
> My child, do not be a liar, for lying leads to theft, nor avaricious nor conceited, for from all these thefts are produced.
>
> My child, do not be a complainer, since it leads to blasphemy, nor self-willed nor evil-minded, for from all these blasphemies are produced.
>
> Be meek, for the meek will inherit the earth.
>
> Be long-suffering and merciful and guileless and peaceable and good, and revere always the words you have heard.[1]

The *Didache* is the teaching of the Apostles and, as such, it is the teaching of the Church. Accordingly, this book series makes extensive use of the most recent comprehensive catechesis provided to us, the *Catechism of the Catholic Church*. The *Didache* series also relies heavily on Sacred Scripture, the lives of the saints, the Fathers of the Church, and the teaching of Vatican II as witnessed by the pontificates of St. John Paul II, Benedict XVI, and Francis.

1. Swett, Ben H. "The Didache (The Teaching)." © January 30, 1998. http://bswett.com/1998-01Didache.html

The Sacraments

Source of Our Life in Christ

Author and General Editor: Rev. James Socias

MIDWEST THEOLOGICAL FORUM
Downers Grove, Illinois

Published in the United States of America by

Midwest Theological Forum
4340 Cross Street, Suite 1
Downers Grove, IL 60515

Tel: 630-739-9750
Fax: 331-777-5819
mail@mwtf.org
www.theologicalforum.org

Author and General Editor: Rev. James Socias

Editor in Chief: Jeffrey Cole

Editorial Board: Rev. James Socias, Rev. Peter V. Armenio, Dr. Scott Hahn, Jeffrey Cole

Other Contributors: Rev. Fred Gatschet and Gerry Korson

Design and Production: Marlene Burrell, Jane Heineman of April Graphics, Highland Park, Illinois

Acknowledgements

Excerpts from the English translation of the *Catechism of the Catholic Church* for the United States of America, copyright ©1994, United States Catholic Conference, Inc.—Libreria Editrice Vaticana. Used with permission.

Excerpts from the English translation of the *Catechism of the Catholic Church: Modifications from the Editio Typica*, copyright ©1997, United States Catholic Conference, Inc.—Libreria Editrice Vaticana. Used with permission.

Scripture quotations are adapted from the *Revised Standard Version of the Bible*, copyright ©1946, 1952, 1971, and the *New Revised Standard Version of the Bible*, copyright ©1989, by the Division of Christian Education of the National Council of the Churches of Christ in the United States of America, and are used by permission. All rights reserved.

Excerpts from the *Code of Canon Law, Latin/English Edition*, are used with permission, copyright ©1983 Canon Law Society of America, Washington, DC.

Citations of official Church documents from Neuner, Josef, SJ and Dupuis, Jacques, SJ, eds., *The Christian Faith: Doctrinal Documents of the Catholic Church*, 5th ed. (New York: Alba House, 1992). Used with permission.

Excerpts from *Vatican II: The Conciliar and Post Conciliar Documents, New Revised Edition* edited by Austin Flannery, OP, copyright ©1992, Costello Publishing Company, Inc., Northport, NY, are used with permission of the publisher, all rights reserved. No part of these excerpts may be reproduced, stored in a retrieval system, or transmitted in any form or by any means—electronic, mechanical, photocopying, recording or otherwise, without express written permission of Costello Publishing Company.

Disclaimer: The editor of this book has attempted to give proper credit to all sources used in the text and illustrations. Any miscredit or lack of credit is unintended and will be corrected in the next edition.

Library of Congress Cataloging-in-Publication Data
Socias, James.
    The Sacraments : source of our life in Christ / James Socias ; general editor, James Socias. – 1st ed.
       p. cm. – (The Didache series)
    Includes bibliographical references and index.
    ISBN 978-1-890177-92-8 (hardcover : alk. paper)
    1. Sacraments – Catholic Church. 2. Catholic Church – Doctrines. 3. Catholic Church – Liturgy.
  4. Christian life – Catholic authors. I. Title.
BX2200.S59 2009
264'.02 – dc22

                        2009017362

TABLE OF CONTENTS

The Crucifixion by Bernardo Daddi, ca. 1340

TABLE OF CONTENTS

TABLE OF CONTENTS

TABLE OF CONTENTS

TABLE OF CONTENTS

ABBREVIATIONS USED FOR THE BOOKS OF THE BIBLE

OLD TESTAMENT

Genesis	Gn	Tobit	Tb	Ezekiel	Ez
Exodus	Ex	Judith	Jdt	Daniel	Dn
Leviticus	Lv	Esther	Est	Hosea	Hos
Numbers	Nm	1 Maccabees	1 Mc	Joel	Jl
Deuteronomy	Dt	2 Maccabees	2 Mc	Amos	Am
Joshua	Jos	Job	Jb	Obadiah	Ob
Judges	Jgs	Psalms	Ps	Jonah	Jon
Ruth	Ru	Proverbs	Prv	Micah	Mi
1 Samuel	1 Sm	Ecclesiastes	Eccl	Nahum	Na
2 Samuel	2 Sm	Song of Songs	Sg	Habakkuk	Hb
1 Kings	1 Kgs	Wisdom	Wis	Zephaniah	Zep
2 Kings	2 Kgs	Sirach	Sir	Haggai	Hg
1 Chronicles	1 Chr	Isaiah	Is	Zechariah	Zec
2 Chronicles	2 Chr	Jeremiah	Jer	Malachi	Mal
Ezra	Ezr	Lamentations	Lam		
Nehemiah	Neh	Baruch	Bar		

NEW TESTAMENT

Matthew	Mt	Ephesians	Eph	Hebrews	Heb
Mark	Mk	Philippians	Phil	James	Jas
Luke	Lk	Colossians	Col	1 Peter	1 Pt
John	Jn	1 Thessalonians	1 Thes	2 Peter	2 Pt
Acts of the Apostles	Acts	2 Thessalonians	2 Thes	1 John	1 Jn
Romans	Rom	1 Timothy	1 Tm	2 John	2 Jn
1 Corinthians	1 Cor	2 Timothy	2 Tm	3 John	3 Jn
2 Corinthians	2 Cor	Titus	Ti	Jude	Jude
Galatians	Gal	Philemon	Phlm	Revelation	Rev

GENERAL ABBREVIATIONS

AG   *Ad Gentes Divinitus* (Decree on the Church's Missionary Activity)

CA   *Centesimus Annus* (On the Hundredth Anniversary)

CCC   *Catechism of the Catholic Church*

CDF   Congregation for the Doctrine of the Faith

CIC   Code of Canon Law (*Codex Iuris Canonici*)

CPG   *Solemn Profession of Faith*: Credo of the People of God

CT   *Catechesi Tradendæ* (On Catechesis in our Time)

DCE   *Deus Caritas Est* (God is Love)

DD   *Dies Domini* (The Lord's Day)

DH   *Dignitatis Humanæ* (Declaration on Religious Freedom)

DoV   *Donum Vitæ* (Respect for Human Life)

DV   *Dei Verbum* (Dogmatic Constitution on Divine Revelation)

DS   Denzinger-Schonmetzer, *Enchiridion Symbolorum, definitionum et declarationum de rebus fidei et morum* (1985)

EV   *Evangelium Vitæ* (The Gospel of Life)

FC   *Familiaris Consortio* (On the Family)

GS   *Gaudium et Spes* (Pastoral Constitution on the Church in the Modern World)

HV   *Humanæ Vitæ* (On Human Life)

IOE   *Iura et Bona* (Declaration on Euthanasia)

LE   Laborem Exercens (On Human Work)

LG   *Lumen Gentium* (Dogmatic Constitution on the Church)

MF   *Mysterium Fidei* (The Mystery of Faith)

PH   *Persona Humana* (Declaration on Sexual Ethics)

PL   J.P. Migne, ed., *Patrologia Latina* (Paris: 1841-1855)

PT   *Pacem in Terris* (On Establishing Universal Peace)

QA   *Quadragesimo Anno* (The Fortieth Year)

RP   *Reconciliatio et Pænitentia* (On Reconciliation and Penance)

RH   *Redemptor Hominis* (The Redeemer of Man)

SC   *Sacrosanctum Concilium* (The Constitution on the Sacred Liturgy)

SRS   *Sollicitudo Rei Socialis* (On Social Concerns)

SS   *Spe Salvi* (In Hope We Are Saved)

USCCB   United States Conference of Catholic Bishops

VS   *Veritatis Splendor* (Splendor of the Truth)

Foreword

What are the Sacraments? Why are they important? From the beginning, God desired to share his friendship and his divine life with his people. Although our first parents lost this intimate communion with their Creator, God did not abandon them. Rather, he promised a Redeemer, who would one day reconcile God and man. His plan of salvation was gradually unfolded through the covenants of the Old Testament and reached its fulfillment with the Incarnation of Jesus Christ—true God and true man.

Through his life, Passion, Death, and Resurrection, Jesus Christ merited the Redemption of all people and made possible our reconciliation with God. He founded the Church to continue his salvific ministry until he comes again and entrusted the Church with the Seven Sacraments as a primary means of continuing this ministry throughout the ages. In the sacraments, the faithful receive God's grace and assistance, and are privileged to have a personal encounter with Jesus Christ.

> **"The sacraments are efficacious signs of grace, instituted by Christ and entrusted to the Church, by which divine life is dispensed to us" (CCC 1131).**

The primary aim of religious education is to lead the student into an intimate relationship with Jesus Christ, who is "the key, the center and the purpose of the whole of human history" (*GS* 10). It is my hope that this text will lead all who read it toward a fuller understanding of the sacramental mysteries of the Church and a more intimate encounter with Christ in the Sacraments and the liturgical life of the Church. I warmly recommend *The Sacraments: Source of Our Life in Christ* for use by high schools, parishes, and Catholic families. Readers of this text will find a treasure of information about the meaning and the importance of the Sacraments.

Bishop Thomas J. Paprocki
Auxiliary Bishop of Chicago

Introduction

POPE BENEDICT XVI TO THE YOUTH ON THE IMPORTANCE OF THE SACRAMENTS IN THE CHRISTIAN LIFE

Just as he once encountered the young Paul, Jesus also wants to encounter each one of you, my dear young people. Indeed, even before we desire it, such an encounter is ardently desired by Jesus Christ. But perhaps some of you might ask me: How can I meet him today? Or rather, in what way does he approach me?

The Church teaches us that the desire to encounter the Lord is already a fruit of his grace. When we express our faith in prayer, we find him even in times of darkness because he offers himself to us. Persevering prayer opens the heart to receive him, as St. Augustine explains: "Our Lord and God…wants our desire to be exercised in prayer, thus enabling us to grasp what he is preparing to give" (*Letter* 130: 8, 17). Prayer is the gift of the Spirit that makes us men and women of hope, and our prayer keeps the world open to God (cf. *Spe Salvi*, n. 34).

Make space for prayer in your lives! To pray alone is good, although it is even more beautiful and fruitful to pray together, because the Lord assured us he would be present wherever two or three are gathered in his name (cf. Mt 18: 20). There are many ways to become acquainted with him. There are experiences, groups and movements, encounters and courses in which to learn to pray and thus grow in the experience of faith.

Take part in your parish liturgies and be abundantly nourished by the word of God and your active participation in the Sacraments. As you know, the summit and centre of the life and mission of every believer and every Christian community is the Eucharist, the sacrament of salvation in which Christ becomes present and gives his Body and Blood as spiritual food for eternal life. A truly ineffable mystery! It is around the Eucharist that the Church comes to birth and grows—that great family of Christians which we enter through Baptism, and in which we are constantly renewed through the Sacrament of Reconciliation.

The baptised, through Confirmation, are then confirmed in the Holy Spirit so as to live as authentic friends and witnesses of Christ. The Sacraments of Holy Orders and Matrimony enable them to accomplish their apostolic duties in the Church and in the world. Finally, the Sacrament of the Sick grants us an experience of divine consolation in illness and suffering.

—Pope Benedict XVI, Message for the 24th World Youth Day: Palm Sunday 2009.

Photo: At the end of the Palm Sunday Eucharistic Concelebration in St. Peter's Square, the World Youth Day Cross and the Icon of Our Lady were passed on from the youth of Sydney to those of Madrid for World Youth Day 2011.

The Sacraments
Source of Our Life in Christ

Introduction

*Through the grace transmitted to us through Christ in the sacraments,
we are formed into the image of Christ.*

The Sacraments
Source of Our Life in Christ

Introduction

All authority in heaven and on earth has been given to me. Go therefore and make disciples of all nations, baptizing them in the name of the Father and of the Son and of the Holy Spirit, teaching them to observe all that I have commanded you; and lo, I am with you always, to the close of the age. (Mt 28:18-20)

Forty days after his Resurrection, Jesus Christ came to his disciples who had gathered on a mountain and issued them a single command before he ascended into Heaven. It is of no little significance that this final instruction contains a twofold message. First, Jesus told his followers to spread the Good News: that God so loved the world that he sent his only Son to live with us, die for us, and conquer sin by rising from the dead so that we may know God and share in his eternal life. The second part of the command instructs the Apostles to baptize, "in the name of the Father, and of the Son, and of the Holy Spirit,"[1] those who, through the power of the Holy Spirit, have come to believe in Jesus Christ.

In this command, Jesus was telling his followers two things. First, the necessity of spreading God's word of salvation to all people and indeed to the ends of the earth; and secondly, that Jesus alone is the way for all humanity to achieve eternal salvation and happiness.

Uniting us by faith and Baptism to the Passion and Resurrection of Christ, the Spirit makes us sharers in his life. (CCC 2017)

In instructing his Apostles to baptize, Christ was providing the way for those who come to believe in him to enter into the mystery of his own life. Here, at the very moment of Christ's physical departure from the earth, he provides a guide with which his believers may continue to encounter him in a real way.

It was God's plan that his reconciliation with mankind be accomplished through Jesus Christ. However, the work of Christ's redemption did not end with his Ascension into Heaven. It was just the beginning. Jesus founded his Church, the Body of Christ, to continue his saving work, and through the sacraments, and with the other means of sanctification that he bestowed on the Church, Christ continues to convey the grace of God until he comes again.

Our goal in this study of the sacraments is to come to a clear understanding as to the terms and definitions of the sacraments, and at the same time to apply them to our lived experiences as Christians. In other words, we will study the theology of the sacraments in a clear and systematic way, and then apply what we have learned to the pastoral situations in which the sacraments are celebrated and lived in the lives of the faithful.

IN THIS CHAPTER, WE WILL ADDRESS SEVERAL QUESTIONS:

✣ What is a sacrament? How and when were the sacraments established? How are they celebrated?

✣ How is Christ present in the world, and how does he act in our lives?

✣ How are the sacraments an "encounter" with Jesus Christ that transforms us?

✣ Why do we need the sacraments in the Christian life?

God Creates Man by Michelangelo.
God loves his creation more than we can imagine.

THE ROLE OF GRACE IN SALVATION HISTORY

We look to the *Catechism of the Catholic Church* to find out more about the Sacraments—also called "Mysteries" in the Eastern Rites of the Catholic Church, which are celebrated in a similar but not essentially different way. The Sacraments are:

> Efficacious signs of grace, instituted by Christ and entrusted to the Church, by which divine life is dispensed to us. The visible rites by which the sacraments are celebrated signify and make present the graces proper to each sacrament. They bear fruit in those who receive them with the required dispositions. (CCC 1131)

Let us start with a question absolutely central to any inquiry into the sacraments: What is grace? Perhaps the easiest way to begin to think about grace is to understand it as a gift given to us by God.

God loves his creation more than we can imagine, and that love, being perfect love, cannot simply be a conceptual love, but a love which seeks to intervene in the lives of those he loves. Grace is the active power of that love, a love that wishes to intercede in our lives and help us. Grace describes the aid and comfort God gives us so that we may learn to love him more, and by loving him, do his will.

The Second Letter of St. Peter explains how being a recipient of the gift of God's grace enables us to participate in a special way in God's divine life:

> His divine power has granted to us all things that pertain to life and godliness, through the knowledge of him who called us to his own glory and excellence, by which he has granted to us his precious and very great promises, that through these you may escape from the corruption that is in the world because of passion, and become partakers of the divine nature. (2 Pt 1: 3-4)

God Creates Woman by Michelangelo.
Grace is the active power of God's love.

ADAM AND EVE AND THE FIRST SIN

To look at the history of mankind through the Scriptures is to encounter a similar story about the grace of God again and again. Man turns away from God, and God reaches out to man to bring him back to God.

In his plan of creation, God made all things as an expression of his divine love. Mankind, as the culminating act of creation, was made in the image and likeness of God. That is to say, Adam and Eve were created with intelligence, self-knowledge, the ability to reason and love, and the freedom to choose and were the only creatures able to know and love their Creator and to be called to share in his life.[2] Divine Revelation informs us that, before Original Sin, our first parents enjoyed a state of original holiness and justice, and "from their friendship with God flowed the happiness of their existence in paradise."[3] This state of original holiness enjoyed by our first parents meant that Adam and Eve shared in the divine life of God, and, through original justice, there was an inner harmony between man and woman, and between them and all of creation.[4]

> The "mastery" over the world that God offered man from the beginning was realized above all within man himself: *mastery of self*. The first man was unimpaired and ordered in his whole being because he was free from the triple concupiscence[5] that subjugates him to the pleasures of the senses, covetousness for earthly goods, and self-assertion, contrary to the dictates of reason. (CCC 377)

Adam and Eve in the Garden of Eden by Jan Brueghel the Elder.
The Book of Genesis opens with a vision of the Garden of Eden, a place where the first man and the first woman were to live that original partnership in the creation and stewardship of the world envisioned by God.

Their intended role was to participate with God in his Creation and to share in his friendship. The Book of Genesis opens with a vision of the Garden of Eden, a place where the first man and the first woman were to live that original partnership in the creation and stewardship of the world envisioned by God.

However, Adam and Eve misused their free will to disobey God. By disobeying God's single command to not eat of the Tree of Knowledge of Good and Evil, Adam and Eve gave into the temptation of making themselves the arbiters of good and evil, choosing to place themselves at the center of Creation. In saying "No" to God, they ruptured their friendship with him and disrupted the harmony of Creation. Through this first sin, called Original Sin, our first parents lost the original holiness and justice in which they had been created, not only for themselves, but for all of their descendents.[6] All sin finds its origin in this act of disobedience to God's will.

> Adam and Eve transmitted to their descendants human nature wounded by their own first sin and hence deprived of original holiness and justice; this deprivation is called "original sin." (CCC 417)

But as we know, this is not the end of the story, but rather the beginning. Although Adam and Eve sought to abandon God, God did not abandon his children. In the Scriptures, we see how throughout the history that unfolds after the "fall of man", God reaches out to individuals, seeking to restore his relationship with humanity and urging us towards obedience. In fact, immediately after Adam and Eve committed the first sin, God set in motion his plan for bringing about the restoration of the damage caused by that sin.

We read in Genesis that at the moment of their disobedience, God promised our first parents a Redeemer, who would reconcile mankind with himself:

> I will put enmity between you [Satan] and the woman, and between your seed and her seed; he shall bruise your head, and you shall bruise his heel. (Gn 3:15)

In this passage, which has come to be known as the *Protoevangelium*, or first Gospel, we see the first prophecy of a Messiah. Knowing the full story of the coming of Christ, we can recognize in these words a prophesy of Our Lady, the Blessed Virgin Mary, whose Son, Jesus Christ, came to destroy the effects of sin. However, at that moment in history, mankind was not yet ready for the promised Redeemer. God needed to prepare the way for the eventual triumph of his Son.

GOD CONTINUES TO LEAD HUMANITY BACK TO HIM

The history of this preparation is the history of God's saving grace active in the world. It is the story of the all-powerful, ever-living God humbling himself to place his power at the service of his Creation. It is also the story of a Father leading his children back to him through an abundant outpouring of his grace. The all-loving God does not limit his grace to those who know him or love him. Everyone who is alive cannot help but be the recipient of graces because God knows no limit to the active power of his love.

In Sacred Scripture, we read that through Abraham, God established a special covenantal relationship with his people, promising them the land of Canaan. Through Isaac, he established the twelve tribes of Israel. In choosing Moses, God gave his people the Commandments, setting down in written language the divine moral order, the Law of God.

When God's people failed to keep his law, he sent prophets to bring them back to his chosen path. These prophets spoke to the people about God's plan of a promised Messiah.

> The Lord himself will give you a sign. Behold, a young woman [virgin] shall conceive and bear a son, and shall call his name Immanuel. (Is 7:14)

In these prophesies and through the covenants which God made with his people in the Old Testament, we see how he prepared humanity for the coming of his Son.

IN THE COVENANT THAT HE ESTABLISHED, GOD MADE THREE PROMISES TO ABRAHAM:

1. *Go from your country and your kindred and your father's house to the land that I will show you. (Gn 12:1)*

2. *I will make of you a great nation, and I will bless you, and make your name great, so that you will be a blessing. (Gn 12:2)*

3. *I will bless those who bless you, and him who curses you I will curse; and by you all the families of the earth shall bless themselves. (Gn 12:3)*

1. God's promise of a land and a nation was fulfilled in Moses.

2. His promise of Kingship and a name was fulfilled in David.

3. His promise of a Blessing for all nations was fulfilled in Jesus Christ.

The Three Angels Appearing to Abraham by Tiepolo.

The Annunciation by Fra Angelico.
In this "Yes" of Mary, the Only-Begotten Son of God, the Eternal Word, became Incarnate.

MARY'S "YES" TO GOD'S PLAN OF SALVATION

In the same way that God had interceded in the lives of so many of the figures of the Old Testament, the New Testament opens with God choosing a young woman to play a vital role in his plan of salvation for mankind. However, unlike our first parents who said "No," unlike Abraham who disbelieved, unlike Moses who hesitated, Mary responded:

> **Let it be to me according to your word.** (Lk 1: 38)

In this "Yes" of Mary, the Only-Begotten Son of God, the Eternal Word, became Incarnate. It was in him, before the foundation of the world, that the Father had chosen us and predestined us to become his adopted sons and daughters. It was Jesus who would re-establish all things, repairing the damage of sin, and restoring God's original plan of Creation. It was Christ who would perfectly fulfill the will of the Father, establishing the Kingdom of Heaven on earth and revealing to mankind the eternal mysteries of God. It was by his obedience that mankind's redemption was to be achieved.[7]

In his life, Jesus showed us the way to human perfection. In his teachings, Jesus perfected the Old Commandments with the Commandment of Love. In his Death and Resurrection, Christ gave us the perfect atonement for sin. It is in the sacrifice of Christ that man's reconciliation with the Father can be accomplished, and it is through the merits of Jesus Christ that we can have the forgiveness of sins. Christ is our way to salvation. If we define a sacrament as an outward sign conveying grace, then Christ is the living sacrament of God, for it is only through Christ that we can receive God's grace.

CHRIST FOUNDS THE CHURCH AS AN INSTRUMENT OF GRACE

When he had accomplished his salvific mission on earth, Christ ascended into Heaven, where he took his place at the right hand of the Father. It was with us in mind that Christ founded his Church to continue both his message and his saving actions on earth until he comes again. He granted the Apostles his own divine authority, telling them to teach and baptize all nations in the name of the Father and of the Son and of the Holy Spirit.

Although at the moment of his Ascension into Heaven, Christ commanded the Apostles to spread the Good News, the Apostles did not, at first, set out to accomplish this mission. Rather, they huddled together in the upper room in Jerusalem, unsure of what to do next. Their beloved leader had risen from the dead, but was now gone again.

But as we read in the Acts of the Apostles, God intervened yet again, sending his Holy Spirit, as Jesus had promised, to fill the Apostles with the grace and courage necessary to go out into the world and accomplish their great mission. At the Jewish feast of Pentecost, St. Peter preached to the multitudes visiting Jerusalem, telling them to repent and to be baptized for the forgiveness of sins. That day, three thousand responded to Christ's message and were baptized. Their numbers grew daily, and, with the guidance of the Apostles, these new believers met in the Temple for prayer and in their homes for the breaking of the bread. The presence of the sacraments in the life of the Church from the very beginning is a strong indication of the vast importance they play in the lives of the faithful.

It was God's plan that his reconciliation with mankind be accomplished through Jesus Christ. However, this Redemption of Christ did not end with his Ascension into Heaven. It was just the beginning. Jesus founded his Church, the Mystical Body of Christ, to continue his saving work until he comes again. Through the assistance of the Holy Spirit, the Church continues the mission of Jesus Christ, conveying the grace of God through the sacraments, which he established.

> From the beginning to the end of time, whenever God sends his Son, he always sends his Spirit: their mission is conjoined and inseparable. (CCC 743)

In the celebration of the sacraments, the mystery of salvation is made effective through the power of the Holy Spirit.

THE CHURCH CONTINUES THE SAVING ACTIONS OF CHRIST THROUGH THE SACRAMENTS, WHICH HE INSTITUTED.

BAPTISM: *Go therefore and make disciples of all nations, baptizing them in the name of the Father and of the Son and of the Holy Spirit. (Mt 28:19)*

CONFIRMATION: *And when Paul had laid his hands upon them, the Holy Spirit came on them. (Acts 19:6)*

EUCHARIST: *Take, eat; this is my body...Drink of it, all of you; for this is my blood of the covenant, which is poured out for many for the forgiveness of sins. (Mt 26:26-28)*

PENANCE: *If you forgive the sins of any, they are forgiven. (Jn 20:23)*

MATRIMONY: *What therefore God has joined together, let not man put asunder. (Mk 10:9)*

HOLY ORDERS: *Do this in remembrance of me. (Lk 22:19)*

ANOINTING OF THE SICK: *And let them pray over him, anointing him with oil in the name of the Lord. (Jas 5:14)*

Institution of the Eucharist by Poussin. Like Christ himself, his Mystical Body the Church is a sacrament, a sign which conveys grace. Sacraments are the actions of Jesus Christ made present in our lives.

In this sacramental dispensation of Christ's mystery the Holy Spirit...prepares the Church to encounter her Lord; he recalls and makes Christ manifest to the faith of the assembly. By his transforming power, he makes the mystery of Christ present here and now. (CCC 1092)

The Spirit and the Church cooperate to manifest Christ and his work of salvation in the liturgy. Primarily in the Eucharist, and by analogy in the other sacraments, the liturgy is the *memorial* of the mystery of salvation.[8] (CCC 1099)

Like Christ himself, the Church is a sacrament, a sign which conveys grace, and it is in the sacraments of the Church, and in the very life of the Church herself, where the believer can have a personal encounter with Jesus Christ. It is Christ himself who creates us anew in Baptism, who forgives our sins in Confession, and who gives us the spiritual nourishment of his own Body and Blood in the Eucharist. Sacraments are the actions of Jesus Christ made present in our lives through the Holy Spirit, and it is from these sacraments that Christians receive the grace of God to live their Christian vocation. For this reason, the Church is the Sacrament of our communion with the Blessed Trinity (cf. CCC 774).

Christ's work in the liturgy is sacramental: because his mystery of salvation is made present there by the power of his Holy Spirit; because his Body, which is the Church, is like a sacrament (sign and instrument) in which the Holy Spirit dispenses the mystery of salvation; and because through her liturgical actions the pilgrim Church already participates, as by a foretaste, in the heavenly liturgy. (CCC 1111)

SACRAMENTS: TRANSFORMING ACTIONS OF CHRIST

Grace is our sharing in the divine life of God. It is God giving himself to us. Through this free and undeserved help that God gives us, we are enabled to respond to his call to become his children. But how does God give us this grace? He does so primarily through the sacraments that Christ established in the Church. The word "sacrament" is derived from the Latin word *sacramentum*. In ancient Rome, the *sacramentum* was the initiation oath taken by soldiers upon entering the Roman army in which they pledged allegiance to the emperor and promised to devote their lives to the empire and their fellow soldiers. No longer ordinary citizens, they were transformed into something greater than themselves with a mission vital to the Roman Empire.

Like the Roman soldiers, Catholics too believe that the sacraments signify our transformation into something different. However, more than simply a human oath, Christian sacraments not only signify that transformation but also convey supernatural grace which allows that transformation to take place. Through the grace transmitted to us through Christ in the sacraments we are formed into the *imago Christi*, the image of Christ. We are incorporated into the Church, the Mystical Body of Christ, with a mission to transform all of God's Creation. This is to say the sacraments are not merely signs but efficacious signs; that is, they are signs in which Christ himself is at work.[9]

SACRAMENTS AS SIGNS

As human beings, we are comprised of body and soul, and each depends upon the other. Without the body and the material information that we receive from our senses, we cannot learn, develop our intellect, or grow in a meaningful way. Our participation in creation, the choices that we make, our relationships, and our being itself, depend on the material.

Signs and symbols also occupy an important place in human life. Not only do we need signs and symbols in order to communicate and understand the world around us, but we approach our understanding of the spiritual world through physical signs and symbols. Therefore, when God wants us to know him, he appeals to us through our senses.

One could say that creation itself is sacramental. Since the beginning of the universe, God has always acted through material reality. Each time that God manifested himself or intervened in the course of humanity, he did so in a physical way that could be comprehended by mankind. This use of a physical sign was central to the covenants that God made with his people in the Old Testament (Noah and the rainbow, Abraham and circumcision, Moses and the tablets).

Likewise, in the institution of the sacraments, Christ employed a *material* or *physical sign*, which was to be used as a channel of God's grace. In fact, each of the Seven Sacraments has a material element that is central to the nature of the sacrament.

Through the eyes of faith, we can see the reality of God behind signs, and we can come to a better understanding of him through his Creation. This way of seeing God occurs more than we realize. How often does a believer in God see the beauty of a sunrise, the architectural genius of a strand of DNA, or the love of a parent and child and recognize the reality of God? At the same time, a nonbeliever may see nothing but the sign itself.

Understood in this way, the appearance of Christ was a sacramental sign. While the world saw a newborn baby lying in the poverty of a manger, the Magi saw the King of the Jews and came bearing gifts. St. Thomas Aquinas put it eloquently in his well-known hymn of the Eucharist, *Adoro Te Devote*, when he said "On the cross was veiled thy Godhead's splendor."

MATERIAL SIGNS USED IN THE SACRAMENTS

BAPTISM – water

CONFIRMATION – Sacred Chrism (oil)

EUCHARIST – wheat bread and grape wine

RECONCILIATION AND PENANCE – oral confession

HOLY ORDERS – the laying on of hands

MARRIAGE – exchange of vows and consummation

ANOINTING OF THE SICK – oil and laying on of hands

Sacred Chrism

The *Adoro Te Devote* also speaks of the Eucharist, singing "here thy manhood lies hidden too." In his lyric, St. Thomas Aquinas draws a connection between the faith required of the Apostles to see the divinity of Christ where every appearance indicated a mere man, and the faith required in the sacraments, where not only the divinity of Christ is hidden, but his humanity as well. While the physical eyes see nothing more than mere bread, the eyes of faith are called to see the Body, Blood, Soul, and Divinity of Our Lord Jesus Christ.

It is not unreasonable to ask us to see a reality beyond what our eyes are capable of seeing. God understands human nature. In order for him to reveal himself to mankind, he must do so through signs that are perceptible to our senses. In this manner, God touches our lives, not merely on a theoretical or conceptual level, but in a tangible and physical way. All that is required to see the reality within and behind the signs of the sacraments are the eyes of faith.

SACRAMENTS AS EFFICACIOUS SIGNS

Sacrament of Baptism by Longhi.
Through the Sacrament of Baptism, a new creation is born, and the baptized becomes an adopted child of God and a member of the Church.

In each of the sacraments, God uses matter from the physical world as a conduit through which he sends or communicates his divine life (grace) to us.

However, while his presence may be perceived through any number of signs, the sacraments are *efficacious* signs, meaning that they "produce or are sure to produce a desired effect." Adjectives that are used to describe efficacious include effective, productive, successful, efficient, useful, and serviceable.

Simply put, efficacious signs mean that the sacraments cause something to happen; they bring about something that was not present before. They are sources of grace that bring about what they signify. The sacraments are efficacious because in them Christ himself is at work: it is he who acts in the sacraments in order to communicate the grace that each sacrament signifies.[10] While we see the visible sign and the visible actions of the minister, it is Christ who accomplishes the sacramental action.

Through the loving and powerful presence of Christ the sacraments cause something to happen for our good that never would have happened had the sacrament not been celebrated. The visible rite of each sacrament makes present the particular graces conferred by the sacrament and accomplishes much through the cooperation of those who receive it with the proper attitude. Each sacrament in its own way enables us to serve God as he intended, while supplying us with grace to help us accomplish his plan for our salvation and the salvation of others.

To better understand how Christ is at work in the sacraments, let us look at the Sacrament of Baptism. The sign of Baptism is water, which is poured on the head or in which a person is immersed, along with the repetition of the Trinitarian formula, "N. I baptize you in the name of the Father and of the Son and of the Holy Spirit." Water signifies life and cleansing or washing. When Baptism by immersion is practiced, it has the additional significance of burial and resurrection. However, in addition to these symbolic meanings contained in the action, in Baptism, we believe a person is cleansed of sin. The "old man" dies and a new creation is born, and the baptized becomes an adopted son or daughter of God the Father, a member of Christ, and a temple of the Holy Spirit. None of these realities were present before the Sacrament was received but were brought about precisely through the Sacrament of Baptism.

In the Latin Church this triple infusion is accompanied by the minister's words: "N., I baptize you in the name of the Father, and of the Son, and of the Holy Spirit." In the Eastern liturgies the catechumen turns toward the East and the priest says: "The servant of God, N., is baptized in the name of the Father, and of the Son, and of the Holy Spirit." At the invocation of each person of the Most Holy Trinity, the priest immerses the candidate in the water and raises him up again. (CCC 1240)

The fruit of Baptism, or baptismal grace, is a rich reality that includes forgiveness of original sin and all personal sins, birth into the new life by which man becomes an adoptive son of the Father, a member of Christ and a temple of the Holy Spirit. By this very fact the person baptized is incorporated into the Church, the Body of Christ, and made a sharer in the priesthood of Christ. (CCC 1279)

Christ works in our lives through the sacraments, and we are called to respond. In the sacraments, we see Jesus as the kind and gentle Shepherd seeking out that which is lost and inviting us back into communion with the Trinity. Through the eyes of faith, we are called to see the reality of Christ in the sacraments and to realize that it is he who transforms us. He is the initiator of all that is good for our sake. It is up to us to respond to his grace.

As Catholics, we understand that it is not we who cause the change, but Christ working in our lives. Simply put, we cannot change ourselves without God's help. God calls us, gives us his grace, and transforms us. While we are certainly called to respond to God's grace, we are changed precisely because of the fact that we have received his grace in the sacraments.

SACRAMENTS AS ACTIONS OF JESUS CHRIST

In the sacraments, it is Christ who is the primary minister. Just as he acts through material signs, he acts through the human instrument of the minister. In this way, each of the sacraments can properly be seen as an "encounter" with Christ. For example, in Confession the penitent has an opportunity for a personal encounter with Jesus Christ and can experience his healing grace. With this in mind, we can see the great benefits gained from the frequent reception of the sacraments.

However, understanding that Christ is the principle minister of the sacraments also has another important implication. With complete faith in the grace received from the sacraments, a person does not have to worry about or even consider the particular holiness of the minister who is the human instrument of this grace. Of course, every priest should live a prayerful and holy life, but the Church has long affirmed that when a sacrament is celebrated with the intention of the Church, the power of Christ and his Spirit act in it and through it, independently of the personal holiness of the minister.[11] It would be quite discomforting to have to consider the state of holiness of the priest each and every time that we

A story from the life of St. Francis of Assisi tells of a village whose priest was not living a holy life. The townspeople learned that St. Francis was coming to their town, and frustrated with their priest's behavior, they decided to bring St. Francis to him, hoping to shame him into changing his ways. However, instead of ridiculing him, St. Francis responded by dropping to his knees, taking the priest's hands and proclaiming, "These are the hands that bring me Jesus!"

St. Francis of Assisi, who himself never became a priest, understood that it is Jesus who works through the human minister, regardless of the character of the person, who is merely God's instrument. The story continues that after his encounter with St. Francis, the priest repented of his former life and became a model of holiness and piety.

St. Francis of Assisi

receive a sacrament. We can be assured that as long as we have the proper disposition, we can receive all of the benefits promised by Christ.

It should give us great comfort to know that God frequently makes use of inadequate instruments. Throughout the Old Testament, he chose imperfect men and women to do great things. St. Paul, in his letter to the Corinthians, praises them for seeing the wisdom of God in spite of his infirmity.[12] Likewise, our own inadequacies and failings do not prevent us from doing God's work. It is Christ who acts through us and who can do wonderful things through our humble efforts.

God the Eternal Father by Guercino.
Grace is first and foremost the gift of the Holy Spirit, who justifies and sanctifies us.

THE NECESSITY OF THE SACRAMENTS

We receive millions of these graces called actual graces. Everyone receives them. You need not be a Christian. Everyone in the world receives actual grace. Here we are speaking of what is called now a habitual grace, a more permanent grace; that which creates in us a likeness that remains. And that brings up this particular problem. How is this grace communicated to us? How does it get into the soul?[13]

Earlier in the chapter, we saw how God has never hesitated to intervene in creation on behalf of his beloved children. Through grace, God places himself at the service of mankind, freely offering his divine assistance.

There are two principal types of grace: actual grace and sanctifying grace. As described in the above quote from Archbishop Fulton Sheen, actual graces are those many blessings and gifts we receive from God. As stated by the *Catechism*:

> Sanctifying grace is the gratuitous gift of his life that God makes to us; it is infused by the Holy Spirit into the soul to heal it of sin and to sanctify it. (CCC 2023)

> Sanctifying grace makes us "pleasing to God." Charisms, special graces of the Holy Spirit, are oriented to sanctifying grace and are intended for the common good of the Church. God also acts through many actual graces, to be distinguished from habitual grace which is permanent in us. (CCC 2024)

Grace is first and foremost the gift of the Holy Spirit, who justifies and sanctifies us. The grace received through the sacraments, called sacramental grace, is of a somewhat different nature than the graces we receive daily. The *Catechism of the Catholic Church* tells us that by the sacraments, "divine life is dispensed to us," which is literally "God's life." Through the sacraments, God actually reaches into his own unlimited and inexhaustible supply of life and shares it with us in order to justify and sanctify us. It is God giving himself to us. Our own free response to his wonderful initiative is the only necessary condition of receiving this grace.[14]

Both kinds of grace are necessary to live the Christian life. However, a look at the theology of sanctifying grace reveals just how vital the sacraments are to the life of a Catholic.

Actual Grace

Actual grace is given to us every time God wishes us to do a good work or to overcome a temptation to do wrong. When temptations occur, we may give into an attitude of laziness, conformity, or peer pressure to avoid the demands of Christian discipleship. This attitude denies our serious responsibility to choose between sinning and returning God's freely given love to us through cooperation with his grace. However, every temptation presents an opportunity to demonstrate our love for God.

Actual grace is the intervention of God in our lives that propels us towards goodness. This actual grace given by God does not force us to choose good over evil; rather, it enables us to make the right moral decisions. Actual grace is freely given and is available to every man, woman, and child in the world, Christians and non-Christians alike. We succeed in the service of God only by opening our hearts and actions to his grace. Each person has a serious responsibility to choose between sinning and returning God's freely given love to us through cooperation with his grace, but ultimately, we have to choose to respond to this grace or not. When we consistently rely on God's help, especially in moments of small temptations, he will give us the grace needed when larger temptations come our way.

Sanctifying Grace

The graces we receive in the sacraments are called *sanctifying graces*. The *Catechism of the Catholic Church* describes sanctifying grace as a "stable and supernatural disposition that perfects the soul itself to enable it to live with God, to act by his love."[15]

Unlike actual grace, which prompts us towards good actions, sanctifying grace establishes in us a permanent disposition to live and act in keeping with God's call. Because this grace is a habitual gift, it is also called *habitual grace*.[16]

Describing sanctifying grace as a "permanent disposition" does not mean that the recipient of such grace is permanently engaged in the active will of God and no longer sins. After the reception of the sacraments, we can often succumb again to our weak natures. We continue to sin as well as experience doubts and crises of faith.

Sanctifying grace is a supernatural reality, which allots us a share in God's own divine life. It prepares our hearts so that we can become Temples of the Holy Spirit, adopted sons and daughters of God. While we receive biological life from our parents, God gives us a share in his own divine life through the sacraments.

Sanctifying grace establishes in us a permanent disposition to live and act in keeping with God's call.

Without this grace, we would live a purely natural level of life, bound to earth with no direct connection to God. When we are baptized, we become directly connected to God through his Son, Jesus Christ, as members of his Mystical Body, the Church. Since his life is above and beyond ours, we can say that we share in his supernatural life. This participation in God's life enables us to accomplish things beyond the capacity of natural human beings. We need only to remember the accomplishments of saints who lived and died for Christ to see a human life that has achieved this communion of love. Through the lives of the saints, and indeed in the lives of all Christians, Christ's love and life is brought to every corner of the world, regardless of conditions and hardships.

While God offers his own divine life through these "Sacraments of Faith," the graces received are dependent on man's free response to his call. Through sanctifying grace, God moves the recipient's heart, but the recipient must respond to this first movement by strengthening his or her faith and striving to avoid sin. If sanctifying grace simply "programmed" us to permanently live holy and perfect lives, it would deprive us of our ability to give to God what he desires most of all: our unrestricted and uncompromised love of him. But what sanctifying grace does accomplish is to enable us to enter freely into God's "communion of love."[17]

This active power of sanctifying grace in the soul is weakened by venial sins and can be lost through mortal sin, which is a grave offense against God that destroys our relationship with him. In committing a mortal sin, a person willingly chooses a disordered act, which separates the person from God and his divine love.[18] However, through a worthy reception of the Sacrament of Penance or Reconciliation, sanctifying grace and our relationship with God can be restored. In addition to the confession of mortal sins, the Church recommends frequent Confession as a means of obtaining grace to avoid future sins and to keep smaller sins from growing into more serious ones.[19]

NEW CREATURES IN CHRIST

All Christians, especially those entering adulthood, need the graces of God to respond to their Christian vocation. Unfortunately, the sacraments are sometimes sought not out of a desire for or need of the grace of God, but out of a feeling of social, cultural, or familial expectations.

But the sacraments are much more than this. They are encounters with Christ, and they enable us to be more united to God and to be Christ to others. It is Christ himself who is waiting patiently for us in the sacraments. To receive the fullness of his love, his blessings, and his graces, we need only to respond to his call to become new creatures in Christ.

By the action of Christ, each sacrament gives a particular grace of the Holy Spirit that enables a person to cooperate with the plan of God. The sacraments are associated with three divine calls:

Baptism is a Sacrament of Initiation. In Baptism, we become members of a community and new creatures in Christ.

✤ **A CALL TO PERSONAL HOLINESS**
The "Sacraments of Initiation" (Baptism, Confirmation, and the Eucharist) call each person to a life of personal holiness to accomplish a mission known to God, which will be worked out over a lifetime.

✤ **A CALL TO WORSHIP**
A crucial aspect of this call is to worship God as his Church indicates in order to acquire the graces necessary to accomplish his call.

✤ **A CALL TO CORRECT MORAL ATTITUDE**
The moral teachings of the Church instruct Catholics about the will of Christ concerning moral choices.

The Church teaches that the sacraments are treasures that Christ gave to his Church. They unite us to God through the mystical union of Christ with his Body, the Church, to which we are joined in loving communion through Baptism, and to which we are continually strengthened in the Eucharist.

As actions of the Church, the sacraments also possess an important communal value. In Baptism, we become members of a community. In the Eucharist we are united together in Christ. In Reconciliation we are reconciled with God and neighbor. The sacraments grant us the graces to live this communal dimension of the Church, enabling us to live with charity toward all and binding each member of the community to one another.

CELEBRATION OF THE SACRAMENTS

Up until now, we have discussed what the sacraments are and how they convey the graces of God. But since the sacraments are physical signs of God's love for us, it is also important to look at the actual celebration of the sacraments, for it is in these real and physical acts that God is made present in our lives.

Matter, Form, and Minister

Each of the Seven Sacraments has three requisite elements that characterize their celebration: matter, form, and minister. As previously discussed, for a sacrament to be a visible sign of God's grace, it must have a material or physical sign. This is the *matter* of the sacrament. For example, in Baptism, the matter is water. In the Eucharist, it is bread and wine, and so on.

Like the meaning of the sacrament itself, the holiness of the material objects used in the sacraments can only be seen with the eyes of faith. If we were to do a scientific chemical analysis on water before it was blessed for Baptism, and then after, there would be no difference. Likewise, if we were to look at a piece of Eucharistic bread under a scanning electron microscope before the Consecration at Mass and then after it had become the Body of Christ, we would not detect any difference.[20] Yet, it is through the matter of the sacraments that God sends us grace.

The various signs used in the celebration of the sacraments are taken from everyday life, and on their own there is nothing extraordinary about them. For example, a basin of water is nothing more than water and may be used for drinking, washing, or watering plants. Yet when this same water is used in Baptism it is elevated to a supernatural purpose. Likewise, bread and wine may be used for any ordinary meal or for the Most Holy Sacrifice of the Mass. For them to be effective signs, there must be accompanying words, which make them a sign of something much deeper.

In addition to the physical objects or materials that constitute the visible sign of the sacraments, each sacrament has words that are said as part of its celebration. These words are called the *form* of the sacrament. It is the form of the sacrament, prayers said by the celebrant, that allow for the material elements of the sacrament to become efficacious signs.

The celebration of each sacrament contains specific words that constitute its form. In Baptism, it is, "I baptize you in the name of the Father and of the Son and of the Holy Spirit," repeated while water is being poured over the person's head or while the person is being immersed. In the Eucharist, the form is, "This is my Body...This is the cup of my Blood..." Without the form, or the words of Christ, the sign is not present, and the matter is not sacramental.

Out of respect for the "matter," water from the baptismal font goes into a sacrarium.

THE SACRARIUM

Because the "matter" used in the sacraments is made holy through its being used to convey God's grace, it is treated with respect, even when the sacramental action has been finished. For example, one would never pour water that was used in Baptism down the drain so that it would go into the sewer. For this reason, many churches are equipped with what is called a *sacrarium*. This is a special sink whose drain goes directly into earth. Baptismal or other holy water can be reverently disposed of by pouring it into the *sacrarium*, or, in the absence of a *sacrarium*, it can be poured onto the soil outside the church or on other consecrated ground. We observe this piety out of respect for what is holy.

The final requirement for a sacrament is that it must be performed by someone. This person who performs the sacramental action is called the *minister*. As previously discussed, Christ is ultimately the means through which grace comes to us through the sacraments. As eternal High Priest, he is the principal minister of God both in the institution of the sacraments and in their celebration. Christ granted his authority to his Apostles and to their successors to act in his name and to continue his saving mission until he comes again.

As will be examined in more detail later in the book, the minister of the sacrament depends on the particular sacrament that is being celebrated. For example, in the case of impending death, anyone may baptize, even a non-Christian, as long as the requisite intent (i.e., to act with the intentions of the Church regarding Baptism) is present. In the Latin Rite of the Catholic Church, it is the couple themselves who are the ministers of the Sacrament of Matrimony. In the case of Holy Orders, in which a man is ordained as a deacon, priest, or bishop in the Catholic Church, only a bishop, who has the fullness of Holy Orders, may be the minister.

RECEIVING THE SACRAMENTS WITH THE PROPER DISPOSITION

For a person to receive the fullness of the graces intended by Christ, the sacrament must be received with the proper disposition. This means that we must not only have the intentions to receive the promised graces, but be in the proper spiritual condition to receive them.

> Celebrated worthily in faith, the sacraments confer the grace that they signify.[21] (CCC 1127)

> The fruits of the sacraments also depend on the disposition of the one who receives them. (CCC 1128)

To prepare for the sacraments, one must seek an awakening of faith, a conversion of heart, and an adherence to God's will. These dispositions are a precondition not only for the graces conferred by the

A sacrament must be received with the proper disposition. God's assistance is available to us even in our preparation for the sacraments.

celebration of the sacrament, but also of the new life in Christ for which the sacrament is intended. We can also take heart that God's assistance is available to us even in our preparation for the sacraments. The grace of the Holy Spirit will awaken our faith, convert our hearts, and conform our wills to God's will. We only need the desire and predisposition to seek it.

> The Holy Spirit prepares the faithful for the sacraments by the Word of God and the faith which welcomes that word in well-disposed hearts. Thus the sacraments strengthen faith and express it. (CCC 1133)

This required disposition is a manifestation of God's desire for us to freely participate in his work of salvation. While Christ always gives us his grace through the sacraments, we are left free to choose it. For example, if an atheist were to receive the Body and Blood of Our Lord in the Eucharist, it would be of no more benefit than a mere piece of bread. It is even worse for those who receive the sacraments in a state of mortal sin, because, in the words of St. Paul, "Whoever, therefore, eats the bread or drinks the cup of the Lord in an unworthy manner will be guilty of profaning the body and blood of the Lord."[22]

To receive the Eucharist in a state of mortal sin of which one has no intention of repenting closes the door to God's grace. Furthermore, receiving the Eucharist unworthily (i.e., in a state of mortal sin) only makes matters worse since such an act itself is a serious sin called a *sacrilege*. To receive the grace of God, one must have faith and the intention to receive the graces that are offered through the particular sacrament.

The Chrism Mass. Sacred oil used in the Sacraments is consecrated by the bishop of the diocese during the Chrism Mass on Holy Thursday. Sacred oil or chrism is used for Confirmation, Baptism, Holy Orders, and Anointing the Sick. Chrism is olive oil scented with a sweet perfume, usually balsam. The holy oils are usually stored in special vessels known as chrismaria and kept in a cabinet known as an ambry. When the oils are distributed to a priest to use in his ministry, they are kept in a smaller vessel with three compartments, known as an oil stock.

CONCLUSION

Understanding the sacraments is intricately connected to understanding God's plan for salvation as it has unfolded through the centuries and continues to unfold in our own lives. The Seven Sacraments celebrated by the Church are the mark of the New Covenant instituted by Jesus Christ during his life on earth. Indeed, it is Jesus Christ who is the Primary Sacrament of God, the source of all grace flowing from God to the universe. Through his Life, Death, and Resurrection he has gained for a fallen humanity the grace needed for Redemption and reconciliation with the Father. Christ, who acts in the sacraments through the Holy Spirit, dispenses grace to the faithful, assisting them in their journey toward holiness.

We must never forget that it is Jesus who is the ultimate minister and cause for each sacrament, and it is in the reception of the sacraments that the believer can have a personal encounter with Christ himself, who promised to remain with us "until the end of time."[23] The sacraments are intricately connected to our understanding of the risen Christ, and they offer us the path for our continuing spiritual education and perfection. The *Catechism of the Catholic Church* tells us that our lives on earth can be understood as sacramental lives; that is, we come to encounter Christ as he is present on earth in the sacraments. Once we are incorporated into "new life" with Christ in Baptism, our earthly lives become a period of preparation and anxious anticipation for the fulfillment of that new life in Christ in Heaven.

> For the Christian the day of death inaugurates, *at the end of his sacramental life*, the fulfillment of his new birth begun at Baptism, the definitive "conformity" to "the image of the Son" conferred by the anointing of the Holy Spirit, and participation in the feast of the Kingdom which was anticipated in the Eucharist—even if final purifications are still necessary for him in order to be clothed with the nuptial garment. (CCC 1682)

THE EASTERN RITES OF THE CATHOLIC CHURCH

Throughout much of this book we will be referring to the Latin Rite of the Catholic Church and the Eastern Rites of the Catholic Church. This terminology may lead one to think that there are two Catholic Churches, but nothing could be further from the truth. In the early years of Christianity, certain cities rose to great prominence and became leading centers of Christianity. Jerusalem, Alexandria, Antioch, and Constantinople contributed greatly to the development of Christianity in their respective regions, and their Patriarchs were regarded as a source of authority. However, it was Rome, led by the successor of St. Peter, which was given pre-eminence as the center of Christian unity.

Each of these Churches originated from the same apostolic source and, therefore, were united in Christian faith. However, in time, each developed certain local customs contributing to the richness and diversity in the celebration of their one faith. For example, there were differences in language, architecture, sacred music, and priestly vestments. Although the manner of celebrating the sacraments was quite similar and expressed a unity of faith, local variations developed in time.

In the following centuries, the influence of Jerusalem, Alexandria, and Antioch became less significant, while Rome continued to grow in importance. Constantinople, which was founded by the Emperor Constantine, also became a significant religious center, especially after the Roman Empire was divided into East and West. Furthermore, the great missionary efforts of the Church also brought new peoples and lands into the fold of the Catholic Church, which added to the richness and cultural diversity of Christian worship.

Unfortunately, the Church began to divide along the lines of the Roman Empire, with the final break, called the *Great Schism* occurring in AD 1054. While the West continued to look to the Pope as the universal shepherd of the Church, much of the East adhered to the Patriarch of Constantinople. However, some of the Eastern Churches, both at the time of the Great Schism, and in the centuries that followed, wished to be united to the Bishop of Rome. These Churches became known as the Eastern Churches.

Although having various local customs itself, the Church in the West gradually adopted the Latin Rite as the primary way of celebrating the sacraments. However, the Catholic Churches in the East retained their unique liturgical customs. While these differences have at times caused confusion and misunderstandings, the Catholic Church has always valued the diverse customs that are used by Catholics in celebrating their one Faith. With respect for the great gift that these various traditions give to the Catholic Church, the *Catechism of the Catholic Church* states:

> The liturgical traditions or rites presently in use in the Church are the Latin (principally the Roman rite, but also the rites of certain local churches, such as the Ambrosian rite, or those of certain religious orders) and the Byzantine, Alexandrian or Coptic, Syriac, Armenian, Maronite, and Chaldean rites. In "faithful obedience to tradition, the sacred Council declares that Holy Mother Church holds all lawfully recognized rites to be of equal right and dignity, and that she wishes to preserve them in the future and to foster them in every way." [24] (CCC 1203)

SUPPLEMENTARY READING

BL. OTTO NEURURER

The first priest to be killed in the Nazi concentration camps, Otto Neururer, was hung upside down until he died on May 30, 1940, at Buchenwald, having previously endured hideous torture there and in Dachau.

Otto Neururer was born on the Feast of the Annunciation in 1882, the last of twelve children in a peasant Austrian family. His upbringing and early priesthood were unremarkable, and while he was a zealous young priest especially committed to the Church's social doctrine, no one would have figured the somewhat timid Otto for a hero. Yet when the Nazis took over Austria in 1938 and began a bloody persecution of the Church, Otto, by then a parish priest in Götzens, a town near Innsbruck, was not intimidated.

He advised a young woman in his parish not to marry a certain German who was already divorced and leading a notorious life. The spurned suitor became enraged and urged his friend, the local Nazi governor, to take action. Otto was arrested on the peculiar charge of "slander to the detriment of German marriage"—ironic since he had defended the sanctity of Christian marriage in advising against what would have been an adulterous relationship in the eyes of God. He was sent to Dachau, and subsequently to Buchenwald where the cause of his death was his commitment to another sacrament.

A fellow prisoner had requested to be baptized. Otto suspected a trap, but acceded to the request out of a sense of priestly duty. Two days later as a consequence, he was taken to the "bunker of extreme punishment" where he died.

"Otto Neururer lived a priestly life, always simple, discrete, ordinary, but characterized by an extraordinary fidelity to his priestly work," wrote Reinhold Stecher, the bishop of Innsbruck on the occasion of Otto's beatification on November 24, 1996. His words were poignant, for the new Blessed had prepared Bishop Stecher for First Communion as a child, and much later, they were both imprisoned together as priests.

The sacraments are at the heart of the Catholic Faith, and are of infinite value. Sacraments take what is ordinary—bread, wine, oil, water,

BL. OTTO NEURURER
March 25, 1882 – May 30, 1940

gestures, words—and, by the institution of Christ, transform them into avenues of grace. In the death camps, Otto used God's grace to transform what was ordinary—toil, torture, hunger, disease, filth, and hatred—into something glorious: a place of redemption and the antechamber of Heaven.

Pope St. John Paul II's homily at the beatification of Otto Neururer, Sunday, November 24, 1996

"Today, the Church presents to us as models two men and one woman who, precisely through the works of generous self-giving to God and their brothers, have realized—each in his own sphere—the Kingdom of God and have become its heirs."

Referring to the priests, he said in German: "A ray of the light of the eternal Kingdom of Christ is projected on these two martyrs, who belong to the group of those who are seated with him, alongside the Throne, because, as the Apocalypse says, they did not adore the beast or his image."

"The two martyrs, Otto Neururer and Jakob Gapp, have given us a witness of integral fidelity to the truth of Jesus, in which they shine as such, in an era in which Christianity found itself immersed in neglect and was relativizing all obligations. In this way, they are patrons of courage in the proclamation…of the priestly mission."

SUPPLEMENTARY READING

Adoro Te Devote (I Devoutly Adore You)
by St. Thomas Aquinas

I devoutly adore you, O hidden God,
truly hidden beneath these appearances.
My whole heart submits to you
it surrenders itself completely.

Sight, touch, taste are all deceived
in their judgment of you,
but hearing suffices firmly to believe.
I believe all that the Son of God has spoken:
there is nothing truer than this word of Truth.

On the Cross only the Divinity was hidden,
but here the Humanity is also hidden.
I believe and confess both
and I ask for what the repentant thief asked.

I do not see the wounds as Thomas did,
but I confess that you are my God.
Make me believe more and more in you,
hope in you, and love you.

O Memorial of our Lord's Death!
Living bread that gives life to man,
grant my soul to live on you
and always to savor your sweetness.

Lord Jesus, good Pelican,
wash me clean with your blood,
one drop of which can free
the entire world of all its sins.

Jesus, whom now I see hidden,
I ask you to fulfill what I so desire:
that on seeing you face to face,
I may be happy in seeing your glory.
Amen.

VOCABULARY

ACTUAL GRACE
This supernatural, free, and undeserved help
from God is given for specific circumstances
to help us choose what is good and avoid what
is evil.

CHARISM
A specific gift or grace of the Holy Spirit which
directly or indirectly benefits the Church, given
in order to help a person live out the Christian
life, or to serve the common good in building up
the Church.

CHURCH
The name given the assembly of people whom
God has called together from the ends of the
earth. This word has three meanings: the people
that God gathers together, the local church
(diocese), and the liturgical assembly. Also,
the name given to a building used for public
Christian worship.

CONCUPISCENCE
Human appetites or desires remain disordered
due to the temporal consequences of Original
Sin; Concupiscence remains even after Baptism
and constitutes an inclination to sin. It is
often used to refer to desires resulting from
strong sensual urges or attachment to things
of this world.

COVENANT
A solemn agreement between people or between
God and man involving mutual commitments
and guarantees.

EX OPERE OPERATO
A term in sacramental theology (literally,
"by the work done"), meaning that sacraments
are effective by means of the sacramental rites
themselves, and not because of the worthiness
of the minister or recipient.

FORM
The necessary ritual words and signs that
accompany a sacrament.

VOCABULARY Continued

HABITUAL GRACE
An infused gift of the Holy Spirit by which a person receives the divine life of God in one's soul. This grace is also called "sanctifying" grace and through it a person receives the three theological virtues of faith, hope, and charity. Habitual grace enables one to live as a true disciple of Christ.

IMAGE OF GOD *(IMAGO DEI)*
The image of God, present in all humans by virtue of their creation by Almighty God, is made even more explicit through the Sacrament of Baptism, whereby one is "baptized into" Christ and made "a new creation." That image of Christ is enhanced through living a life of grace or marred by the commission of sin.

MATTER
The material or physical sign of a sacrament. Examples include water (Baptism) and bread and wine (the Eucharist).

MESSIAH
Hebrew for "anointed." This is used in reference to Jesus because he accomplished perfectly the divine mission of priest, prophet, and king, signified by his being anointed as Christ.

MINISTER
The person who administers or celebrates a sacrament.

MYSTICAL BODY OF CHRIST
Based on the teaching of St. Paul found in his First Letter to the Corinthians, this doctrine holds that believers are united to Christ as branches to a vine and, due to that union, united to one another.

ORIGINAL SIN
Adam and Eve's abuse of their human freedom in disobeying God's command. As a consequence, they lost the grace of original holiness and justice, and became subject to the law of death; sin became universally present in the world; every person is born into this condition. This sin separated mankind from God, darkened the human intellect, weakened the human will, and introduced into human nature an inclination toward sin.

PROTOEVANGELIUM
From the Greek *proto* meaning "first" and *evaggelos* meaning "bringing good news." The first message of Good News—the first Gospel—is Genesis 3:15 in which the promise of the Messiah and Redeemer is foretold.

REDEMPTION
Literally meaning "being bought back," the act by which Jesus Christ, through his sacrificial Death on the Cross, set us free from the slavery of sin, thus redeeming or "buying us back" from the power of the Devil.

RESURRECTION
The bodily rising of Jesus from the dead, as he had foretold, on the third day after his Death on the Cross and burial in the tomb. By virtue of his Resurrection, Christians have the hope of resurrection with Christ on the last day (cf. CCC 997).

SACRAMENT
An efficacious sign of grace, instituted by Christ and entrusted to the Church, by which divine life is dispensed through the work of the Holy Spirit. There are seven sacraments.

SACRAMENTAL CHARACTER
An indelible mark, i.e., a permanent and unrepeatable spiritual quality, imprinted on the soul by the Sacraments of Baptism, Confirmation, and Holy Orders, that gives the Christian a share in the priesthood of Christ.

SACRILEGE
Profaning the sacraments or other liturgical actions, or things consecrated to God in a special way, such as priests, religious women and men, churches, shrines, convents or monasteries, icons, statues, etc. Extreme irreverence by word or deed.

SANCTIFYING GRACE
The free and unmerited favor of God given through the sacraments. This heals human nature wounded by sin by giving man a share in the divine life infused into the soul by the Holy Spirit to heal from sin and sanctify.

STUDY QUESTIONS

1. What command did Jesus give to his disciples at the moment of his Ascension into Heaven?

2. What is grace?

3. How were Adam and Eve different from the rest of God's creation? What was the implication of their choice to eat from the Tree of Knowledge of Good and Evil?

4. Describe the ways God intervened in the lives of the faithful before Christ.

5. Many times in the Old Testament God manifested himself to man through physical objects. List three examples of this and describe the significance of the particular physical manifestation. Why did God choose to appear in these ways?

6. What does it mean when Christ is called a "living sacrament?"

7. How do the sacraments resemble Christ's ministry on earth?

8. How did the Apostles initially react after Christ's Ascension? How and when did that attitude change?

9. What role does the Catholic Church play in the continuing life of the sacraments?

10. What is the origin of the word *sacrament*?

11. Why are signs important in how we understand the world? How do sacraments fulfill the role of a sign or symbol?

12. What does it mean that sacraments are efficacious signs?

13. How is Christ at work in the sacraments?

14. What is the difference between actual and sanctifying grace?

15. Why is sanctifying grace also called habitual grace?

16. Describe the three divine calls associated with the sacraments.

17. What three common elements do the sacraments share? Choose a sacrament and describe how these three elements are contained in its celebration.

18. What does it mean to receive the sacraments with a proper disposition? Why is it important to receive the sacraments with a proper disposition?

The Last Communion of St. Joseph of Calasanz by Goya.

In the history of education, Joseph Calasanz (also Calasanctius) is today known as the great educator of the poor, offering education free of charge to all classes of society without discrimination. On August 13, 1948, Pope Pius XII declared St. Joseph "Universal Patron of all Christian popular schools in the world." Pope St. John Paul II affirmed that St. Joseph Calasanz tried to transmit to the youth the wisdom of the Gospel, teaching them to grasp the loving harmony of God.

PRACTICAL EXERCISES

1. List three sacraments that you have received. What is the meaning of these sacraments in your life? (Alternatively, list three sacraments that you have seen celebrated. What do you think is the meaning of these sacraments in the lives of the people who received them?)

2. Explain why we can only learn through the physical. What implications does this have for God acting in our lives?

3. What advice could you give a friend who received the Sacrament of Confirmation in a state of mortal sin?

4. What could you say to someone who says that they do not want to go to Mass because he thinks it is boring?

5. A person refuses to go to Church because the priest isn't living a holy life. What would you say to her?

6. A Lutheran friend tells you that in her church they only have three sacraments (Baptism, Eucharist, and Confirmation). Where can you look in the Bible to help show her that Jesus instituted four other sacraments? You may also want to use other writings from the early Church Fathers (try *The Faith of the Early Fathers* by William Jurgens).

7. You have another friend who attends non-denominational Christian services. He says he wants a personal relationship with Jesus. He claims that Jesus is the only Mediator between God and men, and that he does not need a priest to be close to Jesus. How can you use the Bible to help your friend see that Jesus intended us to be helped by others, beginning with his Apostles? How can you help your friend see that Jesus gave us the gifts of the sacraments so that we could have a personal relationship with him?

FROM THE CATECHISM

1077 "Blessed be the God and Father of our Lord Jesus Christ, who has blessed us in Christ with every spiritual blessing in the heavenly places, even as he chose us in him before the foundation of the world, that we should be holy and blameless before him. He destined us before him in love to be his sons through Jesus Christ, according to the purpose of his will, to the praise of his glorious grace which he freely bestowed on us in the Beloved."[25]

1080 From the very beginning God blessed all living beings, especially man and woman. The covenant with Noah and with all living things renewed this blessing of fruitfulness despite man's sin which had brought a curse on the ground. But with Abraham, the divine blessing entered into human history which was moving toward death, to redirect it toward life, toward its source. By the faith of "the father of all believers," who embraced the blessing, the history of salvation is inaugurated.

1081 The divine blessings were made manifest in astonishing and saving events: the birth of Isaac, the escape from Egypt (Passover and Exodus), the gift of the promised land, the election of David, the presence of God in the Temple, the purifying exile, and return of a "small remnant." The Law, the Prophets, and the Psalms, interwoven in the liturgy of the Chosen People, recall these divine blessings and at the same time respond to them with blessings of praise and thanksgiving.

1114 "Adhering to the teaching of the Holy Scriptures, to the apostolic traditions, and to the consensus...of the Fathers," we profess that "the sacraments of the new law were...all instituted by Jesus Christ our Lord."[26]

1115 Jesus' words and actions during his hidden life and public ministry were already salvific, for they anticipated the power of his Paschal mystery. They announced and prepared what he was going to give the Church when all was accomplished. The mysteries of Christ's life are the foundations of what he would henceforth dispense in the sacraments, through the ministers of his Church, for "what was visible in our Savior has passed over into his mysteries."[27]

FROM THE CATECHISM Continued

1116 Sacraments are "powers that comes forth" from the Body of Christ,[28] which is ever-living and life-giving. They are actions of the Holy Spirit at work in his Body, the Church. They are "the masterworks of God" in the new and everlasting covenant.

1122 Christ sent his apostles so that "repentance and forgiveness of sins should be preached in his name to all nations."[29] "Go therefore and make disciples of all nations, baptizing them in the name of the Father and of the Son and of the Holy Spirit."[30] The mission to baptize, and so the sacramental mission, is implied in the mission to evangelize, because the sacrament is prepared for by *the word of God and by the faith* which is assent to this word:

> The People of God is formed into one in the first place by the Word of the living God.... The preaching of the Word is required for the sacramental ministry itself, since the sacraments are sacraments of faith, drawing their origin and nourishment from the Word.[31]

1123 "The purpose of the sacraments is to sanctify men, to build up the Body of Christ, and, finally, to give worship to God. Because they are signs they also instruct. They not only presuppose faith, but by words and objects they also nourish, strengthen, and express it. That is why they are called 'sacraments *of faith*.'"[32]

1131 The sacraments are efficacious signs of grace, instituted by Christ and entrusted to the Church, by which divine life is dispensed to us. The visible rites by which the sacraments are celebrated signify and make present the graces proper to each sacrament. They bear fruit in those who receive them with the required dispositions.

1133 The Holy Spirit prepares the faithful for the sacraments by the Word of God and the faith which welcomes that word in well-disposed hearts. Thus the sacraments strengthen faith and express it.

1134 The fruit of sacramental life is both personal and ecclesial. For every one of the faithful on the one hand, this fruit is life for God in Christ Jesus; for the Church, on the other, it is an increase in charity and in her mission of witness.

1149 The great religions of mankind witness, often impressively, to this cosmic and symbolic meaning of religious rites. The liturgy of the Church presupposes, integrates and sanctifies elements from creation and human culture, conferring on them the dignity of signs of grace, of the new creation in Jesus Christ.

ENDNOTES – INTRODUCTION

1. Mt 28:18-20.
2. Cf. CCC 356.
3. CCC 384.
4. Cf. CCC 375; CCC 376.
5. Cf. 1 Jn 2:16.
6. Cf. CCC 416.
7. LG 1, 3.
8. Cf. Jn 14:26.
9. Cf. CCC 1127.
10. Cf. CCC 1127.
11. Cf. CCC 1128.
12. Cf. 1 Cor 2:1-5.
13. Fulton Sheen, *A Catholic Catechism, Sacraments.*
14. Cf. CCC 2002.
15. CCC 2000.
16. Cf. CCC 2000.
17. Cf. CCC 2003.
18. Cf. *RP* 17.
19. Cf. CIC, 988.
20. NB. There is a substantial change in the wheat bread and grape wine of the Eucharist by which they become not only holy, but the Body, Blood, Soul, and Divinity of Jesus Christ. This will be studied in more detail in the chapter on the Eucharist.
21. Cf. Council of Trent (1547): DS 1605; DS 1606.
22. 1 Cor 11:27.
23. Mt 28:20.
24. *SC* 4.
25. Eph 1:3-6.
26. Council of Trent (1547): DS 1600-1601.
27. St. Leo the Great, *Sermo.* 74, 2: PL 54, 398.
28. Cf. Lk 5:17; 6:19; 8:46.
29. Lk 24:47.
30. Mt 28:19.
31. *PO* 4 §§ 1, 2.
32. *SC* 59.

Baptism

Through the Sacrament of Baptism, a person is cleansed of all sin, both original and actual, becomes a member of the Body of Christ, and receives the grace needed to enter Heaven.

The Sacraments

CHAPTER 1

Baptism

After the Ascension of Jesus into Heaven, the Apostles were hesitant and unsure about how to proceed with the mission that Christ had given them. It was at Pentecost that Jesus fulfilled his promise of sending the Holy Spirit who inspired them to begin the work of the Church. Leaving the upper room where they had been hiding in fear, the Apostles went out into the streets to announce the Good News. St. Peter, speaking for the twelve, addressed the crowds, saying:

> Repent, and be baptized every one of you in the name of Jesus Christ for the forgiveness of your sins; and you shall receive the gift of the Holy Spirit. For the promise is to you and to your children and to all that are far off, everyone whom the Lord our God calls to him. (Acts 2: 38-39)

The Acts of the Apostles tells us that "those who received his word were baptized, and there were added that day about three thousand souls. And they devoted themselves...to the breaking of bread and the prayers."[1]

The story of Pentecost gives us a clear description of how the Sacraments of Initiation were celebrated in the earliest Christian community in Jerusalem. Beginning on the day of Pentecost, the Sacraments of Baptism, Confirmation, and the Holy Eucharist have always laid the foundation of the Christian life. The faithful are born anew in the Sacrament of Baptism, strengthened by the Holy Spirit in the Sacrament of Confirmation, and spiritually nourished by the Holy Eucharist.[2]

Just as it was in the early Church, the Sacrament of Baptism is the first Sacrament we receive, ushering us into the Church and new life in Christ. In this chapter we will look at the origins of the practice of Baptism, the theology behind the Sacrament, and the way it is practiced in the Catholic Church.

IN THIS CHAPTER, WE WILL ADDRESS SEVERAL QUESTIONS:

✛ What is the Sacrament of Baptism?

✛ Why is it necessary?

✛ What is the meaning of Baptism in the life of a Christian?

✛ How is Baptism celebrated?

✛ What is the role of parents and godparents in the Baptism of a child?

✛ What does the Church teach about those who have not received Baptism?

INTRODUCTION

Truly, truly, I say to you, unless one is born of water and the Spirit, he cannot enter the kingdom of God. That which is born of the flesh is flesh, and that which is born of the Spirit is spirit. Do not marvel that I said to you, "You must be born anew." (Jn 3: 5-7)

When the Pharisee Nicodemus secretly came to see Jesus at night he was confused and surprised by what he heard. No one can enter the kingdom of God, Jesus told him, without being "born anew." Nicodemus did not understand what Jesus meant by being "born anew," which seemed to imply that we must be reborn to have hope of eternal life with God.

A person is first born from his or her mother's womb. This birth, common to all human beings, gives biological life to the individual and membership in the human community. However, Jesus was speaking about a different kind of birth, a birth through the water of Baptism, by which the Holy Spirit gives supernatural life and membership in the family of God.

Baptism is the doorway into the life of Christ and his Mystical Body, the Church. Through Baptism, the individual receives membership in the Church and access to the other sacraments, in particular the Eucharist and Confirmation. Therefore, Baptism is seen as the basis and foundation of the Christian life.

The Great Flood by Bonaventura Peeters. In the Old Testament, there are many examples in which events connected to water prefigure the Sacrament of Baptism.

PREFIGURATION OF BAPTISM IN THE OLD TESTAMENT

In the Easter Vigil liturgy, the Church reminds us that "water" has long held an important role in the history of salvation as a symbol of the creative power of God and of purification. The first reading at Easter Vigil from the Book of Genesis describes how, at the dawn of Creation, the Spirit breathed on the waters, making them a wellspring of holiness.

Water is a source of life and fruitfulness on earth. Because of its vitality to human life, it has also been at the center of religious expression and has played a particularly central role in some of the most significant events recorded in Sacred Scripture.

In the Old Testament, there are many examples in which events connected to water prefigure the Sacrament of Baptism. In particular, we see Baptism prefigured in the story of Noah and the flood; in the crossing of the Red Sea; and in the crossing of the River Jordan when the Israelites arrived in the Promised Land.

During the time of Noah, Sacred Scripture tells us that humanity was wicked and evil, and that God decided to purge the world of this wickedness by sending a great flood. However, he decided to spare one righteous man, Noah, and his family. He instructed Noah to build an ark, which would save him and his family from the waters of the flood.

In the story of Noah, water is the means by which God brings about a cleansing of the earth. As in Baptism, the sins of the world are washed away by water. Additionally, one can also see in the image of the ark a "type" for the Church. While the waters raged around them, Noah and his family were safe within the walls of the ark.

In his first epistle, St. Peter draws the connection between the meaning of the story of Noah and the Sacrament of Baptism.

> God's patience waited in the days of Noah, during the building of the ark, in which a few, that is, eight persons, were saved through water. Baptism, which corresponds to this, now saves you, not as a removal of dirt from the body but as an appeal to God for a clear conscience, through the resurrection of Jesus Christ. (1 Pt 3: 20-21)

Similarly, in the story of the exodus of the Israelites from slavery in Egypt, we can see how God's Chosen People were saved by water. Having endured generations of slavery, God sent Moses to lead his Chosen People out of captivity. However, this could only be accomplished after God had sent plagues upon Egypt, which initially prompted Pharaoh to allow the Israelites to leave.

Moses Drawing Water from the Rock by Tintoretto. "They drank from the supernatural Rock which followed them, and the Rock was Christ." (1 Cor 10:4)

However, once the Israelites left their captivity, Pharaoh changed his mind, and sent his armies to track down the Israelites and slaughter them. Surrounded and facing certain annihilation, the Israelites escaped when God parted the Red Sea. Once they had safely crossed, the waters closed in on the pursuing Egyptian forces.

In this episode from the Book of Exodus, we can see a prefiguration of Baptism. Those who pass through the waters of Baptism are freed from the slavery of sin, while their former lives and habits are washed away. St. Paul refers to this event when speaking to the Corinthians about Baptism and the Eucharist.

> I want you to know, brethren, that our fathers were all under the cloud, and all passed through the sea, and all were baptized into Moses in the cloud and in the sea, and all ate the same supernatural food and all drank the same supernatural drink. For they drank from the supernatural Rock which followed them, and the Rock was Christ. (1 Cor 10: 1-4)

After forty years of wandering in the desert, the Israelites crossed the River Jordan and entered into the land, which had been promised to them by God. This event again prefigures Baptism, which is understood as the beginning of a Christian's journey toward the Kingdom of Heaven.

As we saw in the previous chapter, God uses the materials of the physical world to reveal himself and to touch our lives. In these stories from the Old Testament, God demonstrates his mercy and forgiveness both to the participants of the event and to those who would hear about it. He also uses a physical experience as a means to usher his people into their new life. In Baptism, God offers every believer the opportunity to experience this same forgiveness, initiating them into new life in Christ.

JEWISH RITES OF PURIFICATION AT THE TIME OF CHRIST

The Sacrament of Baptism receives its name from the Greek verb *baptizein* which means "to plunge," "to immerse," or "to dip." In the Septuagint translation of the Old Testament, the Greek *baptizein* was used to translate the Hebrew word *tabal*, which was often used to describe various religious rites and actions.

✠ In the first Passover, a branch of hyssop was *baptized* (dipped) in the blood of the Passover victim and placed on the doorposts and lintels of the home. (cf. Ex 12:22)

✠ If a person were to touch the dead, they were considered under Jewish law to be ritually unclean. A branch of hyssop would be *baptized* (dipped) in water and sprinkled over the person to ritually purify them. (cf. Nm 19:18)

✠ If a priest were to sin, he was instructed to *baptize* (dip) his finger in the blood of a young bull, sprinkling blood on the veil of the temple seven times. (cf. Lv 4:3-6)

As seen clearly in these passages, the Old Testament often used the word *baptize* to designate a ritual act or ceremony associated with the sprinkling of sacrificial blood or water to purify a person or thing of uncleanliness or to deliver God's people from evil. It is this meaning of purification, or the washing away of sins, with which Baptism is associated in the New Testament. Since water is used to cleanse oneself physically, its use in ritualistic practice allows the symbolic physical action to transcend into metaphysical reality.

ST. JOHN THE BAPTIST AND THE BAPTISM OF CHRIST

At the time of Christ, there existed within Judaism the practice of ritual washings for purification and the forgiveness of sins. One group in particular that practiced these ritual washings was a sect called the Essenes. Flourishing in Palestine at the time of Christ, they practiced daily washings for purification, and then, dressed in white garments, would share a common meal.

Some scholars believe that St. John the Baptist may have been a member of this group or at least spent some time living with them in the deserts around the Dead Sea. Although there is no conclusive evidence to connect John the Baptist with this group, we do know that John, like the Essenes, lived an ascetic life in the wilderness and practiced a ritual baptism for the forgiveness of sins.[3]

Although the baptism practiced by John the Baptist was for the forgiveness of sins, it was not yet a sacrament. John did not hesitate to emphasize the distinction between his baptism, which he said was meant to prepare the way for the Lord, and the Baptism that would be established by the coming of Christ.

I baptize you with water for repentance, but he who is coming after me is mightier than I, whose sandals I am not worthy to carry; he will baptize you with the Holy Spirit and with fire. (Mt 3:11)

St. John the Baptist by El Greco. Although the baptism practiced by John the Baptist was for the forgiveness of sins, it was not yet a sacrament.

When St. John the Baptist saw Jesus coming from a distance, he recognized the Lord and told the crowds, "Behold, the Lamb of God, who takes away the sin of the world!"[4] Understanding his own unworthiness, John tried to persuade Jesus to baptize him. However, in order that the will of the Father might be perfectly fulfilled, Jesus insisted that he be baptized by John.

It may seem strange that Christ was baptized by John. If John's baptism was a call to repentance, why would Christ, who is unblemished by sin, require baptism?

Jesus did not need to be baptized. But one might remember that throughout their lives, Jesus and Mary fulfilled the Law, even when it did not necessarily apply to them. Jesus, who was the Son of God, was circumcised, entering into the covenant that God had established with Abraham and his descendants.[5] Later, he was brought to the Temple to be consecrated to God.[6] Mary, following the virgin birth of Christ, presented herself in the Temple for the ritual purification and sacrifice, which was prescribed by the Law of Moses.[7]

In the moment of his baptism, Jesus, who was without sin, submitted himself to the prophet chosen by God, thereby associating himself with the condition of mankind. Even though Jesus was perfect in every way, his baptism was an affirmation of his humanity.

The Presentation of Christ by Broederlam. Throughout their lives, Jesus and Mary fulfilled the Law established in the Old Testament.

After rising from the water, the Holy Spirit, in the form of a dove, descended upon him, and a voice from Heaven proclaimed, "Thou art my beloved Son; with thee I am well pleased."[8] Here we see Christ, the Son of God, using baptism as an indication of the beginning of his earthly mission.

INSTITUTION OF BAPTISM BY CHRIST

It is through Jesus Christ that mankind has hope of the forgiveness of sins and eternal salvation. This saving work of God was accomplished by Jesus through his sacrifice on the Cross. The *Catechism of the Catholic Church* relates how the blood and water which flowed from the pierced side of Christ were "types" for the Eucharist and Baptism.

However, it was after his Death and Resurrection that Jesus instituted the Sacrament of Baptism. After his Resurrection, Christ instructed his Apostles to meet him in Galilee, where he instructed them to "Go therefore and make disciples of all nations, baptizing them in the name of the Father and of the Son and of the Holy Spirit."[9]

But the Baptism that Jesus commanded his disciples to preach and to practice was fundamentally different from the baptism performed by John the Baptist or the water rituals, which had been celebrated by the Jews for centuries.

Appearance on the Mountain of Galilee by Duccio. It was after his Death and Resurrection that Jesus instituted the Sacrament of Baptism.

The Resurrection of Christ by Veronese. The risen Christ elevated Baptism to a Sacrament.

Because of Jesus' Death on the Cross and the salvation that he won for mankind, Baptism was no longer a simple rite of ritual purification. The risen Christ elevated Baptism to a Sacrament, a sign through which he transmits the grace of God to his people.

The Baptism of Christ by Carracci.
Baptism leaves an indelible mark designating the Christian as belonging to Christ.

BAPTISM AS A SACRAMENT

As we saw in the previous chapter, sacraments are efficacious signs through which Christ conveys God's grace to his people. Through the Sacrament of Baptism, a person is cleansed of all sin, both Original and actual, becomes a member of the Body of Christ, and receives the grace needed to enter Heaven.

> Through Baptism we are freed from sin and reborn as sons of God; we become members of Christ, are incorporated into the Church and made sharers in her mission: "Baptism is the sacrament of regeneration through water and in the word."[10] (CCC 1213)

The Sacrament of Baptism has been given many names, each describing the different effects that it has upon the recipient. Baptism is called the following:[11]

✠ a grace, which bestows on the baptized the divine life of God making us his children;

✠ a washing of regeneration, in that through Baptism, the old person dies to sin and a new person is raised up in Christ;

✠ a renewal by the Holy Spirit, for it is in Baptism that a person receives the Holy Spirit promised by Christ;

✠ an enlightenment, because those who have prepared for Baptism have been instructed in the Faith: further, the baptized becomes a son or daughter of light, and, in effect, light itself;

✠ a gift, because the grace conferred on the baptized is freely bestowed by God and can in no way be merited or earned by our own efforts;

✠ an anointing, because the baptized is made a participant in the kingly, priestly, and prophetic mission of Jesus Christ;

✠ a clothing, in that the person puts on Jesus Christ;

✠ a bath, as it washes us clean of all sin, both Original and actual; and

✠ a seal, because it leaves an indelible mark designating the Christian as belonging to Christ.

EFFECTS OF BAPTISM

Each sacrament carries with it a number of gifts of the Holy Spirit, which are associated with that sacrament's particular salvific grace. The grace of Baptism is called the grace of *justification*, for it is through this Sacrament that an individual is justified in the eyes of God, becoming a "new creation."[12] Thus, the whole origin of the Christian's supernatural life has its roots in Baptism.[13]

> The fruit of Baptism, or baptismal grace, is a rich reality that includes forgiveness of original sin and all personal sins, birth into the new life by which man becomes an adoptive son of the Father, a member of Christ and a temple of the Holy Spirit. By this very fact the person baptized is incorporated into the Church, the Body of Christ, and made a sharer in the priesthood of Christ. (CCC 1279)

The baptized person receives many gifts through the Sacrament of Baptism:

✠ removal of Original Sin and of actual sin, if present;

✠ imprinting of an indelible sign that consecrates the person for Christian worship;

✠ a member of Christ;

✠ entry into Christ's Mystical Body, the Church;

✠ sanctifying grace, which is a share in God's own life;

✠ made a sharer in the priesthood of Christ;

✠ adoption by God the Father as his child;

✠ becoming a temple of the Holy Spirit, capable of worshiping God as he desires;

✠ actual grace, which is the assistance from God to resist sin;

✠ the infused theological virtues of faith, hope, and charity;

✠ the moral virtues of prudence, justice, temperance, and fortitude, which help to perfect the theological virtues;

✠ the gifts of the Holy Spirit; and

✠ entry into Paradise after a life lived in Christ.

Baptism, along with Confirmation and Holy Orders, imprints the soul with a permanent mark or character designating one as a follower of Christ. This character or mark is imparted *ex opere operato*, i.e., by the very fact of receiving the Sacrament. For this reason, Baptism can only be received once. Persons wishing to become Catholic are not re-baptized, if they have received a valid Baptism in another Christian denomination.

Through the Sacrament of Baptism, the person is infused with the theological virtues: faith, hope, and charity.

ORIGINAL SIN AND ITS CONSEQUENCES

Christ's sacrifice on the Cross ultimately won for us the forgiveness of sin, and it is through Baptism that we receive the forgiveness of sins: both actual sins (i.e., those sins we commit) and Original Sin (i.e., that sin inherited from Adam and Eve).

In order to better understand the significance of the Sacrament of Baptism, we first need to examine the nature of sin and its effects. The *Catechism of the Catholic Church* states:

> Sin is an offense against reason, truth, and right conscience; it is failure in genuine love for God and neighbor caused by a perverse attachment to certain goods. It wounds the nature of man and injures human solidarity. It has been defined as "an utterance, a deed, or a desire contrary to the eternal law."[14] (CCC 1849)

In short, sin is any chosen action by which a person effectively places his or her own will before the will of God. It breaks (mortal sin) or damages (venial sin) the friendship that God has created with his people. It also harms ourselves and others. In this sense, we can say that every sin violates not only the Greatest Commandment ("Love the Lord your God with all your heart…"), but also the Second Greatest Commandment ("Love your neighbor as yourself").[15]

In the Book of Genesis, we read of the sin committed by our first parents. Disobeying God's command, Adam and Eve ate from the Tree of Knowledge of Good and Evil. That first or Original Sin had profound consequences not only for Adam and Eve, but for all of their descendents.

As a result of Original Sin, Adam and Eve lost the Paradise that God had prepared for humanity since the beginning of time. They lost the grace of original holiness and justice in which they had been created and introduced sin, suffering, and death into God's Creation.

> Adam and Eve transmitted to their descendants human nature wounded by their own first sin and hence deprived of original holiness and justice; this deprivation is called "original sin." (CCC 417)

Expulsion of Adam and Eve by Milani. As a result of Original Sin, Adam and Eve lost the Paradise that God had prepared for the human race since the beginning of time.

Due to this Original Sin, each person is born in a fallen state, having lost the grace of original holiness and justice, and friendship with God. Effectively, this means that each person is conceived needing God's help, or saving grace. Additionally, "as a result of original sin, human nature is weakened in its powers; subject to ignorance, suffering, and the domination of death; and inclined to sin (This inclination is called *"concupiscence*.")."[16] As we shall see in more detail later in the chapter, Baptism cleanses a person of Original Sin and grants the gift of sanctifying grace, which restores the friendship with God.

While Baptism removes Original Sin and restores a person's friendship with God, the attraction to sin, called concupiscence, remains. The Christian life consists in large part in the struggle to overcome concupiscence. In Baptism, the "new person" created in Christ Jesus, aided with sure knowledge, faith, and the grace of God, must still struggle with the "old person" bound in slavery to sin.

Baptism initiates a person into a life-long process of continuing conversion. Through prayer, frequent reception of the sacraments, and mortification, i.e., the practice of self-denial to overcome desire for sin and to strengthen the will, we can steadily model ourselves on the life of Christ, choosing actions that reflect our Christian calling.

CELEBRATION OF BAPTISM

The essential rite of Baptism consists in immersing the candidate in water or pouring water on his head, while pronouncing the invocation of the Most Holy Trinity: the Father, the Son, and the Holy Spirit. (CCC 1278)

Matter

Water is one of the most plentiful substances found on Earth, and all living beings depend on it as a life-giving source. It is used not only for its life-sustaining qualities, but also for washing and cleansing. Therefore, as Baptism bestows supernatural grace and a cleansing from sin, it is only natural that the matter, or the material sign, used for this Sacrament is water.

St. Paul, in many of his letters, writes symbolically about the life-giving power of water.

> Let us draw near with a true heart in full assurance of faith, with our hearts sprinkled clean from an evil conscience and our bodies washed with pure water. (Heb 10: 22)

> Husbands, love your wives, as Christ loved the church and gave himself up for her, that he might sanctify her, having cleansed her by the washing of water with the word. (Eph 5: 25-26)

In order for water to be an effective sign of cleansing in Baptism, it must have contact with the body in some manner. In the early Church, Baptism was typically practiced through complete bodily immersion. Those receiving the Sacrament would be submerged under the water, emerging as newly born members of the Body of Christ.

However, Baptism by affusion, or pouring water over the candidate, was also seen as a valid form of Baptism which the early Christians employed when immersion was not possible; for example, in the case of a deathbed conversion, or if the person was in prison awaiting martyrdom. The *Didache*, an important early Christian text written in the first century, offers a unique glimpse into the practices and beliefs of the early Christians regarding Baptism.

> Concerning baptism, baptize thus: (After you have repeated all these things) Baptize in the name of the Father, the Son, and the Holy Spirit in running water. If you do not have running water, baptize in other water; if you cannot in cold, then in warm. But if you have neither, pour water on the head three times in the name of Father, Son, and Holy Spirit. (*Didache*, 7.1-7.3)

Since the late medieval era, Baptism by affusion (pouring water over the head) has become the norm in the Latin Rite of the Catholic Church. However, in recent years, Baptism by immersion has seen a resurgence in the Western Church. Rich in symbolism, this method concretely acts out our burial into Christ's Death and our rising into new life.[17]

In the Eastern Orthodox Church as well as the Eastern Rites of the Catholic Church, Baptism by triple immersion is the norm, with affusion being employed only in the case of an emergency.

Form

> "N., I baptize you in the name of the Father, and of the Son, and of the Holy Spirit." (CCC 1240)

The form, or words, used in the Sacrament of Baptism come directly from the Apostolic mandate, which Christ gave to his Apostles before his Ascension. Ultimately, it is only these words, the use of water, and the presence of a proper minister that are necessary for the celebration of the Sacrament.

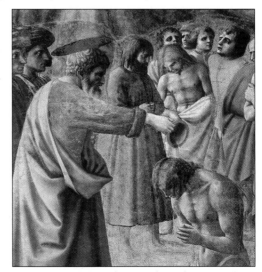

St. Peter Baptizes the Neophytes by Masaccio. Since the late medieval era, Baptism by affusion (pouring water over the head) has become the norm in the Latin Rite of the Catholic Church.

Celebration of the Sacrament of Baptism. Pope St. John Paul II acts as the celebrant (the minister) at this Baptism by affusion (the matter) and speaks (the form): "I baptize you in the name of the Father, and of the Son, and of the Holy Spirit."

Minister

The ordinary minister of Baptism is a bishop, priest, or deacon. However, in the case of necessity, anyone may baptize, even a non-baptized person, provided that he or she intends to accomplish what the Church intends by Baptism. In such a situation, the person would pour water over the recipient's head three times while saying the Trinitarian formula of the Sacrament.

Such might be the case of a person seriously injured in an accident or of a newly born infant who is in danger of death. If there is no priest available, a doctor or nurse could perform an emergency Baptism. As it is possible that any person could be called upon to be an extraordinary minister of Baptism, every Catholic should be familiar with the basic rite.

RITE OF BAPTISM

Although adult Baptism is becoming a more common occurrence in parish life, for most Catholics it is the Baptism of an infant that is by far their most common encounter with this Sacrament. The Baptism of an infant is not simply a matter of bringing the child to church for the ceremony. As we shall see, the *Rite of Baptism for Children* is very clear in its demands that first and foremost the parents, secondly the godparents, and finally all assembled renew their own baptismal promises and then pledge to be living examples of Christian virtue for the baptized child.

a. What Name Have You Given to Your Child?

The *Rite of Baptism for Children* begins with the celebrant asking the parents for the name they have chosen for their child. During the first centuries of Christianity, we see the development of the custom of receiving a new name at Baptism. In the case of the Baptism of infants, the giving of a name would naturally occur during the ceremony. The name would express the hope that the person would exhibit the characteristics of the saint after whom he or she was named.

Pope St. John Paul II spoke of the importance of a name in a homily, which he gave during a visit to Westminster Cathedral in London on May 28, 1982.

> Another aspect of Baptism, perhaps the most universally familiar, is that we are given a name— we call it our Christian name. In the tradition of the Church it is a saint's name, a name of one of the heroes among Christ's followers—an apostle, a martyr, a religious founder, like Saint Benedict, whose monks founded Westminster Abbey nearby, where your sovereigns are crowned. Taking such names reminds us again that we are being drawn into the Communion of Saints, and at the same time that great models of Christian living are set before us.[18]

b. What Do You Ask of God's Church?

The parents come freely and voluntarily to ask the Church for the Baptism of their child. In doing so, they understand that they are also freely and voluntarily assuming the great responsibility of raising the child in the Catholic Faith. In particular, the parents agree

> ✠ to accept the responsibility of training the child in the practice of the Faith; and

> ✠ to teach the child to keep God's Commandments as Christ taught, by loving God and neighbor.

As Christians, parents not only have the responsibility for the physical well-being of their children, but also the responsibility for their spiritual well-being. Pope St. John Paul II, in his encyclical *Familiaris Consortio*, referred to the Christian home and family as the domestic Church. Christian parents have the role of teaching, governing, and sanctifying their children.

All of this assumes that the parents are practicing the Faith themselves. When parents who are not seriously practicing their Faith ask for the Baptism of their children, it is questionable whether they fully understand their responsibility of setting a Christian example. In such situations, it is the responsibility of the deacon or priest to explain that asking for the Baptism of a child involves the grave responsibility of a genuine Christian upbringing.

There must be a founded hope that the infant will be brought up in the Catholic religion; if such a hope is altogether lacking, the baptism is to be put off according to the prescriptions of particular law and the parents are to be informed of the reason. (CIC, 868 § 1, 2)

By insisting that the parents of a baptized child take their Faith seriously, the Church is simply exercising common wisdom. If parents say one thing to their child and then do another, children will most often imitate what they see before they obey what they hear.

c. Godparents and Sponsors

During the celebration of the Sacrament, godparents stand beside the parents and assume a specific responsibility in the religious upbringing of their godchild. This is not just an honorary position. The role of a godparent is to help the baptized child lead a Christian life.[19]

Baptism requires either two sponsors, or one sponsor and a Christian witness. The sponsor must have the intention of performing the duties of a godparent and, therefore, must be at least sixteen years old (exceptions can be made for just cause). The sponsor must also be a confirmed Catholic who has received First Holy Communion and who lives a life that is in harmony with the role he or she is undertaking.

By its nature, the role of godparent is supplementary to that of the parents. Therefore, the father and mother of the child cannot also be the godparent. Because of the responsibilities undertaken, a non-Catholic may act as a Christian witness to the Baptism, but may not be a godparent.[20]

d. Ceremony

After the initial introduction involving the parents and godparents, the baptismal ritual continues as the celebrant claims the child for Christ by tracing the *Sign of the Cross* on the child's forehead. The parents and godparents are also invited to do the same.

Following this, there is a celebration of the *Word of God*. If the Baptism takes place during Mass, the readings for that Mass are used. Otherwise, the readings may be selected by the parents from among the many options available for the ceremony. After the readings, the celebrant gives a homily explaining the readings and encouraging the parents and godparents to accept the responsibilities that arise from Baptism.

There are then a series of *petitions* in which we find some of the blessings and benefits of Baptism. These petitions ask that

✠ the Lord look lovingly upon the child and all who are baptized;

✠ the child be bathed in light, be given the new life of Baptism, and welcomed into Christ's Holy Church;

✠ the child be made a faithful follower of Christ and a witness to the Gospel;

✠ the parents and Godparents be examples of faith to inspire the child; and

✠ the grace of Baptism be renewed in all present.

The petitions are followed by a *Litany of the Saints*. In the litany, the help and prayers of the saints are invoked on behalf of the one to receive Baptism. These prayers ask that the baptized be set free of Original Sin and ask for the indwelling of the Holy Spirit.

The litany is followed by an *anointing with the Oil of Catechumens*, i.e., olive or plant oil that has been blessed by the bishop on Holy Thursday. At this point in the ceremony, the priest is ready to begin the blessing of the baptismal water. The blessing is filled with rich images, mostly from the Old Testament, showing how water has been used by God in the past to prefigure Baptism. As we look back into the history of God's people, we see how God has used water to cleanse and purify in the same way that the waters of Baptism do for the baptized.

BAPTISMAL CEREMONY IN THE EASTERN CHURCHES

Both the Eastern Rites and Latin Rite of the Catholic Church share identical beliefs regarding Baptism. However, there are slight differences in the Baptismal ceremony, which stress different aspects of the Church's teaching about the Sacrament.

In the Eastern Rites, the child is held facing east by the godparents in the esonarthex (entrance) of the Church. This follows the ancient liturgical custom of facing east in recognition of the Resurrection of Christ, which symbolically, like the rising sun, comes from that direction. Beginning in the esonarthex also symbolizes that Baptism is the gateway into the Church.

The priest then blows into the face of the child in the form of a cross. This represents the driving away of Satan and his dominions.

At this point in the ceremony, the two traditions more or less coincide with the exorcisms, confession of faith, blessing of water, and anointing with oil.

While in the Latin Rite of the Catholic Church, parents may choose between Baptism by immersion or by affusion, the Eastern tradition always performs Baptism by a triple immersion, except in the case of emergency.

One other significant difference between the rites concerns the other two Sacraments of Christian Initiation. In the Eastern Rites, the Sacraments of Confirmation, called Chrismation (from the oil of chrism used in the anointing) and the Holy Eucharist, are received by the infant immediately following Baptism. In the Western tradition, this is only the case in the Baptism of adults, as First Communion and Confirmation are deferred until children have received instruction in the Faith.

Following the reception of the Sacraments, a male child is tonsured by cutting some of his hair signifying that he is now a child of God. As in the Latin Rite of the Catholic Church, the baptized will be dressed in white symbolizing purity, and presented with a baptismal candle representing the light of Christ. Finally, a gold cross will be blessed and placed on the child showing that he or she now belongs to Christ.

This Eastern Rite Crucifix has a crossbeam at the top representing the headboard and a slanted crossbeam toward the bottom representing the footboard. The image of Christ is usually painted on the face of the cross.

The center dome of St. Joseph the Betrothed Ukrainian Greek Catholic Church in Chicago, IL.

Having blessed the baptismal water, the celebrant again addresses the parents and godparents, repeating the responsibilities, which they have freely undertaken. All present *renew their baptismal promises*.

The celebrant turns to the parents and godparents one last time asking them if it is their wish that their child be baptized in the Faith of the Church, which they have just professed.

The celebrant then *baptizes* the child saying,

"(Name), I baptize you in the name of the Father, and of the Son, and of the Holy Spirit."

During the repetition of the Trinitarian formula, water is poured over the forehead three times, or the child is immersed three times.

Following the Baptism, the celebrant *anoints* the child on the crown of his or her head with Holy Chrism, i.e., olive oil mixed with balsam that has been consecrated by the bishop on Holy Thursday. The baptized is then *clothed with a white garment* symbolizing purity and that the person has been clothed in Christ. *A small candle is then lit* from the Easter candle, which has been burning throughout the ceremony. This symbolizes that the baptized has been given the light of Christ. The accompanying prayer asks that the child keep the flame of faith alive in his or her heart. Keeping and using this candle throughout life for important events such as First Communion and Confirmation is a meaningful connection to the day when the child was first received into the Faith.

The rite concludes with the celebrant addressing the gathered people, reminding them that the newly baptized is reborn and is now a child of God. The Lord's Prayer is prayed together, followed by three blessings: one over the mother, one over the father, and one over all who are gathered for the Baptism.

BAPTISM AND CHRISTIAN VOCATION

When a person is baptized, he is made a member of the Church, the same Church that was established by Christ and led by the Apostles and their successors. It is this membership that joins all the People of God in the Mystical Body of Christ: "For by one Spirit we were all baptized into one body."[21]

When the Body of Christ gathers to celebrate the liturgy, above all the Easter Vigil, they renew their baptismal promises. The Rite for the Blessing and Sprinkling of Water at the beginning of Mass is "a memorial of Baptism" (*Roman Missal*, Third Edition, Appendix II, no. 1). (cf. CCC 281, 1217, 1254, 1668, 2719)

By its very nature, our membership in the Body of Christ through Baptism cannot be passive. We are called to be living stones in a spiritual house and to share in the life of Christ and his priestly, prophetic, and royal mission. This role is both a great blessing and a great responsibility. We no longer belong to ourselves but to Christ and to his Church, which we must work to build up. We are therefore called to submit ourselves to Christ and to the commands of his Church. Baptism is the entryway into our Christian vocation.

> Baptism is birth into the new life in Christ. In accordance with the Lord's will, it is necessary for salvation, as is the Church herself, which we enter by Baptism. (CCC 1277)

BAPTISM AS A SACRAMENT OF FAITH

Baptism is a Sacrament of Faith. The one receiving Baptism must have an active faith in God as revealed by Jesus Christ, and have the intention, at least implicit, of receiving the benefits and graces promised in the Sacrament. In the case of adults, Baptism is preceded by a period of prayer, reflection, and instruction in the Catholic Faith. This preparation, which is called the catechumenate, is aimed at bringing the conversion and faith of the candidate to maturity.

The catechumenate is a response to God's action, performed in union with the whole Church community. It includes an introduction into the life of faith, the liturgy, and the love of the People of God through successive rites of initiation. By accepting a catechumen, i.e., a person preparing for Baptism, the local church manifests Christ's love as reflected in the community. The whole Church community, in fact, bears some responsibility for the development and safeguarding of the grace given at Baptism.

This faith is expressed in the Baptismal promises, which the candidate makes immediately preceding their Baptism:

I believe and profess all that the holy Catholic Church believes, teaches, and proclaims to be revealed by God. (Rite of Christian Initiation of Adults)

For children, who are not capable of explicitly expressing their faith or of requesting Baptism, this Profession of Faith is made by the parents and godparents in their name. In addition, they agree to undertake the responsibility of instructing the child in the Faith so that as he or she grows and matures, he or she becomes capable of living out the Baptismal promises, which were made for them. In this case, Baptism is followed by several years of post-baptismal instruction.

WHO CAN RECEIVE BAPTISM?

Both adults and infants have received the Sacrament of Baptism since the early days of the Church. On the day of Pentecost, the Apostles offered Baptism to anyone who believed that Jesus was the promised Messiah. Following the example of the Apostles, the Church makes Baptism available to anyone who believes and requests the Sacrament.

In the case of infants, the Church recognizes their need of the priceless gift of Baptism, as well as the responsibility of parents, as nurturers of the life that God has entrusted to them, to have their children baptized. Therefore, Baptism should be administered as soon as possible after birth.

The practice of infant Baptism is an immemorial tradition of the Church. There is explicit testimony to this practice from the second century on, and it is quite possible that, from the beginning of the apostolic preaching, when whole "households" received baptism, infants may also have been baptized.[22] (CCC 1252)

The practice of infant Baptism is also attested to in early Church writings. St. Irenæus, who wrote his book *Against Heresies* about AD 180, stated that "All who through Christ are born again to God, infants and children and boys and young men and old men are born again to God."[23] St. Hippolytus, writing about AD 215 states, "Baptize first the children, and if they can speak for themselves let them do so. Otherwise, let their parents or other relatives speak for them."[24]

St. Philip Baptizing the Ethiopian by Rembrandt. Following the example of the Apostles, the Church makes Baptism available to anyone who believes and requests the Sacrament.

Out of both duty and love, parents do what is best for their children. They make choices in many areas of their children's lives such as nutrition, education, and medical care. These choices are seen as essential for the well-being of their children, and no loving parent would consider deferring these important decisions until the child is old enough to make up their own mind. The same love and duty motivate parents to have their children baptized, for they understand that Baptism is best for their children's souls.

Each child will some day have to take personal responsibility for the decisions that were made for him or her in childhood, and decide whether to continue with the gifts he or she has received. This is true in all areas of life. In regard to Baptism, each person will someday have to personally choose to be a follower of Christ. Rather than enabling a child to make good choices in the future, parents who defer the religious upbringing of their children are, in a certain sense, making the choice for them.

By its very nature, infant Baptism requires a post-baptismal catechumenate, that is, a continuing religious education as the child matures. Not only is there a need for instruction in the Faith, but also the example of Christian life originating in the home. In addition to strengthening the infant recipient with the graces of Baptism for their ongoing conversion, the Sacrament offers an opportunity for an entire family to refocus on living a Christian life more profoundly, both as individuals and in the life of the family.

NECESSITY OF BAPTISM

Truly, truly, I say to you, unless one is born of water and the Spirit, he cannot enter the kingdom of God. (Jn 3: 5)

Baptism initiates us into the life of faith by transmitting the grace of God mediated by Christ on the Cross. For those who have heard the Gospel and have had the possibility of asking for it, Baptism is necessary for salvation. It was Christ's plan to convey his salvation through the Sacrament of Baptism. In this regard, the Church cannot teach any other means that assures entry into eternal life in Heaven.[25]

Baptism is necessary for salvation; however, it is important to remember that God himself is not bound by the sacraments. While an individual should seek God's grace in the way and in the manner that Christ instructed, God can choose any means to convey his grace in accordance with his divine wisdom.[26]

With this omnipotence and benevolence of God in mind, the Tradition of the Church has outlined certain situations in which the eternal salvation of God, offered through the Sacrament of Baptism, may be conveyed to those who have not received the Sacrament. In addition to Baptism by water, the Church recognizes that *Baptism of desire* and *Baptism of blood* allow the recipient to obtain salvation.

Baptism of blood occurs when a person who has not been baptized with water suffers death for the sake of his or her faith in Jesus Christ. This person is baptized by and for his or her death, a martyrdom suffered for and with Christ which configures the person to the Death of Christ.[27] Baptism of blood was common in the early days of the Church when many Christians, living in the Roman Empire, were martyred for Christ before having the opportunity to be baptized with water.[28]

Likewise, those catechumens preparing for Baptism who die before receiving the Sacrament are assured of eternal salvation as a result of their explicit desire for Baptism, along with their personal conversion and repentance of sins. Such a Baptism is called a *Baptism of desire*.[29]

In regard to non-Christians, the teaching of the Church allows for instances when God may generously dispense his salvific grace to those who, for no fault of their own, do not know Christ Jesus. In the *Catechism of the Catholic Church*, we read that:

> "Since Christ died for all, and since all men are in fact called to one and the same destiny, which is divine, we must hold that the Holy Spirit offers to all the possibility of being made partakers, in a way known to God, of the Paschal mystery."[30] Every man who is ignorant of the Gospel of Christ and his Church, but seeks the truth and does the will of God in accordance with his understanding of it, can be saved. It may be supposed that such persons would have *desired Baptism explicitly* if they had known its necessity. (CCC 1260)

Similarly, the Church entrusts infants who die before receiving Baptism to the mercy of God who desires that all should be saved. In this is the hope that God provides another means of salvation for children who have died without receiving Baptism.

CONCLUSION

God has called us into existence to share his love, and he desires that we be the source of his love to others. He has chosen to give us himself in the sacraments, the first of which is Baptism, which grants us the grace needed to enter Heaven and makes us members of Christ's Church. However, not everyone has had the opportunity to hear the saving message of Jesus Christ. As part of our Baptismal vocation, we must realize that we are called personally to be part of God's plan of salvation for all men, bringing the light of Christ into the world.

Although Baptism is a gift beyond our understanding, we are obligated to use the graces we have received through Baptism to live a life that reflects our belief in the living God. In the Sacrament of Baptism, all are given the grace to love him and to accomplish his will. This Sacrament marks a permanent change in who we are and what we can accomplish. We must accept this gift and treasure it for the whole of our lives.

ST. FRANCIS XAVIER

Before his Ascension into Heaven, Christ commanded his followers to "make disciples of all nations, baptizing them in the name of the Father, and of the Son, and of the Holy Spirit, teaching them to observe all that I have commanded."[31] Few Christians have followed these instructions with more passion than St. Francis Xavier.

Born into a noble family in what is now Spain, St. Francis showed a strong mind even as a young boy. When his older brothers took up military careers, St. Francis was sent to Paris to study. While living there, he befriended St. Ignatius of Loyola, who was forming what would become the Society of Jesus. St. Ignatius was in Paris to complete his education, since extensive learning was essential for the members of the order he wished to establish.

St. Ignatius recognized the brilliance of St. Francis, and the two enjoyed each other's company. However, St. Francis initially found St. Ignatius's life of poverty and self-denial unattractive, for St. Francis' mind was on worldly things. Infatuated with his own intelligence, St. Francis wanted recognition and praise for his genius.

Eventually St. Francis experienced a change of heart, prompted by St. Ignatius's repeated question, "For what will it profit a man, if he gains the whole world and forfeits his life?"[32] St. Francis renounced his desire for praise and reputation, studied for the priesthood, and traveled to Italy, where, with the pope's permission, he was ordained a priest. St. Francis worked in Rome for a short time until he was chosen to replace another future Jesuit who had fallen ill and went as a missionary to the East Indies.

With great perseverance, St. Francis instructed those who had fallen away from the Faith and baptized new converts. In his own letters, he wrote of baptizing so many people that he could barely move his arms, weary from having poured out so much holy water. On one island, he baptized a woman who was enduring a painful childbirth, and she delivered her child quickly, without further pain. This miracle helped to convert most of the village.

ST. FRANCIS XAVIER
April 7, 1506 – December 3, 1552

In these new lands, language barriers might have hindered St. Francis from converting and baptizing, but he received the gift of tongues and so was able to speak and understand languages he had never learned.

St. Francis Xavier performed many other miracles during his missionary work. Once he raised a man from the dead, thus converting an entire village. Another time, when his ship was on the verge of sinking, St. Francis' prayers brought the vessel safely to shore.

In the final ten years of his life, St. Francis Xavier left his homeland and family, traveled thousands of miles, baptized tens of thousands of people, and risked violent death, all so that he could bring people from faraway lands into the Catholic Church.

SUPPLEMENTARY READING

A BRIEF HISTORY OF CHRISTIAN INITIATION

Throughout its history, the Catholic Church has learned through countless experiences that in the celebration of the sacraments, one size does not fit all. Rituals have been developed for the Baptism of one child and many children at the same time. There is a ritual for the Baptism of adults, as well as an emergency ritual for someone to be baptized, confirmed, and to receive his or her first Holy Communion when in danger of death. With the re-establishment of the *Rite of Christian Initiation for Adults* (RCIA) after the Second Vatican Council (1962-1965), more Catholics are witnessing adult baptisms at Easter Vigil.

Through the Sacraments of Baptism, Confirmation, and the Eucharist, people have come into the fold of the Catholic Church since the day of Pentecost. The early Christian communities were often small and suffered persecution from the Roman Empire. For this reason, converts were brought into the Church in a personal and intimate way. These catechumens, or people preparing for Baptism, were admitted to the Liturgy of the Word while receiving instruction in the Faith. However, admission to the Liturgy of the Eucharist was reserved for the baptized.

Following the legalization of Christianity by the Edict of Milan AD 313, the Church saw dramatic growth. This changed the initiation process in two ways. First, there was no longer a need for the secrecy required by a persecuted Church, and the smaller and more informal communities gave way to larger more organized parishes. Secondly, with much of the Roman Empire converted, the Baptism of infants soon became the norm.

After centuries of disuse, Vatican II decreed that the *Rite of Christian Initiation for Adults* (RCIA) be restored. This rite closely follows the ancient practices of the early Church.

Period of Inquiry

After making known the desire to become a Christian, an individual would be presented to the local bishop who would question him or her about this desire and the reasons for wanting to join the Catholic Church. Accompanied and aided by another well respected and established member of the Christian community, an individual (known as an inquirer at this point) would answer the bishop's questions. The bishop in turn would commend the inquirer to the care of a Christian sponsor who would continue to lead, teach, and form the inquirer in the ways of Christianity.

The Catechumenate

Once the bishop and the sponsor were convinced that the enquirer was ready, he or she would be admitted into the Order of the Catechumens. The person, now a catechumen, would spend the next few years being instructed in the ways of the Gospel. Remember that during this time, Christianity was a fairly new phenomenon. It took considerable time not only to teach the story of salvation to would-be Christians, but also for a person to adopt a Christian way of life and to leave behind his or her former pagan ways.

Period of Purification and Enlightenment

After an indefinite period as a catechumen (usually about three years), the Rite of Election would be celebrated. In this ritual, the bishop would receive the catechumens, now referred to as "the elect," and admonish them to intensify their spiritual preparation for entry into the Church. This shorter period, usually some forty days before Easter, is what has come to be observed in the Church as Lent. In a series of scrutinies, the bishop would question the elect and their sponsors as to their progress in living the Christian way of life.

Celebration of the Sacraments and Post-Baptismal Catechesis

The Baptism took place on Holy Saturday night. As the bishop and faithful were beginning the Easter Vigil, the elect, their sponsors, and some deacons would be assembled in a baptistery, which was usually separate from the main area of worship. There, the deacons would baptize the elect. Coming out of the baptismal waters, they would be clothed in a white garment and then taken to the doors of the Church where the Easter Vigil Mass was already in progress. As their presence was announced, they would approach the bishop, who would seal or confirm their Baptism by anointing them with perfumed oil. They would then remain with the congregation, and for the first time, participate in the Sacrament of the Eucharist. This great event was followed by a period of further teaching and formation in the Faith known as *mystagogia*.

VOCABULARY

ACTUAL SIN
A thought, word, deed, or omission contrary to God's eternal law. It is a human act that presumes (a) knowledge of wrongdoing, (b) awareness of malice in one's conduct, and (c) consent of the will. It damages a person's relationship with God.

AFFUSION
The practice of baptizing by means of pouring water over the head of the baptized. The Catholic Rite of Baptism provides for Baptism by immersion or affusion (also known as infusion).

ASCENSION
Forty days after his Resurrection, the entry of Jesus' humanity into divine glory.

BAPTISM
The first of the Seven Sacraments that gives access to the other sacraments; first and chief Sacrament of Forgiveness of Sins because the baptized Christian receives the remission of both personal and Original Sin. It incorporates him or her into the Church, the body of Christ. (cf. CCC 977, 1213)

BAPTISM OF BLOOD
One who suffers death for the sake of the Faith, without having been baptized, is "baptized" by his or her death for and with Christ.

BAPTISM OF DESIRE
For those who strive to serve God as best they are able but die before having been baptized, their implicit desire to receive Baptism—together with repentance for their sins and charity—assures them the salvation that they were not able to receive sacramentally.

CATECHUMEN
From the Greek for "one being instructed." This new convert is being instructed in the Christian Faith before Baptism.

CATECHUMENATE
The instruction and formation of catechumens, those being prepared for Baptism. This also refers to the catechumens collectively and their position with respect to the Church.

COMMUNION OF SAINTS
The unity in Christ of all the redeemed, those on earth and those who have died, especially the unity of faith and charity through the Eucharist.

CONCUPISCENCE
The disordered human appetites or desires which remain even after Baptism due to the temporal consequences of Original Sin and which constitute an inclination to sin. This is often used to refer to desires resulting from strong sensual urges or attachment to things of the world.

CONDITIONAL BAPTISM
Conditional Baptism is administered when there is a doubt that Baptism was validly conferred and so is done "conditionally," that is, on the condition that the Sacrament was not previously received.

DIDACHE
An early Christian writing (ca. AD 60) of unknown authorship. It summarizes morality as a choice between the path of life and the path of death, liturgical practice, and disciplinary norms.

DOMESTIC CHURCH
An ancient expression for the Christian family. The family manifests and lives out the communal and familial nature of the Church as the family of God. Each family member, in accord with his or her own role, exercises the Baptismal priesthood and contributes toward making the family a community of grace and prayer, a school of human and Christian virtue, and the place where the Faith is first proclaimed to children.

EASTER VIGIL
The great celebration that takes place after sundown on Holy Saturday before Easter Sunday. In this Mass, the wonders of our salvation are celebrated. Those wishing to become Christians through Baptism as well as those already baptized who desire full communion with the Catholic Church are welcomed into God's family.

ENLIGHTENMENT
Another name for the Sacrament of Baptism. Those who receive catechetical instruction are enlightened in their understanding. The person baptized has been enlightened becoming a son or daughter of light.

VOCABULARY Continued

EPHPHATHA
An Aramaic word that means literally "be opened!" It is the word that Jesus spoke when he cured a deaf-mute. It is the prayer said over the mouth and ears of a newly baptized infant asking that his or her ears may be opened to hear God's word, and his or her mouth be opened to sing God's praises.

EX OPERE OPERATO
A Latin phrase that means literally, "by the very fact of the action's being performed." (CCC 1128) This is a guarantee to the faithful that if they are properly disposed, they will receive grace through the sacraments regardless of the personal sanctity of the person conferring the sacrament, since it is really Jesus who is acting through the minister.

EXORCISM
The public and authoritative act of the Church to protect or liberate a person, place, or object from the power of the devil (demonic possession) in the name of Christ.

GODPARENT
The sponsor of one who is baptized. A godparent assumes the responsibility to assist the newly baptized child or adult in the practice of the Christian Faith.

IMMERSION
A method of baptizing whereby the whole person is submerged in water. The Catholic rite of Baptism provides for Baptism by immersion or affusion (infusion).

JUSTIFICATION
Being made right (righteous) with God. It is a free and undeserved gift of God through the sacrifice of Jesus Christ.

MORAL EVIL
Evil consequences or suffering that is a direct effect of sinful behavior.

PREFIGURE (TYPE)
An event or person in Scripture that points forward to a later event or person.

PROFESSION OF FAITH
A synthesis or summary of the Faith professed by Christians. Professions of Faith are also known as "Symbols of Faith" or "Creeds," derived from the Latin *credo*, meaning "I believe." The most common Creeds are the Apostles' Creed and the Nicene Creed.

SACRAMENTAL CHARACTER (SEAL)
An indelible mark imprinted on the soul by the Sacraments of Baptism, Confirmation, and Holy Orders that gives the Christian a greater share in the priesthood of Christ.

SPONSOR
A baptized, confirmed, and practicing Catholic who presents a child or adult for Baptism or Confirmation (and professes the Faith in the case of an infant). This person prays for the one being sponsored and helps with his or her religious instruction.

TRINITARIAN FORMULA
Part of the form used in the Sacrament of Baptism: "I baptize you in the name of the Father, and of the Son, and of the Holy Spirit." "The essential rite of Baptism consists in immersing the candidate in water or pouring water on his head, while pronouncing the invocation of the Most Holy Trinity: the Father, the Son, and the Holy Spirit" (CCC 1278).

VOCATION
The particular plan or calling that God has for each individual in this life and hereafter. All people have a vocation to love and serve God and are called to the perfection of holiness. The vocation of the laity consists in seeking the Kingdom of God by engaging in temporal affairs and by directing them according to God's will. Priestly and religious vocations are dedicated to the service of the Church.

STUDY QUESTIONS

1. What is a "type"?

2. List three events from the Old Testament and explain how they are "types" for Baptism.

3. What does the word baptize (*baptizein*) mean in Greek? What kind of actions was it used to describe in the Old Testament? In what way are these actions of the Old Testament similar to Baptism in the New Testament?

4. Who were the Essenes, and what is one characteristic that they shared with Christians?

5. What was the significance or meaning of the Baptism practiced by St. John the Baptist?

6. If Jesus was sinless, why was he baptized by St. John the Baptist?

7. What is sin?

8. What are the effects of sin?

9. Define Original Sin.

10. How does Original Sin affect people today?

11. What do we need in order to repair the damage of Original Sin in our lives?

12. What is concupiscence?

13. How is a person enabled to follow Christ in his or her actions?

14. What is actual sin?

15. Why do we commit actual sins?

16. What is the source of salvation from sins?

17. When did Jesus institute the Sacrament of Baptism?

18. When did the Church begin to baptize? Describe this event in a few words.

19. What are the principal effects of Baptism?

20. Why can Baptism be received only once?

21. If a validly baptized non-Catholic wishes to be received into the Catholic Church, must they be re-baptized? Explain.

22. What would happen if a person received the Sacrament without the proper dispositions? For an adult, what would be the proper dispositions for Baptism?

23. What is the difference between immersion and affusion?

24. Why is water an effective sign for Baptism?

25. What is the most usual method for Baptism in the Latin Rite of the Catholic Church? How long has this method of Baptism been practiced?

26. What is the usual method for Baptism in the Eastern Rites of the Catholic Church?

27. What are the matter, form, and minister of Baptism?

28. Who can baptize in the case of an emergency?

29. What does it mean that Baptism is a Sacrament of Faith?

30. Describe the process involved for an adult who wishes to be baptized.

31. How is Baptism still a Sacrament of Faith in the case of infants?

32. What is the obligation undertaken by the parents of a baptized child?

33. Why should infants be baptized? When did the practice of infant Baptism begin?

34. Why would it be wrong for Christian parents to simply let their child make up their own mind? Compare this to other important decisions in a child's life.

STUDY QUESTIONS Continued

35. Why does infant Baptism require a post-baptismal catechumenate?

36. What is meant by baptism of blood and baptism of desire?

37. Is it possible for non-Christians to receive eternal salvation? Explain.

38. What happens to children who die without being baptized?

39. In what ways is a baptized person expected to act differently?

40. What is the Rite of Christian Initiation for Adults (RCIA)?

41. What is the role of the godparents in a Christian Baptism?

42. What must the parents agree to before their child can be baptized? Why?

43. What is the importance of a Christian name?

44. What are two differences between a Baptism in the Latin Rite and in the Eastern Rites of the Catholic Church?

PRACTICAL EXERCISES

1. Write a news story about the day you were baptized. Be sure to include who baptized you, the name of the church where you were baptized, the names of your godparents, and some recollections of those who were present.

2. Adults who want to enter the Church must learn about the Faith by attending the Rite of Christian Initiation for Adults. These adults will then be brought into full communion with the Church during the Easter Vigil. Talk to your parents, pastor, or spiritual director about becoming an RCIA sponsor either this year or in the future, especially if you know someone who wants to be Catholic but is not sure how to take the first step.

3. Can a person who has tried to live a good life by following his conscience and searching for the truth get into Heaven without receiving sacramental Baptism? Explain your answer.

4. Is it good for parents to have their children baptized as infants, before the children can make the decision on their own? Why or why not? Use the Bible to defend your answer.

Detail from *Disputation of the Holy Sacrament (La Disputa)* by Raphael.

FROM THE CATECHISM

1256 The ordinary ministers of Baptism are the bishop and priest and, in the Latin Church, also the deacon.[33] In case of necessity, anyone, even a non-baptized person, with the required intention, can baptize,[34] by using the Trinitarian baptismal formula. The intention required is to will to do what the Church does when she baptizes. The Church finds the reason for this possibility in the universal saving will of God and the necessity of Baptism for salvation.[35]

1257 The Lord himself affirms that Baptism is necessary for salvation.[36] He also commands his disciples to proclaim the Gospel to all nations and to baptize them.[37] Baptism is necessary for salvation for those to whom the Gospel has been proclaimed and who have had the possibility of asking for this sacrament.[38] The Church does not know of any means other than Baptism that assures entry into eternal beatitude; this is why she takes care not to neglect the mission she has received from the Lord to see that all who can be baptized are "reborn of water and the Spirit." *God has bound salvation to the sacrament of Baptism, but he himself is not bound by his sacraments.*

1275 Christian initiation is accomplished by three sacraments together: Baptism which is the beginning of new life; Confirmation which is its strengthening; and the Eucharist which nourishes the disciple with Christ's Body and Blood for his transformation in Christ.

1276 "Go therefore and make disciples of all nations, baptizing them in the name of the Father and of the Son and of the Holy Spirit, teaching them to observe all that I have commanded you."[39]

1277 Baptism is birth into the new life in Christ. In accordance with the Lord's will, it is necessary for salvation, as is the Church herself, which we enter by Baptism.

1278 The essential rite of Baptism consists in immersing the candidate in water or pouring water on his head, while pronouncing the invocation of the Most Holy Trinity: the Father, the Son, and the Holy Spirit.

1279 The fruit of Baptism, or baptismal grace, is a rich reality that includes forgiveness of original sin and all personal sins, birth into the new life by which man becomes an adoptive son of the Father, a member of Christ and a temple of the Holy Spirit. By this very fact the person baptized is incorporated into the Church, the Body of Christ, and made a sharer in the priesthood of Christ.

1280 Baptism imprints on the soul an indelible spiritual sign, the character, which consecrates the baptized person for Christian worship. Because of the character Baptism cannot be repeated.[40]

1281 Those who die for the faith, those who are catechumens, and all those who, without knowing of the Church but acting under the inspiration of grace, seek God sincerely and strive to fulfill his will, can be saved even if they have not been baptized.[41]

1282 Since the earliest times, Baptism has been administered to children, for it is a grace and a gift of God that does not presuppose any human merit; children are baptized in the faith of the Church. Entry into Christian life gives access to true freedom.

1283 With respect to children who have died without Baptism, the liturgy of the Church invites us to trust in God's mercy and to pray for their salvation.

1284 In case of necessity, any person can baptize provided that he have the intention of doing that which the Church does and provided that he pours water on the candidate's head while saying: "I baptize you in the name of the Father, and of the Son, and of the Holy Spirit."

Baptism of Christ by Bellini. Through Baptism we are called to be living stones in a spiritual house and to share in the life of Christ and his priestly, prophetic, and royal mission.

ENDNOTES – CHAPTER ONE

1. Acts 2:41-42.
2. Cf. CCC 1212.
3. Cf. Lk 3:3.
4. Jn 1:29.
5. Lk 2:21.
6. Lk 2:23.
7. Lk 2:22-24.
8. Lk 3:22.
9. Mt 28:19; cf. 3:13-17; Mk 1:9-11; Jn 1:22-34.
10. Roman Catechism, II, 2, 5; cf. Council of Florence: DS 1314; CIC, Cann. 204 § 1; 849; CCEO, can. 675 § 1.
11. Cf. CCC 1214-1216.
12. 2 Cor 5:17.
13. Cf. CCC 1266.
14. St. Augustine, *Contra Faustum* 22: PL 42, 418; St. Thomas Aquinas, *STh* I-II, 71, 6.

15. Mt 22:34-40.
16. CCC 418.
17. Cf. CCC 1214.
18. Pope St. John Paul II, homily given in Westminster Cathedral, London, May 28, 1982.
19. Cf. CIC, 872.
20. Cf. CIC, 874.
21. 1 Cor 12:13.
22. Cf. Acts 16:15, 33; 18:8; 1 Cor 1:16; CDF, instruction, *Pastoralis Actio*: AAS 72 (1980) 1137-1156.
23. St. Irenæus, *Against Heresies* 2:22:4.
24. Hippolytus, *Apostolic Tradition*, 21:15, ca. AD 215.
25. Cf. CCC 1257.
26. Cf. CCC 1257.

27. Cf. Mt 10:32, 39; Lk 9:24.
28. Cf. CCC 1258.
29. CCC 1259.
30. *GS* 22 § 5; cf. *LG* 16; *AG* 7.
31. Mt 28:19-20.
32. Mt 16:26.
33. Cf. CIC, can. 861 § 1; CCEO, can. 677 § 1.
34. CIC, can. 861 § 2.
35. Cf. 1 Tm 2:4.
36. Cf. Jn 3:5.
37. Cf. Mt 28:19-20; cf. Council of Trent (1547) DS 1618; *LG* 14; *AG* 5.
38. Cf. Mk 16:16.
39. Mt 28:19-20.
40. Cf. DS 1609 and DS 1624.
41. Cf. *LG* 16.

Confirmation

*In receiving the Sacrament of Confirmation and the promised gift of the Holy Spirit,
we take on the same role as the Apostles after Pentecost...spreading the Faith as disciples of Christ.*

The Sacraments
CHAPTER 2
Confirmation

On the day of Pentecost the Apostles received the Holy Spirit as the Lord had promised. They also received the power of giving the Holy Spirit to others and so completing the work of Baptism. This we read in the Acts of the Apostles. When Saint Paul placed his hands on those who had been baptized, the Holy Spirit came upon them, and they began to speak in other languages and in prophetic words. (*Rite of Confirmation*)

he Christian life is not an easy life. We can see from the Acts of the Apostles that even those who knew Jesus while he was on earth had trouble beginning to live according to Christ's teachings. For the Apostles, it took the day of Pentecost, the outpouring of the Holy Spirit promised to them by Christ, to start them on their way. For Christians today, the situation is not that different.

In Baptism, we are initiated into new life in Christ, but that initiation is only the beginning of our lives as Christians. The Christian life is an ongoing journey towards holiness and perfection, a perfection that cannot be realized in this world, but which is reserved for eternal life. Christ knows that living this life is not easy, and that our time on earth, like his, is filled with temptation. He knows we must struggle with ourselves and the world to avoid sin. This is why there is not just a single sacrament, Baptism, but rather seven sacraments, each containing special graces that aid us in living our life in Christ.

The Sacrament of Confirmation is necessary for the completion of baptismal grace.[1] The person confirmed is more perfectly bound to the Church and strengthened in the Holy Spirit.[2] Like Baptism, the Sacrament of Confirmation has its roots in the day of Pentecost, when the Apostles received the outpouring of the Holy Spirit and began the work of the Church.

Confirmation is the sacrament that gives people courage: courage to do what they know is right, even when others mock their beliefs; courage to defend the truth, even when people deny that truth exists; courage to profess their faith in Jesus, even when no one else around them believes. In short, Confirmation gives us the tools, which we need to live the fullness of the Catholic Faith.

IN THIS CHAPTER, WE WILL ADDRESS SEVERAL QUESTIONS:

✢ What is the meaning of Confirmation?

✢ Why is Confirmation essential in a person's life?

✢ What are the gifts of the Holy Spirit?

✢ How does one receive the Sacrament of Confirmation (preparation and the rite)?

The Tree of Jesse. Artists of the Middle Ages were inspired by Isaiah 11:1-3 to illustrate the family tree of Jesus Christ. The tree grows from a sleeping Jesse ("…the father of David the king." Mt 1:6). Among the tree branches sprout the kings of Judah and the Old Testament prophets. The tree is crowned with The Blessed Virgin Mary and Infant Jesus, the "anointed one."

JESUS THE "CHRIST"

In the Old Testament, the faithful of Israel waited patiently for God's promised Messiah. The word Messiah (*Christ* in Greek) means "the anointed" and was used frequently in the Old Testament to designate those chosen by God to be kings, priests, and prophets, signifying not only their office, but the divine nature of their calling. The prophets had foretold that God's spirit would come to rest upon the chosen Messiah, his "Anointed One."[3]

> There shall come forth a shoot from the stump of Jesse, and a branch shall grow out of his roots.
> And the Spirit of the LORD shall rest upon him, the spirit of wisdom and understanding, the spirit
> of counsel and might, the spirit of knowledge and the fear of the LORD. (Is 11:1-2)

This prophecy from the Book of Isaiah speaks in detail about the gifts of the Holy Spirit: wisdom, understanding, counsel, might, knowledge, and fear of the Lord, which would characterize the Messiah. At the baptism of Christ in the River Jordan, we see this prophesy fulfilled when the Holy Spirit, in the form of a dove, came and rested upon him. At Pentecost, St. Peter announced to the assembled crowds in Jerusalem that Christ was this promised Messiah:

> Let all the house of Israel therefore know assuredly that God has made him both Lord and Christ,
> this Jesus whom you crucified. (Acts 2:36)

The outpouring of the Holy Spirit was not to be reserved for Christ alone, but was intended for all of God's chosen, who were called a *messianic people*.[4] Beginning at Pentecost and continuing throughout the history of the Church through the Sacrament of Confirmation, Christians have been "anointed" to share in Jesus' kingly, priestly, and prophetic mission and strengthened through the gifts of the Holy Spirit.

Pentecost by Zurbaran.
"And there appeared to them tongues as of fire.... And they were all filled with the Holy Spirit." (Acts 2: 3-4)

THE PROMISED SPIRIT

Suddenly a sound came from heaven like the rush of a mighty wind, and it filled all the house where they were sitting. And there appeared to them tongues as of fire, distributed and resting on each one of them. And they were all filled with the Holy Spirit and began to speak in other tongues, as the Spirit gave them utterance. (Acts 2: 2-4)

At Pentecost, God poured out the Holy Spirit upon the Apostles in order to provide them with the strength to participate in accomplishing his will and to proclaim his word to all who would hear and believe. A profound transformation occurred in the lives of the Apostles that day and continues to occur in the lives of Christians today. The Apostles, filled with courage, went out into the streets of Jerusalem, and, led by St. Peter, fearlessly preached the message of Christ to all who would listen.

Repent, and be baptized every one of you in the name of Jesus Christ for the forgiveness of your sins; *and you shall receive the gift of the Holy Spirit.* [emphasis added] (Acts 2: 38)

Three thousand accepted the message of Jesus Christ that day and were baptized, receiving the promised gifts of the Holy Spirit.

THE LAYING ON OF HANDS
AND THE ANOINTING OF THE HOLY SPIRIT

Following the Story of Pentecost in the Acts of the Apostles, we read about Baptism being followed by a laying-on of hands to confer the gifts of the Holy Spirit.

> When the apostles at Jerusalem heard that Samaria had received the word of God, they sent to them Peter and John, who came down and prayed for them that they might receive the Holy Spirit; for it had not yet fallen on any of them, but they had only been baptized in the name of the Lord Jesus. Then they laid their hands on them and they received the Holy Spirit. (Acts 8:14-17)

> Henceforth, the Apostles—following the will of Christ—communicated to the newly baptized Christians the gift of the Holy Spirit by the laying on of hands. This gift was to complete the grace of Baptism.[5] This explains why, in the letter to the Hebrews,[6] the doctrine on Baptism and the laying on the hands is mentioned among the first elements of Christian formation. (Paul VI, Ap. Const. *Divinæ Consortium Naturæ*: AAS 63 [1971] 659)

The Sacrament of Confirmation finds its origin in this laying-on of hands used by the Apostles to convey the Holy Spirit to the newly baptized. While the New Testament refers to the Sacrament as the "laying on of hands," the early Church added an anointing of perfumed oil, known as *Chrism*, to the imposition of hands to better signify the "anointing" of the Holy Spirit. This anointing with oil strongly illustrated the name "Christian," which was given to the followers of Christ, the Anointed One.[7]

The name "Confirmation" itself was first coined by St. Ambrose of Milan (AD 340-397) when describing the practice of this anointing ritual:

> You have received the spiritual sign, the sign of wisdom; God the Father has sealed you, Christ the Lord has *confirmed* you and has given you the gift of the Spirit in your heart.[8]

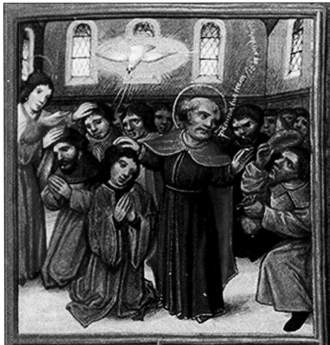

St. Peter and St. John laying their hands upon the people. Illustration from a Book of Hours made in Flanders, ca. 1484-1529.

The use of the word confirmation conveys the meaning of a "confirming" or completion of the faith begun at Baptism, accompanied by a strengthening of baptismal grace.[9] The Eastern Rites of the Catholic Church refer to the Sacrament as *Chrismation*, which finds its origin in the Oil of Chrism used in the anointing.

Throughout the first few centuries of Christianity, the Sacrament of Confirmation was celebrated immediately following the reception of Baptism. The close relationship between the two sacraments led to their being referred to as a "double sacrament." The Eastern Rites of the Catholic Church still confer Confirmation immediately after the reception of Baptism, even in the case of infants. The Latin Rite of the Catholic Church, on the other hand, often defers the reception of Confirmation until a later age, except when an infant is in danger of death, although some dioceses have restored the order of the Sacraments of Initiation to Baptism, Confirmation, and First Eucharist. Additionally, when a person enters the Church as an adult, he or she receives all three of the Sacraments of Initiation, Baptism, Confirmation, and the Holy Eucharist, during the Easter Vigil Mass.

Christ Carrying the Cross by Tiepolo. The Sacrament of Confirmation aids Christians to carry their own crosses.

THE SACRAMENT OF CONFIRMATION

"By the Sacrament of Confirmation, [the baptized] are more perfectly bound to the Church and are enriched with a special strength of the Holy Spirit."[10] (CCC 1285)

The story of Pentecost is truly amazing: men and women speaking dozens of languages, invalids and sick people healed, thousands flocking to hear the inspired preaching of the Apostles. After reading that the Holy Spirit inspired such a fantastic event, it may be difficult to imagine that it is this same Spirit who is made present to us in the Sacrament of Confirmation.

Over the past two thousand years, ever since the day of Pentecost, the Holy Spirit has inspired followers of Christ in many different ways. It is understandable that at the founding moment of Christ's Church, the gifts necessary to spread the Christian message were particularly spectacular. But at different times and for different individuals, different charisms or gifts have been needed to carry on the work of God. Whatever the outward manifestation of the inspired work of the Holy Spirit, all who seek Christ in the Sacrament of Confirmation receive the gifts of the Holy Spirit, which strengthen our inward disposition in the Faith of Jesus Christ.

As seen in the first chapter, sacraments are encounters with Jesus Christ, and as efficacious signs, they cause a change in the person who receives them. Through the Sacrament of Confirmation a person receives special graces that are called the gifts of the Holy Spirit. These seven gifts are wisdom, understanding, counsel, fortitude, knowledge, piety, and fear of the Lord.

As Christians, we are called to follow Christ as he carries his Cross to Calvary. This means having the strength and courage to pick up our own crosses. As we grow older, we learn that it is not difficult to encounter the occasions of suffering and hardship that afford us the opportunity to follow in the way of Christ. What we require, however, is the ability to willingly accept these struggles—even embrace them—and unite them to the suffering of Jesus. By imparting the gifts of the Holy Spirit, the Sacrament of Confirmation aids the Christian in bearing the struggles, temptations, and sufferings that are encountered in life.

St. Thomas Aquinas calls Confirmation the "Sacrament of the fullness of grace," meaning that the graces of Baptism reach their proper end and perfection in the reception of Confirmation.[11] The Sacrament is conferred in order to give the baptized the fullness of the Holy Spirit, the fullness of grace, and the fullness of gifts needed to live the Christian vocation in the world. The individual, who began his or her spiritual journey in Baptism, is now directed towards its completion, as he or she is conformed to the image of Christ.

Confirmation is not necessary for salvation in the same way as Baptism, but there is no doubt that the gifts given by the Sacrament help the Catholic in his or her journey toward Heaven. In fact, the Church teaches that it is necessary to receive this Sacrament for the completion of baptismal grace.[12]

> Every baptized person not yet confirmed can and should receive the sacrament of Confirmation.[13] Since Baptism, Confirmation, and Eucharist form a unity, it follows that "the faithful are obliged to receive this sacrament at the appropriate time,"[14] for without Confirmation and Eucharist, Baptism is certainly valid and efficacious, but Christian initiation remains incomplete. (CCC 1306)

EFFECTS OF CONFIRMATION

Confirmation perfects Baptismal grace; it is the sacrament which gives the Holy Spirit in order to root us more deeply in the divine filiation, incorporate us more firmly into Christ, strengthen our bond with the Church, associate us more closely with her mission, and help us bear witness to the Christian faith in words accompanied by deeds. (CCC 1316)

✠ Baptismal grace is perfected, enabling a person to be an apostle of Christ.

✠ An indelible mark is imprinted on the soul, and because of this permanence, Confirmation can be received only once.

✠ A person is rooted more deeply as a child of the Father and more closely united to Christ.

✠ The gifts of the Holy Spirit (wisdom, understanding, counsel, fortitude, knowledge, piety, and fear of the Lord) and the twelve fruits of the Holy Spirit are increased.

✠ A person's bond with the Church is perfected.

✠ A person is given stewardship over his or her spiritual well-being: "Guard what you have received" (St. Ambrose, *De Myst.* 7, 42: PL 16, 402-403; quoted in CCC 1303).

✠ Special graces are given to a person to enable him or her to spread and defend the faith by word and deed as a true witness to Christ.

THE SEVEN GIFTS OF THE HOLY SPIRIT

Through the Sacrament of Confirmation a person receives the gifts of the Holy Spirit. The Prophet Isaiah had foretold of the Anointed One, who would bear the fullness of these gifts. As Christians we profess that Jesus is the Messiah (Christ), and it is through Confirmation that we too become "anointed," sharing in these gifts of the Spirit.

In order to make full use of these gifts, it is important that we understand their meaning and see how they are interconnected, working together as an integrated whole. Understanding the gifts of the Holy Spirit allows us to more fully receive their benefits in our daily lives.

1. Wisdom

In Latin, the word for wisdom is *sapientia*, which is derived from the verb "to taste." In the Epistle of St. James, we learn that wisdom comes *from above* as a gift of the Holy Spirit that is infused into the soul.[15] In this way we can understand Christian wisdom as tasting, or experiencing in an intimate way, the mind and nature of God, which is revealed to us through the Holy Spirit.

Wisdom is the ability to judge correctly, to discern what is just, not only through human reason, but also in the light of God's will. As such, true wisdom is bound up in an understanding of the Divine Will as revealed in the Person of Jesus Christ. Although its origin is in the intellect, wisdom can only grow and bear fruit when the will is conformed to Jesus Christ.

The gift of wisdom, made available through the Sacrament of Confirmation, allows us to know God and savor his presence. This divine wisdom helps us understand that our happiness comes from God and that true happiness is obtained by orienting our lives with God at the center.

The gift of wisdom, in which a person cooperates freely in God's grace, ultimately leads to a life of holiness modeled on Jesus Christ. Like St. Augustine, the recipient of this gift is led to proclaim, "Lord, you have made us for yourself. Our hearts are restless until they rest in you."[16]

2. Understanding

The divine mysteries, the nature of God, and divine truth, are, by definition, difficult to comprehend. By reason and intellectual effort alone we are able to obtain a certain level of knowledge about God. However, it is the gift of understanding that allows us to penetrate more deeply into these divine mysteries and to reach the fullness of the Catholic Faith.

When we participate in the life of the Church and in the sacraments and study the Faith and Sacred Scripture, the Holy Spirit comes to our aid, granting us the grace needed to increase our understanding of the sacred mysteries. In addition, the Holy Spirit helps us to understand the events that occur in our own lives, judging them according to the life of Christ. As we read in the letter of St. Paul, this gift of understanding comes from the Holy Spirit:

> No one comprehends the thoughts of God except the Spirit of God. Now we have received not the spirit of the world, but the Spirit which is from God, that we might understand the gifts bestowed on us by God. (1 Cor 2:11-12)

We see this gift of understanding at work in the lives of the Apostles. On the road to Emmaus, the disciples did not recognize the Lord. In the breaking of the bread, however, "...their eyes were opened and they recognized him;"[17] and later, "he opened their minds to understand the scriptures."[18] Christ promised his disciples that the Holy Spirit would come after he had ascended into Heaven.

> These things I have spoken to you, while I am still with you. But the Counselor, the Holy Spirit, whom the Father will send in my name, he will teach you all things, and bring to your remembrance all that I have said to you. (Jn 14: 25-26)

Our Lord will usually multiply his gifts in a soul that is sufficiently prepared. Such preparation is accomplished through meditating on our Lord's words in prayer. We can also ask the Holy Spirit for a greater understanding of the meaning of those things, which we find in our daily lives, or in the teachings of the Church. The gift of understanding also prompts us to study the Faith and to consider our own desires with reference to the teachings of Christ.

3. Counsel

I will instruct you and teach you the way you should go; I will counsel you with my eye upon you.
(Ps 32: 8)

The gift of counsel helps Christians to know what we should or should not do in every situation that demands a moral decision. This gift of the Spirit helps us to find our way along the winding and confusing paths of life. To fully utilize the great benefits of this gift a person must seek advice from the teachings of Christ. It involves weighing matters before making a choice and a resolute determination to carry the correct decision through to completion. The key to living a Christian life is to let oneself be led by the Holy Spirit, and the gift of counsel makes this possible.

4. Fortitude

Before the Second Vatican Council, Confirmation included a light slap on the cheek to remind the recipient that he or she was now a soldier of Christ and that Christian service is sometimes difficult. Although this slap has disappeared from the celebration of the Sacrament, Confirmation is a time when we need to understand ourselves as soldiers of Christ.

Throughout history, the Church has always been under attack by those who despised her mission and truth. This is no less true today. Newspapers and television often attack the Church for daring to defend the teachings of Jesus Christ on many issues, such as abortion, marriage, and homosexuality. As confirmed Catholics, we should take courage in the fact that through the Sacrament of Confirmation, we are strengthened with the fortitude to stand up and defend the Faith.

We cannot rely on our own strength alone to withstand the many obstacles we will encounter in life. The gift of fortitude strengthens the will and resolve, allowing a follower of Christ to stand firm in his or her convictions as a child of God. The same Holy Spirit who filled the frightened Apostles with courage at Pentecost works through us and grants us the strength to be heroic followers of the will of God.

5. Knowledge

Scientists seek to discover reality by investigating material causes. However, in addition to scientific knowledge (which forms an important part of human knowledge), the wise man seeks an understanding of reality based on Divine Revelation, i.e., those truths made known by God. Enlightened by faith and guided by the Magisterium of the Church, this gift of the Holy Spirit allows a person to achieve a deeper knowledge of revealed truth.

With the gift of piety, Bl. Teresa of Calcutta (Mother Teresa) saw the divine imprint of God in the sick and dying in India.

The gift of knowledge gives the Christian the supernatural light to see that all creation, our good actions, and all the good that has been achieved in history comes from God and is directed toward him. This gift involves a supernatural understanding, which, insofar as it is a God-like way of knowing, surpasses what we are capable of achieving by our own efforts. However, its development is dependent on one's faithfulness in responding to grace.

For the person who has received the gift of knowledge, no aspect of created reality is lacking in meaning. The Christian finds Christ not only in creation, but in every human encounter, event, and activity.

6. Piety

You have received the spirit of sonship. When we cry, "Abba! Father!" it is the Spirit himself bearing witness with our spirit that we are children of God. (Rom 8:15-16)

In Jewish tradition, the name of God revealed to Moses, "I AM WHO I AM," was not pronounced out of a sense of profound reverence. Instead, an abbreviated form, YHWH, or JHVH, was used. However, Christ called God "Abba," the name that a young child gives to his father, similar to the English word "daddy"; and he taught his followers to call God "Father." This idea that we are children of God is at the forefront of the Lord's Prayer, which Christ taught to his disciples.

The Christian understanding that we are sons and daughters of God, called *divine filiation*, is at the center of the gift of piety. This understanding properly aligns our relations with both God and neighbor. Seeing God as our heavenly Father, we can turn to him with full confidence and trust in every circumstance of life. Seeing the divine imprint of God in everything around us, we are able to see God in others. This reality radically changes the way that we treat other people.

The Holy Trinity by Balen. The *gift of fear of the Lord* is bound up in the Christian understanding of a just God.

In the Parable of the Sheep and the Goats, Jesus says, "Truly, I say to you, as you did it to one of the least of these my brethren, you did it to me."[19] Bl. Teresa of Calcutta relied on this teaching of Christ to give her strength in her own work with the sick and the dying in the streets of Calcutta, India. Knowing that her own strength was insufficient, she would pray that she could see Christ in those she encountered. Then, out of an intense love for God, she could treat others with the true dignity that they deserved as sons and daughters of God.

7. Fear of the Lord

The fear of the Lord is the beginning of wisdom. (Ps 111:10)

Closely related to the gift of piety is the gift of fear. This gift of fear of the Lord is bound up in the Christian understanding of a just God—a God who holds authority and dominion over the world. He alone can pass true judgment on the ways of men.

In understanding the gift of fear, we might be aided by a comparison to the relationship between children and parents in a family. Young children inherently acknowledge their parents' right to make decisions for them. In addition, there is also an unquestioned understanding that disobedience will be punished, and that this is just and proper. However, the primary basis of the relationship is defined by a profound love: a love of the parents for their children and a love of the children for their parents.

This example is a reflection of the divine filiation that Christians have with God the Father. Inspired by the Holy Spirit, Christians will acknowledge the authority of God in their lives. Out of a love for God, they will desire to acknowledge their sins and to detest them.

However, in this desire to please God, there are two distinct levels. To go back to our example, a child may act correctly out of love and respect for his or her parents, or out of fear of punishment. While acting out of love is by far the superior motive, at a minimum, both have at least acted correctly. The same can be said of the supernatural life. Christians who act out of a profound love of God do so out of the best motives. However, those who act correctly out of the fear of punishment still acknowledge God's authority, the justice of his punishment, and as a result still act correctly. The Church's teaching on this gift of the Holy Spirit is summed up in the Act of Contrition.

ACT OF CONTRITION

O my God, I am heartily sorry for having offended thee, and I detest all my sins, *because I dread the loss of Heaven, and the pains of Hell; but most of all because they offend thee, my God, who are all good and deserving of all my love.* I firmly resolve, with the help of thy grace, to confess my sins, to do penance, and to amend my life. Amen.

CELEBRATION OF CONFIRMATION

As we saw earlier in the chapter, the first Confirmations were celebrated by Christ's Apostles, who laid their hands on the recipients and prayed for the outpouring of the Holy Spirit. In many ways, this is the same way the Sacrament is celebrated today. A bishop, who is a successor to the Apostles, lays his hands on the recipient and prays that God will send the Holy Spirit upon that person.

Matter

In Confirmation, we are invited to share in the life and mission of Jesus Christ, the Anointed One sent by God. Appropriately, the matter of the Sacrament, that is, the physical sign used in the Sacrament, is sacred oil with which the recipient is anointed.

This oil, called Sacred Chrism, is essentially olive oil mixed with a small amount of balsam. The oil used in Confirmation is consecrated by the bishop of the diocese during the Chrism Mass on Holy Thursday. During this Mass, which also marks the establishment of the priesthood by Christ, other oils are blessed as well, such as the Oil of Catechumens used in the pre-baptismal anointing and the Oil of the Sick used in the Anointing of the Sick.[20]

The oil used in Confirmation contains two meanings derived from Sacred Scripture. The prophet Isaiah indicates that anointing with oil is a sign of abundance and joy, while the balsam, a fragrant perfume, is described by St. Paul as a symbol of the "aroma of Christ."[21] During the celebration of Confirmation, the forehead is anointed with Sacred Chrism at the moment of the laying on of hands. In the Eastern Rites of the Catholic Church, the eyes, nose, ears, lips, chest, back, hands, and feet are also anointed to show that the entire person is consecrated to Christ.

The oil (Sacred Chrism) used in Confirmation is consecrated by the bishop of the diocese during the Chrism Mass on Holy Thursday.

Form

The form, or the words, of Confirmation are those original words spoken by the Apostles at Pentecost: "Be sealed with the gift of the Holy Spirit." These are the words that signify the moment at which the Holy Spirit, promised us by Christ, is poured upon the recipient of the Sacrament. The bishop, who presides over the Sacrament, says these words as he lays hands on the forehead of the individual and anoints him or her with the oil of chrism.

Minister

The minister of the Sacrament of Confirmation is the bishop. After Pentecost, it was the Apostles who administered the Sacrament of Confirmation. Later, in the churches founded by the Apostles, it was the local bishop who administered the Sacrament.[22] Thus, the power to convey the Sacrament of Confirmation comes down to us through the bishops, in an unbroken chain of succession from the Apostles.

Most Catholics who are baptized as infants will be confirmed in young adulthood by the bishop when he visits the parish. However, under certain circumstances the bishop's authority can be delegated to his priests, who are the extraordinary ministers of Confirmation. Such would be the case of an adult who receives all three Sacraments of Initiation at the Easter Vigil, or at another time of the year, or when the Sacraments are given in the case of an emergency.

In the Eastern Rites of the Catholic Church, the priest administers all three Sacraments of Initiation, whether the person is an adult or infant. However, as the oil of chrism has been consecrated by the bishop for this purpose, there is still a unity with the bishop in the celebration of the Sacrament.

Confirmation Sponsor

The Confirmation sponsor fulfills much the same role as the baptismal sponsor, which we examined in the last chapter. For this reason the *Catechism of the Catholic Church* states that it is highly appropriate, whenever possible, that one of the baptismal godparents should also be the Confirmation sponsor.[23]

The role of the sponsor is to make sure that the confirmed person acts as a true witness of Christ and faithfully fulfills the obligations to which the recipient has been called by this Sacrament.[24] For this reason, the Confirmation sponsor should be a practicing Catholic. In some parishes, the sponsors, for both adult catechumens and for high school students, attend the Confirmation or RCIA classes and retreats along with their respective candidates, and, in addition, undertake the obligation of praying for the candidates, in this, their last stage of Christian initiation.

The role of the sponsor is to make sure that the confirmed person acts as a true witness of Christ.

Confirmation Name

Another important element of the Sacrament is the choice of a Confirmation name. It has been a common practice for those being confirmed to choose the name of a saint who they particularly admire. This practice has its roots in ancient Christianity. In the early years of the Church, becoming a Christian meant a complete change in lifestyle and world view. To show their new identity as Christians, many people would abandon their pagan name and adopt a Christian name. This practice fell into disuse as the Baptism of children became the norm, and as children were given Christian names at birth.

When the monastic movement arose in the late fifth century, revitalizing the Western Church, those monks who went out into the desert to devote themselves to prayer and penance would often take a new name as an indication of their new vocation. To this day, it is common for those who join religious orders to take a religious name.

It is out of this history that we have the practice of choosing a Confirmation name. This new name is an expression of a new identity. Confirmation and the taking of a Confirmation name can be a wonderful opportunity to begin living again as a true Christian and friend of Jesus. It can be of great value to study the lives of the saints and to decide upon one who particularly inspires us by setting the kind of example we would like to follow.

Ceremony

Except for extraordinary circumstances, the Sacrament of Confirmation takes place during the celebration of Mass. After the Gospel, the pastor of the parish, another priest or deacon, or a catechist presents the candidates for Confirmation to the bishop. The bishop selects a reading from the Bible or other suitable words to explain the meaning of Confirmation.

Next, all renew their baptismal promises and make a profession of faith. This is particularly relevant for those who were baptized as infants. At that time, their parents and godparents made the baptismal promises for them. Now, as young adults, they are able to complete their Christian initiation by making these same promises themselves.

After a moment of silent prayer, the ritual continues with a prayer detailing the gifts of the Holy Spirit. The bishop extends his hands over those to be confirmed and, as at the baptism of Christ and at Pentecost, prays that the Holy Spirit descend upon them.

All-powerful God, Father of our Lord Jesus Christ, by water and the Spirit you freed your sons and daughters from sin and gave them new life. Send your Holy Spirit upon them to be their helper and guide. Give them the spirit of wisdom and understanding, the spirit of right judgment and courage, the spirit of knowledge and reverence. Fill them with the spirit of wonder and awe in your presence. We ask this through Christ our Lord.[25]

The candidates approach the bishop individually with their Confirmation sponsor behind them. The sponsor places his or her right hand on the shoulder of the candidate.

The bishop then dips his right thumb into the Holy Chrism and makes the Sign of the Cross on the person's forehead saying,

"(Name), be sealed with the gift of the Holy Spirit."

The newly confirmed responds, *"Amen."*

The bishop says, *"Peace be with you."*

The newly confirmed responds, *"And also with you."*

LIVING IN THE FOOTSTEPS OF CHRIST

When Sacred Scripture speaks of Christ as the "Anointed One," it is referring to an ancient tradition and practice that honored and signified a special calling from God. In the Old Testament, kings, priests, and prophets were anointed as part of their initiation into their vocation. As the Anointed One, Christ fulfills all these roles. He is the King of Heaven and Earth, the eternal High Priest, and the Word of God made flesh—the culmination of all the Old Testament prophets and he for whom they were sent to prepare the way.

With the Sacrament of Confirmation, we are reminded that as followers of Christ, Christians are called to a share in his kingly, priestly, and prophetic mission. We too are anointed to signify our initiation into this divinely inspired mission on earth.

The "kingly" aspect of the Christian vocation calls Christians to cooperate in the mission of the Church according to their particular state in life, and with the gifts that they have been given. St. Paul describes the Church as the Body of Christ. Through the Sacrament of Confirmation, each Christian is given gifts, which are meant to be exercised for the good of the Church and the world.

St. Peter Preaching by Masolino. Christ commanded his followers to preach the Good News to the ends of the earth.

As it is, there are many parts, yet one body....Now you are the body of Christ and individually members of it. And God has appointed in the church first apostles, second prophets, third teachers, then workers of miracles, then healers, helpers, administrators, speakers in various tongues. (1 Cor 12: 20, 27-28)

Each person has an important role to play, and, as in the human body, when one part fails, it affects the functioning of the whole. It is through prayer and discernment that one can come to a better understanding of the particular vocation to which God is calling each and every one of us. By making proper use of our particular gifts, our lives become fruitful, and we attain personal fulfillment and happiness.

When we think of priesthood, we most likely think of the ministerial priesthood, i.e., those men ordained to celebrate the sacraments. Properly speaking, a priest is a person who offers sacrifice; and indeed, one of the primary functions of a parish priest is to offer the Holy Sacrifice of the Mass. However, every Christian is called to participate in this priestly ministry of Christ. What this means is that each person is called to take every aspect of his or her life (prayer, work, family life, relationships, hobbies, relaxation, and even struggles, temptations, and sufferings), and to unite these things to the sacrifice of Christ on the Cross.

The Mass is an appropriate place to offer these events and activities up to the Lord. We can place them on the altar, offering them to the Father along with the sacrifice of Christ. In doing so, every human activity, and indeed the world itself, can be identified with the priesthood of Jesus Christ and consecrated to God.[26]

Throughout the Old Testament, God called certain people to reveal his divine truths to the world. This Divine Revelation found its fulfillment in Jesus Christ, the Eternal Word of God made flesh. In this sense, Jesus is the greatest of the Prophets. We can find all we need to know about God in the Person of Jesus Christ. However, Christ himself instituted a new prophetic mission during his Ascension, commanding his followers to preach his Good News to the ends of the earth.

At Pentecost, this command was realized in a very immediate way, and the Apostles took to the streets of Jerusalem to begin the work of spreading the word of Christ. Every Christian is called to participate in this mission of Christ, making his truth known to the world. Through Confirmation, each person is called to be a Christian witness in word and deed, and thereby share in the prophetic mission of Jesus Christ.

PREPARATION FOR CONFIRMATION

Needless to say, with such a noble mission awaiting the newly confirmed, a period of adequate preparation is required to help orient one's life and understanding towards the Christian vocation.

As a minimum requirement, a candidate for Confirmation, who has attained the age of reason, must first have received the Sacrament of Baptism, be in a state of grace, and have the intention to receive the Sacrament.

> A candidate for Confirmation who has attained the age of reason must profess the faith, be in the state of grace, have the intention of receiving the sacrament, and be prepared to assume the role of disciple and witness to Christ, both within the ecclesial community and in temporal affairs. (CCC 1319)

The person should have the proper dispositions in order to receive the graces intended to be conveyed by the Sacrament. For example, a person who receives Confirmation in a state of serious or mortal sin, or who receives the Sacrament only to please a parent or relative, would not receive the benefits of the Sacrament. An indelible mark or sacramental character would be imprinted on the soul, but the graces would not be infused until such a time that the person is properly disposed. If later, the person chooses to receive the spiritual benefits of Confirmation, they would simply need to make a good Confession, mentioning the improper reception of Confirmation.

In the United States, Confirmation may be received between the ages of seven and seventeen by those who earlier received Baptism in the Catholic Church. This means that the recipient is capable of spiritual maturity and responding to the invitation of the Christian life, helped by the grace of God, even in difficult situations. Deferring the reception of this Sacrament also presupposes that the person has received a thorough instruction in the Catholic Faith—the instruction that was promised to them by their parents and godparents at Baptism.

All parishes and many Catholic schools have programs in place to prepare young people, as well as adult candidates and catechumens, to receive the Sacrament of Confirmation. The preparation for this Sacrament should provide an opportunity for a Christian to gain a greater understanding of the benefits of Confirmation. This preparation also helps the person assume the apostolic responsibilities of a Christian life.

Preparation should include sufficient study so that the person being confirmed understands the meaning of the Sacrament, the gifts being received, and the obligations being undertaken. The candidates should also have the opportunity for personal reflection on this new stage in their Christian life. The Sacrament of Reconciliation and a life of personal prayer are indispensable in helping the person to be spiritually prepared to receive the gifts of Confirmation.

Preparation for Confirmation should aim at leading the Christian toward a more intimate union with Christ and a more lively familiarity with the Holy Spirit—his actions, his gifts, and his biddings—in order to be more capable of assuming the apostolic responsibilities of Christian life. (CCC 1309)

The role of the sponsor is also significant during this period of preparation. A Confirmation sponsor should be a practicing Catholic, who can serve as an example of how to live the Catholic Faith, and the candidates should find an opportunity to talk openly with their sponsors about their faith. Often, the sponsor is chosen precisely because he or she is a person the candidate looks up to and has served as a Christian example in his or her life. This time of preparation should be seen as an opportunity to learn even more from the sponsor and to use the wisdom of his or her experience as a way of preparing oneself for the difficulties that will arise after the reception of the Sacrament.

LIVING OUT THE SACRAMENT OF CONFIRMATION

Pentecost by Gaddi.

Confirmation is not only an ending of a journey, but also a new beginning. The confirmed has arrived at a level of maturity in which they can practice the fullness of the Faith as members of the Catholic Church.

Looking back at the Pentecost story, Jesus had trained his disciples personally for three years, carefully instructing them by his word and example. However, it was not until they received the gift of the Holy Spirit that they were filled with the courage to boldly proclaim the Faith.

Here we can find a model for our own Christian formation. It is after receiving the Sacrament of Confirmation and the promised gift of the Holy Spirit, that we can truly begin to live as disciples of Christ. In receiving Confirmation, we take on ourselves the same role as the Apostles in spreading the Faith. We do this by the way that we live our lives and by standing ready to explain to others the reasons why we live as Catholic Christians.

All of the graces received in Confirmation prepare us to practice what is known as the apostolate, that is, the work of evangelization. This evangelization can take the form of the great missionary activities carried out by some of the saints of the Church, or it can simply mean sharing the Faith with those around us.

THE POPE SPEAKS

"The Church which Christ founded by his blood, he strengthened on the day of Pentecost by a special power, given from Heaven...[S]itting now at the right hand of the Father, he wished to make known and proclaim his Spouse [the Church] through the visible coming of the Holy Spirit with the sound of a mighty wind and tongues of fire. For just as he himself when he began to preach was made known by his eternal Father through the Holy Spirit descending and remaining upon him in the form of a dove, so likewise, as the apostles were about to enter upon their ministry of preaching, Christ our Lord sent the Holy Spirit down from Heaven, to touch them with tongues of fire and to point out, as by the finger of God, the supernatural mission and office of the Church." [27] — Pope Pius XII

We are all called to do apostolate with both our fellow Catholics and those whom we meet outside the Faith in whatever way possible. This is the command Christ gave to us at his Ascension, and by our calling as followers of Christ, each Christian shares in the mission of the Church that Christ gave to his Apostles. However, this apostolate must begin with the serious practice of our own faith. Our Christian example in word and deed makes us a "witness" for Christ to those around us.

> The Church was founded for the purpose of spreading the kingdom of Christ throughout the earth for the glory of God the Father, to enable all men to share in his saving redemption.... the Christian vocation by its very nature is also a vocation to the apostolate. (*Apostolicam Actuositatem*, 2; cf. Eph 4:16)

Two important elements of living out the Sacrament are prayer and learning Sacred Scripture. The Scriptures contain a record of salvation history, especially information about the life, teachings, and self-Revelation of the Son of God, with whom we are united in Baptism and Confirmation (cf. CCC 50-51, 94-95, 1066). Prayer is essential to every believer as a foundation to know the actions of God the Holy Spirit and to follow his will (cf. CCC 1309, 1073, 2670-2672).

Living out the Sacrament of Confirmation also means participating in the sacramental life of the Church. Attending Mass on Sundays and Holy Days of Obligation and the frequent reception of the Sacraments of the Eucharist and Reconciliation, are all fundamental to our spiritual growth. Participation in the sacramental life of the Church offers us the opportunity to grow closer to Christ as we continue in our Christian journey.

CONCLUSION

Christ ascended into Heaven nearly two thousand years ago, but promised he would send us the Holy Spirit. As Catholics, we know that this promise is fulfilled in the Sacrament of Confirmation.

Through this Sacrament we receive the Holy Spirit, completing the Christian initiation that was begun in Baptism, and enabling us to become full members of the Body of Christ. As the recipients of this Sacrament, we bear a great responsibility to work towards becoming able and knowledgeable vessels of God's Holy Spirit in order to complete the mission that Christ gave to his Church. The combination of proper preparation for the Sacrament and the gifts we receive from the Holy Spirit will strengthen us to live out our sacred vocation.

The essential effect of Confirmation is to perfect the grace received in Baptism, strengthening the already existing bond that the baptized has with the Church through the power of the Holy Spirit. Its grace enables the confirmed to witness to Christ by word and deed.

As sons and daughters of God, the confirmed are called upon to act in every situation as Christ himself would act. This requires that we use the gifts that were given us by the Holy Spirit in Confirmation. When we cooperate with his grace, God will always grant us the strength to follow his will in our lives.

Ascension of Christ by Garofalo.
Through the Sacrament of Confirmation we become full members of the Body of Christ.

SUPPLEMENTARY READING

ST. THERESE OF LISIEUX

Imagine for a moment that you are in a dimly lit chapel. Candles light the altar as you are engulfed by soft voices praying the Rosary. You promise to focus completely on the prayers. You lift up your heart and...fall asleep. It is just another day in the life of St. Therese of Lisieux, better known as the "Little Flower." More than any other saint, Therese understood and explained the mystery of divine filiation, of living as a child of God. She loved Mary, but did not enjoy the Rosary. She was a mystic, but disliked retreats. St. Therese never got upset about falling asleep, because she was confident that God, like a good parent, loved his children even when they were sleeping.

Commenting on the mystery of her vocation, Therese writes, "Jesus does not call those who are worthy, but those he wants to call." This call began as a call to Carmel, a cloistered convent cut off from the rest of civilization. This call led to her being named the patroness of missionaries by Pius XI. Why would the Church choose as its patroness of missions one who had never physically done a mission? The answer quite simply is that the essence of missions

ST. THERESE OF LISIEUX
January 2, 1873 – September 30, 1897

St. Therese at age 15 before entering the Carmelite order.

is not a technique or a marketing strategy. Evangelization is the transmission of life, not of words. Words are certainly useful, but "the preachers of the Gospel could well tire themselves out, toil and lay down their lives to lead pagans to the Catholic religion; they might be ever so industrious, ever so diligent and use every means known to man; but none of this would be to any avail, everything would be in vain, if God, with his grace, were not to touch hearts, then the toil of missionaries would be in vain." [28]

Therese knew that she must be a child of God and that her only chance at holiness was to trust in God for all things. In the last pages

of her autobiography *The Story of a Soul*, she writes, "[i]n the eve of my life, I will come before you with nothing in my hands because I do not ask you to count the things I've done." Therese's holiness flew in the face of the dominant Pelagian heresy of her (and our) time—that it is better and safer to rely on ourselves than to receive God's grace. She truly lived Jesus' words: "Without me you can do nothing."

Instead, Therese let God act through her. Whenever God inspired her to a certain kind act, Therese shouted "yes!" unreservedly, faithfully, and happily. She did not try to "earn grace" by her sacrifices and exterior acts, but rather saw each trial as a gift from God so that she may be more closely united to her Savior, Jesus Christ. In all things, St. Therese acted as a child of God, and in all things she was rewarded as a child of God.

SUPPLEMENTARY READING

St. Cyril of Jerusalem, *Jerusalem Catecheses*, The anointing with the Holy Spirit

We became "the anointed ones" when we received the sign of the Holy Spirit....after coming up from the sacred waters of Baptism, were anointed with chrism, which signifies the Holy Spirit…

Beware of thinking that this holy oil is simply ordinary oil and nothing else. After the invocation of the Spirit it is no longer ordinary oil but the gift of Christ, and by the presence of his divinity it becomes the instrument through which we receive the Holy Spirit. While symbolically, on our foreheads and senses, our bodies are anointed with this oil that we see, our souls are sanctified by the holy and life-giving Spirit.

From a commentary on the Gospel of St. John by St. Cyril of Alexandria, Bishop

After Christ had completed his mission on earth, it still remained necessary for us to become sharers in the divine nature of the Word. We had to give up our own life and be so transformed that we would begin to live an entirely new kind of life that would be pleasing to God. This was something we could do only by sharing in the Holy Spirit.

It can easily be shown from examples both in the Old Testament and the New that the Spirit changes those in whom he comes to dwell; he so transforms them that they begin to live a completely new kind of life. With the Spirit within them it is quite natural for people who had been absorbed by the things of this world to become entirely other-worldly in outlook, and for cowards to become men of great courage. There can be no doubt that this is what happened to the disciples. The strength they received from the Spirit enabled them to hold firmly to the love of Christ, facing the violence of their persecutors unafraid.

God Inviting Christ to Sit on the Throne at His Right Hand by Grebber. Christ called God "Abba," the name that a young child gives to his father. This idea that we are children of God is at the forefront of the Lord's Prayer, which Christ taught to his disciples.

VOCABULARY

APOSTOLATE
The activity of each Christian that fulfills the apostolic nature of the whole Church by working to extend the reign of Christ to the entire world. Also called Evangelization.

CHRISM
Greek for "anointing." It is oil mixed with balsam, signifying the gift of the Holy Spirit, which is consecrated by a bishop. Chrism is used in the Sacraments of Baptism, Confirmation, and Holy Orders.

CHRISM MASS
The Mass at which a bishop consecrates the Sacred Chrism (mixture of oil and balsam) and blesses the Oil of Catechumens, and the Oil of the Sick, to be used for liturgical anointings.

CHRIST
Greek for "anointed." This is used in reference to Jesus because he accomplished perfectly the divine mission of Priest, Prophet, and King.

CONFIRMATION
One of the Sacraments of Initiation. It completes and confirms sanctifying grace first received in the Sacrament of Baptism by a special outpouring of the gifts and seal of the Holy Spirit. This Sacrament equips the confirmed for worship and apostolic life in the Church.

DIVINE FILIATION
A child of God. This consoling mystery brings each Christian a spirit of sincerity and trust while filling him or her with love for and wonder towards God; see the Parable of the Prodigal Son. (Lk 15:11-32)

FRUITS OF THE HOLY SPIRIT
"Perfections that the Holy Spirit forms in us as the first fruits of eternal glory. The tradition of the Church lists twelve of them: 'charity, joy, peace, patience, kindness, goodness, generosity, gentleness, faithfulness, modesty, self-control, chastity.'" [29] (CCC 1832)

GIFTS OF THE HOLY SPIRIT
The seven gifts of the Holy Spirit are wisdom, understanding, counsel, fortitude, knowledge, piety, and fear of the Lord. They belong in their fullness to Christ, Son of David.[30] They complete and perfect the virtues of those who receive them. They make the faithful docile in readily accepting divine inspirations. (CCC 1831) These gifts are given to Christians to assist them in following Christ and are conferred in a special way in the Sacrament of Confirmation.

LAYING ON OF HANDS
The ritual act, going back to the Old Testament, whereby men were consecrated for sacred duties. From the New Testament onward, it has been the action used to ordain men to the priesthood.

PENTECOST
Originally, a Jewish festival, fifty days after Passover, celebrating the giving of the Law to Moses at Sinai. Fifty days after Jesus' Resurrection, the Holy Spirit was manifested, given, and communicated to the Church, fulfilling the mission of Christ. This is the "birthday" of the Church.

SEAL
A permanent mark which is imprinted on the soul by the Sacraments of Baptism, Confirmation, and Holy Orders.

Pentecost, illustrated in a Book of Hours from France, ca.1450.

STUDY QUESTIONS

1. What are the Sacraments of Initiation?

2. What does the word "Christ" mean?

3. Who was anointed in the Old Testament?

4. How are the followers of Christ also "anointed" ones?

5. Why were the Apostles frightened?

6. How did the Apostles change when they received the Holy Spirit? What were they empowered to do?

7. Why had some of the early Christians not received the Holy Spirit? What did the Apostles do to convey the promised Spirit?

8. Why was perfumed oil added to the Sacrament? What does it symbolize?

9. What meaning does the word "confirmation" convey?

10. Why do the Eastern Rites of the Catholic Church refer to the Sacrament as Chrismation?

11. Why are Baptism and Confirmation sometimes referred to as a double sacrament? How is this meaning still preserved in the Eastern Churches' celebration of the Sacrament?

12. What is the purpose of Confirmation in the Christian journey begun at Baptism?

13. How does the Sacrament help a person in the Christian life?

14. What is apostolate? How does Confirmation help a Christian to do apostolate? Refer to the story of Pentecost.

15. What is the "kingly" aspect of the Christian mission?

16. What does it mean that every Christian participates in the priestly mission of Christ?

17. In what way are we called to be prophets for Christ?

18. What is the matter of Confirmation? Where does the matter come from?

19. What is the form of Confirmation?

20. Who is the minister for Confirmation?

21. Confirmation is usually celebrated by a bishop. When might it be celebrated by a priest in the Latin Rite?

22. What are the proper dispositions for receiving the Sacrament of Confirmation?

23. What is the purpose of deferring the Sacrament of Confirmation in the Latin Rite of the Catholic Church until the person has reached the age of reason?

24. What is the role of a Confirmation sponsor?

25. What would be good qualities to look for in a Confirmation sponsor?

26. What is the origin of a Confirmation name?

27. What is the relevance of the Confirmation name today?

28. What is the goal of preparation for Confirmation?

29. Why are the renewal of baptismal promises and the profession of faith relevant in Confirmation?

30. In what way are those receiving Confirmation made like Christ?

31. Describe the graces given by the Sacrament of Confirmation.

32. How can a Christian experience the wisdom of God?

33. Under what conditions can a person judge wisely?

34. How does a person learn the contents of Divine Revelation?

35. How does the gift of understanding affect the Christian life?

STUDY QUESTIONS Continued

36. How might a person prepare himself or herself to receive the most benefit from the gift of understanding?

37. What is the purpose of the gift of counsel?

38. In what way can a Christian be described as a soldier of Christ?

39. In what way does the gift of fortitude aid a person in the Christian life?

40. Explain how faith based on Divine Revelation can lead to greater knowledge than man is capable of by his own efforts.

41. What does *piety* mean?

42. What is the basis for the gift of piety? How does this affect our relations with God and neighbor?

43. How might Mt 25: 40 have inspired Bl. Teresa of Calcutta (Mother Teresa)?

44. How can fear be a gift, i.e., something positive?

45. Explain how this gift is expressed in the Act of Contrition.

46. What does it mean that love is proactive? What are some concrete ways in which we can be proactive in our love of God?

47. Explain how Confirmation is not an end, but a beginning.

PRACTICAL EXERCISES

1. A family with three children make the important decision to become Catholic. The children, ages fifteen, twelve, and ten, having reached the age of reason, are enrolled as catechumens with their parents. During the Easter Vigil Mass, the entire family is received into the Catholic Church receiving the Sacraments of Baptism, Confirmation, and the Eucharist. Some of the other students in the parish feel that it is unfair that they have to wait until they are 16 years old to receive Confirmation. Explain why these three children could properly receive Confirmation at an earlier age.

2. Think back to the last time that you went to Confession, or told God that you were sorry for your sins. What was your motivation: love of God, fear of punishment, or some degree of each?

3. Select two of the seven gifts of the Holy Spirit. List some concrete ways in which you could foster these gifts in your life.

4. Many people disagree with certain things that the Church teaches are sinful. List two of these and explain why they are wrong. Also come up with realistic situations in which the strength we receive in the Sacrament of Confirmation would be needed to defend the Church's teachings.

5. One of the most beautiful aspects of Confirmation is a deepening of one's roots in divine filiation, which makes one cry, "Abba, Father!" How are we God's children?

6. Because of her writings on being a child of God, St. Therese of Lisieux was made a Doctor of the Church even though she died at the age of twenty-four. Ask your spiritual director, pastor, or teacher to recommend a good book on St. Therese of Lisieux or on divine filiation.

FROM THE CATECHISM

1315 "Now when the apostles at Jerusalem heard that Samaria had received the word of God, they sent to them Peter and John, who came down and prayed for them that they might receive the Holy Spirit; for it had not yet fallen on any of them, but they had only been baptized in the name of the Lord Jesus. Then they laid their hands on them and they received the Holy Spirit."[31]

1316 Confirmation perfects Baptismal grace; it is the sacrament which gives the Holy Spirit in order to root us more deeply in the divine filiation, incorporate us more firmly into Christ, strengthen our bond with the Church, associate us more closely with her mission, and help us bear witness to the Christian faith in words accompanied by deeds.

1317 Confirmation, like Baptism, imprints a spiritual mark or indelible character on the Christian's soul; for this reason one can receive this sacrament only once in one's life.

1318 In the East this sacrament is administered immediately after Baptism and is followed by participation in the Eucharist; this tradition highlights the unity of the three sacraments of Christian initiation. In the Latin Church this sacrament is administered when the age of reason has been reached, and its celebration is ordinarily reserved to the bishop, thus signifying that this sacrament strengthens the ecclesial bond.

1319 A candidate for Confirmation who has attained the age of reason must profess the faith, be in the state of grace, have the intention of receiving the sacrament, and be prepared to assume the role of disciple and witness to Christ, both within the ecclesial community and in temporal affairs.

1320 The essential rite of Confirmation is anointing the forehead of the baptized with sacred chrism (in the East other sense-organs as well), together with the laying on of the minister's hand and the words: *"Accipe signaculum doni Spiritus Sancti"* (Be sealed with the Gift of the Holy Spirit.) in the Roman Rite, or: *"Signaculum doni Spiritus Sancti"* (the seal of the gift of the Holy Spirit) in the Byzantine rite.

1321 When Confirmation is celebrated separately from Baptism, its connection with Baptism is expressed, among other ways, by the renewal of baptismal promises. The celebration of Confirmation during the Eucharist helps underline the unity of the sacraments of Christian initiation.

ENDNOTES – CHAPTER TWO

1. Cf. *Roman Ritual, Rite of Confirmation (OC)* Introduction 1; CCC 1285.
2. Cf. CCC 1285.
3. Cf. CCC 1286.
4. Cf. Ez 36:25-27; Jl 3:1-2.
5. Cf. Acts 8:15-17; 19:5-6.
6. Cf. Heb 6:2.
7. Cf. CCC 1289.
8. St. Ambrose, *De Mysteriis*, 7.42.
9. CCC 1289.
10. *LG* 11; cf. *OC* Introduction 2.
11. *STh* III, 72, 1, ad 2m.
12. Cf. *Roman Ritual, Rite of Confirmation (OC)* Introduction 1; CCC 1285.
13. Cf. CIC, can. 889 § 1.
14. CIC, can. 890.
15. Cf. Jas 1:5.
16. St. Augustine, *Confessions*, I. 1.
17. Lk 24:31.
18. Lk 24:45.
19. Mt 25:40.
20. Cf. CIC, 880.
21. 2 Cor 2:15.
22. CCC 1312.
23. Cf. CIC, 893.
24. CIC, 892.
25. *OC* 25.
26. CCC 901.
27. Pope Pius XII, *The Pope Speaks*, edited by Michael Chinigo, New York, Pantheon, 1957.
28. Pius XI, *Rerum Ecclesiæ*.
29. Gal 5:22-23 (Vulg).
30. Cf. Is 11:1-2.
31. Acts 8:14-17.

The Eucharist

In the Sacrament of the Eucharist, Jesus gives us his own Body and Blood as spiritual nourishment to keep the flame of sanctifying grace burning brightly within us.

The Sacraments

CHAPTER 3

The Eucharist

So they drew near to the village to which they were going. He appeared to be going further, but they constrained him, saying, "Stay with us, for it is toward evening and the day is now far spent." So he went in to stay with them. When he was at table with them, he took the bread and blessed, and broke it, and gave it to them. And their eyes were opened and they recognized him; and he vanished out of their sight. (Lk 24: 28-31)

n the day of Jesus' Resurrection, two of his disciples were on their way to the town of Emmaus, talking about the amazing things they had just heard. Earlier, some of the women disciples had visited Jesus' tomb to anoint his body, but when they arrived they found the tomb empty. Furthermore, they reported seeing an angel who told them that Jesus had risen from the dead.

As the two disciples were discussing these strange events, a stranger approached them. They began to tell him about the news that was quickly spreading throughout Jerusalem. They had hoped Jesus was the promised Messiah who had come to redeem Israel, and yet he had been condemned to death and crucified.

And he said to them, "O foolish men, and slow of heart to believe all that the prophets have spoken! Was it not necessary that the Christ should suffer these things and enter into his glory?" And beginning with Moses and all the prophets, he interpreted to them in all the scriptures the things concerning himself. (Lk 24: 25-27)

But the disciples still did not recognize Jesus. When they reached their destination, they invited him to stay with them and to have dinner.

The two disciples on the road to Emmaus did not recognize the resurrected Christ. However, in the Breaking of the Bread, a term that the early Christians used to refer to the celebration of the Eucharist, Christ's presence was unmistakably revealed. This passage from the Gospel of St. Luke illustrates a great mystery of the Christian Faith: Christ remains physically present with us in the Sacrament of the Eucharist.

The Eucharist is the last of the Sacraments of Christian Initiation. In the Eucharist, Jesus gives us his own Body and Blood as spiritual nourishment to keep the flame of sanctifying grace burning brightly within us and to unite us more fully to himself and to his Body, which is the Church.

Like the other sacraments, the grace of God is mediated through the Eucharist. However, the Eucharist is different from the other sacraments in that it is not just the grace of God that is present in the Eucharist, but Christ himself. The story of the disciples on the road to Emmaus teaches us that we encounter Christ in a real and physical way in the Eucharist and that we need the Eucharist in order to recognize Our Lord.

IN THIS CHAPTER, WE WILL ADDRESS SEVERAL QUESTIONS:

✤ How was the Eucharist instituted?

✤ What is the Real Presence?

✤ What is the importance of the Mass?

✤ How is the Eucharist the center of Catholic life?

✤ How does the Eucharist transform those who receive it?

✤ What are the conditions for receiving the Eucharist?

The Last Supper by Otto van Veen.
Jesus was the sacrifice that would inaugurate a New Covenant in the history of God and his chosen people.

THE INSTITUTION OF THE EUCHARIST

When the time for the Passover had come, Jesus and his Apostles traveled to Jerusalem to celebrate this great Jewish Feast commemorating the deliverance of the Israelites from slavery in Egypt. This was a ritual meal and the evening would have proceeded according to custom, until Jesus did something that was quite different. At the point when the unleavened bread was eaten,

> Jesus took bread, and blessed, and broke it, and gave it to the disciples and said, "Take, eat; this is my body." And he took a cup, and when he had given thanks he gave it to them, saying, "Drink of it, all of you; for this is my blood of the covenant, which is poured out for many for the forgiveness of sins. (Mt 26: 26-28)

There must have been a shocked silence. Had Jesus really said that the bread and wine were his Body and Blood? What did he mean? The disciples were familiar with the Scriptures. "Blood of the covenant"[1] was referring to the establishment of the covenant between God and Israel. Was Jesus really saying that the cup of his own Blood was the ratification of a *New Covenant*? Was Jesus himself the *sacrifice* that would inaugurate a new age in the history of God and his Chosen People?

Christ in the Garden of Gethsemane by Conca.
"And there appeared to him an angel from Heaven, strengthening him." (Lk 22:43)

Then, there was another surprise. After the cup of blessing, the Passover meal called for the singing of a hymn, which would be followed by the drinking of the "cup of consummation." However, Scripture tells us that "when they had sung a hymn, they went out to the Mount of Olives."[2]

Jesus had dismissed the Apostles before the most important part of the meal—the culminating act of the Passover ritual. Jesus had decided that it was not yet time to drink the "cup of consummation," and in fact he said, "I shall not drink again of the fruit of the vine until that day when I drink it new in the kingdom of God."[3]

After the meal, in the Garden of Gethsemane, Jesus spoke again of this fourth and final cup, when, praying to his Father in Heaven, he said, "Father, if thou art willing, remove this cup from me; nevertheless not my will, but thine, be done."[4]

Later, speaking to St. Peter after he had cut off the ear of the high priest's slave, Jesus said, "Put your sword into its sheath; shall I not drink the cup which the Father has given me?"[5] In these verses, it becomes increasingly clear that the "cup of consummation," left untouched at the meal, would be his own Death, which would inaugurate a New Covenant with God.

It is when Jesus is on the Cross that we read about him drinking the fourth cup, bringing the Passover Feast begun nearly a day earlier to a close. Jesus said, "I thirst,"[6] and the soldiers offered him a sponge of sour wine on a branch of hyssop[7]—the same kind of branch that was used for sprinkling the blood of the Passover lamb.[8] As soon as he had tasted the sour wine, Jesus said, "It is finished."[9]

By choosing to institute the Eucharist in the context of a Passover meal and linking it to his Death on the Cross, Jesus was indicating that he would be the Lamb who takes away the sins of the world. In fact, St. John's Gospel relates how Pilate ordered the crucifixion on the Day of Preparation at the sixth hour; the very hour that the Passover lambs were sacrificed. Through his Death on the Cross, the Old Covenant was fulfilled and the New Covenant established—a covenant that would last until the end of time.

Jesus on the Cross by Rembrandt.
"When Jesus had received the vinegar, he said, 'It is finished';
and he bowed his head and gave up his spirit." (Jn 19:30)

THE PROMISE OF THE EUCHARIST: THE BREAD FROM HEAVEN DISCOURSE

The Last Supper was not the first time that Jesus had spoken about eating his Body and drinking his Blood. Earlier in the Gospel, we read about the miraculous multiplication of the loaves and fishes, which fed the multitude that had come to hear Jesus preach. Following this meal, Jesus spoke to the crowds about bread from Heaven.[10]

In this pivotal chapter of St. John's Gospel, Jesus refers to himself as the "Bread from Heaven." Just as their ancestors had been sustained in the desert by manna from Heaven, Jesus would offer his Body and Blood for the nourishment of the soul. However, unlike their ancestors who died, Christ was offering them food of everlasting life.

At this point in his public ministry, Jesus was at the peak of his popularity, with thousands eagerly gathering around him to hear his teaching. Amazed at his feeding of the five thousand, the crowds sought him out, and questioned Jesus about the miracle of the multiplication of the loaves and fishes. Jesus used this opportunity to tell them about another, greater miracle to come:

> I am the bread of life; he who comes to me shall not hunger, and he who believes in me shall never thirst. (Jn 6:35)

It was hard for the crowds to understand what he meant. But he repeated himself, becoming more and more specific. The crowd became upset with Jesus' claim that he had come down from Heaven. However, Jesus did not back down from his original claim, nor did he explain it away as a metaphor. Rather, he said,

> I am the living bread which came down from heaven; if any one eats of this bread, he will live for ever; and the bread which I shall give for the life of the world is my flesh. (Jn 6:51)

The Jews began to dispute among themselves, asking how he could give his flesh for the life of the world. Jesus must have known full well that he would soon lose this large group of followers unless he backed down from this difficult teaching. However, instead of softening the message, he went even further, comparing himself to the manna, which their ancestors ate in the desert.

The Miracle of the Loaves and Fishes by Lombard.
"Do not labor for the food which perishes, but for the food which endures to eternal life." (Jn 6:27)

> Truly, truly, I say to you, unless you eat the flesh of the Son of man and drink his blood, you have no life in you; he who eats my flesh and drinks my blood has eternal life, and I will raise him up at the last day. For my flesh is food indeed, and my blood is drink indeed. He who eats my flesh and drinks my blood abides in me, and I in him. As the living Father sent me, and I live because of the Father; so he who eats me will live because of me. This is the bread which came down from heaven, not such as the fathers ate and died; he who eats this bread will live forever. (Jn 6: 53-58)

Now the Jews were amazed and most likely disturbed at what they were hearing. Jesus expected them to eat him? They were not cannibals! It was even more shocking because the word we translate from the Greek as "eat" was an especially vivid word, similar to the English word "munch." These statements proved too much for many of them to accept and so the large crowd began to disperse.

Those who had been following Christ and had come to believe that he was a great prophet were dismayed by this new teaching, and so they pushed him further, demanding an explanation. But Jesus did not change his words. Soon, they too began leaving him, unable to accept this teaching. From the dizzying heights of success, Jesus now had only the twelve at his side. He turned to them and said,

> "Do you also wish to go away?" Simon Peter answered him, "Lord, to whom shall we go? You have the words of eternal life; and we have believed, and have come to know, that you are the Holy One of God." (Jn 6: 67-69)

St. Peter did not claim to understand Jesus' teaching on the bread of life. However, he trusted that what Jesus was saying was true. He had faith and would remain with Jesus. It would only be later, at the Last Supper, that the full meaning of Jesus' words would be revealed to him and the other Apostles.

In this narrative given to us by St. John, we see two essential, interrelated teachings on the Eucharist. The first is that the Eucharist is a spiritual food, which gives us the graces needed for everlasting life. The second is that the Eucharist is truly the Body and Blood of Our Lord, Jesus Christ.

THE REAL PRESENCE

The sacraments are a continuation of the saving ministry of Jesus Christ, and through the sacraments we can encounter him. In Baptism, it is Christ who cleanses us from sin, and in Confirmation, it is Christ who mediates his Holy Spirit.

The Sacrament of the Eucharist differs from the other sacraments in one significant way. The baptismal water, while holy, is still only water, and the oil, which marks the seal of the confirmed, is still only oil. When the priest repeats the words of Consecration during the celebration of the Mass, however, the bread and wine become the Body and Blood of Christ, along with his soul and divinity, present in a true, real, and substantial manner. Only the appearance of bread and wine remain. This mystery of Faith is known as the "Real Presence" of Christ in the Eucharist.

> It is highly fitting that Christ should have wanted to remain present to his Church in this unique way. Since Christ was about to take his departure from his own in his visible form, he wanted to give us his sacramental presence; since he was about to offer himself on the cross to save us, he wanted us to have the memorial of the love with which he loved us "to the end,"[11] even to the giving of his life. In his Eucharistic presence he remains mysteriously in our midst as the one who loved us and gave himself up for us,[12] and he remains under signs that express and communicate this love. (CCC 1380)

This understanding of the Real Presence of Christ in the Eucharist is detailed in Sacred Scripture. In fact, every verse of Scripture that speaks about the Eucharist demands that it be understood in literal, rather than symbolic, terms.

In his accounts of the Last Supper and the Bread of Life discourse, St. John used the Greek verb "to be," which has a literal, rather than a symbolic, connotation. Furthermore, the reaction of Jesus' audience to the Bread of Life discourse indicates that they understood his words literally. Both the crowd and his own disciples understood that Jesus meant that we must really eat his Flesh and drink his Blood. Had they misunderstood him, it stands to reason that Jesus would have tried to clarify his message, but he instead allowed them to leave.

The Emmaus Disciples by Bloemaert. In the Breaking of the Bread, Christ's presence was revealed.

The first detailed account of the Christian celebration of the Eucharist comes from the First Letter of St. Paul to the Corinthians. At the time, these early followers of Christ were meeting in homes to celebrate the Eucharist in much the same way that Jesus did in the Last Supper. Writing to the Church in Corinth, Paul addressed certain abuses that were occurring in these early Christian Eucharistic celebrations.

> The cup of blessing which we bless, is it not a participation in the blood of Christ? The bread which we break, is it not a participation in the body of Christ? (1 Cor 10:16)

> As often as you eat this bread and drink the cup, you proclaim the Lord's death until he comes. Whoever, therefore, eats the bread or drinks the cup of the Lord in an unworthy manner will be guilty of profaning the body and blood of the Lord. Let a man examine himself, and so eat of the bread and drink of the cup. For any one who eats and drinks without discerning the body eats and drinks judgment upon himself. (1 Cor 11:26-29)

St. Paul compares the Eucharist to the sacrifices of the Old Testament and to pagan sacrifices as well. When one eats the food, which has been sacrificed, one participates in the sacrifice itself. By consuming the Eucharistic "bread and wine," we participate in the sacrifice of the Body and Blood of Our Lord.

Furthermore, St. Paul uses the word "discern" when speaking about recognizing Christ in the Eucharist. The word "discern" means to perceive the difference between things. For example, a person who can distinguish good food from bad is said to have discerning taste. St. Paul is saying that the Christian must recognize that the Eucharist is the Body and Blood of Christ and distinguish it from ordinary bread and wine.

It is evident in a number of other early Christian letters and writings that the Eucharist was understood as a transformation of the bread and wine into the Body and Blood of Jesus Christ. St. Ignatius of Antioch (AD 107), writing to the Philadelphians, stated,

> Be careful, therefore, to take part only in the one eucharist; for there is only one flesh of our Lord Jesus Christ and one cup to unite us with his blood, one altar and one bishop with the presbyters and deacons, who are his fellow servants. Then, whatever you do, you will do according to God.

Further elaborating on the Real Presence of Christ in the Eucharist, St. Irenæus of Lyon, writing around the end of the second century, said,

> He declares that the cup, taken from the creation, is his own blood, by which he strengthens our blood, and he has firmly assured us that the bread, taken from the creation, is his own body, by which our bodies grow....the mixed cup and the bread that has been prepared received the Word of God,...becomes the Eucharist, the body and blood of Christ.[13]

The early Christians understood that the Eucharist established at the Last Supper fulfilled the words spoken by Jesus about the bread of life in the Gospel of St. John. This belief went to the root of their faith, forming the foundation of their prayer, community, and religious practice. Gathered around the Eucharist, and strengthened by its spiritual nourishment, they grew strong in faith.

Further explaining the belief in the Real Presence, the *Catechism of the Catholic Church* states,

> "Because Christ our Redeemer said that it was truly his body that he was offering under the species of bread, it has always been the conviction of the Church of God...that by the consecration of the bread and wine there takes place a change of the whole substance of the bread into the substance of the body of Christ our Lord and of the whole substance of the wine into the substance of his blood." [14] (CCC 1376)

Trusting in the words of Jesus, the Catholic Church teaches that by the Consecration, the whole and entire substance of bread and wine is changed in a true, real, and substantial manner into the Body and Blood of Christ, with his soul and divinity. This change from one substance to another is called

By an act of God, after the words of consecration, there is no longer bread or wine present. They have truly become the Body and Blood of Christ.

transubstantiation. By an act of God, after the words of Consecration, there is no longer bread or wine present. Every single piece of bread and every single drop of wine have been changed.

> Under the consecrated species of bread and wine Christ himself, living and glorious, is present in a true, real, and substantial manner: his Body and his Blood, with his soul and his divinity. [15] (CCC 1413)

Regarding the Real Presence of Christ in the Eucharist, the Church teaches the following:

✤ the whole of Christ is present as a substance (i.e., the Eucharist is truly the Body, Blood, Soul, and Divinity of Christ, although the accidents or material appearance of bread and wine remain);

✤ the whole of Christ is present in each and every part of the Eucharist;

✤ the whole of Christ is present even if the parts are divided;

✤ the Presence of Christ is sacramental (i.e., the reality comes to us through a sign, in this case bread and wine); and

✤ the Presence of Christ endures as long as the appearance of bread and wine remain.

NAMES OF THE EUCHARIST

Because of the unique nature of the Eucharist, the Sacrament has been given many names throughout the history of the Church. [16]

✤ The word *Eucharist* comes from the Greek *eucharistein*, meaning to "give thanks." This term finds its origin in the words of Scripture, preceding the Consecration, "When he had *given thanks*...." [17] St. Ignatius of Lyon (ca. AD 107) referred to the Body and Blood of Our Lord as the Eucharist, and this terminology has been commonly used in the Church since that time.

✤ The sacrament is called the *Lord's Supper*, because of its connection to the Last Supper of Our Lord. This name also refers to the Eucharistic celebration as an anticipation of the wedding feast of the Lamb in the heavenly Jerusalem.

THE MIRACLE OF LANCIANO

In the village of Lanciano, Italy, in the 8th century, a monk was struggling with his belief in the Real Presence of Christ in the Eucharist. Though he prayed for faith, he was continually plagued by lingering doubt. One morning while celebrating Mass, he said the words of Consecration, wondering whether it was truly the Body and Blood of our Lord Jesus Christ. At that moment, before his very eyes, the bread turned into real flesh and the wine into real blood. Trembling from shock and amazement, he turned to the people gathered at Mass and announced that a great miracle had occurred. His prayers had been answered in an unexpected way. His doubts had now completely vanished and his faith had been fully restored. News of the miracle quickly spread throughout the village and indeed throughout all of Italy.

What makes this miracle particularly amazing is that it continues to our own day. Nearly 1,300 years later, the flesh and blood, which should have decomposed within days, are in the same perfect condition as at that first moment of Consecration. Modern scientific examinations can not explain it.

The miracle of Lanciano was a gift, not only to the doubting monk, but to the entire Church to strengthen the faith of all believers.

As Catholics, we have been given a great privilege. To witness the miracle of the Eucharist, it is not necessary to travel to Lanciano in pilgrimage. One can witness the miracle of the Eucharist at each and every Mass celebrated anywhere throughout the world. We should give thanks for this tremendous gift each time that we attend the celebration of the Most Holy Eucharist.

The Host, now changed to Flesh, is contained in a silver Monstrance. The wine, now changed to Blood, is contained in a crystal chalice. The actual spot of the Miracle is located beneath the present day tabernacle of the Church of St. Francis (built on top of the 8th century church) in Lanciano, Italy.

The Miracle is preserved in the second tabernacle, which is found in the high altar (left).

✠ The Eucharistic celebration, the *Mass*, is called the *Breaking of the Bread*, because it was when Jesus broke bread that the disciples recognized him on the road to Emmaus. This was the term most often used by the first Christians following Pentecost.

✠ *Eucharistic assembly* refers to the fact that the Eucharist, like all of the sacraments, is an action of the Christian community.

✠ In receiving the Eucharist, a Christian is united to Christ and to the other members of the Christian community. Therefore, the sacrament is rightfully called *Holy Communion*.

✠ The entire celebration of the Eucharist is called the *Holy and Divine Liturgy* (*Liturgy of the Eucharist*), because the Mass is an action of the Church. In the Church's liturgy, we encounter the sacred mysteries of Christ and participate in the liturgy celebrated by the angels and saints in Heaven.

✠ The Eucharist is called the *Holy Sacrifice*, because it completes, surpasses, and perfects the sacrifices of the Old Testament, each of which foreshadowed the one and eternal sacrifice of Christ.

✠ The Eucharist is also called a *memorial*, because it reminds us of the Lord's Passion, Death, and Resurrection.

✠ The name *Holy Mass* is derived from the Latin *mittere*, meaning to send forth. This comes from the last words of the Mass, "*Ite, missa est,*" in which Catholics, transformed by the Eucharist, are sent forth in the peace of Christ to transform the world.

✠ The Eucharist is also called the *bread of angels, bread from Heaven*, and *medicine of immortality*, because in the Eucharist we receive the spiritual graces needed to live the Christian vocation.

THE HOLY SACRIFICE OF THE MASS

The celebration of the Eucharist serves as a memorial, or a reminder, of Christ's Passion and Death on the Cross, which brought us our salvation. But it is more than just an ordinary memorial: the actual sacrifice of Christ is re-presented to us in the Liturgy of the Eucharist.

> In the sense of Sacred Scripture the *memorial* is not merely the recollection of past events but the proclamation of the mighty works wrought by God for men.[18] In the liturgical celebration of these events, they become in a certain way present and real. This is how Israel understands its liberation from Egypt: every time Passover is celebrated, the Exodus events are made present to the memory of believers so that they may conform their lives to them. (CCC 1363)

Christ's command at the Last Supper to "do this in memory of me" was profound. In celebrating the Liturgy of the Mass, Christians participate in the primary religious expression of the New Covenant. Indeed, it is this covenant, this saving and redemptive action of Christ, which is proclaimed at each Mass.

Adoration of the Lamb by Van Eyck. Jesus Christ, the last Passover Lamb, will never be sacrificed again. Each time the Liturgy of the Mass is offered, Calvary is present on our altar.

The Last Supper was a celebration of the Passover meal, which commemorates the Israelites' passage out of slavery in Egypt. Christ's command, "Do this in memory of me," transformed the Passover sacrifice into the sacrifice of the Eucharist.

Sacrifices in the Old Covenant

Christ told his disciples that he had not come to destroy the Old Law, but to fulfill it. In the Last Supper, we see how Christ embraced the tradition of the Jewish Passover, while at the same time transforming it, making it new.

The use of bread and wine offers rich symbolic meaning associated with certain Jewish traditions, especially the Passover meal, which commemorated the Israelites' passage out of slavery in Egypt. The offering of bread and wine was also foreshadowed by the Priest/King Melchizedek, who offered a sacrifice of bread and wine with Abram in thanksgiving for Abram's defeat of four kings.[19]

There were many sacrifices and rituals in the Jewish religion. These sacrifices, practiced by the Israelites in the Old Testament, had four distinctive characteristics. The Eucharist, which Christ commanded his Apostles to celebrate, fulfills these requirements of a sacrifice:

✤ *It is offered by a priest.* In the Mass it is Christ, the eternal High Priest, who offers the sacrifice through the ministry of the human priesthood.

✤ *The victim is an unblemished male.* The victim of the Eucharistic sacrifice is Christ himself. Although present in his resurrected form, he is the Lamb of God "standing as though it had been slain." (Rev 5:6)

✤ *It is offered in remission for sin.* The Redemption earned by Christ on Calvary becomes our sacrifice for the redemption of sins in the Holy Mass.

✤ *It is destroyed in some manner.* This signifies that the offering is not for our own use but is intended for God. On Calvary, Christ's Body was broken. Though now in his resurrected form, this same victim is present on our altar at Mass. This is the offering we make to the Father.

The victim (i.e., the animal or object of sacrifice) in the Old Testament was destroyed in some manner. For example, a lamb would be slaughtered and then be given to God as a burnt offering. Then, following the sacrifice, the flesh of the lamb would be consumed by the priests. This act of consuming the victim united the priest to the sacrifice. In the words of St. Paul, "...are not those who eat the sacrifices partners in the altar?"[20] We become united to the sacrifice of Christ precisely when we receive the Eucharist in the reception of Holy Communion.

There is also another symbolic meaning of the bread and wine offered in the Eucharist. In making bread, many grains of wheat are ground and destroyed, being transformed into one loaf. In like manner, many grapes are crushed and destroyed, being transformed into one wine. By analogy, Christians, through the Sacrament of the Eucharist are transformed into the one Body of Christ.

The New Covenant Sacrifice

While the sacrifices of the Old Testament were imperfect, needing to be repeated time and time again, the sacrifice of Christ, the Son of God, is perfect. Like God himself, Christ's sacrifice is eternal and has infinite value, its benefits encompassing all of human history. Its merit is enough to repair the damage caused by the sin of the world, and it contains enough grace for every man, woman, and child until the end of time. In this sense, Jesus will never be sacrificed again, and in this light, we can properly understand the meaning of Jesus as the eternal High Priest.

The sacrifice of the Mass is Christ's gift, which allows us to participate in his sacrifice and to receive the benefits won for us on Calvary. The Eucharist makes Christ's eternal sacrifice, offered once and for all on Calvary, real and present to us in our own lives. For this reason, "the Eucharist is the heart and the summit of the Church's life."[21]

Each time the Holy Sacrifice of the Mass is offered, the Eucharist transcends time and place, making that moment on Calvary, two thousand years ago, present on our altar. "The sacrifice of Christ and the sacrifice of the Eucharist are *one single sacrifice*."[22] The unique sacrifice of Christ on the Cross is re-presented (made present) in each and every Mass that is validly celebrated. Each time we attend the Liturgy of the Eucharist, Christ invites us to participate in the Body and Blood given up for us so that we may have a share in his divine life.

Crucifixion by Nardo di Cione. The sacrifice of the Eucharist and the sacrifice of Christ on the Cross are one and the same.

> The Eucharist is the heart and the summit of the Church's life, for in it Christ associates his Church and all her members with his sacrifice of praise and thanksgiving offered once for all on the cross to his Father; by this sacrifice he pours out the graces of salvation on his Body which is the Church. (CCC 1407)

The *Didache*, a first-century Christian text, speaks of this understanding of the Mass as a sacrifice:

> On every Lord's Day—his special day—come together and break bread and give thanks, first confessing your sins so that your sacrifice may be pure. Anyone at variance with his neighbor must not join you, until they are reconciled, lest your sacrifice be defiled. For it was of this sacrifice that the Lord said "Always and everywhere offer me a pure sacrifice; for I am a great King, says the Lord, and my name is marveled at by the nations."[23] (*Didache* 14:1-4)

The sacrifice of the Eucharist and the sacrifice of Christ on the Cross are one and the same. On Calvary, Christ offered himself to the Father. In the Eucharist, the resurrected Christ gives himself to us sacramentally, under the appearance of bread and wine, to be offered as a perfect and living sacrifice to our Father in Heaven.

> The sacrifice of Christ and the sacrifice of the Eucharist are *one single sacrifice*: "The victim is one and the same: the same now offers through the ministry of priests, who then offered himself on the cross; only the manner of offering is different." "And since in this divine sacrifice which is celebrated in the Mass, the same Christ who offered himself once in a bloody manner on the altar of the cross is contained and is offered in an unbloody manner...this sacrifice is truly propitiatory."[24] (CCC 1367)

In offering the sacrifice of Mass, the Redemption, which was earned by Christ is applied to our lives. In this sense, the most Holy Sacrifice of the Mass is a renewal of the one sacrifice of Christ. The words "representation" and "reenactment" are used to describe the sacrifice of the Mass. Each of these words, however inadequate, attempts to express the idea that the Mass makes present and effective in our lives the one redeeming sacrifice of Christ on Calvary.

As a gift from God, the Mass directly benefits every believer. As often as the sacrifice of the Mass is celebrated, the work of our salvation is carried out. The sacrifice of the Mass is offered for all people, including the faithful departed (the Holy Souls in Purgatory) who have not yet entered Heaven.

What is accomplished by the Eucharistic liturgy is truly amazing. Through the Death and Resurrection of Jesus, the whole of creation is presented as a gift to the Father. For just as everything was tainted by the fall of man in his Original Sin, so all of creation has been redeemed by Christ's Sacrifice.

By sharing in the priesthood of Christ, we can offer God our joys, sufferings, work, anxieties, relationships, and ourselves. United with the Eucharist, these gifts will be transformed and found acceptable to our Father in Heaven. In this way, the Mass becomes a primary means to holiness for the People of God.

THE CELEBRATION OF THE MASS IN THE EARLY CHURCH

The form of the Eucharistic celebration familiar to Catholics today has its roots in the ancient celebrations of the early Christians. In the Acts of the Apostles, we read that the first Christians in Jerusalem met each day in the Temple for prayer and later in their homes for the breaking of bread, a practice that laid the foundation for the two parts of the Mass: the Liturgy of the Word and the Liturgy of the Eucharist.[25]

The early Christians considered themselves to be Jews, the difference being that they recognized Jesus as the promised Messiah. For this reason, they continued to meet in their local synagogue for the Sabbath worship on Saturday. Then, early on Sunday morning, the Day of the Lord, they would meet in someone's home, under the leadership of one or more of the Apostles or a person who had been appointed by them. There they would tell the stories of Jesus (as of yet there were no written books of the New Testament, only the oral Tradition), and the celebration would culminate in the Breaking of the Bread.

The two parts of the Mass came to be united early in the history of the Church. The eventual expelling of the Jewish Christians from the synagogues, as well as the influx of Gentile Christians, meant that they needed a new place to worship. The liturgical service of the synagogue (the Liturgy of the Word) was followed by the Breaking of Bread (the Liturgy of the Eucharist), both occurring now in one celebration on Sunday morning.

The writings of St. Justin Martyr (ca. AD 155) give us detailed information regarding the celebration of the Liturgy of the Eucharist. This basic structure, whether celebrated in the Latin Rite, or the various rites of both East and West, has remained fundamentally the same.

THE HOLY CHALICE OF VALENCIA

In July 2006, at the closing Mass of the fifth World Meeting of Families in Valencia, Spain, Pope Benedict XVI celebrated the Eucharist with the Holy Chalice of Valencia, saying "this most famous chalice," words in the Roman Canon said to have been used by the first popes until the fourth century in Rome. Venerated by millions of believers and displayed at the Cathedral of Valencia, many consider that this agate cup is the same cup that was used by the Lord at the Last Supper, then was taken to Rome by St. Peter and kept by subsequent popes up to Pope St. Sixtus II.

THE CELEBRATION OF THE EUCHARIST

From *The First Apology* (In Defense of the Christians) by St. Justin Martyr (ca. AD 155)

We do not consume the Eucharistic bread and wine as if it were ordinary food and drink, for we have been taught that as Jesus Christ our Savior became a man of flesh and blood by the power of the Word of God, so also the food that our flesh and blood assimilates for its nourishment becomes the flesh and blood of the incarnate Jesus by the power of his own words contained in the prayer of thanksgiving....

On Sunday we have a common assembly of all our members, whether they live in the city or the outlying districts. The recollections of the apostles or the writings of the prophets are read, as long as there is time. When the reader has finished, the president of the assembly speaks to us; he urges everyone to imitate the examples of virtue we have heard in the readings. Then we all stand up together and pray.

On the conclusion of our prayer, bread and wine and water are brought forward. The president offers prayers and gives thanks to the best of his ability, and the people give assent by saying, "Amen." The Eucharist is distributed, everyone present communicates, and the deacons take it to those who are absent.

The wealthy, if they wish, may make a contribution, and they themselves decide the amount. The collection is placed in the custody of the president, who uses it to help the orphans and widows and all who for any reason are in distress, whether because they are sick, in prison, or away from home. In a word, he takes care of all who are in need.

We hold our common assembly on Sunday because it is the first day of the week, the day on which God put darkness and chaos to flight and created the world, and because on that same day our Savior Jesus Christ rose from the dead. For he was crucified on Friday and on Sunday he appeared to his apostles and disciples and taught them the things that we have passed on for your consideration.

THE ANTIOCH CHALICE

Byzantine, first half of the sixth century
The Metropolitan Museum of Art, Cloisters Collection

Discovered at the beginning of the twentieth century, this chalice was claimed to have been found in Antioch, a city so important to the early Christians that it was recognized with Rome and Alexandria as one of the great sees of the Church and St. Peter's first see. The chalice's plain silver interior bowl was then identified as the Holy Grail, the cup used by Christ at the Last Supper. The elaborate footed shell enclosing it was thought to have been made within a century after the death of Christ to encase and honor the Grail. The identification of the "Antioch Chalice" as the Holy Grail has not been sustained. It is now considered to be a sixth century chalice used for the Eucharist in or near the churches of Antioch.

Comments provided by The Metropolitan Museum of Art

SCRIPTURE READINGS
Lay readers may proclaim all of the Scripture readings except for the Gospel, which is reserved for a deacon or priest.

THE LITURGY OF THE MASS
(The Ordinary Form of the Latin Rite)

The Liturgy of the Word

PREPARATION FOR MASS – It is customary for people to gather for Mass a few minutes before it is time to begin. Entering the church they dip their fingers in the holy water font, making the Sign of the Cross. This is a sign of one's Baptism and a prayer asking for purity in preparation for the Eucharistic celebration. Before sitting down, each person genuflects in the direction of the tabernacle, silently acknowledging the Real Presence of Christ in the Eucharist. A few minutes should be spent in silent prayer preparing for the Most Holy Sacrifice of the Mass.

THE ENTRANCE – The Mass begins with a procession. On solemn occasions this might consist of altar servers carrying the cross, lighted candles, and incense, and a lector carrying the Book of the Gospels, followed by the priest and deacon. They will proceed from the narthex in the back of the church to the altar. During the procession, the congregation sings hymns, which reflect either a particular theme of the Mass or the liturgical season. On weekdays, the Mass begins with the entrance of the priest from the sacristy into the sanctuary.

VENERATION OF THE ALTAR – The priest enters the sanctuary and kisses the altar. On solemn occasions he may also incense the altar. When the entrance song finishes, the priest begins with the Sign of the Cross.

PENITENTIAL RITE – The penitential rite is comprised of the *Confiteor* ("I Confess...") and the *Kyrie Eleison* ("Lord have mercy..."). These prayers ask God and neighbor to forgive our sins and our failures to perform the obligations of the Christian life.

HOMILY
The priest or deacon gives a commentary on the readings and applies them to our lives.

GLORIA – The *Gloria* ("Glory to God…") is a song of praise to each person of the Blessed Trinity.

COLLECT (Opening Prayer) – The Collect is a prayer summarizing the intentions suggested by the feast or particular celebration.

SCRIPTURE READINGS – The Scripture readings are from The Old Testament, the Book of Psalms, the Epistles, and the Gospels. Lay readers may be used for all of the Scripture readings, except for the Gospel, which is reserved for a priest or deacon. The readings are selected according to a three-year cycle (a two-year cycle is used for weekday Masses), which reflect the theme of the particular Mass and stress the relationship between the Old and New Testaments.

HOMILY – The priest or deacon gives a commentary on the readings.

PROFESSION OF FAITH – During Sunday Mass and on major feast days, the Nicene Creed is said. (In Masses with children, the Apostles' Creed is permitted.) This is a concise statement of the Catholic Faith.

GENERAL INTERCESSIONS – These are a series of prayers for the good of individuals, the world, and the Church.

The General Intercessions bring the Liturgy of the Word to a close. In the early days of Christianity, only the baptized were allowed to remain for the Liturgy of the Eucharist. In fact, the word Mass itself comes from the Latin *mittere* meaning dismissal. Because of the dismissal of the Catechumens, the Liturgy of the Word was sometimes known as the Mass of the Catechumens.

Today, generally speaking, anyone may now stay throughout the entire Mass. However, there is still a transition between the Liturgy of the Word and the Liturgy of the Eucharist. The priest prepares the altar, while the congregation sings a hymn. A collection is also taken at this time to support the parish and those in need.

INSTITUTION NARRATIVE AND CONSECRATION
This prayer recalls the Last Supper of the Lord in which the celebration of the Eucharist was instituted.

The Liturgy of the Eucharist

PRESENTATION OF THE OFFERINGS (Offertory) – Members of the congregation bring gifts of bread, wine, water, and donations to the altar. The priest prays that the gifts of bread and wine might be acceptable to God and become the Body and Blood of Our Lord Jesus Christ.

EUCHARISTIC PRAYER – This is the primary prayer of the Liturgy of the Eucharist and contains several parts:

✠ **Thanksgiving** – The priest gives thanks (Greek *eucharistia*) to the Father for his gift of salvation.

✠ **Acclamation** – In recognition that the Celebration of the Mass is a participation in the heavenly liturgy, the people join the choirs of angels in singing the *Sanctus* (Holy, Holy, Holy...). (Rev 4: 8)

✠ **Epiclesis** – The priest prays that the Holy Spirit may come down to change the bread and wine into the Body and Blood of Our Lord.

✠ **Institution narrative and Consecration** – This prayer recalls the Last Supper of the Lord in which the celebration of the Eucharist was instituted. It ends with the priest repeating the words of Our Lord, "This is my Body...This is the cup of my Blood." With the words of Consecration, the bread and wine become the Body and Blood of Our Lord Jesus Christ.

✠ **Anamnesis** – The Church recalls the suffering, Death, Resurrection, and Ascension of Jesus.

✠ **Offering** – The entire Church offers the sacrifice of Jesus Christ, asking that it be acceptable to God the Father. The people offer themselves, along with their joys, sufferings, work, and indeed all human activities to God, joined with the sacrifice of Christ. In this manner, all the faithful are part of the priesthood of Christ.

COMMUNION
The Mass is a sacrificial meal in which we partake of the Victim we have offered, transforming us into the Body of Christ.

✣ **Intercessions** – In acknowledgment of the Communion of Saints, the Church joins the fellowship of the saints in the heavenly liturgy. The Church shows its unity with the holy souls in Purgatory by praying that all who sleep in Christ find happiness in the presence of God.

✣ **Final Doxology** – The Eucharistic prayer ends with a praise to God for all of his gifts and blessings.

COMMUNION RITE:

✣ **Lord's Prayer** – The people join together to pray as Jesus taught.

✣ **Rite of Peace** – Remembering the words of St. Paul that the Eucharist is a sign of unity in Christ, the members of the congregation greet each other with a sign of peace before approaching the Eucharistic table.

✣ **Breaking of Bread** – In imitation of the action of Christ at the Last Supper and remembering the broken Body of Christ on the Cross, the host is broken. A small piece is placed in the chalice signifying the unity of the Church.

✣ **Agnus Dei (Lamb of God)** – The congregation acknowledges that Jesus is the Lamb of God, whose sacrifice is the source of our forgiveness and salvation, and asks Jesus for his mercy.

✣ **Communion** – God invites us to the heavenly banquet. The Mass is a sacrificial meal in which we partake of the victim we have offered, transforming us into the Body of Christ.

After the Holy Eucharist is distributed, the Mass ends with the Concluding Rite, which includes a blessing and a command to the congregation to go forth into the world as witnesses to the love of Christ whom they have received. Here again the meaning of the word "Mass" as dismissal bears significance. This Concluding Rite is not, in a certain sense, the ending of Mass, but rather a beginning. Transformed into the Body of Christ by the Eucharist, the People of God bring Christ into the midst of world, transforming it into the City of God, the New Jerusalem.

BYZANTINE RITE LITURGY OF THE EUCHARIST

The Trinity. Russian icon by Andrei Rublev, ca.1410.

Although it may seem quite different in appearance, the Byzantine Rite Liturgy (called the Divine Liturgy) is essentially the same in order and content as the Latin Rite Mass, which we have just seen. The Byzantine Rite emphasizes that the earthly liturgy is a participation in the heavenly liturgy, and thus, an encounter with a mystery. The use of an *iconostasis*, a screen of icons separating the people from the sanctuary, reinforces the idea that in the Eucharist, the people are approaching the altar of Heaven and communion with the saints.

The Divine Liturgy begins in the sacristy (a room where the vestments and Holy objects used in the liturgy are kept). The Rite of Vesting emphasizes that the priest is performing a sacred action. Washing his hands, the priest says the prayers of preparation. He then proceeds to the sanctuary where he prepares the altar. These rites of preparation end with prayers of petition for the gathered people and the world.

The participation of the laity in the liturgy begins with the blessing by the priest. Like the Latin Rite, penitential prayers, including the *Kyrie Eleison* are said. In preparation for the Word of God, antiphons from the Psalms are prayed.

The Liturgy of the Word begins with a procession. This continues the practice of the early Church, when the sacred writings, kept by the deacon for safekeeping, were brought into the Church. Like the Latin Rite, there are readings from the Old Testament, Psalms, New Testament, and Gospels, followed by a homily, and the recitation of the Nicene Creed.

The Liturgy of the Eucharist begins with the procession of the gifts to the altar. The Eucharistic prayer is said, including the words of institution. This is followed by the Lord's Prayer, the Lamb of God, and prayers before communion. Following a Profession of Faith, Communion is received. A prayer of Thanksgiving is prayed after Communion, and the liturgy concludes with a final blessing and hymn.

An Eastern Rite Catholic Bishop celebrating the Divine Liturgy in a Greek Catholic church in Presov, Slovakia.

PARTICIPATION IN THE MASS

Like the reception of the Eucharist, the celebration of the Mass is a communal action. Our participation in the Mass is meant to be total, a participation of body and soul. This begins when we enter the church, blessing ourselves with holy water, a reminder of our own Baptism and an act of petition, asking for the purity of heart and mind to approach the table of the Lord.

Before sitting, we genuflect, greeting Our Lord present in the Blessed Sacrament, and spend a few moments in prayer to prepare ourselves for the sacred mysteries. We may also look over the readings prior to the beginning of Mass. The readings are specifically chosen, because they relate to the Mass of the day and to each other.

During the Mass, it is good to meditate on the great mystery unfolding in the celebration.

During the Mass, it is good to meditate on the great mystery unfolding in the celebration: we will be receiving Christ, the God of all, in the Eucharist. The Lord loves us so much that he wishes to be truly, really, and substantially united with us. If we understand that the Eucharist is the summit of Christian life, it should be clear that frequent reception of the Eucharist, daily when possible, will bring us closer to the risen Christ. Under certain conditions, e.g., if a person participates in a second Eucharistic celebration, or a person in danger of death receives the Viaticum, the Eucharist can be received twice in one day (cf. CIC, 917).

Internal Preparation

To celebrate and to offer the Holy Mass with greater fruitfulness, we may consider the following:

✠ The Eucharistic sacrifice is the most important event of each day.

✠ The Eucharistic sacrifice is the center of the Christian life. All the sacraments, prayers, visits to the Blessed Sacrament, devotions, and mortifications offered to God, as well as the apostolate, have the Mass as their central point of reference. If it were to disappear and if attendance at Mass were consciously abandoned, then the whole Christian life would collapse.

✠ The Eucharistic sacrifice is the most pleasing reality we can offer to God. Every member of the Mystical Body of Christ receives at Baptism the right and duty of taking part in the sacrifice of the Head of that Body. Our Mother the Church wants us to assist at the Mass, not as strangers or passive spectators, but with the effort to understand it better each time. We are to participate in the Mass in a conscious, pious, and active manner, with right dispositions and cooperating with divine grace.

✠ It is a good habit to pray on the way to Mass. Whether you drive or walk, turn your attention to the coming celebration. Pray for the priest, that he will minister to the needs of the parish. It is the mission of the Holy Spirit to prepare the faithful to encounter Christ in the liturgy. Pray for the congregation, that they will open their minds and hearts to what is being taught at the Mass and may experience the saving work and transforming power of Christ.[26] In the sacrifice of the Mass, the priest asks the Holy Spirit to bless the offerings so that they become acceptable to God the Father.

✠ We offer this sublime sacrifice in union with the Church. Live the Holy Mass feeling part of the Church, the Mystical Body of Christ, the People of God. Be united to the bishop of the diocese where the Mass is being offered and to the pope, the Vicar of Christ for the universal Church.

✠ We must be united to the Sacrifice of Jesus. Through him, we also offer to God the Father, with the Holy Spirit, all the sacrifices, sufferings, self-denials, and tribulations of each day.

✠ To receive Holy Communion, we need—besides being in the state of grace—to have the right intention and to keep the Eucharistic fast.

The Mass: External Participation

We should also participate in the Mass externally, paying special attention to several important details.

✠ Attend the Mass with a spirit of prayer, praying as the Church teaches us to pray, avoiding distractions. Be one with the words, actions, and gestures of the celebrant, who acts in the person of Christ. Give up personal preferences; accept the option that the celebrant, considering the circumstances of the people in each community, has chosen from among the legitimate possibilities that the liturgy offers to us.

✠ Listen, respond, acclaim, sing, or keep opportune silence, in order to facilitate union with God and to deepen your reflection on the Word of God.

✠ Stand, sit, and kneel—and be serene—even if you see someone who does not do so.

✠ Be punctual. This is a considerate detail for Christ our Lord, himself, and for others who are attending Mass. Arrive before the priest goes to the altar. Depart only after the priest has left.

✠ Use your missal, or the missalette available in the church. By following the prayers of the priest, you can avoid distractions.

✠ Dress properly as for an important meeting and not, for instance, as if you were going to participate in a sport. Dress ought to convey the respect, solemnity, and joy of the Mass.

DEVOTIONS OUTSIDE OF MASS

The Church and the world have a great need for Eucharistic worship. Jesus awaits us in this sacrament of love. Let us not refuse the time to go to meet him in adoration, in contemplation full of faith, and open to making amends for the serious offenses and crimes of the world. Let our adoration never cease.[27] (CCC 1380)

The transformation of the bread and wine offered in the sacrifice of the Mass is profound and lasting. The essence of the bread and wine are fundamentally changed, and after the Consecration, the matter of bread or wine no longer remains: the Eucharist is the Body, Blood, Soul, and Divinity of our Lord Jesus Christ.

Even outside of the Mass, Christ remains in our presence in this visible form. He remains as a proof of his love, reminding us that he will be with us until the end of time and that he wishes to share himself with us as often as possible.

It became the custom in the early Church to reserve, or set aside, the Eucharist when the Mass had ended. The Eucharist could then be taken to those who were not able to attend the Mass. This allowed them to share in the "one bread," uniting them to the Christian community.

The acknowledgement of the Real Presence of Christ in the Eucharist led to the development of a number of Eucharistic devotions, which are an expression of our love and gratitude to Christ present with us in the Blessed Sacrament. Some common Eucharistic devotions include Benediction, Eucharistic adoration, Eucharistic processions, and Forty Hours' Devotion.

Eucharistic adoration is a devotion during which the Eucharist is placed on the altar in a monstrance, an adorned container that holds up and protects the Eucharistic host. Believers gather to pray and meditate in front of Christ's presence in the Eucharist.

Eucharistic processions sometimes take place through the streets of the town or city. The faithful line the street awaiting the passing of the Eucharist, and some faithful will follow the procession.

Benediction is a liturgical service whose name is derived from the Latin meaning "to bless." Often occurring at the conclusion of a period of adoration, the priest or deacon conducting the service blesses all present with the Eucharist.

Eucharistic processions often take place on the Feast of the Body and Blood of Christ, also known as Corpus Christi. The Eucharist will be placed in a monstrance, which is then carried either through the Church, around the Church, or through the streets of the town or city. In some places, the faithful line the streets to wait for the passing of the Eucharist, and some may follow the Eucharist in solemn procession. The Eucharistic procession is usually accompanied by homilies explaining and inspiring reverence and devotion for Jesus Christ present in the Blessed Sacrament.

All of this should make us realize how close the Lord is to us. Jesus Christ is truly, really, and substantially here—a presence in the truest sense, as present as the person sitting next to you in Mass. Belief in the transubstantiation of the Body and Blood of Jesus is demonstrated in the liturgy when people kneel during the Consecration and genuflect or bow when approaching the altar, indicating their adoration of Our Lord.

THE MINISTERIAL PRIESTHOOD

It is not man that causes the things offered to become the Body and Blood of Christ, but he who was crucified for us, Christ himself. The priest, in the role of Christ, pronounces these words, but their power and grace are God's. This is my body, he says. This word transforms the things offered.[28] (CCC 1375)

While the minister of the Sacrament is a bishop or priest, it is ultimately Christ, the eternal High Priest, who presides over the Mass. Seated at the right hand of the Father, Christ continues offering his eternal sacrifice of Calvary through the Holy Sacrifice of the Mass. The priest participates in this priesthood of Christ, offering the sacrifice of the Mass and repeating the words of Christ in the Consecration, through which the bread and wine are transformed into the Body and Blood of Christ. For this reason, "only validly ordained priests can preside at the Eucharist and consecrate the bread and the wine so that they become the Body and Blood of the Lord."[29]

The Eucharist (detail) by Fra Angelico.
The Eucharist is the Body and Blood of Christ and therefore
is the most sacred thing in the world.

Although the priest leads the congregation in the celebration of Mass and consecrates the Holy Eucharist, everyone who is present plays an important role. The whole People of God participate by their prayers, by the offering of gifts and spiritual sacrifices, and by uniting their hearts and minds in praise and thanksgiving.

The ordinary Eucharistic ministers who distribute Holy Communion to the faithful are bishops, priests, and deacons. However, the Church permits the use of extraordinary ministers of Holy Communion at celebrations where there are large numbers of the faithful present or when the ordained ministers present at a liturgical celebration are unable to distribute Holy Communion. Also, Eucharistic ministers are sometimes needed to help bring the Eucharist to those unable to attend Mass because of infirmity or old age.

Because of the ministerial priesthood, which is preserved by Apostolic Succession, we can be sure that Holy Communion received in the Catholic Church is the Body and Blood of Christ. Christian ecclesial bodies and communities without Apostolic Succession do not have this gift; there are real differences between Holy Communion in the Catholic Church and communion services in Protestant communities. Receiving Holy Communion is, among other things, a statement and action of belief in the Real Presence of Christ in the Eucharistic species, uniting all Catholics throughout the world, which is why Catholics must not receive communion in Protestant communities and non-Catholics must not receive Holy Communion in a Catholic church.

A SOURCE OF UNITY IN CHRIST

> Because there is one bread, we who are many are one body, for we all partake of the one bread.
> (1 Cor 10:17)

St. Paul taught that the Church is the Body of Christ. Though there are many parts, all are united in Christ, who is the head. This unity (comm-union) of the faithful is established through Baptism and finds its full expression in the Eucharist.

As we read earlier, St. Paul admonished the Corinthians against approaching the Eucharist while the community is divided—it would be dishonest. Participation in the Eucharist expresses a unity which, in their case, did not exist. First, the divisions in the community must be healed, and only then can we approach the Eucharist, which is a sign and expression of unity.

Through the Eucharist, we participate in the deepest mystery of the Christian Faith, and through that participation, we are strengthened in our communion and love of God and with each other.

In his book *On the Way to Jesus Christ*, Pope Benedict XVI speaks about how the communion of Christians is bound up in the mystery of the Eucharist:

> The word *koinonia*—in Latin, *communio*—occurred to me as the fundamental concept that expresses the very essence of the Church.[30] The cup of blessing which we bless, is it not a participation [in Greek, *koinonia*; in Latin, *communicatio*] in the blood of Christ? The bread which we break, is it not a participation in the body of Christ?[31]

At the time of Christ, the Greek word *koinonia* was used to indicate a joint venture, such as a business partnership, in which joint owners worked together for a common good. This was the word chosen by the New Testament writers to illustrate the relationship existing between the members of the Church. Its usage points to the two distinct dimensions of this concept: one vertical and the other horizontal.

As an owner of a business, one has a personal stake in the profits of the business. As a partner, there is a relationship and shared interest with the other owners as well. In a similar way, we see these same two dimensions in the Christian community. Each Christian has a personal (vertical) relationship with Christ and is responsible for responding to Christ's call. In addition, there is a shared (horizontal) relationship between the members of the Christian community who share a complementary goal: love for others.

In the Eucharist, a person receives individual graces from Christ, strengthening his or her relationship with God. At the same time, the members of the Church are united in Christ through the Eucharist. In modern terms, we might say, "you are what you eat" when referring to the Eucharist. By receiving the Eucharist, we are transformed into Christ, becoming more firmly united to the Church, to God, and to neighbor. The more we receive the Eucharist prayerfully, the more we can bring about the unity among all who believe in Christ, which is desired by Christ himself.

FRUITS OF REGULAR RECEPTION OF THE EUCHARIST

The infinite graces available to us in the Eucharist should encourage us to receive this Sacrament often, even daily if we are properly disposed and if it is possible. Whenever we receive the Eucharist while in a state of grace, our intimate union with Christ is strengthened. This union preserves, increases, renews, and nourishes the life of grace received at Baptism. Among these graces, the Eucharist

✠ stabilizes and increases the intimate union with Christ;

✠ reinforces the unity of the Church as the Mystical Body of Christ;

✠ forgives venial sins;

✠ strengthens us to avoid grave sins;

✠ diminishes sinful love of self while committing us to the poor;

✠ strengthens against temptation;

✠ decreases purgatorial debt; and

✠ reduces concupiscence.

St. Paul, Icon by Andrei Rublev. St. Paul warned against receiving the Eucharist unworthily.

Receiving the Eucharist also unites the faithful more closely to each other, while incorporating them more deeply into the Church. Since receiving the Eucharist fulfills the call to become one body in Christ, the Church highly recommends that the faithful receive the Eucharist whenever they participate at Mass (providing they are sufficiently prepared and in a state of grace), and requires that Catholics receive the Eucharist at least once a year during the period from Ash Wednesday to Trinity Sunday. The Eucharist is food for the spirit and should be received as often as possible to strengthen the spirit, particularly when the moment of death is imminent.

The Eucharist is the Body and Blood of Christ and therefore is the most sacred thing in the world. Because of this, we must treat it with the utmost respect, which is why it is good to respond immediately to this immense gift with a prayer of thanksgiving and a renewed purpose of amendment. Any act of sacrilege or disrespect towards the Eucharist is a very serious offense against God. It is therefore necessary to reflect on the meaning of the Death and Resurrection of Christ so we can petition him for the grace to give ourselves to others as he did. Each recipient must closely examine his or her conscience in preparation for Holy Communion. St. Paul warned against receiving the Sacrament unworthily when he said,

> Whoever, therefore, eats the bread or drinks the cup of the Lord in an unworthy manner will be guilty of profaning the body and blood of the Lord. Let a man examine himself, and so eat of the bread and drink of the cup. For any one who eats and drinks without discerning the body eats and drinks judgment upon himself. (1 Cor 11: 27-29)

However, it is important that we not let an unwarranted or excessive sense of guilt keep us from receiving the Eucharist. This may be a trick to keep us from communing with Christ in his Sacrament. Frequent Confession will help ensure that one's soul is properly prepared. Seeking spiritual advice and direction will also assist in ensuring one's soul is properly oriented towards the desire to love Christ.

A FIRST COMMUNION
In the Latin Rite of the Catholic Church, a person must have reached the age of reason to receive Holy Communion.

As Christ himself, the Eucharist has infinite graces. Each time we receive Holy Communion there are enough graces present to make us a saint. We are limited only by our own capacity to receive these graces. For this reason, the more properly disposed or spiritually prepared we are to receive Holy Communion, the greater the benefit we receive.

In order to help guide the faithful in the proper reception of the Eucharist, the Church has set forth a number of requirements. A person receiving Holy Communion must

✠ be a baptized Catholic;

✠ have attained the age of reason (usually seven years);
(This does not apply to Catholics of the Eastern Rites who receive First Communion following their Baptism as infants.)

✠ have received first Reconciliation prior to first reception of the Eucharist;
(This does not apply to those who receive First Communion following the reception of Baptism.)

✠ fast from all food and drink except for water or medicine for one hour prior to reception—this reminds us that we are receiving Christ and not ordinary food; and

✠ make a sacramental Confession, if a mortal sin has been committed.

CONCLUSION

Before Christ ascended into Heaven, he promised to be with us until the end of time. He has kept his promise by remaining present in the Eucharist. When the words of Consecration are spoken, Christ becomes truly present in Flesh and Blood.

There is no greater love on earth than the love of God for his people. Christ demonstrated this great love for us on Calvary and continues to offer his love through the Sacrifice of the Mass. Through the Eucharist, Christ unites himself to us and strengthens the unity of his Church. In receiving the Eucharist, we are privileged to participate in the life of the Blessed Trinity, foreshadowing the complete and eternal participation that we will enjoy in Heaven.

The Eucharist is the center, the source, and the summit of the Christian life. The graces offered by Jesus Christ have the power to transform us. In the sacrifice of the Mass, Christ becomes our Redemption and our strength, giving us the spiritual nourishment needed to live each day as his disciples, and creating us anew in his image as members of his Mystical Body, the Church.

SUPPLEMENTARY READING

POPE ST. PIUS X

When the great bell of St. Peter's began tolling on August 19, 1914, it summoned the faithful of Rome to pray for Pope Pius X, who was unexpectedly on his deathbed. The great bell could also be said to have been tolling for the "long nineteenth century," the period from the French Revolution of 1789 to the outbreak of

POPE ST. PIUS X
June 2, 1835 – August 20, 1914

the First World War in the summer of 1914. The "long nineteenth century" had been a nightmare for the Church in Europe. Pius X opened the twentieth century facing a new crisis in France. He condemned the French government's recent decision to secularize the schools, subject religious orders to state control, and create state controlled "cultural associations" to seize Church properties. His refusal to accept the government's policy reduced the Church in France to material poverty, but it also secured the Church's independence from the state. Pius also acted forcefully to end the "imperial veto" that allowed the Holy Roman Emperor to veto

any candidate that the conclave might choose as pope.

These and other moves enabled the Church, unencumbered by state support and entanglement with the high politics of the European powers, to speak with greater freedom—and greater moral authority—in the twentieth century. In a century in which the state was to become the major enemy of human life and liberty, the Church was able to stand resolutely against the evils of Fascism and Communism.

Pius' internal governance of the Church could be severe, and never more so than in his condemnation of "Modernism" as the "synthesis of all heresies." Modernism was an intellectual movement that generally measured Church teaching against the standard of modern philosophy, science, and historical criticism, and undermined traditional doctrine. Pius imposed an "anti-modernist" oath on all clergy. The action was effective in stamping out Modernism in the Catholic Church.

Pius' most important reform, however, was in the norms for the reception of Holy Communion. For quite some time even devout Catholics received Holy Communion infrequently, motivated by an improper sense of unworthiness. Pius encouraged frequent, even daily, reception of Holy Communion, and he lowered the age of reception of First Holy Communion as well. No other decree in the history of the Church resulted in such an increase in reception of the sacraments throughout the whole Church. Whatever else Pius may have done as pope, nothing unleashed the floodgates of grace in the Church as much as the practice of frequent Holy Communion. All of this century's saints nourished their souls on the Holy Eucharist—a grace made available to them by the pastoral wisdom of Pius X.

Pope St. Pius X was canonized in 1954—the first pope to be canonized since Pope St. Pius V (d. 1572)—because of his personal holiness. A saint was needed at the end of the "long nineteenth century" to prepare the Church for the horrors of the twentieth, already underway as the bell tolled in St. Peter's that day in 1914.

VOCABULARY

ADORATION
Worship. This is the humble acknowledgment by human beings that they are creatures of the thrice-holy Creator. By obeying the First Commandment, people acknowledge and respond to the revelation of the glory and power of God.

AGE OF REASON
The age at which a person becomes morally responsible for his or her actions. It is also the age at which people are eligible to receive the Sacraments of Eucharist, Confirmation, and the Anointing of the Sick. In most parts of the world, this age is set at seven years.

ANAPHORA
The Eucharistic prayer that is prayed by the priest at Mass. It begins with the preface and ends with the Great Amen.

BENEDICTION
A prayer invoking God's power and care upon some person, place, thing, or undertaking. The prayer of Benediction acknowledges God as the source of all blessing.

COMMUNION
From the Latin for "mutual participation" or "oneness together": in the sense of Holy Communion, the reception of the Body and Blood of Christ in the Eucharist; in the sense of fellowship, the bond of union with Jesus and all baptized, faithful Christians in the Church.

CONSECRATION
Dedication to a sacred purpose; to sanctify. This can refer to a church building, person, or object set aside for worship. It can refer specifically to entry into a permanent state of life entered freely in response to the call of Christ and characterized by the profession of vows. In the Mass, Consecration refers to the moment when the bread and wine are transformed into the Body and Blood of Christ.

COVENANT
A solemn promise or contract regarding future action binding on the participants and fortified by an oath, expressed either in words or in symbolic action.

EPICLESIS
The calling down of the Holy Spirit. During Mass, as the priest extends his hands over the gifts of bread and wine, he calls down the Holy Spirit to change them into the Body of Blood of Jesus.

EUCHARIST
From the Greek for "thanksgiving"; also called the Mass or Lord's Supper. It is the principal sacramental celebration of the Church, established by Jesus at the Last Supper, in which the mystery of salvation through participation in the sacrificial Death and glorious Resurrection of Christ is renewed and accomplished. This term applies to the species consecrated during the Mass.

EXCOMMUNICATION
Excommunication is a censure by means of which a person is excluded from the communion of the faithful in response to a grave, habitual, public sin. An excommunicated person is forbidden to have a ministerial role in the celebration of the sacraments and other public ceremonies, to receive the sacraments, or to exercise church offices or ministries (cf. CIC, 1331). Excommunication can be *latæ sententiæ* (i.e., automatic for certain intrinsically evil acts, such as abortion or the desecration of the Eucharist) or *ferendæ sententiæ* (i.e., imposed by ecclesiastical authority).

KOINONIA (COMMUNIO)
Communio is the Latin translation of the Greek *koinonia*, meaning communion, fellowship, or association. This term was used by St. Luke to describe both the fellowship of believers and the relationship between the Father, the Son, and the Holy Spirit. St. Paul used *koinonia* to denote the intimate union of the believer with Christ and the community that exists among all the faithful themselves.

MASS
Also called the Eucharist or Lord's Supper. This name is derived from the Latin dismissal of the faithful, *"Ite, missa est."* It is the principal sacramental celebration of the Church, established by Jesus at the Last Supper, in which the mystery of salvation through participation in the sacrificial Death and glorious Resurrection of Christ is renewed and accomplished.

VOCABULARY Continued

MISSAL
Sometimes called a Sacramentary, a liturgical book which contains the prayers of the Mass for the use of the priest at the altar, along with instructions for the celebrant of the liturgy. Scripture readings are contained in a book called a Lectionary.

MISSALETTE
A booklet for the use of the laity which generally contains the prayers, songs, and Scripture readings used at Mass.

MONSTRANCE
A vessel of precious metal used for exposing the Blessed Sacrament for adoration. At the center of the monstrance is a glass disc which allows the faithful to view the Blessed Sacrament during exposition.

PASCHAL LAMB
The pure and spotless lamb prepared for the ritual Passover meal by the Jews. It also refers to Jesus, the sacrificial Lamb of God who takes away the sins of the world and establishes a new covenant between God and his people.

PASSOVER
Pesach, Pesah, Pascha—a Jewish feast commemorating the deliverance of their first-born males from death by the blood of the lamb sprinkled on the doorposts while in bondage in Egypt. The angel of death passed over their homes, allowing them to leave Egypt for the Promised Land. This was a type of the sacrificial Passion and Death of Jesus Christ, saving mankind from bondage to sin. The Eucharist celebrates Christ's Passover.

REAL PRESENCE
The unique and true presence of the Body, Blood, Soul, and Divinity of Christ in the Eucharist under the appearances of bread and wine. The Church invites the faithful to deepen their faith in the Real Presence of Christ through worship and communion in the Eucharistic liturgy, and through acts of adoration outside of Mass.

SACRAMENTAL PRESENCE
The real, true, and substantial existence of Christ's divinity and humanity in the Holy Eucharist under the appearances of bread and wine.

SACRIFICE
A ritual offering made to God by a priest on behalf of the people as a sign of adoration, thanksgiving, supplication, and communion. The perfect sacrifice was offered by Christ, the High Priest of the new and eternal covenant. This sacrifice of the Cross is commemorated and made present sacramentally in the Eucharistic Sacrifice of the Mass.

SPIRITUAL COMMUNION
A conscious, burning desire to receive Holy Communion when unable to do so physically.

STATE OF GRACE
The condition whereby one enjoys the friendship of God. One who possesses "sanctifying grace" or "habitual grace" is enabled to know, love, and serve God and others in reference to him. The state of grace is lost by committing mortal sin but may be regained through the Sacrament of Penance or by an act of perfect contrition.

TABERNACLE
An ornamented receptacle in the church in which the consecrated Eucharist is reserved for Communion for the sick and dying as well as for adoration. In Israelite history, the tabernacle was the curtained tent containing the Ark of the Covenant and other sacred items. This portable sanctuary was taken throughout their wandering in the wilderness until the building of the Temple in Jerusalem.

TRANSUBSTANTIATION
The scholastic term used to designate the unique change, in a true, real, and substantial manner, of the entire substance of the Eucharistic bread and wine into the Body and Blood of Christ, with his soul and divinity, leaving intact the accidents.

VICTIM
A living being sacrificed to a deity in the performance of a religious ritual. For Christians, Jesus is the victim, *par excellence*, by his loving and freely made offering of himself on the Cross to his Father for the salvation of the world.

STUDY QUESTIONS

1. What does the "Real Presence" mean?

2. What do Christians mean by the word "communion"?

3. How does the Eucharist transform a person?

4. What was the Exodus?

5. Briefly describe the Passover meal.

6. What did Jesus do in the Passover meal that was different?

7. What is the "cup of consummation" for Christians?

8. Explain the significance of the Mass as a memorial and as a sacrifice.

9. What are the four requirements of a sacrifice? Explain how the Sacrifice of the Mass fulfills these requirements.

10. How is a Christian united to the sacrifice of Christ?

11. If Christ was sacrificed only once, then how can we speak of the Mass as a sacrifice?

12. What meaning is being conveyed with the words "representation" and "re-enactment" when applied to the Mass?

13. Explain the analogy between Jesus and manna.

14. In the Bread from Heaven discourse, the thousands who had been following Jesus turned away and left. Why did he not just explain his words in a way that would have been acceptable to them? Apply this to some teachings of the Church today.

15. What can we learn about the Eucharist from the Bread from Heaven discourse?

16. Select three of the fruits of receiving the Eucharist and explain them in your own words.

17. What happens when the priest says the words of Consecration?

18. What words of St. Paul reaffirm the early Christian belief in the Real Presence, rather than explaining it as a metaphor?

19. What is meant by the word "transubstantiation?"

20. How did the custom of reserving the Eucharist outside of Mass arise in the early Church?

21. What are ways in which the Church shows respect for the Holy Eucharist?

22. Describe three different types of Eucharistic adoration.

23. The word *koinonia*, or *communio*, was used to describe the early Church. Explain the use of these words.

24. How is the meaning of *communio* expressed in the Eucharist?

25. What does the word "eucharist" mean? Why was this word chosen to designate the Body and Blood of Our Lord?

26. How did the Liturgy of the Eucharist come to be called the Mass?

27. Why is it important to fast before receiving the Eucharist?

28. What is the significance of being free from mortal sin when receiving the Eucharist?

29. Who is the high priest who presides over the Eucharist?

30. Who may celebrate the Liturgy of the Mass?

31. What are some external ways in which the faithful can participate in the Mass?

32. List several ways in which a person may privately or internally participate in the Mass.

33. What are the two parts of the Mass? What is the origin of each of these two parts?

34. How did the early Christians fulfill the Commandment to keep the Sabbath?

35. How did the custom of worshiping on Sunday arise?

36. Why were the Liturgy of the Word and the Liturgy of the Eucharist united into one liturgical service?

PRACTICAL EXERCISES

1. List four things that we can do to prepare for receiving the Eucharist. Do at least one of them this Sunday.

2. Why do you think it is a sin to receive the Eucharist without "discerning" it as the Body and Blood of Christ? Does this have anything to do with respect and love for Jesus?

3. Other Christian communities have ceremonies that seem like Eucharistic Communion but are not. Why are they not? Who has to consecrate the bread and wine for Jesus to actually be present?

4. Eucharistic miracles exist throughout the world. Go online and see what Eucharistic miracles you can find outside of Ostia, Italy. How do these miracles help reveal Jesus' true presence in the Eucharist?

5. The next time that you pass by a Church, stop for a few minutes to make a visit to Christ who is waiting for you in the Blessed Sacrament.

FROM THE CATECHISM

1406 Jesus said: "I am the living bread that came down from heaven; if any one eats of this bread, he will live for ever;...he who eats my flesh and drinks my blood has eternal life and... abides in me, and I in him." [32]

1408 The Eucharistic celebration always includes: the proclamation of the Word of God; thanksgiving to God the Father for all his benefits, above all the gift of his Son; the consecration of bread and wine; and participation in the liturgical banquet by receiving the Lord's body and blood. These elements constitute one single act of worship.

1409 The Eucharist is the memorial of Christ's Passover, that is, of the work of salvation accomplished by the life, death, and resurrection of Christ, a work made present by the liturgical action.

1410 It is Christ himself, the eternal high priest of the New Covenant who, acting through the ministry of the priests, offers the Eucharistic sacrifice. And it is the same Christ, really present under the species of bread and wine, who is the offering of the Eucharistic sacrifice.

1411 Only validly ordained priests can preside at the Eucharist and consecrate the bread and the wine so that they become the Body and Blood of the Lord.

1412 The essential signs of the Eucharistic sacrament are wheat bread and grape wine, on which the blessing of the Holy Spirit is invoked and the priest pronounces the words of consecration spoken by Jesus during the Last Supper: "This is my body which will be given up for you....This is the cup of my blood...."

1413 By the consecration the transubstantiation of the bread and wine into the Body and Blood of Christ is brought about. Under the consecrated species of bread and wine Christ himself, living and glorious, is present in a true, real, and substantial manner: his Body and his Blood, with his soul and his divinity. [33]

1414 As sacrifice, the Eucharist is also offered in reparation for the sins of the living and the dead and to obtain spiritual or temporal benefits from God.

FROM THE CATECHISM Continued

1415 Anyone who desires to receive Christ in Eucharistic communion must be in the state of grace. Anyone aware of having sinned mortally must not receive communion without having received absolution in the sacrament of penance.

1416 Communion with the Body and Blood of Christ increases the communicant's union with the Lord, forgives his venial sins, and preserves him from grave sins. Since receiving this sacrament strengthens the bonds of charity between the communicant and Christ, it also reinforces the unity of the Church as the Mystical Body of Christ.

1417 The Church warmly recommends that the faithful receive Holy Communion when they participate in the celebration of the Eucharist; she obliges them to do so at least once a year.

1418 Because Christ himself is present in the sacrament of the altar, he is to be honored with the worship of adoration. "To visit the Blessed Sacrament is…a proof of gratitude, an expression of love, and a duty of adoration toward Christ our Lord."[34]

1419 Having passed from this world to the Father, Christ gives us in the Eucharist the pledge of glory with him. Participation in the Holy Sacrifice identifies us with his Heart, sustains our strength along the pilgrimage of this life, makes us long for eternal life, and unites us even now to the Church in heaven, the Blessed Virgin Mary, and all the saints.

ENDNOTES – CHAPTER THREE

1. Ex 24:8.
2. Mk 14:26.
3. Mk 14:25; cf. Mt 14:13-21; Mk 6:30-33; Lk 9:10-17; Jn 2:1-12.
4. Lk 22:42.
5. Jn 18:11.
6. Jn 19:28.
7. Cf. Jn 19:29.
8. Ex 12:22.
9. Jn 19:30.
10. Cf. Jn 6.
11. Jn 13:1.
12. Cf. Gal 2:20.
13. St. Irenæus, *Against Heresies*.
14. Council of Trent (1551): DS 1642; cf. Mt 26:26ff.; Mk 14:22ff.; Lk 22:19ff.; 1 Cor 11:24ff.
15. Cf. Council of Trent: DS 1640; 1651.
16. Cf. CCC 1328-1332.
17. Lk 22:19.
18. Cf. Ex 13:3.
19. Cf. Gn 14.
20. 1 Cor 10:18.
21. CCC 1407.
22. CCC 1367.
23. Mal 1:11,14.
24. Council of Trent (1562): *Doctrina de SS. Missæ Sacrificio*, c. 2: DS 1743; cf. Heb 9:14, 27.
25. Cf. Acts 2:46; cf. Acts 3:1.
26. Cf. CCC 1112.
27. St. John Paul II, *Dominicæ Cenæ*, 3.
28. St. John Chrysostom, *prod. Jud.* 1:6: PG 49, 380.
29. CCC 1411.
30. Ratzinger, Cardinal Joseph, *On the Way to Jesus Christ* (San Francisco, California: Ignatius Press, 2005), p.113.
31. Ibid., p. 115; 1 Cor 10:16ff
32. Jn 6:51, 54, 56.
33. Cf. Council of Trent: DS 1640; 1651.
34. Paul VI, *MF* 66.

Reconciliation

The Sacrament of Reconciliation is the way in which God heals our souls and reconciles sinners to himself.

The Sacraments

CHAPTER 4

Reconciliation

he Parable of the Prodigal Son is one of the most enduring stories in the Gospel. In a simple narrative, Jesus captures a key aspect of the nature of God that he was sent to reveal: that the one true God is a Father who offers love and forgiveness to his children.

Like the father in the parable, God gives everything to his children. Even when they squander their wonderful inheritance, God always welcomes them back with open arms and calls their brothers and sisters to celebrate their return.

For the followers of Christ, this belief in God's forgiveness became the foundation of Christian hope and love. After Jesus' Resurrection and Ascension into Heaven, the Apostles took to the streets preaching the message: "Repent, and be baptized every one of you in the name of Jesus Christ for the forgiveness of your sins."[1]

In Baptism, our sins are forgiven and the stain of Original Sin is washed away. However, Christ knew that even his most sincere followers would continue to struggle against their weakened natures, and it was for this reason that he instituted the Sacrament of Reconciliation and granted his Apostles the authority to forgive sins.

In this chapter, we will look at the first of the two Sacraments of Healing. The Sacrament of Reconciliation, or Penance, is the Sacrament in which Jesus Christ, through the ministry of his Church, forgives those sins committed after Baptism. It is the way in which God heals our souls and reconciles sinners to himself. Jesus, out of his great love for us, died for our sins on Calvary, and it is through the saving power of his sacrificial love that we can seek God's forgiveness through the Sacrament of Reconciliation.

IN THIS CHAPTER, WE WILL ADDRESS SEVERAL QUESTIONS:

✛ When did Christ give the Apostles the authority to forgive sins?

✛ How does the Church mediate God's forgiveness in the Sacrament of Reconciliation?

✛ Why is Confession necessary in the Christian life?

✛ How does one prepare for a good Confession?

✛ What are the benefits of frequent Confession?

THE PARABLE OF THE PRODIGAL SON

And he [Jesus] said, "There was a man who had two sons; and the younger of them said to his father, 'Father, give me the share of property that falls to me.' And he divided his living between them. Not many days later, the younger son gathered all he had and took his journey into a far country, and there he squandered his property in loose living. And when he had spent everything, a great famine arose in that country, and he began to be in want. So he went and joined himself to one of the citizens of that country, who sent him into his fields to feed swine. And he would gladly have fed on the pods that the swine ate; and no one gave him anything. But when he came to himself he said, 'How many of my father's hired servants have bread enough and to spare, but I perish here with hunger! I will arise and go to my father, and I will say to him, "Father, I have sinned against heaven and before you; I am no longer worthy to be called your son; treat me as one of your hired servants."' And he arose and came to his father. But while he was yet at a distance, his father saw him and had compassion, and ran and embraced him and kissed him. And the son said to him, 'Father, I have sinned against heaven and before you; I am no longer worthy to be called your son.' But the father said to his servants, 'Bring quickly the best robe, and put it on him; and put a ring on his hand, and shoes on his feet; and bring the fatted calf and kill it, and let us eat and make merry; for my son was dead, and is alive again; he was lost, and is found.' And they began to make merry."

"Now his elder son was in the field; and as he came and drew near to the house, he heard music and dancing. And he called one of the servants and asked what this meant. And he said to him, 'Your brother has come, and your father has killed the fatted calf, because he has received him safe and sound.' But he was angry and refused to go in. His father came out and entreated him, but he answered his father, 'Lo, these many years I have served you, and I never disobeyed your command; yet you never gave me a kid, that I might make merry with my friends. But when this son of yours came, who has devoured your living with harlots, you killed for him the fatted calf!' And he said to him, 'Son, you are always with me, and all that is mine is yours. It was fitting to make merry and be glad, for this your brother was dead, and is alive; he was lost, and is found.'" (Lk 15:11-32)

"And the son said to him, 'Father, I have sinned against heaven and before you; I am no longer worthy to be called your son.'"

THE ORIGINS OF RECONCILIATION IN SALVATION HISTORY

Adam and Eve were created in a state of original holiness and justice. God gave them the Garden of Eden, and while they lived in the garden, there were no barriers between them and God. Filled with sanctifying grace, our first parents enjoyed an intimate relationship with their Creator and were completely happy.

By eating of the Tree of Knowledge, Adam and Eve questioned the justice of God. They placed their own will before that of God.

Unfortunately, this state of original holiness and justice did not last. God had given Adam and Eve one commandment. He forbade them to eat of the fruit of the Tree of Knowledge of Good and Evil. The Book of Genesis tells us that Adam and Eve disobeyed God.

The First Sin

The first or Original Sin seems like such a simple transgression, and yet the act goes deeply into the heart of the nature of sin. By eating of the Tree of Knowledge, Adam and Eve questioned the justice of God and chose to be their own arbiters of right and wrong. They placed their own will before that of God.

Man, tempted by the devil, let his trust in his Creator die in his heart and, abusing his freedom, disobeyed God's command. This is what man's first sin consisted of.[2] All subsequent sin would be disobedience toward God and lack of trust in his goodness. (CCC 397)

As a result of this choice, Adam and Eve not only lost their state of original holiness and justice and complete happiness, but they introduced sin and suffering into the world. The consequences of this sin would not only affect Adam and Eve, but also all of their descendants. Thus, every individual is conceived in a state of Original Sin, inheriting the fallen condition introduced into the world by Adam and Eve.

Adam and Eve transmitted to their descendants human nature wounded by their own first sin and hence deprived of original holiness and justice; this deprivation is called "original sin." (CCC 417)

Although it is proper to each individual,[3] original sin does not have the character of a personal fault in any of Adam's descendants. It is a deprivation of original holiness and justice, but human nature has not been totally corrupted: it is wounded in the natural powers proper to it, subject to ignorance, suffering, and the dominion of death; and inclined to sin—an inclination to evil that is called "concupiscence." Baptism, by imparting the life of Christ's grace, erases original sin and turns a man back towards God, but the consequences for nature, weakened and inclined to evil, persist in man and summon him to spiritual battle. (CCC 405)

The Sacrament of Baptism cleanses us of Original Sin. Indeed, all sins, both Original and actual, are washed away through Baptism, and we are filled with God's sanctifying grace—the divine life of God present in the soul. Despite this, each person still suffers from the effects of concupiscence—a weakened will and disordered desire that we possess as a result of our fallen state.

This means that even after Baptism, each person still struggles to live a life modeled on Jesus Christ. In others words, we continue to sin. Because of this, Christ understood that those striving to live a Christian life would need a means of receiving God's forgiveness, even after Baptism.

The *Catechism of the Catholic Church* speaks of two conversions in the Christian life. The first conversion, the result of Christian Baptism, gives us new life in the Spirit. Created anew in the image of Christ, the Christian is made "holy and without blemish."[4] However, the effects of sin remain, making the Christian life a struggle.

The second conversion spoken about in the *Catechism* is the ongoing work of daily Christian life in which the baptized person responds to the call of Christ "to be holy." This "universal call to holiness" is the vocation of all Christians, which beckons us to an intimate union with Jesus Christ.[5] Through the Sacrament of Reconciliation we are called to participate in this ongoing conversion by continually reflecting upon and amending our lives.

The Forgiveness of Sin

In the Father's great love for mankind he sent his only Son to reconcile a fallen humanity with himself; and indeed, the mission of Jesus Christ was one of forgiveness and reconciliation. The Book of Isaiah foretells how the promised Messiah will "make himself an offering for sin,"[6] and the angel tells St. Joseph that "…you shall call his name Jesus ('Yahweh saves') for he will save his people from their sins."[7]

When he began his public ministry, Jesus sought out sinners and those who were lost. He scandalized the scribes and Pharisees, not only by associating with sinners, but by claiming to forgive their sins as well.

"Take heart, my son; your sins are forgiven."
By claiming to forgive sins, Jesus was proclaiming his divinity.

> Behold, they brought to him a paralytic, lying on his bed; and when Jesus saw their faith he said to the paralytic, "Take heart, my son; your sins are forgiven." And behold, some of the scribes said to themselves, "This man is blaspheming." But Jesus, knowing their thoughts, said, "Why do you think evil in your hearts? For which is easier, to say, 'Your sins are forgiven,' or to say, 'Rise and walk?' But that you may know that the Son of man has authority on earth to forgive sins"— he then said to the paralytic—"Rise, take up your bed and go home." And he rose and went home. When the crowds saw it, they were afraid, and they glorified God, who had given such authority to men. (Mt 9: 2-8)

The scribes were not bothered that Jesus healed the sick, but to heal the soul was the work of God alone. By claiming to forgive sins, Jesus was proclaiming his divinity. Such a claim would be blasphemous— unless it was true.

As Christians, we believe that Jesus is divine. He is the eternally begotten Son of God, who does have the authority to forgive sins. Indeed, Jesus is the Lamb of God who takes away the sins of the world.

> Only God forgives sins.[8] Since he is the Son of God, Jesus says of himself, "The Son of man has authority on earth to forgive sins" and exercises this divine power: "Your sins are forgiven."[9] Further, by virtue of his divine authority he gives this power to men to exercise in his name.[10] (CCC 1441)

The Good News of the Death and Resurrection of Jesus Christ is that by dying he conquered sin and offered mankind hope that we may find forgiveness in him. The power of that forgiveness is made manifest in the Sacrament of Reconciliation, and it is through this Sacrament that all are called to renew their desire to follow the will of God.

The Institution of the Sacrament

Throughout his public ministry on earth, Jesus forgave the sins of many of the people he encountered. By invoking the authority to forgive sins, Jesus revealed his divine authority, and it is this authority that Jesus handed down to his Apostles.

We first see Jesus imparting his divine authority to forgive sins in an episode recounted in the Gospel of St. Matthew. After hearing the opinions of the multitudes concerning his identity, Jesus asked his Apostles, "But who do you say that I am?"[11] St. Peter, speaking for the other eleven, made a profession of faith that Jesus was the promised Messiah, the Son of the living God. In doing so, St. Peter, still known at this time as Simon, implicitly acknowledged Jesus' divine authority. Jesus in turn explicitly bestowed his own authority on Simon, changing his name to Peter (meaning rock).[12]

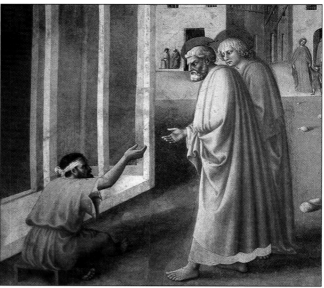

> You are Peter [rock], and on this rock I will build my church, and the powers of death shall not prevail against it. I will give you the keys of the kingdom of heaven, and whatever you bind on earth shall be bound in heaven, and whatever you loose on earth shall be loosed in heaven. (Mt 16:18-19)

Christ bestowed on the Apostles his authority to forgive sins. St. Peter, following the outpouring of the Holy Spirit at Pentecost, healed a man lame from birth.

This is a great responsibility that Jesus gave to St. Peter. It is on him that Christ founded his Church, placing him in the position of leadership in this new community. The giving of keys is an ancient sign of granting one's authority to another to act as a steward or minister in one's absence.

Christ vested St. Peter with his authority and gave him responsibility for his Church on earth. Jesus desired that his authority to forgive sins continue in the ministry of the entire Church.

We first hear of the keys in Isaiah 22:22, when the Lord says, "And I will place on his shoulder the key of the house of David; he shall open, and none shall shut; and he shall shut, and none shall open." In doing this, he is placing his servant Eliakim in charge of the house of Judah and the inhabitants of Jerusalem.

However, the keys that Christ gave St. Peter are not for the earthly City of Jerusalem, but for the New Jerusalem. They are the keys to the Kingdom of Heaven. Jesus designated St. Peter to act as his steward or minister when he ascended into Heaven. He vested St. Peter with his authority and gave him responsibility for his Church on earth. Referring again to the verse from Isaiah, Jesus told St. Peter, that what he binds or looses on earth will be ratified in Heaven. St. Peter received his authority from Christ, who received it from the Father. The origin of all authority is God, but he wishes to exercise it through those he has chosen.

While the keys and the leadership of the Christian community were given to St. Peter alone, Jesus desired that his authority to forgive sins continue in the ministry of the entire Church. After his Resurrection, he appeared to his Apostles and said:

> Receive the Holy Spirit. If you forgive the sins of any they are forgiven: if you retain the sins of any, they are retained. (Jn 20:22-23)

The words of Jesus are very clear. He was bestowing on the Apostles his authority to forgive sins. We saw earlier how Christ forgave the sins of the paralytic. As evidence that he had the authority to forgive sins—spiritual healing—he also offered the paralytic physical healing. In a similar way, St. Peter, following the outpouring of the Holy Spirit at Pentecost, healed a man lame from birth,[13] and later raised a woman from the dead.[14]

Handed Down by the Apostles

It is true that God can forgive any sin in any way he wants—even directly—he knows what we need even better than we do and has thus revealed us his plan for the forgiveness of sins; he instituted the Church to mediate this ministry. It was the intent of Christ that the authority he bestowed on his Apostles as the leaders of the Church would continue to be passed down through the generations until he comes again. The mercy of God in the forgiveness of sins was not intended for the contemporaries of the Apostles alone, but was meant for all people until the end of time.

This authority to forgive sins has been handed down from the Apostles to their successor bishops through apostolic succession. Through the Sacrament of Holy Orders, all bishops and priests participate in the ministry of Christ's forgiveness. As the visible head of the local community, it is the bishop who exercises the primary authority of forgiving and retaining sins. The priests, acting under the authority of the bishop, cooperate in this ministry, bringing the Sacrament of Reconciliation and the forgiveness of sins to the people.

THE HISTORY OF THE SACRAMENT OF PENANCE

As previously mentioned, the authority to forgive sins, which Christ bestowed on the Apostles, was handed down and exercised through the succession of bishops. However, the way in which the Sacrament was celebrated evolved during the first centuries of the Church.

Reconciliation in the Early Church (AD 50-400)

Christ had given the Apostles the ability to forgive sins, but how and when was this authority to be exercised? We see in the New Testament that those who were guilty of serious and unrepentant sins were excluded from the Christian community. In fact, the Church took its mission of calling its own members to repentance and forgiveness very seriously, and asked that sins be confessed to one another.[15]

St. Augustine (AD 354-430), Doctor of the Church, framed important concepts of Original Sin. He wrote, "Love the sinner and hate the sin."

> I wrote to you not to associate with any one who bears the name of brother if he is guilty of immorality or greed, or is an idolater, reviler, drunkard, or robber—not even to eat with such a one. For what have I to do with judging outsiders? Is it not those inside the Church whom you are to judge? God judges those outside. "Drive out the wicked person from among you." (1 Cor 5: 11-13)

In the years that followed, more formal methods of celebrating the Sacrament of Reconciliation were developed. Ordinarily, a person who had committed a grave sin would be called to present himself or herself before the local bishop, where the sin would be confessed in front of the gathered community. The bishop would then impose a penance that would be carried out publicly.

The penances were severe by modern standards and might include months of prayer and fasting. While the penitents could attend the celebration of the Eucharist, they would be separated from the congregation and could not receive Holy Communion. This was an acknowledgement that they had separated themselves both from Christ and his Body, the Church. Once the period of penance was completed, they would again present themselves to the bishop, who would pronounce absolution of their sins and welcome them back into the Christian community.

One of the benefits of such a lengthy process of Reconciliation was that once having performed the penance required, it was unlikely that such persons would repeat the sin again. Great Christian thinkers such as Origen, St. Ambrose, and St. Augustine feared that if penance were allowed to be repeated, people would become accustomed to it, and not take sin as seriously as they should.

On the other hand, this type of public penance also proposed some difficulties. For one thing, a sinner could only avail himself of the Sacrament once in a lifetime. If a person were to fall into serious sin again, he or she would be permanently excluded from the Church.

The public nature of this form of Reconciliation no doubt also discouraged many people who needed to be reconciled with God. In fact, it became the practice of many to delay even their Baptism until their deathbed, thinking that it would be better to have all their sins forgiven immediately before death rather than risk committing a serious sin after Baptism. This, of course, amounted to gambling with one's salvation. What if someone died unexpectedly, or was not able to be baptized before death? Obviously another solution was needed.

Reconciliation in the Irish and the British Church (AD 400-700)

By the fifth century, Christian missionaries began to arrive in Ireland. The most famous of these, of course, was St. Patrick (d. 493), who established monasteries and evangelized the people of Ireland. One of the great developments that came out of this evangelization was the creation of a new form of Reconciliation. The missionaries to these lands saw a need for a form of Penance that was private and repeatable. Instead of receiving absolution from sin after performing a long penance, the penitent's sins were forgiven immediately following Confession, with the penance to be performed afterwards.

Just as the confession was now private, the penance too would be performed privately. Typically, this would consist of prayer and fasting. Although still severe by modern standards, the nature of the penance was determined by the seriousness of the sin and the rank of the person committing it. For example, if a priest and a peasant both committed the same sin, the priest would receive the harsher penance.

As the centuries unfolded, Irish missionaries like St. Columbanus (d. 615) began to leave Ireland to re-evangelize other parts of Europe. They brought with them this practice of frequent and private Confession through the ministry of a priest. This form of celebrating the Sacrament of Reconciliation soon became the norm throughout the Western Church. The actual practice of going to Confession in the Church today has changed little since the fifth century.

Christian missionary St. Patrick, Patron Saint of Ireland. Irish missionaries practiced a form of Reconciliation which survives today. Instead of receiving absolution from sin after performing a long penance, the penitent's sins were forgiven immediately following Confession, with the penance to be performed afterwards. Just as the confession was now private, the penance would also be private.

INDULGENCES

As a result of inordinate attachments to created things, sin distorts the image of Christ that has been imprinted on our soul. These inordinate attachments can be purified and the image of Christ restored through acts of penance while on this earth, or in Purgatory after death. In either event, our soul must be perfected before we can have complete unity with Christ in Heaven.

All sins damage us and our relationship with God and neighbor. Penance, then, springs from the desire to repair the damage caused by our sins. As we saw earlier, penances, in the early Church, ordinarily involved a particular period of time. It was in this context that the practice of gaining indulgences was introduced as a means to shorten or fulfill a prescribed penance.

For example, if someone was assigned a penance of fasting for one year, the period of time could be shortened by making a pilgrimage to a Christian shrine. In other words, the temporal or earthly punishment due to sins already forgiven was reduced by obtaining an indulgence.

By gaining an indulgence and applying the merits that Jesus Christ gained on the Cross, a person becomes purified of his or her inordinate attachments to creatures and the image of Christ is more fully restored in the soul, thereby reducing or eliminating the need for further purification in this life or in Purgatory.

Indulgences are said to be *plenary* when they remove all of the temporal punishment due to sin. A person who dies after obtaining a plenary indulgence would go to Heaven with no need for any purification in Purgatory. To gain a plenary indulgence, however, one must be completely detached from all sin, including venial sin. Because this is rarely the case, most indulgences are *partial*, removing part of the temporal punishment due to sin.

Let us look at an example. Paul, who is a practicing Catholic, has just been to Confession. Although he had no mortal sins to confess, he has an inordinate attachment to certain vices, such as laziness. To be purified of these faults and to be more closely united to Christ, he would need to perform acts of penance. Shortly after his Confession, Paul goes on a trip to Rome with the youth group at his local parish. While there he learns that one can gain a plenary indulgence by making a pilgrimage to St. Peter's Basilica.

With the intention of obtaining an indulgence he fulfills all of the necessary requirements, i.e., Confession, reception of the Eucharist, and praying for the pope. Additionally, while visiting the tomb of St. Peter in the Basilica, he finds his heart touched with a new love for Christ and the desire to make spiritual progress in his Christian life. In obtaining this indulgence, Paul has reduced the amount of purification needed on this earth, or in Purgatory after death, to detach himself from his laziness. If he was to be completely detached from all desires of sin and abhorred all sin, then the indulgence would be plenary, eliminating all of the purification needed. If not, the indulgence would be considered partial, removing some of the purification needed. In either situation, the indulgence has brought him closer to a life in Christ.

The Creation and the Expulsion from the Paradise by Giovanni di Paolo. Because of free will, we can say that sin is always the result of a free choice. We sin when, by a deliberate act of the will, we make a choice in opposition to God's moral law.

MORALITY AND RESPONSIBILITY

God created us as rational beings endowed with free will. This great gift allows us the privilege of freely responding to God's great love, participating with him in his act of creation, and sharing a personal relationship with him. However, it also allows for the possibility of rejecting God, his love, and his plan for us in our lives.

Because of free will, we can say that sin is always the result of a free choice. We sin when, by a deliberate act of the will, we make a choice in opposition to God's moral law. In doing so, we are implicitly or explicitly rejecting his Will and his Divine Wisdom.

Sin is a personal act, and the first and most important consequence of sin is in the sinner himself or herself. Each sin damages our relationship with God, and also damages our spirit, weakening the will and clouding the intellect.[16]

We must also remember that no sin affects the sinner alone. While some sins directly impact others, every sin, even ones of thought, affects who we are and therefore our relationships with those around us. For example, the scandal caused by the sin of a Christian gives a bad example, offers nonbelievers a ready excuse not to follow Christ, and lowers the general morality of society. Like a pebble thrown into a pond, the effects of sin reverberate outwards eventually affecting everyone.

WHAT IS SIN?

Sin is any act, word, or desire that violates moral law.

Moral law is the law of God, which directs all of creation according to his Divine Wisdom. As the ultimate guide for all of creation, including human beings who are endowed with free will, it concerns mankind and the moral decisions that we make.

Man is perfected when his actions are in accordance with the moral law. In doing so, he acts according to the purpose and plan of divine wisdom for which he was created. In like manner, when man acts contrary to the moral law he is degraded. He loses his dignity as a child of God, suffers a reduction in freedom and self-control, loses grace, and distances himself from God.

Sin is a violation of moral law.

The moral law is referred to as *natural moral law* when it is applied to human conduct. Natural moral law prohibits those evils that are easily deduced from human reason (e.g., murder is wrong), but it finds its ultimate expression in Divine Revelation as expressed in the Ten Commandments and the teachings of Jesus Christ.

Any thought, word, or action that violates moral law harms us, other people, and our relationship with God. It is important to stress that sin is not limited to only those instances in which our intention is to offend God, but also when, out of weakness, we perform an act knowing that we will offend him. As in human relationships, we harm others and our relationships with them by our wrongdoing, even when it is not our intention. Therefore, every sin is an offense against God, damaging our relationship with him, even if our intentions are not malicious.

Sin is a disordered love of creatures over God.

The story of Original Sin teaches us that human beings sin when they place themselves and their desires before the will of God. When we allow created things to become more important than God in our lives, our relationship with God is damaged. This attachment to creatures also includes those instances when we place ourselves and our own desires, especially our disordered passions, before God's will in our lives.

This particular aspect of sin is specifically addressed in the First Commandment's prohibition against idolatry. An idol can be defined as any created thing that takes the place of God in our lives. In such a case, we are giving to a created thing that which belongs only to God, the Creator.

Creation of the Animals by Raphael. The Story of Original Sin teaches us that human beings sin when they place themselves and their desires before the will of God. When we allow created things to become more important than God in our lives, our relationship with God is damaged.

Creation of the Sun, Moon, and Planets by Michelangelo.
There are no limits to God's mercy. However, there can be no forgiveness of sins without sorrow.

In summary, the *Catechism of the Catholic Church* states that sin is:

✠ an offense against reason, truth, and right conscience;

✠ a failure in genuine love of God and neighbor;

✠ a word, act, or desire against moral law; and

✠ an offense against God.[17]

SIN DAMAGES OUR RELATIONSHIP WITH GOD

Human beings were created for happiness. In the story of creation, our first parents were created in God's friendship, and their happiness was complete. Adam and Eve had an intimate relationship with God and enjoyed a complete sharing of their lives with him.

However, immediately upon sinning, Adam and Eve hid from God. Aware of their sins, they were ashamed to be in God's presence. Their friendship with him was ruptured and an unfathomable gulf now separated them from him, both in heart and mind. This episode illustrates how Original Sin, and indeed all sin, damages our relationship with God, separating us from his love and his will in our lives.

The Old Testament prophets show us clearly that sin is much more than a simple violation of some ethical norm of conduct. It is an offense against God. The prophet Hosea was married to an adulterous wife, a situation that was analogous to the relationship between God and Israel. However, after sending his wife away, Hosea was instructed by God to forgive her and to receive her once again into his household.

In a similar manner, the Israelites were God's Chosen People with whom he had established a covenant. By their sins of disobedience and idol worship, they had, however, betrayed their relationship with him. These sins were likened to the betrayal of an adulterous spouse. Eventually God withdrew his blessings, allowing the Israelites to be conquered and sent into exile in Babylon. However, while in exile, God prepared them once again to be received into his friendship and to return to the Promised Land.

In the New Testament the meaning of sin takes on a much more personal nature. In his plan of salvation God sent his own Son, Jesus Christ, to die on the Cross to redeem us from our sins. In this sense, we can say that our sins are the reason for the suffering and Death of Jesus on the Cross. This sacrifice of Christ was not done out of some vague concept of sin in general, but out of his infinite love for each and every one of us, and to bring us to Heaven. It is our own personal sins that caused him to willingly accept such great suffering and ultimately his Death.

MORTAL AND VENIAL SINS

Although all sins represent a failure to love and are acts offensive to God, the Bible teaches us that there are degrees of severity of sin, and the Tradition of the Church has given us two classifications of actual sin: *mortal* and *venial*.[18]

Venial sin is the result of an unhealthy attachment to created goods, which harms the relationship between God and man. While they are infractions of the moral law, venial sins are not so serious that they separate the sinner from God. However, the fact that venial sin does not completely break our relationship with God does not mean that it can be dismissed as unimportant. They do affect our relationship with God and the practice of the Christian virtues. Additionally, repeated and unrepentant venial sins can lead to mortal sins.

A mortal sin is a deliberate choice in a serious matter which is so contrary to the will of God that it completely ruptures our relationship with him. In order for a sin to be considered mortal, three conditions must be met.[19]

1. **GRAVE OR SERIOUS MATTER:** the matter of the sin in and of itself must be serious. A grave matter would include those proscribed in the Ten Commandments.

2. **FULL KNOWLEDGE:** the person committing the sin must know that it is serious.

3. **COMPLETE CONSENT:** the person committing the sin must, by a free act of human will, commit the act or allow it to happen.

The Murder of Abel by Novelli. A mortal sin is a deliberate choice which is so contrary to the will of God that it completely ruptures our relationship with him. This willful separation from God deprives the soul of eternal life.

If any one of these conditions is missing from an act, while it may still be sinful, it is not mortally sinful. Ultimately, it is up to God as to whether any given act will be judged as mortal or venial.

The effect of mortal sin is a separation of the sinner from God and his sanctifying grace. This willful separation from God deprives the soul of eternal life and merits eternal punishment. This means that if a person were to die in a state of mortal sin, having willingly and unrepentantly chosen to separate himself or herself from God and his mercy, he or she would merit eternal separation from God. This state of eternal separation from God is called Hell.

Venial sins, i.e., those lesser sins, which even the just commit everyday, can be forgiven by repentance, acts of contrition, prayer, works of charity, reception of Holy Communion, and participation in the Holy Sacrifice of the Mass. Although it is not strictly necessary, the Church nevertheless strongly recommends the confession of venial sins.[20] Mortal sins, however, which rupture a person's relationship with God and extinguish the light of sanctifying grace in the soul, require a different remedy. It is in these cases that the penitent can make use of the promise that Jesus made to his Apostles, "Whose sins you forgive they are forgiven,"[21] in the Sacrament of Reconciliation.

HOW TO MAKE A GOOD CONFESSION

The penitent confesses his or her sins to the degree that is necessary for a good Confession and for the priest to be able to offer the best help. The penitent must confess the sins with sufficient detail to explain them, but not so much that it becomes an exercise in scrupulosity.

EXAMINATION OF CONSCIENCE: Confession must be made out of a sincere desire to live the Faith. In preparation to receive Reconciliation, an examination of conscience is made to review one's moral conduct since the last Confession. This involves an examination of one's words, thoughts, actions, and omissions, along with the relevant intentions. By taking a close look at our lives, we can see those areas in which we have failed to live according to our Christian vocation. One of the ways of examining one's conscience is to use the Ten Commandments and the precepts of the Church and reflect on how you may or may not have lived up to these Christian principles.

SORROW FOR SINS: There are no limits to God's mercy. However, there can be no forgiveness of sins without sorrow. Sometimes feeling sorry for a particular sin is easy, especially when we have done something that is particularly repulsive or out of character. Other times, particularly for small moral transgressions or sins that do not seem to affect us or anyone else, it may be more difficult to feel a sense of contrition.

One way we can begin to feel sorrow for our sins is by looking at their true consequences. As Christians, we know that Jesus suffered and died for us. If we meditate on his sufferings, which were caused by our sins, we will begin to be truly sorry for them. In addition, spending time reflecting on our sins will help us understand their true consequence and the harm that we have caused to ourselves and others.

When we are sorry for our sins out of love for God,[22] we are said to have perfect contrition. Such contrition involves an abhorrence of all sin. When we have a relationship with God, who loves us beyond human understanding, we will naturally want to please him and to avoid that which would harm our relationship with him. Upon realizing that we have done something that offends him, we will immediately seek reconciliation out of our great love for him.

As human beings with a weakened will, our contrition is not always perfect, and therefore, the second type of contrition is called imperfect. This type of sorrow is present primarily out of a fear of punishment. While imperfect contrition is inferior to perfect contrition, it is still valid in that we acknowledge that we have done wrong, recognize God's divine justice and his right to punish, and, most importantly, choose henceforth to do what is right.

There are also instances when a person may suffer from a scrupulous conscience. Scrupulosity is the act of judging things to be morally evil when in fact they are not. Sometimes people who suffer from a scrupulous conscience have difficulty with the Sacrament of Reconciliation or may even abuse the Sacrament. Some examples might include the fear that Confession has not forgiven one of their sins, the fear that one is not sufficiently sorry for one's sins, or the mistaking of a venial sin for a mortal sin.

PURPOSE OF AMENDMENT AND THE RESOLUTION TO APPLY THE MEANS TO AVOID SINS IN THE FUTURE: As we strive for ongoing conversion, we need to see our sins for what they are, and by the same act of will that drove us to commit them, we must now, with the grace of God, make a deliberate decision not to do them again. Included in this is the resolution to change our habits, which might lead us into occasions of sin. Acts of atonement (prayer, fasting, and almsgiving) can be of great help in leaving our sins behind for good.

SHORT EXAMINATION OF CONSCIENCE

✠ When was my last good confession? Did I receive Communion or other sacraments while in the state of mortal sin? Did I intentionally fail to confess some mortal sin in my previous confession?

✠ Did I willfully and seriously doubt my faith, or put myself in danger of losing it by reading literature hostile to Catholic teachings or by getting involved with non-Catholic sects? Did I engage in superstitious activities: palm reading, fortune telling?

✠ Did I take the name of God in vain? Did I curse or take a false oath? Did I use bad language?

✠ Did I miss Mass on a Sunday or a holy day of obligation through my own fault, without any serious reason? Did I fast and abstain on the prescribed days?

✠ Did I disobey my parents or lawful superiors in important matters?

✠ Was I selfish in how I treated others, especially my spouse, my brothers and sisters, my other relatives, or my friends? Did I hatefully quarrel with anyone, or intentionally seek or desire revenge? Did I refuse to forgive? Did I cause physical injury or even death? Did I get drunk? Did I take illicit drugs? Did I consent to, advise, or actively take part in an abortion?

✠ Did I willfully look at indecent pictures or watch immoral movies? Did I read immoral books or magazines? Did I engage in impure jokes or conversations? Did I willfully entertain impure thoughts or feelings? Did I commit impure acts, alone or with others?

✠ Did I steal or damage another's property? How much? Have I made reparation for the damages done?

✠ Did I tell lies? Did I slander? Did I reveal unknown grave faults of others without necessity? Did I judge others rashly in serious matters? Have I tried to make restitution for any damage of reputation that I have caused?

If you remember other serious sins besides those indicated here, also include them in your confession.

CONFESSION OF SINS: After having made an examination of conscience, and having expressed sorrow for sins and the resolution to avoid sin in the future, the penitent is now ready to make a good Confession. Upon entering the confessional, the penitent begins by making the Sign of the Cross. In order to better help the priest understand the particular situation of the penitent, it is customary to say how long it has been since the last Confession.

> In the name of the Father, and of the Son, and of the Holy Spirit. Amen. Bless me, Father, for I have sinned. It has been (how long) since my last confession, and these are my sins...

At this point, the penitent confesses his or her sins to the degree that is necessary for a good Confession and for the priest to be able to offer the best help. The penitent must confess the sins with sufficient detail to explain them, but not so much that it becomes an exercise in scrupulosity. For example, to come to Confession and say, "I did bad things," while true, is too general to help the penitent adequately address the sins. On the other hand, to tell every last detail of every sinful act is not of much help either. This will not be the same for every Confession and every penitent. For this reason, the penitent should feel free to ask questions of the priest, and should not feel embarrassed if the priest asks questions for clarity.

One should also confess sins by their number and kind. There is a difference between stealing one dollar from your mother's purse and fifty thousand dollars from a bank. There is also a difference between an impure thought and hours spent viewing pornography. This information will help the priest to assess the severity of our sins and our vulnerability toward repeating them, which will help the priest give appropriate spiritual direction.

Another helpful tool is to identify the root of our sin and then expand upon it. Perhaps someone has a problem with the sin of laziness, greed, pride, or lust. Confessing that sin and then explaining how it manifests itself through concrete acts will help us to overcome that particular fault.

ACT OF CONTRITION: Once the sins have been sufficiently confessed, the priest will give a penance, and then ask the penitent to make an Act of Contrition. This can be a prayer in one's own words expressing sorrow and remorse for sins committed and a resolve to sin no more, or can be a formulary prayer that is memorized. For example:

> O my God, I am heartily sorry for having offended you. And I detest all my sins because I dread the loss of Heaven and the pains of Hell. But most of all, because they offend you my God, who are all good and deserving of all my love. I firmly resolve, with the help of your grace, to confess my sins, do my penance, and amend my life. Amen.

Having received the Act of Contrition the priest then gives the penitent absolution for his or her sins.

> God the Father of mercies, through the Death and Resurrection of his Son has reconciled the world to himself, and sent the Holy Spirit among us for the forgiveness of sins. Through the ministry of the Church, may God give you pardon and peace. And I absolve you from your sins, in the Name of the Father, and of the Son, and of the Holy Spirit. Amen.

After giving absolution, the priest and penitent offer a prayer of thanksgiving and praise to God for his forgiveness and the graces received, and the penitent is dismissed with the words…

> The Lord has freed you from your sins. Go in peace.

PENANCE OR SATISFACTION: The Sacrament of Reconciliation, however, is not yet complete. The last component of Confession is doing the penance assigned by the priest. By doing penance we demonstrate to God and to ourselves that we acknowledge being forgiven through the mercy of God, that we are sorry for our sins, and that we will do everything in our power to make reparation for our sins and to avoid them in the future.

In addition to the penance that is assigned, it is good to voluntarily take upon ourselves other acts of penance. Acts of self-denial, as well as charity towards our neighbor, help to root selfishness out of our lives. Taking regular time for prayer keeps us aware of the actions of God in our lives and how we can best accomplish our small part of his Will.

Having been cleansed of his or her sins in Confession, the penitent is asked to show remorse for the confessed sins by sincerely striving to imitate Jesus in all that we think, say, and do. We reach out with a loving concern for the poor and defend what is just and right. We admit our faults and lovingly correct others. We suffer patiently, enduring persecution for the sake of what is right, taking up our cross daily, and following Jesus.[23]

It comes as no surprise that the Christian life is a process, not a one-time project. As perfect as our intentions may be we cannot help but fail again. For this reason, the Church encourages us to make frequent use of the Sacraments of Penance and the Eucharist. These are great gifts that God has given us to become more like his Son each and every day.

Acts of self-denial, as well as charity towards our neighbor, help to root selfishness out of our lives. The Christian vocation is a call to sacrifice oneself for others. Through self-denial we die to ourselves and live for Christ.

THE MINISTER OF THE SACRAMENT OF RECONCILIATION

The minister of the Sacrament of Reconciliation is a bishop or priest. While human beings cannot forgive sins, Jesus Christ granted his Apostles the authority to forgive sins in his name, making God's forgiveness available in a real and tangible way.

As in the Eucharist, when Jesus works through the priest to transform the bread and wine into his Body and Blood, it is Jesus who is working through the physical presence of the priest to forgive the sins of those seeking forgiveness in the Sacrament of Reconciliation.

Exercising Christ's authority to forgive sins and saying the words of absolution is a grave responsibility. For this reason, the Church has declared that confessors (i.e., those who hear Confessions) are bound by absolute secrecy regarding all sins that have been confessed. There are no exceptions to this "Seal of Confession" and a confessor is subject to the penalty of excommunication should this seal be broken.

A confessor may not reveal what has been told to him in Confession, even upon the threat of death to himself or others as in the story of St. John Nepomucene.

Therefore, a confessor may not reveal what has been told to him in Confession, even upon the threat of death to himself or others. (See the story of St. John Nepomucene in this chapter.)

Given the delicacy and greatness of this ministry and the respect due to persons, the Church declares that every priest who hears confessions is bound under very severe penalties to keep absolute secrecy regarding the sins that his penitents have confessed to him. He can make no use of knowledge that confession gives him about penitents' lives.[24] This secret, which admits of no exceptions, is called the "sacramental seal," because what the penitent has made known to the priest remains "sealed" by the sacrament. (CCC 1467)

Another role of the confessor is that of a spiritual advisor or director. Spiritual direction is a traditional method of forming one's conscience. In simple terms, spiritual direction is spiritual advice given regularly to help a person guide his or her life toward God. Spiritual direction is usually offered by priests, religious, or qualified lay persons.

As an analogy, all who wish to excel in athletics will employ trainers or coaches to help them improve their skill and ability. These trainers are experts who are able to see things that the athlete misses and are able to offer techniques to improve his or her performance. A spiritual director is a coach who guides us in improving our spiritual life and our relationship with God. He or she becomes familiar with our moral strengths and weaknesses and can be a valuable resource in striving towards a more perfect life.

Spiritual direction should be sought regularly if it is to be beneficial. Time should be set aside to discuss any progress since the last meeting, any problems that may have arisen, and what goals should be set for the month ahead. As an ongoing discussion, spiritual direction helps to keep a person accountable for his or her spiritual development.

IMPORTANCE OF THE SACRAMENT

The Sacrament of Reconciliation was instituted by Christ as the means of receiving the forgiveness of sins committed after Baptism. Some people have the attitude that there is no need for the Sacrament, because an all-powerful, all-merciful God does not need to offer his forgiveness through human ministers.

While it is true that God is not bound by the sacraments and can distribute his graces in any manner he sees fit, this mistaken attitude diminishes the true nature of the sacraments and the means that Christ chose to continue his saving actions in the world. Christ founded the Church and its sacraments to offer mankind a tangible experience of his saving grace. The sacraments are the means through which Christ remains present in our lives. Furthermore, as followers of Christ, we have an obligation to be faithful to the means and instructions that he gave us.

What is the significance of having one's sins forgiven in the Sacrament of Reconciliation? In theological terms, it means that the presence of God in the soul and his sanctifying grace is restored, if it has been lost through mortal sin. A person who is reconciled to God and continues in a state of grace will be with God in Heaven upon the completion of his or her life on earth. Furthermore, by conforming more to the image and likeness of Christ, the amount of purification needed in this life, or after death in Purgatory is reduced.

The Sacrament of Reconciliation offers many benefits and graces to Christians in their spiritual life. The Church teaches that the Sacrament:

✛ reconciles God and man;

✛ restores sanctifying grace lost by mortal sin;

✛ forgives all confessed sins;

✛ remits eternal punishment caused by mortal sin;

✛ imparts actual graces to avoid sin in the future;

✛ reconciles the penitent with the Church;

✛ reduces purgatorial purification; and

✛ gives peace of conscience and spiritual consolation.

As Christ instituted the Sacrament of Reconciliation as the ordinary means by which mortal sins are forgiven, the Church teaches that its members should avail themselves of this important Sacrament. Catholics are required to confess all mortal sins in kind and number after having made a diligent examination of conscience.[25]

Furthermore, if we are in a state of mortal sin, we should not receive the Eucharist, until we have received forgiveness in the Sacrament of Reconciliation. Receiving Holy Communion while in the state of mortal sin would constitute another serious sin called a sacrilege.

In addition, the Church has always encouraged its members to seek the graces that God makes available to us through the Sacrament, even when there have been no mortal sins committed. In the encyclical *Mystici Corporis Christi*, Pope Pius XII enumerated some of the benefits of frequent Confession:

✛ genuine self-knowledge is increased;

✛ bad habits are corrected;

✛ the conscience is purified;

✛ Christian humility grows;

✛ the will is strengthened;

✛ lukewarmness and spiritual neglect are resisted; and

✛ self-control is increased.

PENANCE IN THE LIFE OF A CHRISTIAN

The call to follow Christ is a call to conversion. Baptism is just the beginning of this journey, which lasts a lifetime. The sacraments, as encounters with Christ, are vital sources of grace, which help us along the path of Christian perfection. This is especially true in the Sacraments of the Eucharist and Reconciliation.

The Church emphasizes the need for penance and self-denial out of love for God in the life of the Christian. For this reason it has established certain days and seasons throughout the year when Catholics can practice this vital aspect of their spiritual life. In particular, the season of Lent offers an excellent opportunity for conversion. Focusing on the sufferings of Christ and his Redemption, we can use this important time in the Church year to convert our hearts and to identify more closely with our Lord.

The Christian vocation is a call to sacrifice oneself for others. Through self-denial we die to ourselves and live for Christ. This self-denial can take several different forms and is known as *mortification*. Fasting, as a manifestation of self-denial, is an act of giving something up out of love for Christ. Traditionally, fasting has meant giving up food, or at least some food, for a specified period of time.

> ✠ On Ash Wednesday and Good Friday, Catholics are asked to eat only one full meal and two half meals along with an abstinence from meat. This fasting helps us to identify with the sufferings of Christ, the sufferings of others (especially those who are hungry), and makes our life of prayer more effective.[26]

> ✠ In addition, every Friday is a day of abstinence. This means that Catholics are asked to give something up each and every Friday of the year, and specifically meat on Fridays during Lent.[27]

While the precept on Fasting is binding on all Catholics who have reached the age of eighteen (fourteen for Abstinence), these requirements are a minimum for the spiritual life of a Christian. No day should go by without a reflection on the sufferings of Christ and a small mortification, which helps us to identify more closely with him.

Prayer is also a form of penance. Through prayer, we are given God's graces, we become more closely united to him, and we proceed in our journey toward Christian perfection. The tradition of the Church offers us many forms of Christian prayer. To mention only a few, the Church has always recommended the prayerful reading of Sacred Scripture, known as the *lectio divina*. It would be highly beneficial for each Catholic to spend a few minutes each day meditating on the life and teachings of our Lord.

Along with the Scripture, the Church recommends praying the *Liturgy of the Hours*, which are Psalms of praise. Because it is a liturgical prayer, we are united to the entire Church when we pray the Liturgy of the Hours either by ourselves or with others. Other prayers coming from the Church's rich tradition include the Holy Rosary, visits to the Blessed Sacrament, and meditations on the lives and writings of the Saints.

By almsgiving, the Church refers to the practice of Christian charity. As indicated in the Parable of the Sheep and the Goats,[28] these works of mercy have tremendous value when done out of love of God and love of neighbor. The practice of Christian charity depends very much on our particular state in life. While the donation of money is certainly a part of almsgiving, we should also make a contribution of our time and talents. Christians should always be aware of opportunities to express their love of God by helping others. While this can be practiced through the parish or other Catholic organizations, it is also an individual vocation through which we can bring Christ to those whom we meet.

CONCLUSION

In the Sacrament of Baptism, sanctifying grace is infused into the soul and God and man are reconciled. However, concupiscence—the tendency to sin—remains, causing a constant struggle between slavery to sin and new life in Jesus Christ. One part of us wishes to serve Christ, while another part wishes to serve ourselves. It is as if man is at war within himself. It is because of our failings after Baptism that we have been given the wonderful gift of Reconciliation.

When a person realizes he or she has offended God, the ugliness of his or her sins may seem overwhelming. Like Adam and Eve in the garden, we sometimes want to hide from God. However, as taught by Christ in the Parable of the Good Samaritan, God wishes to give us his love and reconcile us to his friendship. God reaches out to embrace us. We must simply respond by seeking his forgiveness in the Sacrament of Reconciliation.

SUPPLEMENTARY READING

ST. JOHN NEPOMUCENE

In Confession, though we tell our sins to the priest, we are really telling them to Jesus, the Lord. What the priest hears in the confessional he can never reveal—for what goes on in Confession is between the person making the confession and the Lord. We have only to look at St. John Nepomucene to see that this is true.

St. John Nepomucene was a priest in Prague, which is in the modern-day Czech Republic. A gifted preacher, St. John was chosen by King Wenzel as the preacher for the royal court. The queen also recognized the wisdom and goodness of John, and she chose him as her confessor.

One day, King Wenzel called John in for a private meeting. When they were alone, the king asked John what his wife had confessed. John was shocked and explained to the King what he already knew: under no circumstances could the priest reveal anything he had heard in Confession, no matter who asked for the information.

The king tried to persuade John to break the rules, just this one time. He even hinted that John might receive the office of bishop if he cooperated. John still refused. This of course brought down the anger of the king upon the upright priest. John was thrown into prison and tortured, but he did not reveal a word of what the queen had told him.

King Wenzel was persuaded to release John, but the saint knew his trials were not yet over. He went to pray for the strength to endure what was coming. Once again the king called John in, demanding to know what the queen confessed. If John refused, he was told, he would be drowned. John had prepared for a martyr's death, and refused the king's demand. The king had his men tie John up and throw him off a bridge into the Moldau River.

As soon as John died, five lights appeared where he had been thrown in the river. The king saw these lights from his palace and fled the city, fearing the people would riot over the saint's murder. John's body was found by fishermen a few days later, and that summer, a horrible drought came upon Prague, practically drying up the river in which John drowned.

ST. JOHN NEPOMUCENE
ca. 1345 – March 20, 1393

Centuries later, when the Church was investigating the life of John Nepomucene to see whether he was worthy to be named a saint, his tomb was opened. His body was nothing but bones and dust, except for one thing. His tongue, which he had kept pure by refusing to reveal the secrets of the confessional, was whole and incorrupt. It had not decayed at all. To this day it remains that way—a sign of God's role in the Sacrament of Confession.

VOCABULARY

ABSTINENCE
A penitential practice, consisting in abstaining from the use of certain kinds of food. Also refraining from sexual activity either before marriage or within marriage for certain periods of time as part of a program of natural family planning.

ALMSGIVING
The practice of Christian charity through the selfless donation of time, money, and other resources. Almsgiving, together with prayer and fasting, are traditionally recommended to foster interior penance.

CONFESSION
An essential element of the Sacrament of Reconciliation (or Penance), which consists in telling one's sins to the priestly minister. By extension, the word Confession is used to refer to the Sacrament itself.

CONSCIENCE
The inner voice of a human being, in whose heart is inscribed the law of God. Moral conscience is a judgment of practical reason about the moral quality of a human action that a person will do, is in the process of doing, or has already done.

CONTRITION
True sorrow for and hatred of committed sins, coupled with the firm purpose to sin no more. Contrition is necessary to make a good Confession and for the priest to absolve a penitent in the Sacrament of Penance.

CONVERSION
A radical reorientation of one's whole life away from sin and evil and toward God. This is a central element of Christ's preaching, of the Church's ministry of evangelization, and of the Sacrament of Penance.

EXAMINATION OF CONSCIENCE
Prayerful self-reflection on one's words and deeds in light of the Gospel to determine how one has sinned against God. This is necessary to prepare for the Sacrament of Penance.

FASTING
Mortification by deprivation of food or drink. This is an ancient religious practice that denies the desires of the flesh in order to strengthen the spirit.

FREE WILL
This gift from God includes the power of directing one's own actions without constraint. It makes possible the choice to love God.

GENERAL ABSOLUTION
A form of the rite of Penance that is rarely used. In extreme circumstances, a group of people may be absolved of their sins without individual confession of sins.

IMPERFECT CONTRITION (ATTRITION)
Sorrow of the soul and detestation of the sin committed together with the resolution not to sin again as a result of fear of God's punishment rather than out of love of God.

INDULGENCE
The remission of the temporal punishment due to sin that has already been forgiven.

LECTIO DIVINA
Reading and meditation on Scripture.

MORAL LAW
The ethical code, authored and revealed by God and safeguarded by the Church, imposing obligations on the conscience of each person.

MORTAL SIN
A grave offense against God that destroys a person's relationship with him by severing him or her from divine love. It destroys charity in the heart of man; it turns man away from God, who is his ultimate end and his beatitude, by preferring an inferior good to him.

PARTIAL INDULGENCE
An indulgence that removes part of the temporal punishment due to sin.

VOCABULARY Continued

PENANCE
A conversion of heart toward God and away from sin; this includes the intention to change one's life because of hope in divine mercy. It is often characterized by fasting, prayer, and almsgiving.

PERFECT CONTRITION
Sorrow of the soul and detestation of the sin committed together with the resolution not to sin again as a result of love for God above all else.

PLENARY INDULGENCE
An indulgence that removes all of the temporal punishment due to sin.

PURGATORY
A state of final purification of the soul after death but before entrance into Heaven; this is for those who died in God's friendship but were only imperfectly purified.

RECONCILIATION
Also called Penance or Confession: the Sacrament by which Christ forgives sins. Jesus gave his Apostles—who passed it on to their successors down to this day—the power to forgive or retain sins.

SATISFACTION
An act whereby the sinner makes amends, especially in reparation to God for offenses against him.

SCRUPULOSITY
The quality of one whose conscience judges an action to be morally evil when in fact it is not or judges a sin to be mortal when it is venial.

SEAL OF CONFESSION (SACRAMENTAL SEAL)
The confessor's obligation to keep absolutely secret what a penitent has told him in the Sacrament of Penance; also known as the sacramental seal.

SENSUALITY
A preoccupation with the senses or appetites; overindulgence in sensual pleasure; the gratification of sensual pleasures, often to the development of deficiencies in the spiritual, moral, or intellectual realms.

SIN OF COMMISSION
Sin by means of committing an evil act such as theft or murder.

SIN OF OMISSION
Sin by means of failure to commit a good act, such as attend Mass on Sunday or forgive a sinner. Willful neglect or positive refusal to perform some good action, such as attending Mass, that one's conscience urges one to do.

SPIRITUAL DIRECTION
Assisting persons to understand themselves and, with divine grace, to grow in the practice of Christian virtue, while acting as a vehicle for the Holy Spirit, the true spiritual director.

TEMPORAL PUNISHMENT
The punishment due to sin in order to heal the rift with God. It is purified either during one's earthly life, through prayer and conversion, or after death in Purgatory.

VENIAL SIN
An offense against the law and love of God that does not deprive the soul of sanctifying grace. It does, however, weaken a person's love for God and neighbor.

The Church has given us the Seal of Confession in order to encourage the use of the great gift of Reconciliation, which Christ has given us for our spiritual benefit.

STUDY QUESTIONS

1. Define the Sacrament of Penance.

2. Sin is the result of a failure to love. Explain.

3. How does Original Sin affect each and every person?

4. Explain the Original Sin of Adam and Eve. How do we still commit the same sin today?

5. What is concupiscence? How does it affect us?

6. What is moral law, and what is its source?

7. How can sin be said to be a form of idolatry?

8. How did the Original Sin affect our first parents' relationship with God? How does sin affect our relationship with God?

9. What does the Old Testament teach us about the nature of sin and our relationship with God?

10. Explain the analogy between sin and an unfaithful spouse.

11. How did the advent of Christ add a new dimension to the nature of sin and our relationship with God?

12. What are the implications of free will?

13. Why would God give us free will if he knew that many would misuse this gift and cause immeasurable human suffering (e.g., Adolf Hitler)?

14. Name at least three people who are affected by every sin. Explain this using an example.

15. What are the conditions for a mortal sin? Choose an example of a mortal sin and a venial sin, and apply these conditions to each.

16. What was the mission of Jesus Christ?

17. If only God can forgive sins then how was Jesus able to forgive the sins of the paralytic?

18. How does Jesus continue to forgive sins in the world today?

19. Describe when Jesus first imparted his divine authority to forgive sins.

20. When is the giving of keys first mentioned in the Bible? What was the meaning of this event?

21. List the signs of authority that Jesus gave to St. Peter and their significance. What was the role of St. Peter to be in the Church?

22. When was the authority to forgive sins given to the rest of the Apostles?

23. How was this authority to forgive sins handed down in the Church? Who has this authority today?

24. Explain what is meant by the "Seal of Confession."

25. Why is this seal necessary for Confession?

26. What is accomplished in the Sacrament of Reconciliation?

27. What is the relationship between the Sacrament of Reconciliation and purgatory?

28. What is the purpose of the graces received in the Sacrament of Reconciliation?

29. Explain how the Sacrament of Reconciliation helps a person to become a better Christian.

30. If God is the one who forgives sins, then why is the Sacrament of Reconciliation necessary?

31. Explain how the Sacrament of Reconciliation addresses the dual nature of sin: sin against God and sin against neighbor.

32. What is an examination of conscience, and why is it important?

33. "Catholics can just go to Confession and then continue sinning." Why is this statement false?

34. Identify some practices that might help us to resolve to avoid sin in the future.

35. Why is it a good idea to confess venial sins?

STUDY QUESTIONS Continued

36. Why should a person perform penance in addition to the penance assigned to him or her in Confession?

37. What is conscience? What is its purpose? And how is it formed?

38. What is the purpose of spiritual direction? Why is it important?

39. Define contrition.

40. What is the difference between perfect and imperfect contrition? Give an example of each.

41. Define fasting, abstinence, and mortification. Give an example of each.

42. What are Catholics asked to do on every Friday of the year? During Lent?

43. It is obvious that almsgiving helps our neighbor, but how does it help our relationship with God? (Hint: refer to the Parable of the Sheep and the Goats.)

44. What is the *lectio divina*? What is its purpose?

45. As long as God has forgiven us, why is it important to try and repair the damage caused by our sins? Explain using an example.

46. What are ways in which we can make satisfaction for our sins?

47. What is the "temporal punishment" due to sin? When and where can it be forgiven?

48. Define an indulgence. Include in your answer the relationship between an indulgence and the temporary punishment due to sin. In your own words and using an example, explain how indulgences work.

49. What is the difference between a plenary and a partial indulgence? What is required to earn a plenary indulgence?

PRACTICAL EXERCISES

1. Suppose a Catholic friend tells you that God will forgive your mortal sins even if you do not go to Confession. Is this ever true? Why should you go to Confession? (Think about who created the Sacrament.)

2. In *The Screwtape Letters*, C. S. Lewis writes from the perspective of the demon Screwtape teaching his nephew how to tempt a human into sin. This demon has the opposite role of a guardian angel. Imagine you are Uncle Screwtape. Write a letter to your nephew describing how you would tempt your classmates, your parents, or yourself.

3. Are the following behaviors sins? If so, what kind of sins are they: venial or mortal, sins of commission or sins of omission?

   Tim was helping his teacher count the money his class collected during a fundraiser. There was a lot of money, and he knew he could get away with taking some. Did he sin by thinking about stealing the money?

Carl learned in religion class that getting drunk was a sin, and he understands that it is sinful and why it is sinful, yet on the weekend, he went over to his friend's house and had too much of his friend's father's beer. Of what, if anything, is Carl guilty?

Max understands that he has a serious obligation to go to Mass on Sunday, yet he skipped Mass the weekend his parents were out of town. Of what, if anything, is Max guilty?

Tom has never been told how important it is to go to Mass, and he skipped one weekend also. Of what, if anything, is Tom guilty?

Chris goes to Confession, but he intentionally does not mention one mortal sin that he does not want to talk about. Is his Confession valid?

FROM THE CATECHISM

1482 The Sacrament of Penance can also take place in the framework of a *communal celebration* in which we prepare ourselves together for confession and give thanks together for the forgiveness received. Here, the personal confession of sins and individual absolution are inserted into a liturgy of the word of God with readings and a homily, an examination of conscience conducted in common, a communal request for forgiveness, the Our Father and a thanksgiving in common. This communal celebration expresses more clearly the ecclesial character of penance. However, regardless of its manner of celebration the Sacrament of Penance is always, by its very nature, a liturgical action, and therefore an ecclesial and public action.²⁹

1483 In case of grave necessity recourse may be had to a *communal celebration of reconciliation with general confession and general absolution*. Grave necessity of this sort can arise when there is imminent danger of death without sufficient time for the priest or priests to hear each penitent's confession. Grave necessity can also exist when, given the number of penitents, there are not enough confessors to hear individual confessions properly in a reasonable time, so that the penitents through no fault of their own would be deprived of sacramental grace or Holy Communion for a long time. In this case, for the absolution to be valid the faithful must have the intention of individually confessing their grave sins in the time required.³⁰ The diocesan bishop is the judge of whether or not the conditions required for general absolution exist.³¹ A large gather of the faithful on the occasion of major feasts or pilgrimages does not constitute a case of grave necessity.³²

1485 "On the evening of that day, the first day of the week," Jesus showed himself to his apostles. "He breathed on them, and said to them: 'Receive the Holy Spirit. If you forgive the sins of any, they are forgiven; if you retain the sins of any, they are retained.'"³³

1486 The forgiveness of sins committed after Baptism is conferred by a particular sacrament called the sacrament of conversion, confession, penance, or reconciliation.

1487 The sinner wounds God's honor and love, his own human dignity as a man called to be a son of God, and the spiritual well-being of the Church, of which each Christian ought to be a living stone.

1488 To the eyes of faith no evil is graver than sin and nothing has worse consequences for sinners themselves, for the Church, and for the whole world.

1489 To return to communion with God after having lost it through sin is a process born of the grace of God who is rich in mercy and solicitous for the salvation of men. One must ask for this precious gift for oneself and for others.

1490 The movement of return to God, called conversion and repentance, entails sorrow for and abhorrence of sins committed, and the firm purpose of sinning no more in the future. Conversion touches the past and the future and is nourished by hope in God's mercy.

1491 The sacrament of Penance is a whole consisting in three actions of the penitent and the priest's absolution. The penitent's acts are repentance, confession or disclosure of sins to the priest, and the intention to make reparation and do works of reparation.

1492 Repentance (also called contrition) must be inspired by motives that arise from faith. If repentance arises from love of charity for God, it is called "perfect" contrition; if it is founded on other motives, it is called "imperfect."

1493 One who desires to obtain reconciliation with God and with the Church, must confess to a priest all the unconfessed grave sins he remembers after having carefully examined his conscience. The confession of venial faults, without being necessary in itself, is nevertheless strongly recommended by the Church.

1494 The confessor proposes the performance of certain acts of "satisfaction" or "penance" to be performed by the penitent in order to repair the harm caused by sin and to re-establish habits befitting a disciple of Christ.

FROM THE CATECHISM Continued

1495 Only priests who have received the faculty of absolving from the authority of the Church can forgive sins in the name of Christ.

1496 The spiritual effects of the sacrament of Penance are:

— reconciliation with God by which the penitent recovers grace;

— reconciliation with the Church;

— remission of the eternal punishment incurred by mortal sins;

— remission, at least in part, of temporal punishments resulting from sin;

— peace and serenity of conscience, and spiritual consolation;

— an increase of spiritual strength for the Christian battle.

1497 Individual and integral confession of grave sins followed by absolution remains the only ordinary means of reconciliation with God and with the Church.

1498 Through indulgences the faithful can obtain the remission of temporal punishment resulting from sin for themselves and also for the souls in Purgatory.

The Expulsion of Adam and Eve by Domenichino. The consequences of their sin would not only affect Adam and Eve, but also all of their descendants.

ENDNOTES – CHAPTER FOUR

1. Acts 2:38.
2. Cf. Gn 3:1-11; Rom 5:19.
3. Cf. Council of Trent: DS 1513.
4. Eph 5:27.
5. CCC 1425-1428, 2013-2014.
6. Is 53:10.
7. Mt 1:21.
8. Cf. Mk 2:7.
9. Mk 2:5, 10; Lk 7:48.
10. Cf. Jn 20:21-23.
11. Mt 16:15

12. In the Aramaic language in which Jesus was speaking, he gave Simon the name *Cephas* meaning rock. In Greek, the word rock is translated as *petra*. Because this is a feminine noun, it was changed to the masculine *Petros*, giving us the name Peter in English.
13. Cf. Acts 3:1-10.
14. Acts 9:40
15. Cf. Mt 18:15-18; 2 Cor 2:10, 5:18; Jas 5:15-16.
16. *RP* 16.
17. Cf. CCC 1849-1850.
18. Cf. CCC 1855.
19. Cf. CCC 1857.
20. Cf. CCC 1458.
21. Jn 20:22-23.

22. Cf. CCC 1452.
23. Cf. CCC 1435.
24. Cf. CIC, can. 1388 § 1; CCEO, can. 1456.
25. CCC 1456, CIC, 988 § 1.
26. CIC, 1250.
27. CIC, 1251-1253.
28. Mt 25:31-46.
29. Cf. *SC* 26-27.
30. Cf. CIC, can. 962 § 1.
31. Cf. CIC, can. 961 § 2.
32. Cf. CIC, can. 961 § 1.
33. Jn 20:19, 22-23.

Anointing of the Sick

The Sacrament of Anointing of the Sick offers the spiritual graces needed when facing sickness and death and passes on the healing touch of Jesus Christ to our souls.

The Sacraments
CHAPTER 5

Anointing of the Sick

Getting into a boat he [Jesus] crossed over to his own city. And behold, they brought to him a paralytic, lying on his bed; and when Jesus saw their faith he said to the paralytic, "Take heart, my son; your sins are forgiven." And behold, some of the scribes said to themselves, "This man is blaspheming." But Jesus, knowing their thoughts, said, "Why do you think evil in your hearts? For which is easier, to say, 'Your sins are forgiven,' or to say, 'Rise and walk'? But that you many know that the Son of man has authority on earth to forgive sins"—he then said to the paralytic— "Rise, take up your bed and go home." And he rose and went home. When the crowds saw it, they were afraid, and they glorified God, who had given such authority to men. (Mt 9:1-8)

n the last chapter, we looked at the first of two Sacraments of Healing—the Sacrament of Reconciliation. During his earthly ministry, Christ performed many miraculous healings, but perhaps even more miraculously, he also performed many healings of the soul—telling those who had been physically cured that they were also freed from their sins.

While spiritual well-being is vital for salvation, it should not be overlooked that Christ offered physical healing as well. God understands human suffering, and he sent his Son into the world not only to endure suffering but also to give it salvific meaning.

Christ, in his great love for mankind, continues his saving actions through the sacraments, touching our lives in a very special way at each critical stage in our journey of life. Each sacrament, in its own particular way, carries on the mission Christ began on earth.

As we have seen in previous chapters, he comes to us first in Baptism, giving us a new birth in the Spirit, restoring our friendship with God, and re-creating us in his own image. In the Eucharist, he gives us spiritual nourishment, uniting us more fully to himself and his Mystical Body, the Church. In Confirmation, he seals us with the promised Spirit, granting us the gifts needed to fully live the Christian life. When we fail, he seeks us out in the Sacrament of Reconciliation, offering us forgiveness and spiritual healing for the soul.

Suffering and death is an unavoidable part of the human experience, and much of Christ's time on earth was devoted to caring for those who were suffering. This vital aspect of Christ's earthly mission did not vanish with his Ascension into Heaven. Indeed, in the days following Pentecost, many people were healed—one of the most powerful signs in the early Church that Christ's power and authority had been handed down to his Apostles.

Later, in the New Testament, we see that the sick were anointed with oil, while the Church prayed for their spiritual and physical well-being. Called the "Anointing of the Sick," this Sacrament offers the spiritual graces needed when facing sickness and death and passes on the healing touch of Jesus Christ to our souls.

Healing the Blind Man by Bloch. The sick and suffering who came seeking Jesus' healing touch were asked only to have faith in him, and those who he touched experienced a personal encounter with the divine. "Jesus said to him, 'Go your way; your faith has made you well'" (Mk 10:52).

IN THIS CHAPTER, WE WILL ADDRESS SEVERAL QUESTIONS:

✤ What are the benefits received from the Anointing of the Sick?

✤ How is it celebrated?

✤ When should it be celebrated?

✤ When does the Sacrament forgive sins?

✤ What is the meaning of suffering?

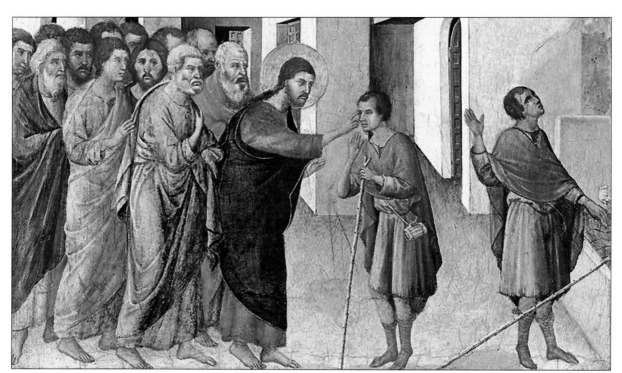

Healing of the Blind Man by Duccio. Jesus showed a special concern and compassion for those who were suffering. Today, Jesus continues his ministry of healing through the Church.

THE MINISTRY OF HEALING

In his public ministry, Jesus showed a special concern and compassion for those who were suffering. His ministry of Redemption and Reconciliation was accompanied by numerous miracles of physical healing. He worked these miracles both to demonstrate that he was the Messiah and to show compassion for those who were suffering. In sending out his disciples he gave them the mission of preaching the Kingdom of God and healing the sick.[1]

> Christ's compassion toward the sick and his many healings of every kind of infirmity are a resplendent sign that "God has visited his people"[2] and that the Kingdom of God is close at hand. Jesus has the power not only to heal, but also to forgive sins;[3] he has come to heal the whole man, soul and body; he is the physician the sick have need of.[4] His compassion toward all who suffer goes so far that he identifies himself with them: "I was sick and you visited me."[5] His preferential love for the sick has not ceased through the centuries to draw the very special attention of Christians toward all those who suffer in body and soul. It is the source of tireless efforts to comfort them. (CCC 1503)

Today, Jesus continues his ministry of healing through the Church, which has always identified closely with Jesus' concern for the sick. Throughout its history, the Church has considered the relief of human suffering to be one of its primary missions. This is attested to by thousands of Catholic hospitals and the many religious congregations and saints who have dedicated their lives to helping the sick. Indeed, all Christians are called to have this same compassion for the sick and suffering.

The goal of these Corporal Works of Mercy, however, is not only the physical healing of the person but spiritual healing as well. This two-part aspect of healing is seen clearly in the Sacrament of the Anointing of the Sick. As an encounter with Christ, the Sacrament makes present Jesus' healing actions. Concerned with both body and soul, Jesus gives the sick the graces needed to face illness and death, preparing them for eternal life in Heaven and healing the body if it is good for the salvation of the soul. This sacrament is administered not only for those at the point of death but also to those afflicted with serious sickness or old age.[6]

LOURDES

Delizia Cirolli was twelve years old when she began to feel a pain in her right knee. As the pains worsened, her parents sought medical help. The examinations showed that she had a malignant tumor, and the doctors recommended an immediate amputation of the leg. Even so, they could not guarantee that the tumor's growth could be stopped.

Although in much pain, Delizia went with her mother to the shrine of Our Lady of Lourdes, in France, before receiving any medical treatment. After praying at the grotto of Our Lady and bathing in the healing waters, the two returned home. A new medical examination confirmed the worst. Not only had there been no miraculous healing, but her condition had deteriorated. The advanced stage of the tumor now made medical treatment impossible, and so without receiving treatment, Delizia returned home to face her impending death. Relying on faith, Delizia's mother continued to wash the leg in the healing water from Lourdes, and family and friends prayed for a miracle.

Delizia eventually was confined to bed. A few days before Christmas, however, everyone was surprised when Delizia announced that she felt better and wished to get up. She walked for the first time in several weeks. A thorough medical examination showed that the tumor had completely vanished, a cure for which there was no scientific explanation. On June 28, 1989 the cure of Delizia Cirolli was declared a miracle.

Lourdes has been a place of healing for over a century. It has been remarked that everyone who goes to Lourdes in a spirit of faith receives a healing, if not of body, then of soul. These healing miracles of Lourdes began in 1858, when the Virgin Mary appeared to a young girl named Bernadette. Our Lady's message was one of penance in reparation for the sins of the world. In addition, she asked Bernadette for a favor. Bernadette dug in the earth at a spot designated by Our Lady, and a spring of pure water rose from the ground. People soon found that those who bathed in its waters were healed from disease and illness.

In a later apparition, Our Lady requested that a chapel be built near the grotto. The parish priest, not yet convinced, requested further proof that the apparitions were authentic. Bernadette was to ask the Lady for her name. Our Lady told Bernadette, "I am the Immaculate Conception." Accompanied by miraculous healings, Our Lady was confirming the title given her by the Church just four years earlier. The Dogma of the Immaculate Conception proclaimed that Mary was preserved free from the stain of Original Sin from the moment of her conception.

A chapel was built, and over the course of the next century, multitudes of pilgrims visited the site dedicated to the Immaculate Conception of the Blessed Virgin Mary. Thousands of people have been cured of disease, and millions have received spiritual benefits. After carefully examining each claim, the Church has officially declared sixty-seven of these cases to be miraculous.

The Raising of Lazarus by Rembrandt. The miracles performed by Christ show us that the Kingdom of God has come upon us, and that this kingdom brings a healing deeper than merely physical cures: it brings healing and victory over sin and death through Christ's own death on the Cross.

ENCOUNTERS WITH CHRIST

In his miracles of healing we see Jesus calling people to faith. The sick and suffering who came seeking Jesus' healing touch were asked only to have faith in him, and those who he touched experienced a personal encounter with the divine. This physical encounter between Christ and those who were suffering was central to his healing actions.

✠ And he stretched out his hand and touched him, saying, "I will; be clean." And immediately his leprosy was cleansed. (Mt 8:3)

✠ And when Jesus entered Peter's house, he saw his mother-in-law lying sick with a fever; he touched her hand, and the fever left her, and she rose and served him. (Mt 8:14-15)

✠ Then he touched their eyes, saying, "According to your faith be it done to you." And their eyes were opened. (Mt 9:29-30)

✠ ...so that all who had diseases pressed upon him to touch him. (Mk 3:10)

✤ She had heard the reports about Jesus, and came up behind him in the crowd and touched his garment. For she said, "If I touch even his garments, I shall be made well." (Mk 5: 27-28)

✤ And taking him aside from the multitude privately, he put his fingers into his ears, and he spat and touched his tongue…and said to him…"Be opened." (Mk 7: 33-34)

✤ And some people brought to him a blind man and begged him to touch him…and when he had spit on his eyes and laid his hand upon him…. (Mk 8: 22-23)

From this small selection of Jesus' miracles we can see a particular pattern emerging. Jesus could have healed in any manner that he wished, even from a distance.[7] The method Jesus used, however, was his physical touch. In other words, Jesus healed sacramentally—he was the sign of God's healing power. It was through an active and personal encounter with Christ that the sick were offered his healing grace, an encounter that "touched" them both in body and soul.

Although Christ showed compassion for those who were suffering, his ultimate concern was for their eternal salvation. He healed, but he also forgave sins. Though it was within his capacity, Jesus did not heal everyone in Palestine. In fact, the reality is that every single person healed by Jesus, even Lazarus who he raised from the dead, eventually died. It was not the mission of Christ to remove all suffering from the world, but to give us the grace to accept it as a means of uniting ourselves with his Redemption.

This reality informs our understanding of the actions of Christ in the Sacrament of Anointing. The Sacrament is primarily concerned with a person's eternal life. It is good to pray for a physical healing, but it is not always the will of God that a person recover. What is always the will of God is that the hearts of mankind are directed toward him in love. By conveying the healing sacramental grace of Christ, the Sacrament of Anointing serves this dual purpose of offering physical and spiritual healing to the recipient and strengthening his or her soul in the Faith of Christ during these difficult times of suffering.

The miraculous healings of Christ also had another meaning. As Jesus told the amazed crowd who witnessed the resurrection of Lazarus, his miracles were worked to demonstrate the glory of God so that people may believe in him.[8] These miracles performed by Christ show us that the Kingdom of God has come upon us, and that this kingdom brings a healing deeper than merely physical cures: it brings healing and victory over sin and death through Christ's own Death on the Cross.

Christ Healing the Leper by Rosselli. The method Jesus used was his physical touch. Jesus healed sacramentally.

Anointing the Sick by Carducho. Suffering is the noble mission of the Christian person. The Sacrament of Anointing of the Sick strengthens the recipient's ability to endure that suffering and unite it to the saving action of Christ on the Cross.

THE SACRAMENT OF THE ANOINTING OF THE SICK

The healing ministry of Jesus Christ is carried on in a real and personal way in the sacraments. By instituting the sacraments, Jesus chose effective signs, which were associated with the effect that each sacrament has on the soul.

At different points in the Gospel story, we see Jesus giving his Apostles a share in his ministry of human compassion and instructing them to heal the sick. The Gospel of St. Mark records how they "anointed with oil many that were sick and healed them."[9] In a similar manner, Jesus appeared to the eleven before his Ascension into Heaven and gave them instructions to preach the Gospel and to baptize, adding that if they laid their hands on the sick they would recover.[10]

The Epistle of St. James details how the administration of this healing action was carried out in the early Church. The epistle gives specific instructions to the *elders* of the Church (called "*presbyters*" in Greek from which word we derive "*priest*") regarding the proper exercise of the Sacrament of the Anointing of the Sick:

> Is any among you sick? Let him call for the elders [*priests*] of the Church, and let them pray over him, anointing him with oil in the name of the Lord; and the prayer of faith will save the sick man, and the Lord will raise him up; and if he has committed sins, he will be forgiven. (Jas 5:14-15)

Following the charge given by Christ to heal the sick, the Church faithfully offers this Sacrament of Healing to all those who are suffering and approaching death.

> This sacred Anointing of the Sick was instituted by Christ our Lord as a true and proper sacrament of the New Testament. It is alluded to indeed by Mark, but is recommended to the faithful and is promulgated by James the apostle and brother of the Lord. (Council of Trent, 1551, DS 1695)

CELEBRATION OF THE SACRAMENT

> The celebration of this sacrament consists especially in the laying on of hands by the priests of the Church, the offering of the prayer of faith, and the anointing of the sick with oil made holy by God's blessing. This rite signifies the grace of the sacrament and confers it. (*Pastoral Care of the Sick*, 6)

The Sacrament of the Anointing of the Sick consists of prayer, the laying on of hands, and an anointing with oil, which is reminiscent of a number of other sacraments, such as Confirmation. As in Reconciliation, words are also said that forgive the recipient of his or her sins.

When possible, the Anointing of the Sick should be received along with the Sacrament of Reconciliation and the Holy Eucharist. Received together, these sacraments offer the graces that will strengthen the recipient at the moment of suffering and assist him or her through the final struggles of life.

Matter

The material or physical matter used in the Sacrament of the Anointing of the Sick is the Oil of the Sick with which the recipient is anointed. In the ancient world, olive oil was used medicinally for its healing properties. In the Parable of the Good Samaritan, we see how oil was poured into the wound of the injured man.[11] Athletes used oil after a competition to rejuvenate their tired bodies and aching muscles. Therefore, it is not surprising that oil would be used as the physical sign for this Sacrament of Healing. In the same manner that oil helps to cure the body, the Sacrament of Anointing helps to heal the soul.

The particular oil used in the Sacrament of Anointing is called the Oil of the Sick, which is blessed by the bishop of the diocese during the Chrism Mass on Holy Thursday. However, in extraordinary circumstances, the Church provides that any plant oil blessed by a priest may be used.

James the Apostle by Veneziano. The Letter of James gives specific instructions to the elders of the Church regarding the proper exercise of the Sacrament of the Anointing of the Sick: "and the prayer of faith will save the sick man..." (Jas 5:15).

Form

In the Sacrament, the anointing is accompanied by words of spiritual healing, spoken by a priest or bishop, who is the minister of the Sacrament. These words call for God to ease the person's sufferings and to give strength in his or her weakness. With the help of the Holy Spirit, the priest then asks that God free the person from sin, grant him or her salvation, and raise him or her up on the Last Day. In the prayers following the anointing, the priest prays for health that the person might be restored to the service of God. It is through the physical anointing with oil, accompanied by words of healing, that the sick encounter Christ and his divine touch.

> The celebration of the Anointing of the Sick consists essentially in the anointing of the forehead and hands of the sick person (in the Roman Rite) or of other parts of the body (in the Eastern rite), the anointing being accompanied by the liturgical prayer of the celebrant asking for the special grace of this sacrament. (CCC 1531)

The priest begins the Sacrament with the anointing of the forehead and hands; however, in cases of necessity a single anointing on the forehead is sufficient. If the condition of the sick person prevents anointing the forehead, then another suitable part of the body may be anointed.[12] This is followed by the prayer:

> *Through this holy anointing, by his most loving mercy, may the Lord assist you by the grace of the Holy Spirit so that freed from your sins he may save you and raise you up.*

In addition to this prayer said by the priest, the Church encourages the faithful to be present and to join in prayer for the sick and suffering. In this way, the Anointing of the Sick more clearly manifests the communal nature of the Church and the sacraments.

> Like all the sacraments the Anointing of the Sick is a liturgical and communal celebration,[13] whether it takes place in the family home, a hospital or church, for a single sick person or a whole group of sick persons. (CCC 1517)

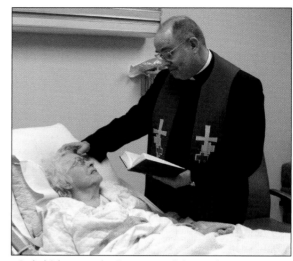

Whenever possible, therefore, the family and friends of the person being anointed should be present for the Sacrament. This is especially true when the Sacrament of Anointing is celebrated at home, though the participation of the faithful should be encouraged no matter where it is celebrated.

Minister

Only bishops and priests can celebrate the Anointing of the Sick. Like Confession and the Eucharistic sacrifice, the presence of the priest as the minister is a reminder that it is ultimately Christ who is the divine physician and the one who mediates God's grace. The role of the priest in the Sacrament is also a reminder of the Apostolic Tradition that has passed down Christ's authority through the bishops to the priests.

Only bishops and priests can celebrate the Sacrament of Anointing of the Sick.

The bishop or priest who is celebrating the Sacrament will also attend to any other spiritual needs of those who are suffering. This includes offering pastoral care, spiritual direction or counseling, *Viaticum* (Holy Communion for the Dying), and offering God's forgiveness in the Sacrament of Reconciliation.

THE EFFECTS OF THE ANOINTING OF THE SICK

The Anointing of the Sick is intended for those who are seriously ill and need the special help of God's grace in this time of anxiety.[14]

> This sacrament gives the grace of the Holy Spirit to those who are sick: by this grace the whole person is helped and saved, sustained by trust in God, and strengthened against the temptations of the Evil One and against anxiety over death. Thus the sick person is able not only to bear suffering bravely, but also to fight against it. A return to physical health may follow the reception of this sacrament if it will be beneficial to the sick person's salvation. If necessary, the sacrament also provides the sick person with the forgiveness of sins and the completion of Christian penance.[15] (*Pastoral Care of the Sick*, 6)

The Sacrament of the Anointing of the Sick forgives part of the temporal punishment due to sins that are already forgiven, and strengthens the person to avoid sins in the future. In particular, the Sacrament

- ✤ unites the sick person to Christ's Passion for his own good and the good of the Church;
- ✤ grants strength, peace, and courage to endure in a Christian manner the sufferings of illness or old age;
- ✤ forgives sins, if the person had contrition and was unable to receive the Sacrament of Penance, restoring sanctifying grace;
- ✤ restores health if it is good for the salvation of the person's soul;
- ✤ prepares the person for passage into eternal life; and
- ✤ reduces or removes the temporal punishment due to sin when the person is properly disposed.

Those who are facing death need the grace of God to ensure that they accept the death that God has permitted them to suffer. From the moment of death, each person will be judged by Christ (*the particular judgment*), and will receive his or her eternal recompense.[16] Those who die in a state of grace, and whose souls are perfectly purified, will be eternally united with God in *Heaven*. "Those who die in God's grace and friendship imperfectly purified, although they are assured of their eternal salvation, undergo a purification after death, so as to achieve the holiness necessary to enter the joy of God."[17] This purification of the soul after death for those who are assured of Heaven is called *Purgatory*. However, those who die in mortal sin without repenting and accepting God's merciful love will be eternally separated from him.[18] This is called Hell. The Sacrament of Anointing of the Sick gives the grace and strength necessary to resist the devil as those preparing for death face passage from this world to the next. Because of its effects, the Anointing of the Sick is an invaluable spiritual help for the sick.

> Every man receives his eternal recompense in his immortal soul from the moment of his death in a particular judgment by Christ, the judge of the living and the dead. (CCC 1051)

> Those who are seriously ill need the special help of God's grace in this time of anxiety, lest they be broken in spirit and, under the pressure of temptation, perhaps weakened in their faith. This is why, through the sacrament of anointing, Christ strengthens the faithful who are afflicted by illness, providing them with the strongest means of support. (*Pastoral Care of the Sick*, 5)

WHEN SHOULD THE SACRAMENT BE ADMINISTERED?

The Sacrament of Anointing of the Sick is most commonly received by baptized Catholics who are in danger of death due to sickness or old age. However, the Sacrament is not only for those who are just moments from death. It is fitting to receive this Sacrament just prior to a serious operation and as soon as there is danger of death from sickness or old age. The Sacrament may be repeated if a person's condition becomes more serious.

Like the Eucharist, Anointing of the Sick may also be received by children as long as they have reached the age of reason. In *Pastoral Care of the Sick*[19] the Church gives the following guidelines indicating when the Sacrament should be administered.

✠ The Letter of St. James[20] states that the sick are to be anointed in order to raise them up and save them. Great care and concern should be taken to see that those of the faithful whose health is seriously impaired by sickness or old age receive this Sacrament.

✠ The Sacrament may be repeated if the sick person recovers after being anointed and then falls ill again or if during the same illness the person's condition becomes more serious.

✠ A sick person may be anointed before surgery whenever a serious illness is the reason for the surgery or if the surgery is a high-risk procedure.

✠ Elderly people may be anointed if they have become notably weakened even though no serious illness is present.

There are also a number of extraordinary circumstances during which the Sacrament may be administered. If an individual is in a coma or in a grave moment of health, which prevents them from going to Confession, they may receive the Sacrament of Anointing. In such cases, the Sacrament will remove all mortal sin, provided the person has or had the proper dispositions required for forgiveness, including contrition and the desire to go to Confession. If the person later recovers, he or she should make a sacramental Confession.

> When a priest has been called to attend to those who are already dead, he should not administer the sacrament of anointing. Instead, he should pray for them, asking that God forgive their sins and graciously receive them into the kingdom. But if the priest is doubtful whether the sick person is dead, he is to confer the sacrament. (*Pastoral Care of the Sick*, 15.)

THE MEANING OF HUMAN SUFFERING

> In the Cross of Christ not only is the Redemption accomplished through suffering, *but also human suffering itself has been redeemed*…In bringing about the Redemption through suffering, Christ *has* also *raised human suffering to the level of the Redemption.* Thus each man, in his suffering, can also become a sharer in the redemptive suffering of Christ. (*Salvifici Doloris*, 19)

Suffering is a fact of human life. While it is natural to question the reason for suffering, it is nonetheless inescapable. In the Book of Genesis, we see how suffering and death entered the world as a result of Original Sin.[21]

Sin is inextricably linked with suffering. We can clearly see that our sins cause suffering for ourselves and others and also affect our relationship with God. However, it should not be mistaken that suffering is a punishment from God in retribution for any particular sin one has committed. The Book of Job illustrates beautifully how even the most upright and just person may endure suffering in this life.

Suffering and death can be one of the most difficult issues encountered in life. It is here, in the contemplation of our own mortality, that we must come to grips with the ultimate meaning of life itself. This struggle with mortality can lead some to despair, hopelessness, and anger. However, it can also cause us to contemplate the purpose of our lives, provoking a search for God and seeking an ultimate union with him.[22]

Here we have no greater inspiration than Jesus Christ, the Son of God who came into this world precisely to suffer and, by suffering, give meaning to our own sufferings. Christ has taught us that we can turn our own sufferings into something positive by uniting them with his suffering on the Cross. When we suffer, we accomplish God's greatest desire for us: to live like Christ. Those who join their suffering to Christ work for the good of his Body, the Church.[23]

> Now I rejoice in my sufferings for your sake, and in my flesh I complete what is lacking in Christ's afflictions for the sake of his body, that is, the church. (Col 1: 24)

Jesus calls us to pick up our cross and follow him.[24] By accepting suffering for the well-being of others, we imitate Christ, who accepted suffering for our salvation, and are given a new outlook on our own sufferings and those of Christ. By imitating Christ and cooperating with him, we will be liberated from sin and death, being raised with him on the last day.

Viewed in this light, suffering can be understood as a means to a more complete union with Jesus Christ and a path for our own spiritual purification. When we accept our own suffering, identifying ourselves both physically and spiritually with Jesus Christ, we can help to spread the grace of God.

> It is when we attempt to avoid suffering by withdrawing from anything that might involve hurt, when we try to spare ourselves the effort and pain of pursuing truth, love, and goodness, that we drift into a life of emptiness, in which there may be almost no pain, but the dark sensation of meaninglessness and abandonment is all the greater. It is not by sidestepping or fleeing from suffering that we are healed, but rather by our capacity for accepting it, maturing through it and finding meaning through union with Christ, who suffered with infinite love. (*Spe Salvi*, 37)

THE CHRISTIAN VOCATION TO SERVE THOSE IN NEED

Jesus taught us that we show our love for him by serving those in need. When we help those who are suffering, we are serving Christ himself: "I was sick and you visited me.…as you did it to one of the least of these my brethren, you did it to me."[25] Likewise, in the Parable of the Good Samaritan, Jesus teaches that we must love our neighbor as ourselves. This Commandment of Love is extended by Christ to each and every human being, even to those that the world considers "unlovable."[26]

Ironically, often the people we find most difficult to love are those who are suffering and, therefore, most in need of our love. In today's world, suffering is viewed as something ugly to be avoided. However, in the Christian view, human suffering is a difficult blessing, which offers the opportunity to be like Christ in his suffering and to atone for our sins and the sins of others. Suffering is the noble mission of the Christian person. The Sacrament of Anointing of the Sick strengthens the recipient's ability to endure that suffering and unite it to the saving action of Christ on the Cross.

BL. TERESA OF CALCUTTA

At the age of twelve, the young Agnes Gonxha Bojaxhiu felt God's call to the missionary life. With a desire to spread the love of Christ throughout the world, she entered the religious life, joining the Sister's of Loreto. After spending a few months in Dublin, she was sent to their missions in India. At the age of twenty-one, Agnes took her initial vows and chose the name Teresa, after St. Therese of Lisieux. For thirteen years, Sister Teresa taught High School geography and religion in Calcutta and later served as the school principal, but she still felt that God was calling her to do something more. Sent to Darjeeling to recuperate from tuberculosis, she received a second calling from God. She was to leave her convent and live among the poor.

In 1948, Mother Teresa received permission to leave the order, and she began her work in the slums of Calcutta. She started a school to teach the children of the poor and began learning medical skills to treat the sick, who had no money for doctors or hospitals. Soon she was joined by several of her former students, and the order that would be known as the Missionaries of Charity slowly began to take shape. Going into the streets and slums of Calcutta, Mother Teresa and her associates would find the sick and the dying who had been rejected by others.

Gathering them up, they would bring them home and give them medical care. But most importantly, they would give them the love of Christ.

In 1950, Mother Teresa received permission to found the Missionaries of Charity, whose primary purpose was to work with the "poorest of the poor." Two years later she founded a home for the dying in a former Hindu Temple. The care that Mother Teresa and the Missionaries of Charity gave to the poor allowed them to die in peace and dignity. For some people, it was the first time in their lives that they had experienced love. Mother Teresa was inspired by the Parable of the Sheep and the Goats (Mt 25: 31-46) to see Christ in the poor and the sick she encountered everyday. For more than fifty years, she continued her work and became an inspiration for millions. By the time of her death in 1997, her small group of followers had grown into thousands with more than five hundred missions throughout the world.

In her own words, Mother Teresa taught that:

At the end of our lives, we will not be judged by how many diplomas we have received, how much money we have made or how many great things we have done. We will be judged by

"I was hungry and you gave me to eat. I was naked and you clothed me. I was homeless and you took me in."

— *Hungry not only for bread, but hungry for love.*

— *Naked not only for clothing, but naked of human dignity and respect.*

— *Homeless not only for want of a room of bricks, but homeless because of rejection.*

This is Christ in distressing disguise.

— **Mother Teresa**

Bl. Teresa of Calcutta dedicated her life to helping the poorest of the poor. Jesus taught us that we show our love for him by serving those in need.

MESSAGE OF A CARDINAL

Joseph Cardinal Bernardin served as the Archbishop of Chicago from 1982 until his death from pancreatic cancer in 1996. In the last weeks of his life, he wrote a book, *The Gift of Peace*, discussing his final trials. He offers a powerful witness to every person's need to reflect prayerfully on the healing power of Christ. He finished the book just thirteen days before he died. In the following passage, Cardinal Bernardin discusses an event that took place immediately after he disclosed that his cancer was terminal:

> On August 31, 1996, the day after I announced that the cancer had spread to my liver and was inoperable, I presided at a communal Anointing of the Sick at Saint Barbara Church in Brookfield, Illinois. I told my fellow sick that, when we are faced with serious illness (or any serious difficulty), we should do several things—things that have given me peace of mind personally.
>
> The first is to put ourselves completely in the hands of the Lord. We must believe that the Lord loves us, embraces us, never abandons us (especially in our most difficult moments). This is what gives us hope in the midst of life's suffering and chaos. It is the same Lord who invites us: "Come to me, all who labor and are heavy laden, and I will give you rest. Take my yoke upon you, and learn from me; for I am gentle and lowly in heart, and you will find rest for your souls. For my yoke is easy, and my burden is light." (Mt 11:12-30)

Joseph Cardinal Bernardin

CONCLUSION

Christ Carrying the Cross by Piombo. "Take my yoke upon your shoulders..." (Mt 11:29)

Just as the Sacraments of Baptism, Confirmation, and the Eucharist form the "Sacraments of Initiation" at the beginning of the Christian life, the Sacraments of Reconciliation, Anointing of the Sick, and the Eucharist form the "Sacraments that prepare [us] for our heavenly homeland" at the end of the Christian journey.[27] This journey is not easy, yet it is a comfort to meditate on the ways Christ has given us to experience his saving love—all the way to the moment of death.

The Anointing of the Sick reminds us that the sacraments are like sign posts on our spiritual journey towards everlasting life. Baptism begins that journey, the Eucharist nourishes us for the journey, Confirmation strengthens us in our maturity, and Confession offers the hope of forgiveness and the grace to renew our efforts. We especially need God's help as we approach the end of our journey. Through the Sacrament of Anointing, Christ makes that grace available to us even at the moment of death.

As a Sacrament, the Anointing of the Sick has been given to us by Jesus to see us safely through our journey into the next life and to enter the presence of the Father for all eternity. Each time that we embrace suffering out of love for God, we are united more closely to the Cross of Christ and participate more fully in his redemptive mission.

SUPPLEMENTARY READING

A SAINT WHO KILLED?

Jacques Fesch
(1930-1957)
Murderer, Convert

On February 25, 1954, Alexandre Silberstein was changing two million francs into gold bars for a customer. The man drew a revolver and demanded money from the register. Silberstein tried to reason with the man, but he was adamant and took about 300,000 francs. The suspect tried to escape into the crowd outside, but Silberstein began shouting that he had been robbed. When a policeman, a widower with a young daughter, ordered him to put his hands up, the robber shot him through the heart.

Jacques was a lost soul, the son of wealthy parents who never took an interest in him. The boy failed to take an interest in his schoolwork or his job at the bank after he graduated. His anti-Semitic parents were horrified when he married Pierrette, a Catholic girl who had a Jewish father. She and Jacques had a daughter together, but he continued to see other women. He had an illegitimate son and his marriage soon broke up.

After this, Jacques decided to purchase a boat and sail around the South Pacific. Unfortunately, his parents refused him the money so he decided to rob Mr. Silberstein. In court, he defiantly declared that his only regret was not carrying a submachine gun. In prison, he told a chaplain, "I've got no faith. No need to trouble yourself about me." Many people made efforts at his conversion—his attorney, a Dominican chaplain named Pere Devoyod, Brother Thomas (a Benedictine and friend of Pierrette), and his mother-in-law Madame Polack—but none were successful.

It was only on February 28, 1955, when as he writes:

> I was in bed, eyes open, really suffering for the first time in my life...It was then that a cry burst from my breast, an appeal for help—My God—and instantly, like a violent

wind which passes over without anyone knowing where it comes from, the spirit of the Lord seized me by the throat. I had an impression of infinite power and kindness and, from that moment onward, I believed with an unshakeable conviction that has never left me.

Later he wrote:

> A powerful hand has seized me. Where is it? What has it done to me? I do not know, for his action is not like the action of men. It is unknowable and effective. It constrains me, and I am free. It transforms my being, yet I do not cease to be what I am.

> Then comes the struggle—silent, tragic— between what I was and what I have become. For the new creature who has been planted within me calls for a response which I am free to refuse.

> My viewpoint has changed, but my habits of thought and action have not. God has left them as they were. I have to fight, adapt, reconstruct my inner being; I cannot be at peace unless I accept to fight.

While in prison, he began to live a very sober life, giving up chocolates and cigarettes, praying often, and going to bed at 7:00 each evening. More than three years after his crime, Jacques was sentenced to death. Overcoming his temptation to hate those who sentenced him, he wrote, "May each drop of my blood wipe out a mortal sin."

On the last night of his life, Jacques wrote, "I wait in the night; I wait in peace. I wait for Love! Within 5 hours...I will see Jesus!" The prison chaplain arrived at 5:30 and gave him the Last Rites (the Sacraments of Confession, the Anointing of the Sick, and the Eucharist). As he was led up the scaffold, he said to the chaplain, "The crucifix, Father, the crucifix," and kissed it fervently. Jacques is often likened to the good thief who died with Jesus on Calvary. Recently his writings have been published as *Light Over the Scaffold* and *Cell 18* by Augustin-Michel Lemmonier.

VOCABULARY

ANOINTING OF THE SICK
One of the Seven Sacraments. It is administered by a bishop or priest to someone who suffers from illness or old age. It includes prayers and anointing of the hands and forehead with the Oil of the Sick. It is usually administered together with Penance and the Eucharist.

COMPASSION
From the Latin meaning "to suffer together with." It is the love, kindness, mercy, or forbearance shown to a neighbor who is suffering in some way.

CONVERSION
A radical reorientation of one's whole life away from sin and evil toward God. This is a central element of Christ's preaching, of the Church's ministry of evangelization, and of the Sacrament of Penance.

MIRACLES
A sign, wonder, or event, which transcends the laws of nature and can therefore only be attributed to divine power. The miracles of Jesus were messianic signs of the presence of God's Kingdom.

PASSION
The suffering and Death of Jesus.

PRAYERS FOR THE DEAD
From the very beginning, the Church (following the practice of Judaism) has offered prayers, especially the Eucharistic Sacrifice, on behalf of the souls in Purgatory, that they might enter into the fullness of heavenly bliss.

SALVIFIC
Pertaining to the salvation of souls: freedom from attachment, enjoying the vision of God, consummating happiness and union with God. All of this is joined to Christ's saving Passion.

VIATICUM
The Eucharist received by a dying person.

STUDY QUESTIONS

1. Why did Jesus work miracles in his public ministry?

2. What are concrete examples of how the Church shows compassion for the suffering?

3. What were the instructions that Jesus gave to his Apostles concerning those who were sick?

4. What instructions did St. James give concerning the sick?

5. Why does God not work a miracle of physical healing each time the Sacrament of Anointing is celebrated?

6. What limitations are there on God's grace?

7. What was the method generally used by Jesus in his healing miracles?

8. What was it that transformed the sick in both body and soul?

9. Why is oil an effective sign for this sacrament?

10. What is Oil of the Sick, and where does it come from?

11. Who are the ministers of the Sacrament of the Anointing of the Sick?

12. If the Sacrament is celebrated by a priest and received by only one person, then how can we say that the Sacrament is an action of the Church as a whole? (Hint: the sacraments are actions of Christ.)

13. Explain what is meant by "sacraments that prepare [us] for our heavenly homeland."

14. What are the essential elements of the celebration of the Sacrament?

15. What could a priest do if he did not have the Oil of the Sick available?

STUDY QUESTIONS Continued

16. Who may receive the Sacrament of Anointing?

17. When should the Sacrament of Anointing be received?

18. Should the Sacrament of Anointing be administered in the following situations: the person is in a coma; the person has just died; the person has been dead for some time?

19. Does the Sacrament remove mortal sin if the person is unconscious? Explain. What should happen if the person later recovers?

20. What other Sacrament should normally be celebrated before the Sacrament of Anointing, and why?

21. What is the primary purpose of the Sacrament of Anointing?

22. List and explain some of the graces conveyed.

23. How can human suffering be "positive"?

24. What can be achieved by "offering up" our suffering to God?

25. What does the Christian vocation demand from Christians regarding the sick and suffering?

PRACTICAL EXERCISES

1. If someone receives the Anointing of the Sick and then dies, does that mean that the Sacrament did not work? What does it mean? What good does the Sacrament do if it does not heal a person physically?

2. Suppose someone were very ill and had only a few weeks left to live. Should this person be told of his condition? Why or why not? How could Anointing of the Sick help this person?

3. Suppose a friend has a parent who is sick and probably going to die. Your friend says he does not believe in God anymore, because his parent is suffering for no reason. What could you say to your friend? What is the source of suffering? Can there be any benefit to suffering?

4. Go with a friend or group of friends to visit someone you know who is sick or visit the gravesite of someone who died—grandparents, other relative, etc.

Christ Healing the Blind Man by Le Sueur. A miracle can only be attributed to divine power.

FROM THE CATECHISM

1022 Each man receives his eternal retribution in his immortal soul at the very moment of his death, in a particular judgment that refers his life to Christ: either entrance into the blessedness of heaven—through a purification[28] or immediately,[29]—or immediate and everlasting damnation.[30]

1051 Every man receives his eternal recompense in his immortal soul from the moment of his death in a particular judgment by Christ, the judge of the living and the dead.

1526 "Is any among you sick? Let him call for the presbyters of the Church, and let them pray over him, anointing him with oil in the name of the Lord; and the prayer of faith will save the sick man, and the Lord will raise him up; and if he has committed sins, he will be forgiven."[31]

1527 The Sacrament of Anointing of the Sick has as its purpose the conferral of a special grace on the Christian experiencing the difficulties inherent in the condition of grave illness or old age.

1528 The proper time for receiving this holy anointing has certainly arrived when the believer begins to be in danger of death because of illness or old age.

1529 Each time a Christian falls seriously ill, he may receive the Anointing of the Sick, and also when, after he has received it, the illness worsens.

1530 Only priests (presbyters and bishops) can give the Sacrament of the Anointing of the Sick, using oil blessed by the bishop, or if necessary by the celebrating presbyter himself.

1531 The celebration of the Anointing of the Sick consists essentially in the anointing of the forehead and hands of the sick person (in the Roman rite) or of other parts of the body (in the Eastern rite), the anointing being accompanied by the liturgical prayer of the celebrant asking for the special grace of this sacrament.

1532 The special grace of the Sacrament of the Anointing of the Sick has as its effects:

— the uniting of the sick person to the passion of Christ, for his own good and that of the whole Church;

— the strengthening, peace, and courage to endure in a Christian manner the sufferings of illness or old age;

— the forgiveness of sins, if the sick person was not able to obtain it through the sacrament of Penance;

— the restoration of health, if it is conducive to the salvation of his soul;

— the preparation for passing over to eternal life.

ENDNOTES – CHAPTER FIVE

1. Cf. Lk 10:9.
2. Lk 7:16; cf. Mt 4:24.
3. Cf. Mk 2:5-12.
4. Cf. Mk 2:17.
5. Mt 25:36.
6. Second Vatican Council, Const. *Sacrosanctum Concilium*, 73: AAS, LVI (1964) [118]-119.
7. Cf. Mt 8:5-13.
8. Jn 11:15, 40.
9. Mk 6:13.
10. Cf. Mk 16:18.
11. Cf. Lk 10:34.
12. Cf. *Pastoral Care of the Sick*, 23.
13. Cf. *SC* 27.
14. Cf. *Pastoral Care of the Sick*, 5.
15. Cf. Council of Trent, sess. 14, *De Extrema Unctione*, cap. 1: Denz.-Schön. 1694 and 1696.
16. Cf. CCC 1051.
17. CCC 1054.
18. Cf. CCC 1033.
19. *Pastoral Care of the Sick*, 8-11.
20. Cf. Jas 5:14-15.
21. Cf. Gn 3:16-19.
22. Cf. CCC 1500-1501.
23. *Salvifici Doloris*, 1.
24. Cf. Mt 10:38.
25. Mt 25:36, 40.
26. Cf. Lk 10:29-37.
27. CCC 1525.
28. Cf. Council of Lyons II (1274): DS 857-858; Council of Florence (1439): DS 1304-1306; Council of Trent (1563): DS 1820.
29. Cf. Benedict XII, *Benedictus Deus* (1336): DS 1000-1001; John XXII, *Ne Super His* (1334): DS 990.
30. Cf. Benedict XII, *Benedictus Deus* (1336): DS 1002.
31. Jas 5:14-15.

Holy Orders

The call of Christ to the Sacrament of Holy Orders is a personal invitation to leave all behind and live a life dedicated entirely to the service of God and his people in his plan of Redemption.

The Sacraments

CHAPTER 6

Holy Orders

Do this in remembrance of me. (Lk 22:19)

I greet you in the Blood of Jesus Christ. You are my abiding and unshakeable joy, especially if your members remain united with the bishop and with his presbyters and deacons, all appointed in accordance with the mind of Christ who by his own will has strengthened them in the firmness which the Spirit gives.

I know that this bishop has obtained his ministry, which serves the community, neither by his own efforts, nor from men nor even out of vainglory, but from the love of God the Father and of the Lord Jesus Christ. I am deeply impressed by his gentleness, and by his silence he is more effective than the empty talkers. He is in harmony with the commandments as is a lute with its strings. I call him blessed, then, for his sentiments toward God, since I know these to be virtuous and perfect, and for his stability and calm, in which he imitates the gentleness of the living God.

As sons of the light of truth, flee divisions and evil doctrines; where your shepherd is, follow him as his flock. For all who belong to God and Jesus Christ are with the bishop; all who repent and return to the unity of the Church will also belong to God, that they may live according to Jesus Christ. Do not be deceived, my brothers. If anyone follows a schismatic, he will not obtain the inheritance of God's kingdom; if anyone lives by an alien teaching, he does not assent to the passion of the Lord.

Be careful, therefore, to take part only in the one Eucharist; for there is only one flesh of our Lord Jesus Christ and one cup to unite us with his blood, one altar and one bishop with the presbyters and deacons, who are his fellow servants. Then, whatever you do, you will do according to God.[1]

— St. Ignatius of Antioch

At the turn of the first century, the world was a hostile place for Christians. The Church, still in its infancy, had watched the last of the Apostles pass away. The Church was being tested both by Roman persecution and by the emergence of a number of schismatic, or heretical, sects of the new Christian religion.

One of the great fathers of the Church, St. Ignatius of Antioch (AD 107), offered guidance to believers who were vulnerable to these powerful forces, which threatened to tear apart the young Church.

At this critical moment in the Church's history, St. Ignatius understood that the role of the Apostle's successors (i.e., the bishops, the presbyters, and the deacons) was crucial for maintaining the Church's unity, preserving the truth of Christ, and continuing the mission that Christ had given them. These bishops, presbyters, and deacons were men whose lives had been consecrated to the service of the Church through the Sacrament of Holy Orders.

There are two Sacraments at the Service of Communion: Holy Orders and Matrimony. By the very nature of Christian Baptism, all of the faithful share in the mission of Jesus Christ. However, Holy Orders and Matrimony *consecrate* a person to the service of others. In the Sacrament of Matrimony, a baptized man and a baptized woman are bound together in a permanent union and given the graces needed for the mutual

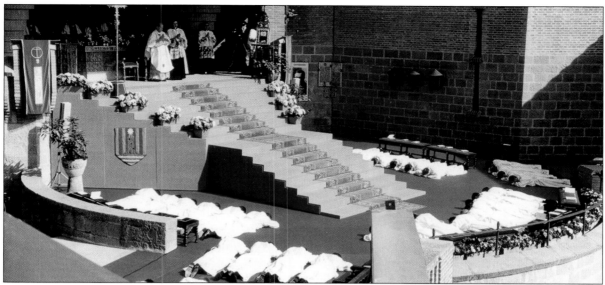

In the Sacrament of Holy Orders, a man is ordained to the ministry of the Church, which, by its nature, is directed toward the service and salvation of the People of God.

good of each other and their children. In the Sacrament of Holy Orders, a baptized man is ordained to the ministry of the Church, which, by its nature, is directed toward the service and salvation of the People of God.[2]

> In order to shepherd the People of God and to increase its numbers without cease, Christ the Lord set up in his Church a variety of offices which aim at the good of the whole body. The holders of office, who are invested with a sacred power, are, in fact, dedicated to promoting the interests of their brethren, so that all who belong to the People of God...may attain to salvation.[3] (CCC 874)

The word *minister* comes from the Latin meaning "servant." As ordained ministers of the Catholic Church, those who have received a vocation to Holy Orders are called to a life of service. First and foremost, they are called to serve Jesus Christ, who desires to continue his saving mission through the ministry of his Church. This ministry of Christ is exercised when the ordained ministers serve the people to whom God has entrusted them. In celebrating the sacraments appropriate to their office and their pastoral ministry, bishops, priests, and deacons, continue the work that Christ did while he was on earth. When Jesus wishes to touch our lives through his word, his forgiveness, his healing, or his own Body and Blood, he does so through those men he has called to the ministry of Holy Orders.

Today, just as in the days of St. Ignatius, those ministers ordained through the Sacrament of Holy Orders continue the vital mission of preserving the Church and passing down the truth of Christ through his word and sacraments.

IN THIS CHAPTER, WE WILL ADDRESS SEVERAL QUESTIONS:

✥ What are the roles of bishops, priests, and deacons in the Catholic Church?

✥ What is a vocation to the priesthood?

✥ Who may receive Holy Orders?

✥ What are the reasons for priestly celibacy in the Latin Rite of the Catholic Church?

THE PRIESTHOOD IN THE OLD TESTAMENT

The institution of the priesthood was not a new development in Judeo-Christian history. God had chosen the Hebrew people, the descendents of Abraham, to be his priestly people, who would reveal God to the world and represent all mankind before him.

God directed Moses to appoint one of the twelve tribes of Israel, the Levites, to act as priests for the Hebrew people. The Levites first served God in the Tabernacle in the desert and then later in the Temple in Jerusalem, presiding at Hebrew feasts, offering sacrifices, and teaching the Word of God to the Hebrew people.[4] However, the Levitical priesthood was never intended to save, nor to sanctify others. Only Christ's redeeming sacrifice could accomplish this.[5]

THE CALL OF THE APOSTLES

> You did not choose me, but I chose you. (Jn 15:16)

The office of priesthood in the Old Testament was handed down from generation to generation. Levite fathers trained their sons in the Torah and in the requirements of priestly service. Jesus, however, called his twelve Apostles in a more personal and profound way. No longer were the priests to be appointed through their hereditary lineage, but through a personal call to the service of God and his people.

The Gospels describe the calling of the twelve Apostles. In the Gospel of St. John, we see how St. Andrew brought his brother Simon to Jesus, telling him that he had found the Messiah.

> Jesus looked at him [Simon], and said, "So you are Simon the son of John? You shall be called Cephas [Aramaic for rock]." (Jn 1: 42)

At their first meeting, Jesus called St. Peter personally by name. He showed a profound understanding of who Simon-Peter was, of who he was capable of becoming, and of the role for which he had been chosen in the plan of salvation. In this episode, Jesus revealed the omnipotence of God, who knows

Calling of the Apostles Peter and Andrew by Lorenzo. The call of Christ is a personal invitation to leave all behind and live a life dedicated entirely to the service of God and his people in his plan of Redemption.

The Sacrament of Ordination by Poussin. In calling his Apostles and instructing them to preach, baptize, celebrate the Eucharist, forgive sins, and administer all of the other sacraments, Jesus called them to participate in his own priestly ministry.

us more than we can ever know ourselves. Simon-Peter must have been astounded by this call, and he immediately recognized that it came from God.

In the Gospel of St. Mark, we read that Sts. Peter and Andrew were "casting a net into the sea and Jesus said to them, 'Follow me and I will make you fishers of men.' They immediately left their nets and followed him."[6]

What would have caused these two ordinary men—and indeed all of the Apostles—with families, homes, and businesses to leave everything and follow a man whom they had just met? To be called by Christ is a profound and transforming experience. We can only imagine how this personal call by Christ himself would have affected men of faith whose hearts were open to the will of God. Christ's piercing gaze and his extraordinary words moved Peter and Andrew so profoundly that they left everything to follow him.

This call or vocation has been given to those chosen by God throughout the history of the Church and is still given today. It is a personal invitation to leave all behind and live a life dedicated entirely to the service of God and his people in his plan of Redemption. Those who hear his call today and respond to it do so after long periods of discernment, prayer, and time spent seeking to understand God and to recognize his voice.[7] Speaking about the vocation to the priesthood, Pope Benedict XVI commented that when those called by Christ open their hearts to a vocation, they participate in the passing down of Christ's divine authority through the twelve Apostles and in Christ's mandate to spread his Good News to the ends of the earth:

> We cannot find Jesus without the reality that he created and through which he communicates himself. Between the Son of God made man and his Church, there is a profound, inseparable continuity, in virtue of which Christ is present today in his people....He is always our contemporary—our contemporary in the Church built upon the foundation of the Apostles. He is alive in the succession of the Apostles. And his presence in the community, in which he himself always gives himself, is the reason for our joy. Yes, Christ is with us, the Kingdom of God is coming.[8]

THE APOSTOLIC CHURCH:
BISHOPS, PRESBYTERS, AND DEACONS

St. Peter Consecrates Stephen as Deacon by Fra Angelico.

The Acts of the Apostles describes the birth and growth of the Apostolic Church, which was centered on the leadership and ministry of the Apostles. The early followers of Christ met in the Temple for prayer and in their homes for the Breaking of the Bread. As a sign that the mission of Christ was not to die with the twelve, St. Matthias was chosen to replace Judas. Later, Sts. Paul and Barnabas, as well as others, came to be known as Apostles.

Christ's choice of twelve men to carry out his mission had much biblical significance. Just as there were twelve tribes in the Old Covenant, there were to be twelve leaders of the Church in the New Covenant established by Christ. It soon became apparent to the Apostles, however, that the demands of their ministry to spread the word did not allow them the time to minister to the daily needs of the Church. Therefore, they selected seven men to serve the material needs of the Christian community in Jerusalem. As an indication of their responsibilities, these seven were given the name *deacons*, from the Greek word meaning *servers*. The Apostles laid hands on them and ordained them to the service of the Church.

Although selected primarily to minister to the needs of the widows and the daily distribution of bread, we see in the Acts of the Apostles that St. Stephen, a newly ordained deacon, fearlessly preached the Good News. As a result, St. Stephen was greatly persecuted and became the first Christian martyr.

As many of the Apostles left Jerusalem on missionary journeys and established local churches in the various places that they visited, it became clear that additional leaders were necessary to minister to these new congregations. The Apostles appointed and ordained *bishops*, from the Greek word meaning *overseer*, and *presbyters*, from the Greek word meaning *elders* (from which we get the English word *priest*). The Apostles imparted their authority to the leaders of the local community, ordaining them by the laying on of hands.

THE ROLE OF A PRIEST: *In Persona Christi*

In all religions, the priest is a mediator between God and man. However, the Christian priesthood established by Christ is different. For Christians, Jesus Christ is the one true High Priest who restores the unity of God with his people.

God chose to send his Only-Begotten Son into the world to atone for the sins of mankind and to repair his friendship with his people. In this manner, it could be said that Jesus was born to die. The very reason for his Incarnation was to offer himself as a perfect sacrifice for our sins on Calvary. In doing so, Jesus Christ became the source of our salvation and the only mediator between God and man. He is the eternal High Priest.

> For there is one God; there is also one mediator between God and man, the man Jesus Christ, who gave himself as a ransom for all. (1 Tm 2: 5-6)

In the Letter to the Hebrews, St. Paul explained this priestly role of Jesus. The sacrifices offered by the Levitical priests could never satisfy the debt for sin. They were but a foreshadowing of the perfect and spotless sacrifice that would be offered by a perfect and eternal high priest once and for all. It is in the person of Jesus Christ, the promised Messiah, that we find both the priest and the offering for sin, which satisfies the debt incurred by humanity.

Christ's role as priest extended from his sacrifice on the Cross and influenced every action of his life. Jesus' teaching offered the fullness of Divine Revelation. His life gave us an authentic example of how to live God's Commandments. Throughout the course of his public ministry, he showed compassion to the suffering, healed the sick, and forgave sins. His entire mission was directed toward the Cross. Knowing from the beginning that he would give his life as a ransom for many, he desired that his saving ministry be continued after his Death and Resurrection until he comes again. For this reason, he called certain men as his closest associates. He empowered these Apostles with his own divine authority and instructed them to continue his work of Redemption.

The grace needed for our salvation flows directly from the sacrifice of Christ on Calvary. This is the way chosen by God. However, in calling his Apostles and instructing them to preach, baptize, celebrate the Eucharist, forgive sins, and administer all of the other sacraments, Jesus called them to participate in his own priestly ministry. By entrusting them with these sacred actions and the power to "bind and loose," Jesus chose human beings to participate in his own ministry to his Church.

In establishing this relationship with his Apostles, we see that Jesus was imitating the relationship between the Father and the Son. Christ was sent into the world by the Father for its salvation and sanctification. He taught us that the Father and the Son are one and that he received his authority from the Father. He, in turn, bestowed his authority on the Apostles.

Communion of the Apostles by Signorelli. When a priest is celebrating the sacraments, he is acting *in persona Christi* (in the person of Christ).

Therefore, the divine authority of the priest is one and the same with the divine authority of Christ. When a priest is celebrating the sacraments, he is acting *in persona Christi* (in the person of Christ). Christ has profoundly transformed the nature of the priest, who no longer acts as the individual mediator between God and man but participates in the mediation and ministry of Christ himself.

> In the ecclesial service of the ordained minister, it is Christ himself who is present to his Church as Head of his Body, Shepherd of his flock, high priest of the redemptive sacrifice, Teacher of Truth. This is what the Church means by saying that the priest, by virtue of the sacrament of Holy Orders, acts *in persona Christi Capitis*:[9]

> It is the same priest, Christ Jesus, whose sacred person his minister truly represents. Now the minister, by reason of the sacerdotal consecration which he has received, is truly made like to the high priest and possesses the authority to act in the power and place of the person of Christ himself (*virtute ac persona ipsius Christi*).[10]

> Christ is the source of all priesthood: the priest of the old law was a figure of Christ, and the priest of the new law acts in the person of Christ.[11] (CCC 1548)

THE POST-APOSTOLIC CHURCH

Christ told his followers that he must leave them to return to the Father but promised he would come again. The Apostles and many other early Christians felt that this would occur in their own lifetime. However, as the years passed, and as several of the Apostles suffered martyrdom, instructions were given that certain men should succeed the Apostles. Many of these first instructions are found in the earliest Christian documents written shortly after the death of the Apostles.

Among these are the writings of Pope St. Clement I, who was ordained by St. Peter and became the third Bishop of Rome (ca. AD 88-99); St. Ignatius, who was also ordained by St. Peter and became the third Bishop of Antioch (martyred ca. AD 98-117); and St. Polycarp (ca. AD 69-155), who was ordained by St. John the Evangelist and became the Bishop of Smyrna. These earliest post-apostolic writings show that it was by instruction of the Apostles that the bishops exercised the authority of teaching, governing, and sanctifying the local church.

St. Clement by Master of the Castello Nativity. Pope St. Clement I was ordained by St. Peter and became the third Bishop of Rome (ca. AD 88-99).

> Our Apostles knew through our Lord Jesus Christ that there would be strife over the name of the bishop's office. For this cause therefore, having received complete foreknowledge, they appointed the aforesaid persons, and afterwards they provided a continuance, that if these should fall asleep, other approved men should succeed to their ministration. (1 Clement 44:1-2 [ca. AD 96])

Furthermore, these writings clearly detail the hierarchy of bishop, priest, and deacon, which existed in the local church. This hierarchy is mentioned repeatedly by several writers not as an innovation but as a tradition coming from the Apostles themselves. Loyalty and unity to the bishop, presbyters, and deacons was viewed as a definitive sign of the true Christian and of the authentic Church.

> You are my abiding and unshakeable joy, especially if your members remain united with the bishop and with his presbyters and deacons, all appointed in accordance with the mind of Christ who by his own will has strengthened them in the firmness which the Spirit gives. (St. Ignatius of Antioch, *Letter to the Philadelphians* [ca. AD 107])

Later writings toward the end of the second century illustrate the importance of apostolic succession, in which a bishop could demonstrate an unbroken chain, or direct connection, to the Apostles. By tracing the authority of the Apostles from one bishop to the next, one could identify the true Church and be guaranteed that the bishop was acting under the authority of Christ himself.

> Let them produce the original records of their churches; let them unfold the roll of their bishops, running down in due succession from the beginning in such a manner that [their first] bishop shall be able to show for his ordainer and predecessor some one of the apostles or of apostolic men—a man, moreover, who continued steadfast with the apostles. For this is the manner in which the apostolic churches transmit their registers: as the church of Smyrna, which records that Polycarp was placed therein by John; as also the church of Rome, which makes Clement to have been ordained in like manner by Peter. (Tertullian, *Against the Heretics*, 20 [AD 200])

More than eighteen centuries later, Pope Benedict XVI spoke about the importance of apostolic succession in ensuring that the authentic Gospel message is transmitted as instructed by Jesus Christ:

> Through her apostolic ministry the Church, a community gathered by the Son of God who came in the flesh, will live on through the passing times, building up and nourishing the communion in Christ and in the Holy Spirit to which all are called and in which they can experience the salvation given by the Father. The Twelve—as Pope Clement, the third Successor of Peter, said at the end of the first century—took pains, in fact, to prepare successors,[12] so that the mission entrusted to them would be continued after their death.[13]

St. Polycarp by Papas. St. Polycarp (ca. AD 69-155) was ordained by St. John the Apostle and became the Bishop of Smyrna.

As we have seen, Christ bestowed his divine authority on the Apostles, who in turn appointed bishops, priests, and deacons in those churches that they founded. At Mass, it was the bishop who would break the bread, pour the wine, and, to use the term of the day, "make Eucharist." The bishop would be assisted by his priests (presbyters) and the deacons, who were ordained to help with the daily operations of the Church.

Since the first days of Christianity, this was the structure of the local Church. These communities existed primarily in the major cities of the Roman Empire, with one church normally serving the entire Christian population. However, as the Church began to experience rapid growth, the demographics of the local communities began to change as well. The number of Christians in one city soon became too large to be served by only one church; and many of the small towns surrounding the city began to have their own significant Christian populations. In this situation, the bishop, who had been given the pastoral care of the Christians living in that particular area, would send one of his presbyters to assist the new community.

Martyrdom of St. Ignatius. St. Ignatius was ordained by St. Peter and became the third Bishop of Antioch (martyred ca. AD 98-117).

This custom soon became the universal practice throughout the Church and is the form used to this day. Each Catholic belongs to a local church community called a diocese, which is headed by a bishop. The bishop sends his priests to each of the smaller Catholic communities within the diocese, which are called parishes.

THE SACRAMENT OF HOLY ORDERS

It was during the celebration of his Last Supper that Jesus instituted the Sacraments of the Eucharist and Holy Orders. By instructing the Twelve to "Do this in remembrance of me,"[14] Christ called them to a share in his ministerial priesthood.

After his Resurrection, Jesus told the Twelve that he would send them the Holy Spirit and then gave them the authority to forgive sins.[15] He instructed them to go to all nations, teaching and baptizing.[16] These episodes from the Gospel show Christ granting his authority to the Apostles and empowering them to continue his saving ministry through the celebration of the sacraments.

The continuation of this divine mission until Christ comes again requires that the priestly authority given to the Apostles at the Last Supper be passed down to their successors. This action is accomplished in the Sacrament of Holy Orders.

> By divine institution, the sacrament of orders establishes some among the Christian faithful as sacred ministers through an indelible character which marks them. They are consecrated and designated, each according to his grade, to nourish the people of God, fulfilling in the person of Christ the Head the functions of teaching, sanctifying, and governing. (CIC, 1008)

Through the Sacrament of Holy Orders, the priesthood of Christ is made visible in the Church.[17] By the laying on of hands and a consecratory prayer, deacons, priests, and bishops receive the grace from the Holy Spirit that is necessary for them to serve the People of God, along with the ability to celebrate those sacraments appropriate to each one's particular office.[18]

Appearance Behind Locked Doors by Duccio. After his Resurrection, Jesus told the Apostles that he would send them the Holy Spirit and then gave them the authority to forgive sins. "As the Father has sent me, even so I send you.... If you forgive the sins of any, they are forgiven." (Jn 20: 21-23)

Through this Sacrament, an indelible seal is imprinted on the candidate's soul, which marks them as a deacon, priest, or bishop forever, and the man being ordained receives an increase in sanctifying grace so that he might faithfully and courageously accept and carry out the duties that will be expected of him as a servant of the People of God.

> Sacramental ministry in the Church, then, is a service exercised in the name of Christ. It has a personal character and a collegial form. (CCC 879)

The reception of this Sacrament consecrates a person to the Lord. Those who receive this Sacrament become servants of the Word of God and his sacraments. They dedicate themselves to a life of self-denial and sacrifice for the good of the People of God. St. Paul goes so far as to refer to himself as a slave, showing the seriousness of the obligation to serve Christ when a person receives Holy Orders.

This life of service is a great blessing from God. Every ordained person has been personally called by Christ. Priests are called not only to "follow Christ" by what they say and do, but also to "be Christ" to others by the lives they lead.

The word "orders" in the Roman Empire referred to a governing body, membership in which was considered sacred. The Church assumes this term when she speaks of the *ordo episcoporum* (order of bishops), *ordo presbyterorum* (order of priests), and *ordo diaconorum* (order of deacons). "Orders" is now the term used to indicate that a man who has been ordained has also been consecrated by a gift of the Holy Spirit into the service of God, the Church, and his fellow man.

Holy Orders is a Sacrament of three separate degrees. The first degree is that of deacon, the second is the priesthood, and the third is the office of bishop. As such, only a bishop enjoys the fullness of this Sacrament. Deacons and priests are ordained as assistants of the bishop and cannot function apart from him.

While all people have a right to approach the Church for the reception of the other sacraments and cannot be denied them except for serious and compelling reasons, no one has a right to receive Holy Orders. Due to this Sacrament's nature as a vocation from God, only Church authority may call a baptized man to receive the Sacrament of Holy Orders, and only after a candidate's suitability for the priestly ministry has been verified. In fact, it is the sacred duty of the bishop to verify the call as authentic before ordaining a man to the priesthood.

> The Church confers the sacrament of Holy Orders only on baptized men (*viri*), whose suitability for the exercise of the ministry has been duly recognized. Church authority alone has the responsibility and right to call someone to receive the sacrament of Holy Orders. (CCC 1598)

To receive the Sacrament of Holy Orders, a person must possess the following qualifications:

✠ be a baptized male of excellent character;

✠ have received the Sacrament of Confirmation;

✠ have an interior call from God and an exterior call from the bishop;

✠ have the necessary knowledge of the nature of Holy Orders;

✠ have attained the proper age (In the Latin Rite of the Catholic Church, the proper age currently set for ordination is twenty-five years old for priests; twenty-three years old for transitional deacons; and thirty-five years old for permanent deacons, if married, or twenty-five years old for permanent deacons, if celibate. In the Eastern Rites of the Catholic Church, the age is currently set at twenty-three years old for deacons and twenty-four years old for priests.);

✠ have the capacity of living the life of a priest and exercising the priestly ministry, which includes undergoing a mental health screening (cf. *Program of Priestly Formation* 5, 53);

✠ have a commitment to lifelong celibacy (this does not apply to permanent deacons, priests from the Eastern Rites of the Catholic Church, or ministers converting from other denominations, who may be married before, but not after their ordination);

✠ have the theological knowledge and necessary training proper to their particular office; and

✠ have no impediments.

The Sacrament has the following effects:

✠ the conferral of the office of bishop, priest, or deacon;

✠ an indelible mark upon the soul (therefore, it cannot be repeated); and

✠ a sacramental grace proper to the exercise of the recipient's ministry.

The grace given by this Sacrament also strengthens the ordained to live fortitude in his life as another Christ by ministering to all and with a preferential love for the poor and needy.

DEACONS

Now in these days when the disciples were increasing in number, the Hellenists murmured against the Hebrews because their widows were neglected in the daily distribution. And the twelve summoned the body of the disciples and said, "It is not right that we should give up preaching the word of God to serve tables. Therefore, brethren, pick out from among you seven men of good repute, full of the Spirit and of wisdom, whom we may appoint to this duty. But we will devote ourselves to prayer and to the ministry of the word." And what they said pleased the whole multitude, and they chose Stephen, a man full of faith and of the Holy Spirit, and Philip, and Prochorus, and Nicanor, and Timon, and Parmenas, and Nicolaus, a proselyte of Antioch. These they set before the apostles, and they prayed and laid their hands upon them. (Acts 6:1-6)

The first degree in the hierarchy of Holy Orders is that of the deacon, who is united directly to the bishop in service. A special character is conferred on him that configures him to Christ as a servant.

There are two types of deacons: permanent and transitional. A permanent deacon is someone who is ordained to the diaconate with the intention of serving in that capacity for the rest of his life. If the candidate for the permanent diaconate is married, he must be at least thirty-five years old and have the consent of his wife.[19] If his wife should die after his ordination, he may not remarry unless granted a dispensation for a grave reason. If he is unmarried at the time of his ordination, he must assume publicly before God and the Church the obligation of celibacy.[20]

Deacon candidates prostrate before the altar during the diaconate ordination liturgy. A deacon is united directly to the bishop in service. In many parishes, deacons provide vital services such as preparing couples for marriage and parents for the Baptism of their children.

SYMBOLS OF A DEACON

DALMATIC: A sleeved outer garment that has been worn by deacons since the early Church.

STOLE: A long band of cloth worn by deacons over the left shoulder.

BOOK OF THE GOSPELS: As the deacon is the proper minister of the Gospel at Mass, the Book of the Gospels is a symbol of his ministry.

A deacon wearing a dalmatic.

The deacon is the minister of the Book of the Gospels at Mass.

A transitional deacon is ordained to the diaconate for a period of time before progressing on to the priesthood. For those with a vocation to the priesthood, the diaconate is a time of further formation and training. A candidate for the priesthood must spend at least six months as a transitional deacon,[21] and it is common in many dioceses for seminarians to be ordained as transitional deacons during their last year of seminary studies. This gives the candidate ample opportunity to exercise the ministries of the diaconate before being ordained a priest.

Deacons have several duties and responsibilities.

- ✠ Deacons assist the bishop and priests at the celebration of the Mass. Proper to the office of deacon are the proclamation of the Gospel and the distribution of Holy Communion. He may also deliver the homily if the priest wishes, and should be the one to read the petitions.

- ✠ Deacons may preside at the Liturgy of the Hours and impart a blessing at the end of the celebration. They may also bless sacred objects such as rosaries, Bibles, and medals.

- ✠ As ordinary ministers of the Eucharist, deacons not only help in the distribution of Holy Communion but also take Communion to the sick and dying.

- ✠ Deacons preside over services of Exposition and Benediction of the Blessed Sacrament and may give the final blessing over the people with the monstrance.

- ✠ If a wedding is celebrated outside of Mass, the deacon may preside at the ceremony and receive the vows of the couple. He may also preside at funerals if there is no Mass and may always preside at gravesite services at the cemetery.

- ✠ Deacons are a proper minister of the Sacrament of Baptism.

- ✠ In many parishes, deacons provide vital services such as preparing couples for marriage and parents for the Baptism of their children.

- ✠ In places where there is a lack of priests, deacons may act as administrators of parishes, managing day-to-day affairs between visits by a priest for Mass and other ministries that only the priest may provide. Those ministries appropriate only to the priesthood are the Sacrament of Penance, Holy Eucharist, Confirmation, and the Anointing of the Sick.

PRIESTS

Let the elders [presbyters] who rule well be considered worthy of double honor, especially those who labor in preaching and teaching... (1 Tm 5:17)

The second level of Holy Orders is that of priests. As with deacons, the bishop delegates his apostolic authority to the priests, who become his co-workers in his ministry to the Church. Through the Sacrament of Holy Orders, a priest is given a special character or mark upon the soul enabling him to act in the person of Christ. Priests are ordained to preach the Gospel and shepherd the faithful as well as to celebrate the sacraments and lead divine worship.

The most central duty of a Catholic priest is the celebration of the Eucharist.

While priests have a share in the worldwide dimension of the Church's mission, they exercise their ministry in union with the local bishop, to whom they promise obedience. The diocesan priest is, therefore, united to his bishop and to all other priests in the diocese in a collegial way.

The parish priest is the minister of the Church with whom most people have direct contact. This is because it is the parish priest who will be called upon at the most defining moments in their lives. It is the priest who will baptize them at birth and later give them their First Holy Communion. It is the priest who they see each Sunday at Mass and who hears their Confessions. It is the priest who will help them prepare for marriage and who will celebrate the wedding day with them as well as the wedding anniversaries that follow. In times of crisis, it is the priest who is called to the hospital to bring the Sacrament of the Anointing of the Sick to those who are ill, and *Viaticum* to the dying. Finally, it will be the priest who celebrates the funeral Mass and commends the souls of the faithful departed to a merciful and loving God.

The most central duty of a Catholic priest is the celebration of the Eucharist. At each Mass, the priest proclaims and explains the Gospel and gives the Body and Blood of Christ to the faithful to nourish their souls on their pilgrim way to Heaven. Priests also serve as teachers in Catholic schools, universities, and seminaries. They are administrators of their parishes and aid the bishop in the operation of the diocese. Priests have long been associated with championing and defending the poor, the working class, and especially immigrant peoples. The priest is to be a man of God for God's people. He spends a good part of his day in prayer drawing strength and grace from God so that he may, in turn, be a source of grace and strength for those whom he serves.

No one has the right to become a priest. One is called to the Sacrament of Holy Orders by the bishop. When a young man recognizes an interest in the priesthood, he should speak with his pastor or another priest with whom he is comfortable. He should try to foster his spiritual life and attend Mass more frequently, daily if possible. He should also make frequent use of the Sacrament of Reconciliation. At some point, the candidate will be introduced to the diocesan bishop and a vocation director.

The educational requirements for a priest are extensive and demanding. Upon finishing high school, the seminarian must earn a university degree. This may be done at a college seminary, where a seminarian may earn his college diploma and take the courses prerequisite for the next four years of post-graduate theological studies. Many candidates for the priesthood today earn their degrees from public or non-Catholic private colleges or universities. Such candidates are subsequently enrolled in what are called "Pre-Theology" programs, which last one to three years before taking on the final four years of theological studies at the graduate level.

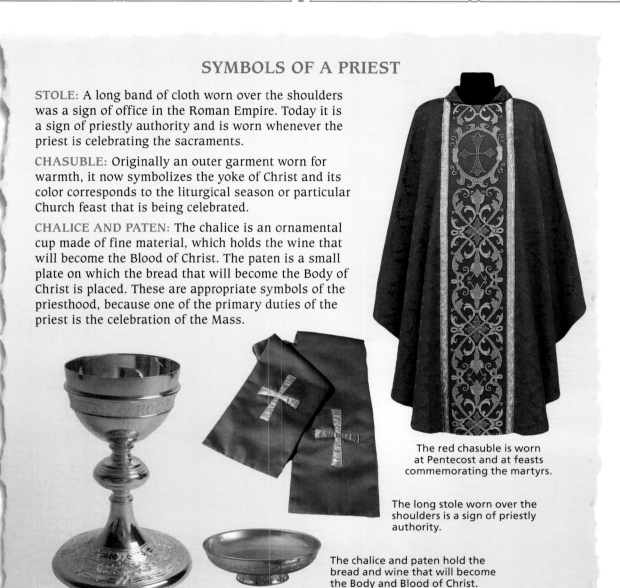

SYMBOLS OF A PRIEST

STOLE: A long band of cloth worn over the shoulders was a sign of office in the Roman Empire. Today it is a sign of priestly authority and is worn whenever the priest is celebrating the sacraments.

CHASUBLE: Originally an outer garment worn for warmth, it now symbolizes the yoke of Christ and its color corresponds to the liturgical season or particular Church feast that is being celebrated.

CHALICE AND PATEN: The chalice is an ornamental cup made of fine material, which holds the wine that will become the Blood of Christ. The paten is a small plate on which the bread that will become the Body of Christ is placed. These are appropriate symbols of the priesthood, because one of the primary duties of the priest is the celebration of the Mass.

The red chasuble is worn at Pentecost and at feasts commemorating the martyrs.

The long stole worn over the shoulders is a sign of priestly authority.

The chalice and paten hold the bread and wine that will become the Body and Blood of Christ.

While in the seminary, young men dedicate themselves to study, prayer, and formation. Formation includes meeting regularly with a spiritual director to discuss, among other things, the seminarian's spiritual life and how it is progressing. Seminarians also participate in other activities such as organized sports, apostolic outreaches to youth, the elderly, and the poor, pro-life activities, and helping with some aspects of running the seminary.

It is important for any young man considering the seminary to understand what it is and what it is not. The seminary is not some kind of "priest factory" where candidates enter one end and come out the other as priests. The very word "seminary" means "seed bed." That is to say, the seminarians are "planted" in the seminary in order to discern their vocation from God to the priesthood. Some enter and discover that they are not called to the priesthood and leave before receiving the Sacrament of Holy Orders. Others continue and are ordained priests.

Any young man who has experienced a "gnawing sense" that God is calling him to something other than a "normal career" should spend time in prayer asking God if he is being called to the priesthood and should seek out a priest with whom he can discuss his vocation to the priesthood.

BISHOPS:
THE FULLNESS OF THE PRIESTHOOD

Hear your bishop, that God may hear you. My life is a sacrifice for those who are obedient to the bishop, the presbyters and the deacons; and may it be my lot to share with them in God. Work together in harmony, struggle together, run together, suffer together, rest together, rise together, as stewards, advisors and servants of God. (St. Ignatius of Antioch, *Letter to Polycarp* [ca. AD 107])

The earliest bishops took their title from the Greek word *episkopos*, which means an "*overseer.*" Bishops continue to oversee their local Christian communities. Through the ministry of the bishop, surrounded by priests, and aided by deacons, the presence of Jesus Christ has been kept alive in the Church by the proclamation of the Gospel and the celebration of the sacraments.

Bishops, who by divine institution succeed to the place of the Apostles through the Holy Spirit who has been given to them, are constituted pastors in the Church, so that they are teachers of doctrine, priests of sacred worship, and ministers of governance. (CIC, 375 § 1)

Through the imposition of hands and the words of Consecration, a bishop is given the power to sanctify, teach, and rule. A sacred character is imparted on his soul, and he receives the grace of the Holy Spirit needed to fulfill his vocation. In a visible manner, he represents Christ as teacher, shepherd, and priest. In virtue of the grace received from the Holy Spirit, a bishop is constituted as a true and authentic teacher of the Faith and a unifier of the Church.

Having received the fullness of Holy Orders himself, a validly ordained bishop is the only minister of this Sacrament. This authority to transmit the Sacrament comes by virtue of his own ordination, which every bishop can trace directly back to the Apostles in an unbroken line of succession. This apostolic line is an indication of the authority and unity maintained by the Church since the time of Christ. All bishops have the power to confer all three levels of Holy Orders—bishop, priest, and deacon—through ordination.

All bishops have the power to confer all three levels of Holy Orders—bishop, priest, and deacon—through ordination.

However, present Church law specifies that a bishop can be ordained only with the permission of the pope, who chooses him for this role.

A diocesan bishop in the diocese entrusted to him has all ordinary, proper, and immediate power which is required for the exercise of his pastoral function except for cases which the law or a decree of the Supreme Pontiff reserves to the supreme authority or to another ecclesiastical authority. (CIC, 381 § 1)

It is for the diocesan bishop to govern the particular church entrusted to him with legislative, executive, and judicial power according to the norm of law. (CIC, 391 § 1)

True to his title, the bishop is an overseer of his diocese. He is the principal pastor and teacher of his flock, and a guide and father to his priests and deacons. As a successor to the Apostles, he fulfills the teaching, governing, and sanctifying role entrusted to him by Christ in his diocese. It is the responsibility of the bishop to know the particular spiritual needs of his flock and to strive to meet them. Having received the fullness of Holy Orders, the bishop presides at the celebration of each of the Seven Sacraments, including the Sacrament of Holy Orders. For Catholics who were baptized

SYMBOLS OF A BISHOP

This Bishop wears the bishop's mitre, the bishop's ring, and carries the crosier.

MITRE: The mitre is a head covering worn by the Pope since the tenth century. By the twelfth century, it became customary for all bishops to wear the mitre as a symbol of their office.

RING: The bishop's ring is a both a symbol of his office as a successor to the Apostles and a symbol of his spiritual marriage to the Church. The ring worn by the Pope is called the Fisherman's ring in recognition of his office as successor to St. Peter.

BISHOP'S CHAIR: The bishop's church, known as a cathedral, comes from the Latin *cathedra* meaning chair. It is the site where the bishop's chair is placed and represents his authority in the diocese.

CROSIER: This is a shepherd's staff, which represents the bishop's role as a pastor or shepherd over his flock.

The Pope's *cathedra* in the Basilica of St. John Lateran, the cathedral of Rome.

in infancy, the bishop is the ordinary minister of the Sacrament of Confirmation, making it an effective sign of membership in the Catholic (universal) Church.

The bishop is involved in parish life in ways that many Catholics might not realize. The bishop spends much time in the education and formation of his priests and decides which priest(s) will be assigned to each parish. In doing so, he must consider the particular needs of the parish and the needs of the diocese as a whole.

It is also the duty of a bishop to visit the parishes in his diocese. During these visits, he will often celebrate Confirmation and will speak with the pastor regarding the state of the parish. Although he delegates much of his responsibility to the priest, the bishop is ultimately responsibility for the parish and the spiritual life of all Catholics in his diocese.

Each bishop has a collegial relationship with all of the other Catholic bishops in the world and a shared responsibility for the entire Church. This unity of Catholic bishops, led by the Pope, makes present the relationship that existed between St. Peter and the Apostles.

In addition to the many informal meetings bishops have with each other, they also convene in councils to study and resolve various issues and conflicts facing the Church. There are two kinds of councils: local councils and ecumenical, or general, councils.

> Although the bishops who are in communion with the head and members of the college, whether individually or joined together in conferences of bishops or in particular councils, do not possess infallibility in teaching, they are authentic teachers and instructors of the faith for the

Christian faithful entrusted to their care; the Christian faithful are bound to adhere with religious submission of mind to the authentic magisterium of their bishops. (CIC, 753)

Local councils often occur between bishops of various regions of the world, and they may address issues and problems particular to local and regional churches. Ecumenical councils involve all the bishops of the world and consider issues facing the entire Church. The decisions made at an ecumenical council come with strong authority as they represent the views of the entire collegiate of bishops. However, decisions made at these councils do not have authority over the entire Church unless they are agreed upon by the Pope, who alone, as the successor to St. Peter, the Vicar of Christ, has authority over the whole Church. There have been twenty-one such councils in the history of the Church, many of which have been instrumental in defining some of the most fundamental doctrines of the Catholic Faith. The last ecumenical council was the Second Vatican Council, which was in session from 1962 to 1965.

THE CELEBRATION OF THE SACRAMENT OF HOLY ORDERS

The celebration of the Sacrament of Holy Orders is an important and wondrous event, similar in both its solemnity and festivity to a wedding. Indeed those receiving the Sacrament are wedding their lives to Christ and his Church. Because the bishop is the minister of the Sacrament, it usually takes place in the cathedral and as many members of the diocese as possible are encouraged to attend. Catholics attending the celebration of the Sacrament of Holy Orders welcome the newly ordained spiritual fathers.

Matter

From apostolic times, the physical symbol of the Sacrament of Holy Orders has been the act of laying on of hands. This is still the case today. The bishop receives the candidates for the Sacrament, calls them to the priesthood, and lays his hands on their heads. This act is an indication that the authority that Jesus gave to the Apostles is in turn delegated by the bishop to those ordained into the priesthood. This symbolic action of laying on of hands is accompanied by the actual outpouring of Christ's grace, which leaves an indelible mark and changes the recipient forever.

Form

The rite of ordination for all three degrees of Holy Orders consists of the bishop's imposition of hands on the head of the ordained and the consecratory prayer asking God to pour out his Holy Spirit and bestow the gifts appropriate to the ministry for which the candidate is being ordained. In addition to this essential action, the celebration of the Sacrament contains a number of complementary rituals and prayers that emphasize the nature of the celebration. The candidates are presented to the bishop, who examines each candidate and then offers an instruction. Both bishops and priests receiving the Sacrament are anointed with holy chrism.

At the ordination elevating a priest to the episcopacy, the new bishop is given a Book of the Gospels, along with a ring, mitre, and crosier, which symbolize his apostolic mission and role as the shepherd of Christ's flock.

The rite of ordination for all three degrees of Holy Orders includes the bishop's imposition of hands on the head of the ordained.

Minister

Bishops receive the fullness of ministry that Christ bestowed on his Apostles. For this reason, the authority to celebrate the Sacrament of Holy Orders resides with the bishops alone. Only a bishop can ordain a man as a deacon, priest, or bishop.

THE PRIESTLY LIFE

Priests live in a great variety of ways. Some are small parish pastors and others cathedral rectors. Some work as chaplains in the military or in hospitals, others teach at universities. Some work in diocesan or Vatican offices as specialists in Canon Law, the liturgy, or numerous other functions, while still others may run soup kitchens in impoverished neighborhoods. Indeed there are as many ways of living out the priestly life as there are various personalities and talents that are called to the vocation. What all priests do have in common is a unique participation in the priesthood of Jesus Christ, exercising their priestly ministry *in persona Christi*.

Diocesan priests in the Latin Rite of the Catholic Church make a commitment to celibacy (to remain unmarried) and of obedience to their bishop. A dispensation to the requirement of celibacy can be made in the case of married Protestant ministers who convert and are ordained to the Catholic priesthood. Also, priests of the Eastern Rites of the Catholic Church may be married before ordination, but they may not marry afterwards.

> In leading their lives, clerics are bound in a special way to pursue holiness…In order to be able to pursue this perfection:
>
> …priests are earnestly invited to offer the eucharistic sacrifice daily and deacons to participate in its offering daily;
>
> …priests and deacons aspiring to the presbyterate are obliged to carry out the liturgy of the hours daily according to the proper and approved liturgical books…. (CIC, 276 § 1 - § 2)

In the exercise of his priestly ministry, a priest is responsible for leading those entrusted to his care in a life of holiness. However, before he can lead others, the priest must first care for his own spiritual life. For this reason, the Church strongly encourages priests to offer daily Mass and requires them to pray the Liturgy of the Hours. Additionally, priests are encouraged to frequently receive the Sacrament of Reconciliation, along with spiritual direction, and to foster their spiritual life through such practices as mental prayer, spiritual reading, and visits to the Blessed Sacrament.

The faithful in the lay state or consecrated life have an essential role in building up and sustaining the ordained deaconate, priesthood, and episcopacy. We should pray for the deacons, priests, and bishops serving the local church and every diocese throughout the world, and we should pray for more vocations to the priesthood and diaconate. In addition to prayer, we should offer our help and support to bishops, priests, and deacons. (cf. CCC 1547-1548).

In the exercise of his priestly ministry, a priest is responsible for leading those entrusted to his care in a life of holiness.

RELIGIOUS LIFE

The life consecrated through the profession of the evangelical counsels is a stable form of living by which the faithful, following Christ more closely under the action of the Holy Spirit, are totally dedicated to God who is loved most of all, so that, having been dedicated by a new and special title to His honor, to the building up of the Church, and to the salvation of the world, they strive for the perfection of charity in the service of the kingdom of God and, having been made an outstanding sign in the Church, foretell the heavenly glory. (CIC, 573 § 1)

St. Francis in Prayer by El Greco. The beauty of religious life is the communal life of prayer and work with each person supporting the others as they strive for holiness.

Religious priests are those who are associated with a particular religious order, such as the Dominicans or Franciscans. They are ordained to serve their order and are not necessarily bound to a particular diocese. Additionally, they take vows of chastity, poverty, and obedience. While their obedience is to their religious superior, they must also be obedient to the local bishop while serving in a given diocese.

Their vow of poverty requires that they own nothing individually, although the order as a whole may own a monastery or friary, as well as cars and other goods necessary for their work. Some religious priests also take additional vows, for example, vows of obedience to the pope or to serve the poor. Part of the beauty of religious life is the communal life of prayer and work with each person supporting the others as they strive for holiness.

CELIBACY

Christ's redemptive mission required a complete giving of himself and ultimately his own Death on the Cross for the sins of the world. As Christians, we are called to imitate Christ. Even during the Church's infancy, many of the Apostles and early followers of Christ sought to imitate Christ's complete self-giving by not marrying for the sake of the Christian ministry.

The practice of celibacy finds its origins in the apostolic Church. In the Gospels we find that Jesus encouraged those who had been given the gift of celibacy to accept it for the good of the Kingdom of Heaven.

He said to them, "Not all men can receive this saying, but only those to whom it is given. For there are eunuchs who have been so from birth, and there are eunuchs who have been made eunuchs by men, and there are eunuchs who have made themselves eunuchs for the sake of the kingdom of heaven. He who is able to receive this, let him receive it." (Mt 19:11-12)

Likewise, in giving advice to the married, those desiring to be married, and to widows and widowers, St. Paul writes:

Are you free from a wife? Do not seek marriage. But if you marry, you do not sin, and if a girl marries she does not sin. Yet those who marry will have worldly troubles, and I would spare you that…I want you to be free from anxieties. The unmarried man is anxious about the affairs of the Lord, how to please the Lord; but the married man is anxious about worldly affairs, how to please his wife, and his interests are divided. (1 Cor 7: 27-28, 32-34)

Those who voluntarily renounce the blessings of marriage and family to dedicate themselves entirely to God's service are living examples of their ministry. By putting aside all to follow Christ, priests demonstrate that whatever is given up in this world is nothing compared to what awaits us in Heaven.

The advantages of a celibate clergy are easily recognized in light of the aspect of service. An unmarried person can dedicate his entire life and all of his time to the service of God and to a life of prayer. He needs little for himself and can always be available whenever or wherever he is needed. By forsaking wife and children, he becomes married to the Church and those whom he serves become his family. Furthermore, this imitation of Christ through celibacy visibly symbolizes the union or spiritual marriage between Christ and his Church.

Far from undermining the value of marriage, the exaltation of celibacy in the Christian life emphatically confirms the great value that the Church places on marital and family life. This is seen clearly in the direct relationship between the sanctity of marriage and religious vocations. In those places and times where marriage and family are held in the highest regard, priesthood and religious life flourish. Likewise, when human sexuality is not respected in society, vocations to the priesthood suffer.

> Virginity or celibacy for the sake of the kingdom of God not only does not contradict the dignity of marriage, but presupposes it and confirms it. Marriage and virginity or celibacy are two ways of expressing and living the one mystery of the covenant of God with his people. When marriage is not esteemed, neither can consecrated virginity or celibacy exist; when human sexuality is not regarded as a great value given by the Creator, the renunciation of it for the sake of the Kingdom of Heaven loses its meaning. (*Familaris Consortio*, 16)

MALE PRIESTHOOD

One of the things that made Jewish and Roman authorities suspicious of Jesus was the way his life and teaching broke from many contemporary social conventions and customs. Nowhere is this more evident than in his treatment and acceptance of women. One example in the Gospel of St. John shows how surprised even Jesus' own disciples were that Jesus evangelized the Samaritan woman he met at the well. Indeed the woman herself was surprised that Jesus would speak with her.[22] This is just one of many instances when Jesus included women in important aspects of his work and teaching. Perhaps most significantly, it was the women who were most faithful to Christ during his Passion and Death and who were the first witnesses of his Resurrection.[23]

Christ was revolutionary in his inclusion of women in his ministry. However, he also specifically chose twelve men to be his Apostles. It was to them that he gave his own divine authority to bind and loose with instructions to lead the Church.[24] He invited these twelve to his Last Supper where he charged them with continuing the celebration of the Eucharist. After his Resurrection, it was again the twelve who were charged with the ministry of forgiving sins.[25]

It is reasonable to believe that if Jesus had intended his faithful women followers to be a part of his priestly ministry, he would have so instructed his Apostles. Jesus did not, and therefore, the Church has no authority to act contrary to her founder's example and design.

Resurrection of Christ and Women at the Tomb by Fra Angelico. Christ was revolutionary in his inclusion of women in his ministry. However, he specifically chose twelve men to be his Apostles.

It is not a question of the Church refusing to ordain women to the ministerial priesthood, rather, it is impossible for the Church to do so.[26]

Calling of the Apostles by Ghirlandaio. The Sacrament of Holy Orders was designed by Christ as the means to provide ministers to his people until he comes again. Through this Sacrament, Christ assured the faithful of his continuing presence in the Church.

CONCLUSION

By virtue of the Sacrament of Baptism, every member of the Church has a share in Christ's role as priest, king, and prophet. This is referred to as the *common priesthood of the faithful*. All Christians have been set apart to bring God to the world and the world to God. By living as Jesus taught, we are to be proof of God's wisdom and goodness, so that seeing us, all may desire his friendship. This priesthood is exercised by all the baptized in their particular state in life, which is a call to bring others to Christ by their prayer and example. It is a call to offer oneself as a living sacrifice, uniting it to the sacrifice of Christ on the Cross.

However, this common priesthood differs in essence from the *ministerial priesthood*. Desiring to continue his salvific ministry, Christ granted his divine authority to the Apostles, who in turn handed this authority on to those they ordained to the ministry. The Sacrament of Holy Orders was designed by Christ as the means to provide ministers to his people until he comes again. The bishop, as a direct successor of the Apostles, has the fullness of Holy Orders, which confers on him a special participation in the priesthood of Christ. Priests are coworkers and assistants in the ministry of the bishop, while deacons are ordained as ministers of service.

Through the Sacrament of Holy Orders, Christ assured the faithful of his continuing presence in the Church. As privileged encounters with Christ, the sacraments grant us the grace necessary to fulfill our own Christian vocation. Those who have been called to celebrate the sacraments and to serve the People of God through ordination to the Christian ministry have been given a great dignity and a great responsibility.

SUPPLEMENTARY READING

POPE ST. JOHN PAUL II

POPE ST. JOHN PAUL II
May 18, 1920 – April 2, 2005

In his book *Gift and Mystery*, Pope St. John Paul II offers many insights into the vocation of the priesthood from his own experience. He explains how the priesthood is not a decision that man makes and God accepts, but rather a decision that God makes so that man may accept:

> A vocation is a mystery of divine election: "You did not choose me, but I chose you and appointed you that you should go and bear fruit and that your fruit should abide."[27] "And one does not take the honor upon himself, but he is called by God, just as Aaron was."[28] "Before I formed you in the womb I knew you, and before you were born I consecrated you; I appointed you a prophet to the nations."[29] These inspired words cannot fail to move deeply the heart of every priest…that God "called us with a holy calling, not in virtue of our works but in virtue of his own purpose and the grace which he gave us."[30]

Later in the book the pope tries to explain the mystery of the priesthood, knowing that human words cannot do it justice. He makes it clear that this vocation is where some young men "will find complete personal fulfillment."

> The priestly vocation is a mystery. It is the mystery of a "wondrous exchange"—admirable commercium—between God and man. A man offers his humanity to Christ, so that Christ may use him as an instrument of salvation, making him as it were into another Christ. Unless we grasp the mystery of this "exchange," we will not understand how it can be that a young man, hearing the words "Follow me!" can give up everything for Christ, in the certainty that if he follows this path he will find complete personal fulfillment.[31]

Pope St. John Paul II entered the seminary when Poland was occupied by Nazi Germany. He and all the other seminarians had to keep their studies secret or face arrest by the Nazis. Here he discusses his realization of his vocation during World War II.

> The outbreak of the war took me away from my studies and from the University. In that period I also lost my father, the last remaining member of my immediate family. All this brought with it, objectively, a process of detachment from earlier plans; in a way it was like being uprooted from the soil in which, up till that moment, my humanity had grown.

> But the process [of detachment] was not merely negative. At the same time a light was beginning to shine ever more brightly in the back of my mind: the Lord wants me to become a priest. One day I saw this with great clarity: it was like an interior illumination bringing with it the joy and certainty of a new vocation.

> And this awareness filled me with a great inner peace.[32]

VOCABULARY

APOSTLES
From the Greek for "one sent forth." It refers to the Twelve chosen by Jesus during the course of his public ministry to be his closest followers, as well as Sts. Matthias, Paul of Tarsus, Barnabas, and the enlighteners of whole nations.

APOSTOLIC SUCCESSION
The handing on of ecclesiastical authority from the Apostles to their successors the bishops through the laying on of hands.

BISHOP
From the Greek for "overseer." By divine institution, he succeeds the Apostles through the Holy Spirit who is given to him. He is constituted a Pastor in the Church, to be the teacher of doctrine, the priest of sacred worship, and the minister of governance. (cf. CIC, 375)

CARDINAL
A member of a special college that elects the pope. This person is available to the pope to deal with issues of major importance or the daily care of the Church. (cf. CIC, 349)

CELIBACY
The state of one who has chosen to remain unmarried for the sake of the Kingdom of Heaven in order to give himself entirely to God and to the service of his people.

CHASTITY
The moral virtue (under the cardinal virtue of temperance) that is directed toward the positive integration of sexuality within a person by moderating the sexual appetite. This virtue leads to truly human sexuality when integrated in a correct way into every relationship. Chastity is a gift of God, a grace, and a fruit of the Holy Spirit.

COLLEGE OF BISHOPS
The body of bishops, united with the Pope as their head, having its origin in the community of the Twelve Apostles with Peter at their head. The college of bishops under the Pope has supreme and full authority in the Catholic Church.

COMMON PRIESTHOOD OF THE FAITHFUL
The participation in the priesthood of Christ, which all of the faithful share through Baptism.

DEACON
From the Greek for "servant": one who has been ordained to the first degree of Holy Orders, ordained not to priesthood but for ministry and service.

DIOCESE
A portion of the People of God that is entrusted to a bishop to be nurtured by him, with the cooperation of his priests, in such a way that, remaining close to its pastor and gathered by him through the Gospel and the Eucharist in the Holy Spirit, it constitutes a particular Church. In this Church, the one, holy, catholic and apostolic Church of Christ truly exists and functions. (cf. CIC, 369)

EPISCOPAL COLLEGE
All bishops collectively in communion with the pope.

FATHERS OF THE CHURCH
Great theologians of the Church following the time of the Apostles. The Patristic age is named for these Fathers (Latin "*patri*").

HOLY ORDERS
The Sacrament of Apostolic Ministry by which the mission entrusted by Christ to his Apostles continues to be exercised in the Church through the laying on of hands, which leaves a sacramental character on the soul.

MINISTER (MINISTRY)
A servant or attendant.

MINISTER OF THE HOLY COMMUNION (extraordinary)
Lay persons or non-ordained religious, who assist the ordinary ministers of Holy Communion in the distribution of the Sacrament when extraordinary circumstances exist, as defined by Canon Law.

MINISTER OF THE HOLY COMMUNION (ordinary)
Bishops, priests, and deacons who, by right of their ordination, have an official function in the celebration of the Mass. One of their responsibilities is the distribution of Holy Communion, both during the Mass and to those who are unable to attend due to illness or other circumstances.

VOCABULARY Continued

OBEDIENCE
Submission to the authority of God, which requires everyone to obey the divine law. For example, a priest obeys his bishop or religious superior as a representative of God.

ORDINATION
The rite of the Sacrament of Holy Orders by which the bishop, through the imposition of hands and the prayer of Consecration, confers the order of bishop, priest, or deacon by the power of the Holy Spirit on behalf of the Church.

POVERTY
The condition of want experienced by those who are poor, whom Christ called blessed, and for whom he had a special love. Poverty of spirit signifies humility and detachment from worldly things.

PRESBYTERATE
From the Greek for "elders": the office of presbyter (priesthood); a body or the order of presbyters. This is one of the three degrees of the Sacrament of Holy Orders.

PRIEST
In the Old Testament, one of the tribe of Levi; in the New Testament, an abbreviation of the Greek *presbyteros*, "elder": A member of the order of presbyters. This baptized and confirmed male is ordained to be a coworker with his bishop, to preside at public liturgies in his stead, and otherwise to assist his bishop in priestly service to the People of God.

RELIGIOUS
One who professes the evangelical counsels of poverty, chastity, and obedience in a canonically recognized institute. Also, a synonym for devout.

STUDY QUESTIONS

1. What does the word "minister" mean?

2. What is the primary role of those receiving Holy Orders?

3. In the Old Testament, what was the role of a priest, and who were chosen to act as priests?

4. What was lacking in the sacrifices of the Old Covenant?

5. What is the reason for God becoming man?

6. Why is Jesus called the "eternal" High Priest? Why was his sacrifice perfect?

7. What were other aspects of Jesus' "ministry" to mankind?

8. How, and through whom, did Jesus plan to continue his ministry to mankind after his Ascension into Heaven?

9. What "method" did Jesus use in calling his Apostles?

10. What was the special role that he gave to St. Peter?

11. What did the Apostles do when they founded churches in their missionary journeys?

12. What was the hierarchy that was established in the apostolic Church?

13. What do the following words mean in their original languages: bishop, priest (presbyter), deacon?

14. What is apostolic succession, and why is it important?

15. When did Jesus institute the Sacrament of Holy Orders? What other Sacrament was also instituted at this time?

16. What happens to a man at his ordination?

17. What does it mean that Holy Orders is a Sacrament of three degrees?

18. What are exceptions to the rule of celibacy in the Catholic Church?

STUDY QUESTIONS Continued

19. What is the role of a deacon?

20. What is the difference between a transitional and a permanent deacon?

21. What are some of the functions that a deacon performs in the parish?

22. Describe the activities performed by a priest in a parish.

23. No one has a right to become a priest. Explain.

24. Explain what is meant by saying that a bishop is a successor to the Apostles (i.e., apostolic succession).

25. How can apostolic succession be demonstrated?

26. Briefly describe the duties of a bishop.

27. In addition to the role that a bishop has in his diocese, what role does a bishop have in the "Catholic" or worldwide Church?

28. Summarize the teachings of Christ and St. Paul regarding celibacy.

29. Does the exaltation of the celibate life undermine the sanctity of marriage? Explain.

30. Briefly explain why the Catholic Church ordains only men in the Sacrament of Holy Orders.

31. What is meant by the "common priesthood of the faithful"? How does an individual participate in this priesthood?

32. What is the difference between the "common priesthood of the faithful" and the "ministerial priesthood"?

PRACTICAL EXERCISES

1. Suppose that two churches exist side by side in the same community. To every appearance they seem identical. Applying the teachings of Tertullian (*Prescription against Heretics*), how could you determine which is the true church acting under the authority of Jesus Christ? What are the implications for a church that cannot demonstrate apostolic succession?

2. Invite a priest to class (or to dinner with your family). Ask him to discuss how he serves the Church and why he loves the celibate life. Ask him about his own vocation to the priesthood.

3. Imagine that you have a non-Catholic friend who thinks that Catholic priests are superior to lay people and try to control them. Explain to him why priests may be called "servants of the servants of God."

4. Priests can trace the roots of their ordination all the way back to the Apostles. Ask your parents, search on the Internet, and/or visit your courthouse to see how far back you can trace your family tree.

FROM THE CATECHISM

1590 St. Paul said to his disciple Timothy: "I remind you to rekindle the gift of God that is within you through the laying on of my hands,"[33] and "If any one aspires to the office of bishop, he desires a noble task."[34] To Titus he said: "This is why I left you in Crete, that you amend what was defective, and appoint presbyters in every town, as I directed you."[35]

1591 The whole Church is a priestly people. Through Baptism all the faithful share in the priesthood of Christ. This participation is called the "common priesthood of the faithful." Based on this common priesthood and ordered to its service, there exists another participation in the mission of Christ: the ministry conferred by the sacrament of Holy Orders, where the task is to serve in the name and in the person of Christ the Head in the midst of the community.

1592 The ministerial priesthood differs in essence from the common priesthood of the faithful because it confers a sacred power for the service of the faithful. The ordained ministers exercise their service for the People of God by teaching (*munus docendi*), divine worship (*munus liturgicum*) and pastoral governance (*munus regendi*).

Through the Sacrament of Holy Orders, a priest is given a special character or mark upon the soul enabling him to act in the person of Christ.

1593 Since the beginning, the ordained ministry has been conferred and exercised in three degrees: that of bishops, that of presbyters, and that of deacons. The ministries conferred by ordination are irreplaceable for the organic structure of the Church: without the bishop, presbyters, and deacons, one cannot speak of the Church.[36]

1594 The bishop receives the fullness of the sacrament of Holy Orders, which integrates him into the episcopal college and makes him the visible head of the particular Church entrusted to him. As successors of the apostles and members of the college, the bishops share in the apostolic responsibility and mission of the whole Church under the authority of the Pope, successor of St. Peter.

1595 Priests are united with the bishops in sacerdotal dignity and at the same time depend on them in the exercise of their pastoral functions; they are called to be the bishops' prudent co-workers. They form around their bishop the presbyterium which bears responsibility with him for the particular Church. They receive from the bishop the charge of a parish community or a determinate ecclesial office.

1596 Deacons are ministers ordained for tasks of service of the Church; they do not receive the ministerial priesthood, but ordination confers on them important functions in the ministry of the word, divine worship, pastoral governance, and the service of charity, tasks which they must carry out under the pastoral authority of their bishop.

1597 The sacrament of Holy Orders is conferred by the laying on of hands followed by a solemn prayer of consecration asking God to grant the ordinand the graces of the Holy Spirit required for his ministry. Ordination imprints an indelible sacramental character.

1599 In the Latin Church the sacrament of Holy Orders for the presbyterate is normally conferred only on candidates who are ready to embrace celibacy freely and who publicly manifest their intention of staying celibate for the love of God's kingdom and the service of men.

1600 It is bishops who confer the sacrament of Holy Orders in the three degrees.

The celebration of the Sacrament of Holy Orders is an important and wondrous event, similar in both its solemnity and festivity to a wedding.

Prayer for Vocations

O loving and gracious God, Father of all, you bless your people in every time and season and provide for their needs through your providential care. Your Church is continually in need of priests, sisters and brothers to offer themselves in the service of the gospel by lives of dedicated love. Open the hearts of your sons and daughters to listen to your call in their lives. Give them the gift of understanding to discern your invitation to serve you and your Church. Give them the gift of courage to follow your call. May they have the spirit of young Samuel who found fulfillment in his life when he said to you, "Speak Lord, for your servant is listening." We ask this through Jesus Christ, our Lord and Redeemer. Amen.

ENDNOTES – CHAPTER SIX

1. St. Ignatius of Antioch, *A Letter to the Philadelphians*, from the Office of Readings, Thursday of the 27th Week in Ordinary Time.
2. Cf. CCC 1533-1535.
3. *LG* 18.
4. Cf. Ex 32:25-29.
5. Cf. CCC 1540.
6. Mk 1:17-18.
7. For further research on vocation see the video: *Fishers of Men* at www.priest4christ.com; or *The Catholic Priest Today* at www.thecatholicpriesttoday.com.
8. Pope Benedict XVI, General Audience, March 15, 2006.
9. Cf. *LG* 10; 28; *SC* 33; *CD* 11; *PO* 2; 6.

10. Pius XII, encyclical, *Mediator Dei*: AAS, 39 (1947) 548.
11. St. Thomas Aquinas, *STh* III, 22, 4c.
12. Cf. 1 Clement 42:4.
13. Pope Benedict XVI, General Audience, March 29, 2006.
14. Cf. Lk 22:19.
15. Jn 20:21-23.
16. Mt 28:18-20.
17. Cf. CCC 1549.
18. Cf. CCC 1573.
19. Cf. CIC, 1031 § 2.
20. Cf. CIC, 1037.
21. CIC, 1031 § 1.
22. Cf. Jn 4:9-27.
23. Cf. Lk 23:49, 55; 24:1-12.
24. Cf. CCC 1575.

25. Cf. Jn 20:19-23.
26. Cf. CCC 1577; Mt 16:18ff.; Lk 6:12-16; Mk 3:14-19.
27. Jn 15:16.
28. Heb 5:4.
29. Jer 1:5.
30. St. John Paul II, *Gift and Mystery: On the Fiftieth Anniversary of My Priestly Ordination* (Doubleday, 1997), pp. 3-4; 2 Tm 1:9.
31. Ibid., pp. 72-73.
32. Ibid., pp. 34-35.
33. 2 Tm 1:6.
34. 1 Tm 3:1.
35. Ti 1:5.
36. Cf. St. Ignatius of Antioch, *Ad Trall.* 3, 1.

1. ST. PETER

THE  POPES

266. FRANCIS I

FIRST CENTURY
St. Peter (AD 33-67)
St. Linus (67-76)
St. Anacletus (76-88)
St. Clement I (88-97)
St. Evaristus (97-105)

SECOND CENTURY
St. Alexander I (105-115)
St. Sixtus I (115-125)
St. Telesphorus (125-136)
St. Hyginus (136-140)
St. Pius I (140-155)
St. Anicetus (155-166)
St. Soter (166-175)
St. Eleutherius (175-189)
St. Victor I (189-199)
St. Zephyrinus (199-217)

THIRD CENTURY
St. Callistus I (217-222)
St. Hippolytus (217-235)
St. Urban I (222-230)
St. Pontian (230-235)
St. Anterus (235-236)
St. Fabian (236-250)
St. Cornelius (251-253)
St. Lucius I (253-254)
St. Stephen I (254-257)
St. Sixtus II (257-258)
St. Dionysius (259-268)
St. Felix I (269-274)
St. Eutychian (275-283)
St. Caius (283-296)
St. Marcellinus (296-304)

FOURTH CENTURY
St. Marcellus I (308-309)
St. Eusebius (309-310)
St. Miltiades (311-314)
St. Sylvester I (314-335)
St. Marcus (336)
St. Julius I (337-352)
Liberius (352-366)
Felix II (353-365)
St. Damasus I (366-384)
Ursinus (366-367)
St. Siricius (384-399)
St. Anastasius I (399-401)

FIFTH CENTURY
St. Innocent I (401-417)
St. Zozimus (417-418)
St. Boniface I (418-422)
Eulalius (418-419)
St. Celestine I (422-432)

St. Sixtus III (432-440)
St. Leo I (440-461)
St. Hilary (461-468)
St. Simplicius (468-483)
St. Felix III (II) (483-492)
St. Gelasius I (492-496)
Anastasius II (496-498)
St. Symmachus (498-514)
Laurentius (498-505)

SIXTH CENTURY
St. Hormisdas (514-523)
St. John I (523-526)
St. Felix IV (III) (526-530)
Boniface II (530-532)
Dioscurus (530)
John II (533-535)
St. Agapitus I (535-536)
St. Silverius (536-537)
Vigilius (537-555)
Pelagius I (556-561)
John III (561-574)
Benedict I (575-579)
Pelagius II (579-590)
St. Gregory I (590-604)

SEVENTH CENTURY
Sabinian (604-606)
Boniface III (607)
St. Boniface IV (608-615)
St. Deusdedit (615-618)
   or Adoedatus I
Boniface V (619-625)
Honorius I (625-638)
Severinus (640)
John IV (640-642)
Theodore I (642-649)
St. Martin I (649-655)
St. Eugene I (654-657)
St. Vitalian (657-672)
Adeodatus II (672-676)
Donus (676-678)
St. Agatho (678-681)
St. Leo II (682-683)
St. Benedict II (684-685)
John V (685-686)
Conon (686-687)
Theodore II (687)
Paschal I (687-692)
St. Sergius I (687-701)

EIGHTH CENTURY
John VI (701-705)
John VII (705-707)
Sisinnius (708)

Constantine (708-715)
St. Gregory II (715-731)
St. Gregory III (731-471)
St. Zachary (741-752)
Stephen II (752)
St. Paul I (757-767)
Constantine (767)
Philip (767)
Stephen III (768-772)
Adrian I (772-795)
St. Leo III (795-816)

NINTH CENTURY
Stephen IV (816-817)
St. Paschal I (817-824)
Eugene II (824-827)
Valentine (827)
Gregory IV (827-844)
John VIII (844)
Sergius II (844-847)
St. Leo IV (847-855)
Benedict III (855-858)
Anastasius III (855)
St. Nicholas I (858-867)
Adrian II (867-872)
John VIII (872-882)
Marinus I (882-884)
St. Adrian III (884-885)
Stephen V (VI) (885-891)
Formosus (891-896)
Boniface VI (896)
Stephen VI (VII) (896-897)
Romanus (897)
Theodore II (897)
John IX (898-900)

TENTH CENTURY
Benedict IV (900-903)
Leo V (903)
Christopher (903-904)
Sergius III (904-911)
Anastasius III (911-913)
Landus (913-914)
John X (914-928)
Leo VI (928)
Stephen VII (928-931)
John XI (931-935)
Leo VII (936-939)
Stephen VIII (IX) (939-942)
Marinus II (942-946)
Agapetus II (946-955)
John XII (955-964)
Leo VIII (963-965)
Benedict V (964-966)
John XIII (965-972)

Benedict VI (973-974)
Benedict VII (974-983)
John XIV (983-984)
Boniface VII (984-985)
John XV (985-996)
Gregory V (996-999)
Sylvester II (999-1003)

ELEVENTH CENTURY
John XVII (1003)
John XVIII (1004-1009)
Sergius IV (1009-1012)
Benedict VIII (1012-1024)
Gregory VI (1012)
John XIX (1024-1032)
Benedict IX (1032-1044)
Sylvester III (1045)
Gregory VI (1045-1046)
   (John Gratian Pierleoni)
Clement II (1046-1047)
   (Suitgar, Count of
   Morsleben)
Damasus II (1048)
   (Count Poppo)
St. Leo IX (1049-1054)
   (Bruno, Count of Toul)
Victor II (1055-1057)
   (Gebhard, Count of
   Hirschberg)
Stephen IX (X) (1057-1058)
   (Frederick of Lorraine)
Nicholas II (1059-1061)
   (Gerhard of Burgundy)
Alexander II (1061-1073)
   (Anselmo da Baggio)
Honorius II (1061-1064)
St. Gregory VII (1073-1085)
   (Hildebrand of Soana)
Clement III (1080-1100)
Bl. Victor III (1086-1087)
   (Desiderius, Prince of
   Beneventum)
Bl. Urban II (1088-1099)
   (Odo of Chatillon)
Paschal II (1099-1118)
   (Ranieri da Bieda)
Theodoric (1100-1102)
Albert (1102)
Sylvester IV (1105)

TWELFTH CENTURY
Gelasius II (1118-1119)
   (John Coniolo)
Gregory VIII (1118-1121)
Callistus II (1119-1124)
   (Guido, Count of Burgundy)

Italicized = Anti-popes

THE ✠ POPES Continued

Honorius II (1124-1130)
(Lamberto dei Fagnani)

Celestine II (1124)

Innocent II (1130-1143)
(Gregorio Papareschi)

Anacletus II (1130-1138)
(Cardinal Pierleone)

Victor IV (1138)

Celestine II (1143-1144)
(Guido di Castello)

Lucius II (1144-1145)
(Gherardo Caccianemici)

Bl. Eugene III (1145-1153)
(Bernardo Paganelli)

Anastasius IV (1153-1154)
(Corrado della Subarra)

Adrian IV (1154-1159)
(Nicholas Breakspear)

Alexander III (1159-1181)
(Orlando Bandinelli)

Victor IV (1159-1164)

Paschal III (1164-1168)

Calixtus III (1168-7118)

Innocent III (1179-1180)
(Lando da Sessa)

Lucius III (1181-1185)
(Ubaldo Allucingoli)

Urban III (1185-1187)
(Uberto Crivelli)

Gregory VIII (1187)
(Alberto del Morra)

Clement III (1187-1191)
(Paolo Scolari)

Celestine III (1191-1198)
(Giacinto Boboni-Orsini)

Innocent III (1198-1216)
(Lotario de Conti di Segni)

THIRTEENTH CENTURY

Honorius III (1216-1227)
(Cencio Savelli)

Gregory IX (1227-1241)
(Ugolino di Segni)

Celestine IV (1241)
(Goffredo Castiglione)

Innocent IV (1243-1254)
(Sinibaldo de Fieschi)

Alexander IV (1254-1261)
(Rinaldo di Segni)

Urban IV (1261-1264)
(Jacques Pantaléon)

Clement IV (1265-1268)
(Guy le Gros Foulques)

Bl. Gregory X (1271-1276)
(Tebaldo Visconti)

Bl. Innocent V (1276)
(Pierre de Champagni)

Adrian V (1276)
(Ottobono Fieschi)

John XXI (1276-1277)
(Pietro Rebuli-Giuliani)

Nicholas III (1277-1280)
(Giovanni Gaetano Orsini)

Martin IV (1281-1285)
(Simon Mompitie)

Honorius IV (1285-1287)
(Giacomo Savelli)

Nicholas IV (1288-1292)
(Girolamo Masci)

St. Celestine V (1294)
(Pietro Angelari da
Murrone)

Boniface VIII (1294-1303)
(Benedetto Gaetani)

FOURTEENTH CENTURY

Bl. Benedict XI (1303-1304)
(Niccolò Boccasini)

Clement V (1305-1314)
(Raimond Bertrand de Got)

John XXII (1316-1334)
(Jacques Dueze)

Nicholas V (1328-1330)
(Pietro di Corbara)

Benedict XII (1334-1342)
(Jacques Fournier)

Clement VI (1342-1352)
(Pierre Roger de Beaufort)

Innocent VI (1352-1362)
(Étienne Aubert)

Bl. Urban V (1362-1370)
(Guillaume de Grimord)

Gregory XI (1370-1378)
(Pierre Roger de
Beaufort, the Younger)

Urban VI (1378-1389)
(Bartolomeo Prignano)

Clement VII (1378-1394)
(Robert of Geneva)

Boniface IX (1389-1404)
(Pietro Tomacelli)

Benedict XIII (1394-1423)
(Pedro de Luna)

FIFTEENTH CENTURY

Innocent VII (1404-1406)
(Cosmato de Migliorati)

Gregory XII (1406-1415)
(Angelo Correr)

Alexander V (1409-1410)
(Petros Philargi)

John XXIII (1410-1415)
(Baldassare Cossa)

Martin V (1417-1431)
(Ottone Colonna)

Clement VIII (1423-1429)

Benedict XIV (1424)

Eugene IV (1431-1447)
(Gabriele Condulmer)

Felix V (1439-1449)
(Amadeus of Savoy)

Nicholas V (1447-1455)
(Tommaso Parentucelli)

Callistus III (1455-1458)
(Alonso Borgia)

Pius II (1458-1464)
(Aeneas Silvio de
Piccolomini)

Paul II (1464-1471)
(Pietro Barbo)

Sixtus IV (1471-1484)
(Francesco della Rovere)

Innocent VIII (1484-1492)
(Giovanni Battista Cibo)

Alexander VI (1492-1503)
(Rodrigo Lanzol y Borgia)

SIXTEENTH CENTURY

Pius III (1503)
(Francesco Todoeschini-
Piccolomini)

Julius II (1503-1513)
(Giuliano della Rovere)

Leo X (1513-1521)
(Giovanni de Medici)

Adrian VI (1522-1523)
(Adrian Florensz)

Clement VII (1523-1534)
(Giulio de Medici)

Paul III (1534-1549)
(Alessandro Farnese)

Julius III (1550-1555)
(Giovanni Maria Ciocchi
del Monte)

Marcellus II (1555)
(Marcello Cervini)

Paul IV (1555-1559)
(Gian Pietro Caraffa)

Pius IV (1559-1565)
(Giovanni Angelo de Medici)

St. Pius V (1566-1572)
(Antonio Michele Ghislieri)

Gregory XIII (1572-1585)
(Ugo Buoncompagni)

Sixtus V (1585-1590)
(Felice Peretti)

Urban VII (1590)
(Giambattista Castagna)

Gregory XIV (1590-1591)
(Niccolò Sfondrati)

Innocent IX (1591)
(Gian Antonio Facchinetti)

Clement VIII (1592-1605)
(Ippolito Aldobrandini)

SEVENTEENTH CENTURY

Leo XI (1605)
(Alessandro de Medici-
Ottaiano)

Paul V (1605-1621)
(Camillo Borghese)

Gregory XV (1621-1623)
(Alessandro Ludovisi)

Urban VIII (1623-1644)
(Maffeo Barberini)

Innocent X (1644-1655)
(Giambattista Pamfili)

Alexander VII (1655-1667)
(Fabio Chigi)

Clement IX (1667-1669)
(Giulio Rospigliosi)

Clement X (1670-1676)
(Emilio Altieri)

Bl. Innocent XI (1676-1689)
(Benedetto Odescalchi)

Alexander VIII (1689-1691)
(Pietro Ottoboni)

Innocent XII (1691-1700)
(Antonio Pignatelli)

EIGHTEENTH CENTURY

Clement XI (1700-1721)
(Gian Francesco Albani)

Innocent XIII (1721-1724)
(Michelangelo dei Conti)

Benedict XIII (1724-1730)
(Pietro Francesco Orsini)

Clement XII (1730-1740)
(Lorenzo Corsini)

Benedict XIV (1740-1758)
(Prospero Lambertini)

Clement XIII (1758-1769)
(Carlo Rezzonico)

Clement XIV (1769-1774)
(Lorenzo Ganganelli)

Pius VI (1775-1799)
(Gianangelo Braschi)

NINETEENTH CENTURY

Pius VII (1800-1823)
(Barnaba Chiaramonti)

Leo XII (1823-1829)
(Annibale della Genga)

Pius VIII (1829-1830)
(Francesco Saverio
Gastiglioni)

Gregory XVI (1831-1846)
(Bartolomeo Alberto
Cappellari)

Bl. Pius IX (1846-1878)
(Giovanni Mastai-Ferretti)

Leo XIII (1878-1903)
(Gioacchino Pecci)

TWENTIETH CENTURY

St. Pius X (1903-1914)
(Giuseppe Sarto)

Benedict XV (1914-1922)
(Giacomo della Chiesa)

Pius XI (1922-1939)
(Achille Ratti)

Pius XII (1939-1958)
(Eugenio Pacelli)

St. John XXIII (1958-1963)
(Angelo Roncalli)

Paul VI (1963-1978)
(Giovanni Battista Montini)

John Paul I (1978)
(Albino Luciani)

St. John Paul II (1978-2005)
(Karol Jozef Wojtyla)

TWENTY-FIRST CENTURY

Benedict XVI (2005-2013)
(Joseph Alois Ratzinger)

Francis I (2013-   )
(Jorge Mario Bergoglio)

Matrimony

The Sacrament of Matrimony joins a man and a woman in a covenant for life with the same self-sacrificing love with which Christ loved his bride the Church.

The Sacraments

CHAPTER 7

Matrimony

How can I ever express the happiness of the marriage that is joined together by the Church strengthened by an offering, sealed by a blessing, announced by angels and ratified by the Father?...How wonderful the bond between two believers with a single hope, a single desire, a single observance, a single service! They are both brethren and both fellow-servants; there is no separation between them in spirit or flesh; in fact they are truly two in one flesh and where the flesh is one, one is the spirit.[1]

he second Sacrament at the Service of Communion is the Sacrament of Holy Matrimony. Much more than a mere contract or agreement, Matrimony is a sacrament that joins a man and woman in a covenant for life—a holy union created by God.

The love that exists between a husband and a wife is expressed in their desire for what is best for the other: to help each other get to Heaven and to raise Christian children who will join them there some day. The Sacrament of Matrimony is a great affirmation of human love and serves a vital role in the lives of two people, while also reflecting the unity of Christ and his Church.

> The sacrament of Matrimony signifies the union of Christ and the Church. It gives spouses the grace to love each other with the love with which Christ has loved his Church; the grace of the sacrament thus perfects the human love of the spouses, strengthens their indissoluble unity, and sanctifies them on the way to eternal life.[2] (CCC 1661)

Since it is a creation of God, Matrimony is endowed with special graces enabling the couple to love each other with the same self-sacrificing love with which Christ loved his bride the Church. This grace enables the spouses to perfect and sanctify their love.

Marriage is a covenant, by which a man and a woman form an intimate communion of life and love, endowed with its own special laws by the Creator. Although it is possible to speak generally about God's design, intent, and grace in marriage, the details of each particular marriage are mysterious. Why are two people drawn to marry each other at a particular time in their own lives and in history? Why does God grant children to a couple at one time and not another? Why does it appear that some families suffer more than others? How does God's plan for marriage help a couple to reach Heaven? What does God wish for a couple to accomplish at their particular time and place in history?

These are difficult questions, but in each individual case they are approached and answered with the aid of God's grace made present in a special way through the Sacrament of Matrimony.

> ### IN THIS CHAPTER, WE WILL ADDRESS SEVERAL QUESTIONS:
> ✠ What is the nature of marriage as created by God?
> ✠ What graces are received in the Sacrament of Matrimony?
> ✠ What does it mean that marriage is a vocation?
> ✠ What does the Church teach about artificial birth control?
> ✠ What does the Church teach about divorce and remarriage?

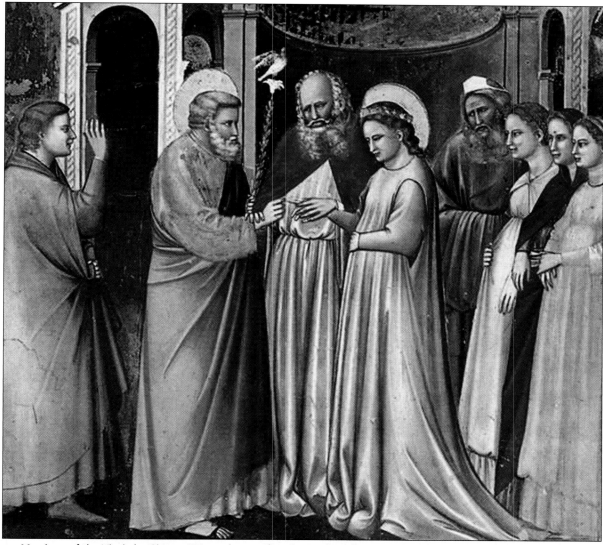

Marriage of the Virgin by Giotto. "My soul magnifies the Lord, and my spirit rejoices in God my Savior, for he has regarded the low estate of his handmaiden." (Lk 1:46-47)

THE ORIGINAL MEANING OF MARRIAGE

The intimate community of life and love which constitutes the married state has been established by the Creator and endowed by him with its own proper laws....God himself is the author of marriage. (*Gaudium et Spes*, 48)

By its very nature, love requires a relationship. Love requires an "other" and seeks union with that person. God, in his triune nature, is a loving community of Persons: Father, Son, and Holy Spirit.

In the Book of Genesis, we see how God made man in his final and culminating act of creation. However, Adam was alone and incomplete. He could find nothing in all of creation to which he could give the fullness of his love. For this reason, God created a companion for him. Created "male and female," they were enabled to become one flesh in a complete union of self-giving love. In referring to our first parents as husband and wife, Scripture indicates that they were created in a "state of marriage," and as an image of God, this unity between man and woman would be permanent.[3]

This state of marital perfection reflected God's love and intentions for man and woman. With the fall, however, the original condition of our first parents in the Garden of Eden, including the state of their

In Matrimony, God joins a man and a woman in an indissoluble bond and gives them the supernatural graces needed to live out their vocation to marriage.

marital union, was changed. Through their act of disobedience, Adam and Eve disrupted the natural unity that existed between themselves and God, and between each other. Rather than a selfless love, which gave itself entirely for the other, they began to look inward, toward themselves and their own desires.

The effects of Original Sin had serious consequences for marriage. Man's heart was hardened against the original love that existed between husband and wife. Among the sins that entered the world were disordered passions and desires as well as the ultimate betrayal of marital love, adultery. To accommodate this fallen state of humanity, the Old Testament tolerated the practice of divorce.

> For the hardness of heart Moses allowed you to divorce your wives, but from the beginning it was not so. (Mt 19: 8)

Throughout the Old Testament, we repeatedly see how the sinful actions of men and women failed to re-create the original beauty of unity and happiness that existed in the beginning. Marriage needed to be elevated once again to the original state for which it had been intended.

THE SACRAMENT OF MATRIMONY

> From the beginning of creation, God made them male and female. "For this reason a man shall leave his father and mother and be joined to his wife, and the two shall become one flesh." So they are no longer two but one flesh. What therefore God has joined together, let not man put asunder. (Mk 10: 6-9)

For marriage to overcome human failings and weaknesses, the couple must cooperate with God's gifts given in the Sacrament of Matrimony and follow the teachings of Christ and his Church.

As part of his redemptive mission, Jesus re-established the permanence of marriage to the original state, which it enjoyed before the Fall, by making it a sacrament. Christ knew, however, that simply declaring that marriage should be a lifelong commitment would not enable people to live up to this high expectation. In making Matrimony a sacrament, Jesus made available the graces necessary for married couples to live as God wants them to live.

> To heal the wounds of sin, man and woman need the help of the grace that God in his infinite mercy never refuses them.[4] Without his help man and woman cannot achieve the union of their lives for which God created them "in the beginning." (CCC 1608)

This grace is needed not only to overcome Original Sin, which all people inherit from our first parents but to overcome the sinfulness that is active in the world. Mankind experiences the evil caused by sin both within himself and in society around him. This "culture of sin" affects both partners in a marriage. Ignoring or rejecting God's plan for family life can cause a marriage to degenerate into discord and jealousy, leading to disunion. Marriages in which the grace of God is not present can easily go wrong, focusing on self-interest instead of self-sacrifice. For marriage to overcome these human failings and weaknesses, the couple must cooperate with God's grace given in the Sacrament and follow the teachings of Christ and his Church.

> The marriage covenant, by which a man and a woman form with each other an intimate communion of life and love, has been founded and endowed with its own special laws by the Creator. By its very nature it is ordered to the good of the couple, as well as to the generation and education of children. Christ the Lord raised marriage between the baptized to the dignity of a sacrament.[5] (CCC 1660)

Sacraments are efficacious signs of grace that transform and bear fruit in those who receive them. In Matrimony, God joins a man and a woman in an indissoluble bond and gives them the supernatural graces needed to live out their vocation to marriage. This vocation is for the good of the spouses and for their children, who are the fruit of their love.

Like the story of creation in Genesis, there are three parties in the covenant of marriage: man, woman, and God. It is God who creates the marriage bond and endows it with its own special laws. Once established, it cannot be broken by man. "By its very nature it is ordered to the good of the couple, as well as to the generation and education of children."[6] Christ "raised marriage between the baptized to the dignity of a sacrament"[7] and gives the couple his graces to help them keep their marital promises and to live out this permanent bond.

All of the attributes of Matrimony point to the same goal: a total gift of self to the other person. The graces given by God in the Sacrament of Matrimony make this gift of self possible. They enable the couple to perfect their love, to strengthen their marriage, to welcome children, and ultimately to attain holiness. This supernatural assistance from Christ also helps a couple to take up their crosses and follow him, forgiving one another, bearing each other's burdens, and loving each other with a supernatural and fruitful love.

In summary, the Sacrament of Matrimony

+ is a sacrament in which God binds a baptized man and a baptized woman together in a permanent union;

+ is an indissoluble covenant established by God, which may not be broken by man;

+ gives the actual graces needed to fulfill one's vocation to the marital state;

+ is directed toward the union of the spouses, their mutual good, and the procreation and education of children; and

+ enables a couple to cooperate with God in his plan of creation. (CCC 1604, 1640-1641)

MARITAL LOVE

The marital act is a renewal of the covenant of marriage and therefore a supernatural action blessed by God.

In the First Epistle of St. John, he tells us that God is love (cf. 1 Jn 4: 8, 16). God is all merciful and all giving. His greatest wish is to give himself entirely to us, whom he loves, and for us to give ourselves entirely to him, loving him with our whole hearts and minds. This love of God manifests itself in many concrete ways, especially in the love of Christ for his Church.

Perhaps there is no greater example of this kind of limitless love than the love between a man and a woman who have given themselves to each other entirely—body and soul—in the Sacrament of Matrimony. In imitation of Christ, each spouse gives himself or herself entirely and unreservedly to the other, promising unending fidelity through the marital vows and giving their bodies to each other in conjugal love.

The word conjugal comes from the Latin *conjungere*, meaning to join together.

While this love can be manifested in many ways, it finds its full expression in the conjugal, or marital, act. This aspect of interpersonal communion, in which the spouses give themselves completely to the other, is so integral to the married state that the marriage bond is not complete until it has been consummated. Furthermore, each time that the couple expresses their marital love in this manner, they renew their marriage covenant. In this way, the marital act can be seen as a supernatural action blessed by God, which increases the love that each spouse has for the other and strengthens the couple's relationship with God.

This love is eminently human, because it is directed from one person to another through an affection of the will. It involves the good of the whole person and can enrich the expressions of body and mind with a unique dignity, ennobling these expressions as special ingredients and signs of the friendship distinctive of marriage.

Such love, merging the human with the divine, leads the spouses to a free and mutual gift of themselves, a gift providing itself by gentle affection and by deed, such love pervades the whole of their lives....This love is uniquely expressed and perfected through the appropriate enterprise of matrimony. The actions within marriage by which the couple are united intimately and chastely are noble and worthy ones. Expressed in a manner which is truly human, these actions promote that mutual self-giving by which spouses enrich each other with a joyful and a ready will. Sealed by mutual faithfulness and be allowed above all by Christ's sacrament, this love remains steadfastly true in body and in mind, in bright days or dark. It will never be profaned by adultery or divorce. (*Gaudium et Spes*, 49)

By its very nature, marital love is directed toward new life and the mutual love and support of the married couple.

THE UNITIVE ASPECT OF MARITAL LOVE

There are two aspects of the conjugal or marital act in marriage: the *unitive* and the *procreative*. The unitive (or love-giving) aspect of the marital act is a physical expression of the one-flesh union that exists by reason of the Sacrament of Matrimony. It is a sign of the self-giving love that each spouse has for the other. This giving is so complete that St. Paul says, "For the wife does not rule over her own body, but the husband does; likewise the husband does not rule over his own body, but the wife does."[8]

By its very nature, marital love is directed toward new life and the mutual love and support of the married couple. This physical expression of human love is raised in dignity and blessed by God, and through it, the bond between husband and wife, which was established by the Sacrament, is renewed and strengthened.

> "Conjugal love involves a totality, in which all the elements of the person enter—appeal of the body and instinct, power of feeling and affectivity, aspiration of the spirit and of will. It aims at a deeply personal unity, a unity that, beyond union in one flesh, leads to forming one heart and soul; it demands *indissolubility* and *faithfulness* in definitive mutual giving; and it is open to *fertility*."[9] (CCC 1643)

The essence of the marital act is corrupted when practiced outside marriage. In the case of premarital sexual activity, the actions of the couple are trying to express a reality that does not exist. They have not given themselves completely to each other in the Sacrament of Matrimony. God has not bound them together in a permanent union. They have not received the graces necessary for marital life. Therefore, the physical expression of the marital act is a deception and a corruption of that act. Instead of renewing and strengthening the marriage bond created and blessed by God, it becomes a profanation of that which is holy. This is even more so in the case of extramarital (adulterous) relations. Not only is the action expressing a reality that does not exist, but it is a violation of the sacred bond that at least one of the partners has with another person.

True love bears fruit. Christian spouses are asked to be generous in their cooperation with God in his act of creation.

THE PROCREATIVE ASPECT OF MARITAL LOVE

True love bears fruit. Creation is an expression of God's great love for mankind. When a person responds to God's love and allows him to work in his or her life, he or she is transformed, producing good fruit, which shows forth in acts of love for God and neighbor. The love between a husband and a wife will manifest itself in deeds of love, respect, and self-sacrifice for each other and the family. This fruitfulness of marital love is especially appropriate when speaking of the marital act in which the couple freely cooperates with God's will for them in his plan of creation.

To some extent, the procreative aspect of the marital act is not really a second or separate attribute, but rather an integral part of the unitive aspect of marriage. The very nature of a complete one-flesh union between the spouses is directed toward the procreation and education of children. The Second Vatican Council spoke of the sanctity of marriage in its document, *Gaudium et Spes*, which discussed how Christian spouses cooperate with God in his act of creation.

> Marriage and conjugal love are by their nature ordained toward the begetting and educating of children. Children are really the supreme gift of marriage and contribute very substantially to the welfare of their parents. The God Himself Who said, "it is not good for man to be alone"[10] and "Who made man from the beginning male and female,"[11] wishing to share with man a certain special participation in His own creative work, blessed male and female, saying: "Increase and multiply."[12] Hence, while not making the other purposes of matrimony of less account, the true practice of conjugal love, and the whole meaning of the family life which results from it, have this aim: that the couple be ready with stout hearts to cooperate with the love of the Creator and the Savior. Who through them will enlarge and enrich His own family day by day.[13]

If the nature of marriage and the marital act created by God is directed toward the unity of the spouses and the procreation and education of children, then any act that intentionally frustrates or prevents this end of marriage violates the nature of marriage.

When artificial birth control is used, the couple, by a positive act of the will, intentionally removes one of the inherent meanings of the marital act, thereby corrupting the meaning of the act itself. By intentionally withholding the complete gift of one's entire being and by refusing to accept the gift of the other in his or her totality as a human person, they distort both the one-flesh and the resultant procreative meaning for which the marital act was intended. For this reason, the Catholic Church teaches that the marital act must always be open to new life. Any use of artificial birth control is contrary to the nature of the marital act and is, therefore, gravely sinful.

While the Church has consistently taught that the use of artificial birth control is a grave violation of moral law, this teaching was re-emphasized by Pope Paul VI in his encyclical *Humanæ Vitæ* (*On Human Life*) in 1968. In addition to explaining the moral reasoning of the Church's teaching, Paul VI prophetically warned of the consequences of widespread use of artificial birth control.

- Adultery (accompanied by a weakness of the family and divorce) would become more common.
- The general level of sexual morality would be lowered.
- There would be a dramatic increase in sexual promiscuity.
- Premarital sex would become widespread.
- Respect for the human person and especially of women would be diminished as the body would be viewed as an object of selfish enjoyment.
- Governments would impose artificial birth control on segments of the population.

The teachings of *Humanæ Vitæ*, along with the importance of the Church's moral guidance on many issues of human sexuality in modern society, was also stressed by Pope St. John Paul II in his 1995 encyclical *Evangelium Vitæ* (*The Gospel of Life*).

NATURAL FAMILY PLANNING

Although the nature of marital love demands a gift of self and openness to new life, it does not mean that every marital act must have conception as its primary or explicit intention.

Christian spouses are asked to be generous in their cooperation with God in his act of creation. In imitation of Christ, they are asked to live a life of self-giving generosity. However, enlightened by the teachings of Christ, and with generous and prayerful hearts, they must sometimes accept that their particular situation in life may discourage, at that moment, the gift of another child. Some of the circumstances that a couple might consider in making this determination are the physical or psychological condition of either partner, the particular needs of their family and children, and the financial resources of the family. While those circumstances that might discourage a couple from accepting the gift of a child are normally temporary in nature, they depend on the unique situation of each individual couple.

In addressing this point, the Second Vatican Council taught

> Let them thoughtfully take into account both their own welfare and that of their children, those already born and those which the future may bring. For this accounting they need to reckon with both the material and the spiritual conditions of the times as well as of their state in life.[14]

What is important to note about NFP is that when used in accordance with God's moral law, it upholds the dignity and sacredness of the marital act as an expression of total self-giving and openness to life.

If for legitimate and serious reasons, the couple, in a spirit of prayer and generosity, decides that, for the welfare of the family, they cannot accept the blessing of another child, they may, in good conscience, practice Natural Family Planning (NFP) for as long as those conditions remain. These methods involve the abstention from the marital act during those times when a pregnancy could occur. Modern science now offers several methods of NFP, which have proven highly effective.

> The practice of using infertile times for expression of marital love is available for those who for serious reasons need to postpone a new birth. This practice expresses in a concrete way the right relationship between spouses in marriage. It calls for a profound respect for each other and a communion of minds and hearts regarding the regulation of births....It respects human nature and moves beyond mechanical ways of expressing human love. The relationship between communion [unitive] and generativity [procreative] is preserved and a new level of understanding between husband and wife is promoted.[15]

What is important to note about NFP is that when used in accordance with God's moral law, it upholds the dignity and sacredness of the marital act as an expression of total self-giving and openness to life. In this regard, NFP is fundamentally different from artificial birth control.

CELEBRATING THE SACRAMENT OF MATRIMONY

In many ways, the celebration of the Sacrament of Holy Matrimony parallels that of Holy Orders. Both are Sacraments at the Service of Communion, and both indicate the beginning of a lifelong commitment to a specific vocation to which an individual or couple has been called by God. Like Holy Orders, the marital commitment is made well before the actual celebration of the Sacrament, and there should be a significant period of preparation for the couple.

Those preparing for marriage are preparing for a life of ministry within their own domestic church, that is, the home they will establish in their family. They are, like candidates for the religious life, preparing for a special Christian vocation. The couple will assume the primary responsibility for the support and development of their spouse's spiritual life as well as the education of their children.

The initial preparation for a Christian marriage begins mainly with the values that we learn at home as children. It is continued in the experience of friendships which we form in life, and even more so when a person begins dating. However, it is when a person meets their potential spouse and begins to enter

into a relationship built on genuine love and respect that this preparation is raised to a higher level. This is the time to discern whether this particular man or this particular woman is the one to whom you can completely give your love and dedicate the rest of your life. If he or she is, then the love that will manifest itself fully in marital life will slowly begin to grow. This love, which is based on self-giving and sacrifice, will show itself through acts of respect, understanding, and self-denial.

If the Catholic Faith is important in your life, it will also be a part of your relationship with a future spouse. Sharing your faith by participating in various activities in the parish, going to Mass, and praying together are just a few of the many patterns and habits that pave the way for a happy marriage.

If a couple discerns that they have a vocation to marry, the preparation for marriage, both spiritual and material, enters into the final stages. The Church requires all pastors to provide personal preparation for couples entering into marriage so that the parties may be predisposed toward holiness and the duties of the married state.[16] All dioceses require that couples asking for marriage participate in a

It is when a person meets their potential spouse and begins to enter into a relationship built on genuine love and respect that the preparation for marriage is raised to a higher level.

In the Sacrament of Matrimony, the couple promises God to remain faithful to their spouse for life. God blesses the couple and sends them countless graces, which enable them to live out their vows, encountering the joy that comes from the total giving of oneself to another.

suitable program of marriage preparation. This marriage preparation is an opportunity for the couple to discuss the responsibilities that they are undertaking and the meaning of a Christian marriage. It is also an opportunity for the pastor to speak to them about their spiritual lives.

Everyone is called to assist other married couples. We should pray for our parents, relatives, friends, and all people who are married (cf. CCC 1657). In addition, we can offer consolation to people when they experience difficulty in their marriages and even help with ongoing marriage enrichment programs (cf. CCC 1632, 1648).

REQUIREMENTS FOR MARRIAGE

In the same manner that each state or country has laws or certain requirements regulating those who can get married, the Catholic Church has developed the Code of Canon Law, which details the necessary conditions required to enter into the Sacrament of Matrimony. Its purpose in doing so is to ensure the validity of the Sacrament and the spiritual welfare of those seeking to get married.

The first requirement for receiving the Sacrament of Matrimony is that the parties are of the proper age. For the Universal Church, the minimum ages required are fourteen for the woman and sixteen for the man. The National Conference of Bishops in each country may raise the minimum age for Catholics in their country but may not lower it. Catholics must also meet the age requirements of the country or state in which they live. In the United States, most states require that the parties be eighteen years old unless they have the consent of the parents, in which case the age requirement is sixteen.[17] People may not be forced or coerced to marry but must enter into marriage as an act of their own free will.[18]

The Church requires that each party have sufficient use of reason. For example, if a person suffers from a mental or psychological problem, which causes a grave lack of discretion and judgment concerning the rights and duties that are essential to marriage, then he or she cannot receive this Sacrament.[19]

If possible, Catholics should receive the Sacrament of Confirmation before getting married. Additionally, in spiritual preparation for the Sacrament of Matrimony, the Church encourages the parties to receive the Sacrament of Reconciliation and the Eucharist.[20]

The Church also requires that certain other elements be present for a marriage to be valid. For example, a visiting priest or deacon must receive permission from the pastor of the parish where the wedding is to take place. If, for example, a couple had recently moved to a new city and wished their former parish priest to preside at their marriage, he would have to obtain the permission of their new parish priest.

Furthermore, the marriage ceremony must follow the accepted rites of the Church. A couple cannot simply design their own ceremony. Finally, there cannot be any canonical impediments to their marriage, e.g., one party has been divorced and has not been granted an annulment. Should any of these required elements be absent, the marriage is not valid.

REQUIREMENTS OF A VALID MARRIAGE

1. CONSENT

Matrimonial consent is a free act of the will by which a man and a woman, in an irrevocable covenant, mutually give and accept each other, declaring their willingness to welcome children and to educate them.

2. FOLLOW THE PROPER MARRIAGE RITES OF THE CHURCH

3. NO IMPEDIMENTS

a. IMPEDIMENTS ARISING UNDER DIVINE LAW

- **Impotence:** inability to have marital relations.

- **Existing Marriage Bond:** unless a Declaration of Annulment has been issued, a previous marriage is presumed valid.

- **Consanguinity:** all relatives originating from a common ancestor, up to and including the second degree (e.g., brothers and sisters).

b. IMPEDIMENTS ARISING UNDER ECCLESIASTICAL (CHURCH) LAW

- **Lack of Valid Age:** Church law requires men to be sixteen years of age and women to be fourteen years of age before entering the Sacrament of Matrimony.

- **Disparity of Cult:** marriage between a baptized Catholic and a non-baptized person.

- **Holy Orders:** those who have been ordained as a bishop, priest, or deacon.

- **Public or Perpetual Vow of Chastity:** those who have made perpetual vows in a religious congregation (e.g., a religious brother or sister).

- **Abduction:** abduction or at least unlawful detention of a woman for the purpose of marrying her.

- **Crime:** bringing about the death of a person's spouse, or one's own spouse, for the purpose of entering marriage with that person.

- **Consanguinity:** descendants from a common ancestor in the collateral line of the third and fourth degree (such as aunt and nephew or first cousins).

- **Affinity:** blood relatives (not relatives by adoption) of the spouse in a previous valid marriage in any degree of the direct line.

- **Public Propriety:** arising from an invalid marriage, after common life has been established, or from notorious and public concubinage, the impediment affects the man and the blood relations of the woman, and vice-versa, in the first degree of the direct line.

- **Legal Relationship:** arising from adoption, within direct line or in the second degree of the collateral line.[21]

MARRIAGES TO NON-CATHOLICS

Marriages between a Catholic and a baptized Christian who is not in full communion with the Catholic Church are called *mixed marriages*. For *mixed marriages* permission from the local Ordinary (bishop), not dispensation, is required. Marriages between Catholics and non-baptized persons (disparity of cult) are invalid unless a dispensation from the local Ordinary is granted.[22]

The local bishop may grant permission or dispensation for such marriages on the following conditions:[23]

✠ The Catholic party declares that he or she is prepared to remove dangers of falling away from the faith and makes a sincere promise to do all in his or her power to have all the children baptized and brought up in the Catholic Church.[24]

✠ The other party is to be informed at an appropriate time of these promises, which the Catholic person is obliged to make. It is important that the other person be fully aware of the commitments and obligations of the Catholic spouse.

✠ Both persons are to be instructed on the essential ends and properties of marriage, which are not to be disregarded by either party.

✠ They should marry in the Catholic Church. The canonical form (Church ceremony with at least two witnesses) is to be followed.

CELEBRATING THE SACRAMENT

The celebration of marriage between two baptized persons normally takes place at Mass. It is in the sacrifice of the Mass that Christ's love for his Church is made manifest.

There is perhaps no other sacrament that is greeted with the same anticipation by the recipients as the Sacrament of Matrimony. Along with the actual Sacrament, there are many cultural customs and practices that shape the ceremony and the accompanying celebrations. This can be a wonderful, joyous time in the life of the couple, but it can also be a trying and distracting one. Considering all of the responsibilities that come with the wedding celebration, it can be a welcomed relief to reflect upon the reality of the Sacrament that seals the love of the couple in the love of Christ.

Matter

The marital bond is symbolized in different ways, depending on the particular culture and rite of Marriage. In the Eastern Church, the priest places a crown upon the heads of the two spouses immediately after they make their vows. In the Western tradition, rings are exchanged as a sign of love and fidelity. The traditional wedding ring, an unadorned gold or silver band, is rich in symbolism. The circle represents the eternity of marriage; the precious metal signifies the elevated dignity of marriage; and the lack of adornments stands for the purity and simplicity of marriage.

Although there are many symbols of marriage, it is the spouses themselves who form the matter or material symbol in the Sacrament of Matrimony. The Sacrament begins when the couple exchanges vows as an expression of their commitment to each other and is completed when it is consummated by the couple through the physical expression of marital love. In light of this, the very bodies of the spouses, given to each other completely, become a powerful and efficacious means by which God's grace is poured out upon the new couple through the Sacrament.

Once all are gathered inside the church, the rite of Matrimony begins like any other celebration of the Holy Mass. The readings follow the same pattern as those used for solemnities with a reading from the Old Testament, a Responsorial Psalm, a second reading from the New Testament, and a Gospel reading.

Form

The form, or words, which are used in the wedding ceremony, is the repetition of the wedding vows. By definition, a vow is a solemn promise made to God in the presence of witnesses. In the Sacrament of Matrimony, the couple promises God to remain faithful to each other for life. God blesses the couple and sends them countless graces, which enable them to live out their vows, encountering the joy that comes from the total giving of oneself to another. The vows are made in the presence of an ordained minister of the Church (a deacon, priest, or bishop) and two witnesses.

Minister

Since priests preside over most of the other sacraments and play such a central role in the celebration of the Sacrament of Matrimony, it is surprising to some that the priest is not, in fact, the minister of this Sacrament. Even though the priest presides at the wedding, celebrates Mass, initiates the vows, and offers a number of prayers for the couple, the priest does not "marry" them. A bishop, priest, or deacon (or in special circumstances a layman designated by the Church) simply witnesses the vows of the couple.

The actual marriage of a man and a woman consists of their expression of commitment to each other through the marital vows. In this sense, it is the man and the woman who are the ministers, administering the Sacrament of Matrimony to each other.

THE WEDDING CEREMONY

The celebration of marriage between two Catholics normally takes place at Mass. The Sacrament of Matrimony is, in a supernatural way, bound up with the union of Christ and his Church, and it is in the sacrifice of the Mass that Christ's love for his Church is made manifest. Through the power of the Sacrament of Matrimony, married couples are empowered to participate in Christ's love, creating the indissoluble bond of marriage and obtaining the sacramental graces needed to perfect human love and to enable the couple to live a life of holiness.

> It is therefore fitting that the spouses should seal their consent to give themselves to each other through the offering of their own lives by uniting it to the offering of Christ for his Church made present in the Eucharistic sacrifice, and by receiving the Eucharist so that, communicating in the same Body and the same Blood of Christ, they may form but "one body" in Christ.[25] (CCC 1621)

The wedding Mass is a joyous and dignified celebration. The dress of the participants should reflect that dignity. The wedding songs should be in accordance with the approved liturgy, and the music should be carefully arranged, keeping in mind the nature of the Sacrament and the norms of the Church.

The Church is a place of worship, and the participants should conduct themselves accordingly. The guidelines for receiving Communion should be followed. Regardless of whether the participants are Catholic or not, they should display both good manners and respect for the beliefs of the Church.

At the end of Mass, before the dismissal and recessional, there is a three part blessing bestowed on the couple and all who are in attendance.

Most parishes allow photographs during the wedding ceremony and also provide ample time for pictures after the wedding. This should be done in such a way that it does not detract from the liturgical celebration.

The Rite of Matrimony

Once all are gathered inside the church, the rite of Matrimony begins like any other celebration of the Holy Mass. The readings follow the same pattern as those used for solemnities with a reading from the Old Testament, a Responsorial Psalm, a second reading from the New Testament, and a Gospel reading. These readings may be chosen by the couple from a wide selection of Scripture passages approved by the Church for use at wedding Masses, each reflecting the meaning of the marriage covenant. After the Gospel, the priest will give a homily, further explaining the mystery of Christian marriage, the dignity of wedded love, the grace of the Sacrament, and the responsibilities of marriage.

After the homily, all stand and the priest addresses the couple. He then questions them about their freedom to enter into marriage, their intentions to be faithful to one another, their acceptance of children, and their responsibility for providing their children a Catholic upbringing. These questions ensure that the couple intends to enter into a valid sacramental marriage, i.e., one entered into freely, for life, which is open to children.

At this time, the priest invites the couple to declare their consent. This consent may take one of two forms. The couple either repeats the entire vow, or the priest declares the vows for them, with each individual saying, "I do." After receiving their consent or vows, the priest says:

> *You have declared your consent before the Church. May the Lord in his goodness fill you both with his blessings. What God has joined, men must not divide.* All respond: *Amen.*[26]

Following the exchange of rings, the petitions are read, and Mass continues with the Presentation of the Gifts and the Liturgy of the Eucharist. The priest gives the couple the Nuptial Blessing after the Lord's Prayer, asking for God's blessing on the couple, their married life, and their children. After the blessing, Mass continues with the sign of peace and Communion. At the end of Mass, before the dismissal and recessional, there is a three-part blessing bestowed on the couple and all who are in attendance.

THE VOCATION TO MARRIAGE AND THE UNIVERSAL CALL TO HOLINESS

It is part of our nature as human beings to ask, "Why was I created?"; What is my purpose in life?"; "In what direction should I go with my life?" God, our loving Father, has a special plan for us. What a wonderful realization it is that God wants each one of us to play a vital role in his plan of creation, a role that was determined before the beginning of time.

Discovering God's plan for us, however, can be difficult. We must take time to pray, reflect, and listen. In doing so, God will reveal his plan, which will bring us true happiness in this life and in the life to come.

The Christian spouse gives himself or herself entirely to the other and to the children with which God blesses them.

The word "vocation" comes from the Latin verb *vocare*, which means "to call." The Church, in the Second Vatican Council, taught with renewed emphasis that each and every person is called to a life of holiness.[27] In other words, we are called to be like Christ in whose image we were re-created in Baptism. God calls everyone to "wholeness" by following his will. It is by following God's plan for our lives that we find our path to him in Heaven. The Church has traditionally recognized four such vocations: a vocation to marriage, a vocation to the priesthood and/or religious vows, and a vocation to the celibate life.

Those whom God calls to the priesthood, the religious, or celibate life have been given a great blessing. God is entrusting them with a special role in establishing his kingdom. The same is true of marriage, a covenant by which a man and a woman form an intimate communion of life and love. This is a special calling that God gives to the vast majority of people. Seen from the perspective of vocation, marriage is also a call to dedicate one's entire life to the service of others. When lived out as God envisions, marriage is a noble path along which spouses love and support one another, serving as living examples of the love that Christ has for the Church.[28] The Christian spouse gives himself or herself entirely to the other and to the children with which God blesses them. It is in the giving of self, an act of love, that one fulfills God's plan and obtains the happiness for which he or she was created.

> Husband and wife are called to sanctify their married life and to sanctify themselves in it. It would be a serious mistake if they were to exclude family life from their spiritual development. The marriage union, the care and education of children, the effort to provide for the needs of the family as well as for its security and development, the relationships with other persons who make up the community, all these are among the ordinary human situations that Christian couples are called upon to sanctify.[29]

The vocation to marriage, by its very nature, involves more than just one person. Husbands and wives are called by God to help each other in living their Christian vocation, the ultimate end of which is to be united to God and to be with him in Heaven. Together, husbands and wives help to bring up their children in the love and instruction of the Lord.

> God who created man out of love also calls him to love—the fundamental and innate vocation of every human being. For man is created in the image and likeness of God who is himself love.[30]

The Christian home is called the domestic church. The mutual self-sacrifice of the spouses will educate the children as to the true nature of love that was demonstrated by Christ.

Since God created him man and woman, their mutual love becomes an image of the absolute and unfailing love with which God loves man. It is good, very good, in the Creator's eyes. And this love which God blesses is intended to be fruitful and to be realized in the common work of watching over creation: "And God blessed them, and God said to them: 'Be fruitful and multiply, and fill the earth and subdue it.'"[31] (CCC 1604)

THE DOMESTIC CHURCH

The family is the first school of life. This statement applies especially to Christian homes, where children will receive their first instruction in the supernatural life as children of God. For this reason, the Christian home is called the domestic church—a community of grace and prayer, a school of human virtues and Christian charity.

Children will learn from the way their parents live out their commitment to each other and to God. If the family is oriented toward Christ and his Church, the children will learn how to live from a Christian perspective, personal priorities will be in order, and life will be viewed as a struggle to get to Heaven through complete involvement in Christ's redeeming love. The mutual self-sacrifice of the spouses will educate the children as to the true nature of love that was demonstrated by Christ. Children will see themselves as gifts from God and blessings to their family, rather than as burdens of questionable value.

It is at home that the children will learn about prayer and the practice of the Faith. From the example of their parents, they will understand the significance of the Mass in their Catholic life. They will see the importance of frequent reception of the Eucharist and Reconciliation. They will have the example and mutual support of a broad network of family and friends to strengthen them in the Faith. A Christian family will also teach its children how to approach the troubles of life. A family that is centered on Christ will bear life's sufferings more easily. Every family has its good and bad times, but if a family endures its trials with a Christian attitude, the times of suffering become redemptive and draw the family closer together. A Christian home, then, must be a place where love of God and obedience to his will are at the center of a marriage, where Christ is the head, and where selfless love can provide happy citizens for the Kingdom of Heaven.

The Church, in the Second Vatican Council, taught with renewed emphasis that each and every person is called to a life of holiness. God created marriage as an indissoluble union of two people that must be open to children, who are gifts from God. All actions contrary to this union are seriously sinful.

SINS AGAINST MARRIAGE

God created marriage between a man and a woman as an indissoluble union of two people that must be open to children, who are gifts from God. All actions contrary to this union are seriously sinful.

- **Artificial birth control** – The deliberate interference with the marital act by artificial means with the intent to prevent conception (e.g., condoms, birth control pill, IUD, etc.).

- **Adultery** – Sexual intimacy between a married person and a party other than his or her spouse.

- **Divorce** – A legal action that claims to break a valid marital bond. (A legal separation or a divorce is sometimes necessary to protect an innocent party or their children, but it can never claim to break the bonds of marriage, which are created by God alone.)

- **Polygamy** – The state or institution of an individual contracting more than one marriage or contracting marriage with an already married individual.

- **Premarital sex** – Sexual relations between unmarried persons.

- **Cohabitation (living together)** – The state of a man and a woman living together in a relationship that involves sexual intimacy outside of marriage.

- **Trial marriage** – Cohabitation for the purpose of evaluating what marriage would be like.

- **Same-sex unions** – The legal recognition of a "marital-like" relationship between persons of the same sex.

- **Improper sexual intimacy** – Improper sexual intimacy while dating grants to another the familiarity with one's body that is proper only to a person's spouse as a preparation for the marital act.

- **Abortion** – The deliberate elimination of a conceived life while still in the mother's womb.

While upholding the permanence of Christian marriage, the Church recognizes that some people find themselves in marriages that do not appear to be working. It recommends that these couples seek the assistance of the Church in counseling, along with recourse to prayer and self-sacrifice, to save the marriage. Making an appointment to speak with their local pastor or seeking help with a qualified counselor should be tried before giving up on a marriage.

However, there are occasions, such as situations involving physical abuse, alcoholism, psychological problems, or unfaithfulness, in which it might be best for a couple to separate or even to seek a legal divorce, understanding that a civil dissolution of marriage does not mean that the marriage is no longer valid. At times, this may be the only option available for the protection of the person and his or her children. This remedy, however, does not dissolve the marriage in the eyes of God, and in no case may the separated or divorced person date third parties with the purpose of entering into a second marriage.

Since the remarriage of persons who have a valid first marriage is a serious offense against God, those who enter into a second marriage, though they are still members of the Church, may not receive the sacraments except for Confession. Furthermore, the obligation that they undertook to educate their children in the Faith remains. The Church offers its members in this difficult situation her love, prayers, and support and encourages them to seek full communion with the Church.

WHAT IS AN ANNULMENT?

Marriage is permanent, because God established it so from the very beginning. The indissolubility of marriage is for the good of husband and wife, their children, and human society as a whole.

The civil government has no power to dissolve a valid marriage, but can only dissolve the civil aspects of marriage, such as ownership of property, or the custody of the children. Even when a civil divorce is granted, a valid marriage, in God's eyes, still exists.

The Church does not have the power to dissolve a valid, sacramental marriage that has been consummated. However, she may declare a marriage *null and void* upon investigation and on evidence that the marriage did not exist from the very beginning. The reasons could be one of the following:

✣ Lack of fully *voluntary and free consent*.

✣ Some deficiency in the *form of the marriage celebration*.

✣ The presence of an *impediment* that makes a marriage invalid.

The *declaration of nullity* (so-called *annulment*) is a very important decision of an ecclesiastical court. A very careful investigation has to be made by the court before that conclusion can be reached, ensuring that no valid marriage is declared *null and void* by mistake.

The indissolubility of marriage is for the good of husband and wife, their children, and human society as a whole.

The Holy Family by Coello.
Christian marriage is a sacrament through which God offers
immeasurable help of sacramental graces.

CONCLUSION

The covenant of marriage is one of the great joys of life, and it is also one of life's greatest mysteries. In this Sacrament, a man and a woman willingly agree to share a life in which their individual wills are put aside for the benefit of their bond and for the earthly and eternal benefit of themselves and their children. They share a love which, to the eyes of the world, seems impossible and idealistic. They share themselves in a way which, through the mystery of creation, may bring forth new life into the world.

An extraordinary commitment is made in marriage. Unfortunately, we see many faltering and failing couples. But great happiness comes from that commitment, which informs and shapes the lives and souls of the spouses. When confronted with the magnitude of undertaking in the Sacrament of Marriage, one can take comfort in the truth that Christian marriage is a sacrament through which God offers immeasurable help of sacramental graces to married couples. Through these graces, God assists the couple in the commitment that they made, allowing the spouses to grow in love for each other throughout their lives.

God watches over each married couple with loving care. As the former marriage rite states, "Nor will God be wanting to your needs; he will pledge you the lifelong support of his graces in the holy sacrament you are going to receive."[32]

SUPPLEMENTARY READING

EXHORTATION BEFORE MARRIAGE
Collectio Rituum, (1964)

DEAR FRIENDS IN CHRIST:

As you know, you are about to enter into a union which is most sacred and most serious, a union which was established by God himself. By it, he gave to man a share in the greatest work of creation, the work of the continuation of the human race. And in this way he sanctified human love and enabled man and woman to help each other live as children of God, by sharing a common life under his fatherly care.

Because God himself is thus its author, marriage is of its very nature a holy institution, requiring of those who enter into it a complete and unreserved giving of self. But Christ our LORD added to the holiness of marriage an even deeper meaning and a higher beauty. He referred to the love of marriage to describe his own love for his Church, that is, for the people of God whom he redeemed by his own blood. And so he gave to Christians a new vision of what married life ought to be, a life of self-sacrificing love like his own. It is for this reason that his Apostle, St. Paul, clearly states that marriage is now and for all time to be considered a great mystery, intimately bound up with the supernatural union of Christ and the Church, which union is also to be its pattern.

This union then is most serious, because it will bind you together for life in a relationship so close and so intimate that it will profoundly influence your whole future. That future, with its hopes and disappointments, its successes and its failures, its pleasures and its pains, its joys and its sorrows, is hidden from your eyes. You know that these elements are mingled in every life and are to be expected in your own. And so, not knowing what is before you, you take each other for better or for worse, for richer or for poorer, in sickness and in health, until death.

Truly, then, these words are most serious. It is a beautiful tribute to your undoubted faith in each other, that, recognizing their full import, you are nevertheless so willing and ready to pronounce them. And because these words involve such solemn obligation, it is most fitting that you rest the security of your wedded life upon the great principle of self-sacrifice. And so you begin your married life by the voluntary and complete surrender of your individual lives in the interest of that deeper and wider life which you are to have in common. Henceforth, you belong entirely to each other; you will be one in mind, one in heart, and one in affections. And whatever sacrifices you may hereafter be required to make to preserve this common life, always make them generously. Sacrifice is usually difficult and irksome. Only love can make it easy; and perfect love can make it a joy. We are willing to give in proportion as we love. And when love is perfect, the sacrifice is complete. God so loved the world that he gave himself for our salvation. "Greater love than this no one has, that one lay down his life for his friends."

No greater blessing can come to your married life than pure conjugal love, loyal and true to the end. May, then, this love with which you join your hands and hearts today, never fail, but grow deeper and stronger as the years go on. And if true love and the unselfish spirit of perfect sacrifice guide your every action, you can expect the greatest measure of earthly happiness that may be allotted to man in this vale of tears. The rest is in the hands of God. [Nor will God be wanting to your needs; he will pledge you the lifelong support of his graces in the holy sacrament which you are now going to receive.]

"No greater blessing can come to your married life than pure conjugal love, loyal and true to the end. May, then, this love with which you join your hands and hearts today, never fail, but grow deeper and stronger as the years go on."

SUPPLEMENTARY READING Continued

MORE ON ARTIFICIAL BIRTH CONTROL

The origin of the contraceptive mentality has its roots in a series of complex events dating to the beginnings of the twentieth century. Its influential advocates promised that once a cheap and dependable contraceptive became available, society would reap untold benefits. Among these were stronger marriages and fewer women and children living in poverty. It all sounded very promising.

In 1930, at the Lambeth Conference, the Anglican Church (Episcopalian Church in the United States) became the first Christian denomination to officially approve the use of contraceptives within marriage. (Before this time, virtually every Christian denomination had actively opposed the use of artificial birth control.) However, it was soon realized that such a solution would be impossible to regulate, and that contraceptives purchased for use in marriage could be used outside of marriage as well. Indeed, both civil governments and the general public were concerned that incidences of adultery and promiscuity would escalate, and, therefore, laws prohibiting the use of artificial contraceptives remained in place in the United States until the 1940s.

Since the legalization of artificial birth control, the strength of the family in modern society has seen a significant decline. First, the divorce rate has skyrocketed, increasing from ten percent at the beginning of the century to fifty percent by century's end. Where the advocates of birth control had promised an end to poverty, the opposite has occurred. As a consequence of the high number of divorces, there are more women and children living in poverty than ever before. In fact, in the United States, seventy percent of those living in poverty are unwed mothers and their children.

Secondly, once the procreative aspect is removed from the marital act, the door is opened to various types of relationships outside the context of marriage. For example, in recent years many couples are simply choosing to forego marriage altogether, opting instead for cohabitation. Additionally, many countries and some U.S. States are beginning to legally recognize same-sex unions. Finally, the availability of abortion became a necessity as a backup plan should birth control fail, leading to a devaluation of the sanctity of human life. It is undeniable that contraceptives have not made for better marriages; in fact, the institution of marriage and human life itself are being challenged.

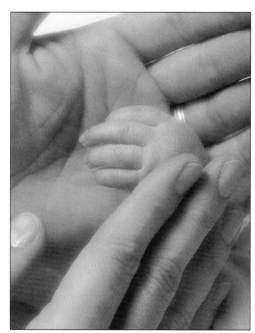

Once the procreative aspect is removed from the marital act, the door is opened to various types of relationships outside the context of marriage.

SUPPLEMENTARY READING Continued

GEORGES AND PAULINE VANIER

Georges and Pauline Vanier were made for each other. He grew up bilingual (French and English) and was a lifelong daily communicant. After earning his degree, he considered entering the priesthood, but when World War I broke out, he chose to serve his country and raised the first French-Canadian battalion. After being made colonel, he married Pauline Archer.

Pauline had contemplated being a nun, but when war broke out, she applied to the army as a foot soldier. Unsuccessful, she enrolled in nursing school and took a job in a military hospital. After their marriage, Pauline went with Georges to Geneva where he was a military advisor for the League of Nations.

As the Canadian ambassador to France in 1939, Georges' warnings of imminent war soon came true. Pauline was given her chance to show her courage, compassion, and complete trust in God in her wartime escape from Paris with her four children. When a German fighter plane crashed in front of her car on the jammed roads out of Paris, Pauline tried to save the pilot, but he was already dead.

With the fall of France, Germany set up a puppet regime known as the Vichy government, and Georges' warnings about this government's treachery proved remarkably accurate. After the Allied liberation of Paris, he was again named Canadian ambassador to France. Although the French capital was still considered too dangerous for women, Pauline persuaded the Red Cross to allow her to be their representative and made her way to her husband. While

Pauline provided food for returning refugees and established an information network to reunite them with their families, Georges worked on international agreements to aid Holocaust survivors, orphans, and the elderly.

The Vaniers' inner prayer life was the wellspring of all their efforts. They rarely made any major decision without first considering it in prayer. In 1959, Georges was made the Governor-General of Quebec. As he took his oath of office, Georges said, "May almighty God in his infinite wisdom and mercy bless the sacred mission which has been entrusted to me...and help me to fulfill it in all humility. In exchange for his strength, I offer him my weakness. May he give peace to this beloved land of ours and...the grace of mutual understanding, respect, and love."

Their efforts to improve Canadian family life led to the Vanier Institute of the Family, where research continues today. Their son Jean founded l'Arche community for mentally handicapped adults. After her husband's death, Pauline held weekly prayer meetings for the next nineteen years because she believed that "Faith, far from being outmoded or old fashioned, imparts a beauty, a richness, and a radiance that can be found in no other source."

These two Christians give all others an example to follow. Their lives were filled with heroic, loving action that came from a life of prayer. Husband and wife understood that God is a necessary ingredient in all our worldly undertakings and the rock upon which we should build lives of virtue.

VOCABULARY

ADULTERY
Sexual relations between a married person and one to whom he or she is not married. Adultery is opposed to the Sacrament of Matrimony, because it contradicts the equal dignity of man and woman and the unity and exclusivity of married love.

ANNULMENT
More properly called a "decree of nullity," a declaration by an ecclesiastical court that a presumed marriage was never valid.

ARTIFICIAL BIRTH CONTROL
The use of mechanical, chemical, or medical procedures to prevent conception from taking place. This is a grave disorder against the openness to life required of marriage and the inner truth of conjugal love.

COHABITATION
The situation in which unmarried individuals live together as "husband" and "wife."

CONJUGAL LOVE
A total, faithful, exclusive, willing, and unitive love that is not only physical but also spiritual. As such, it desires children and is willing to suffer for the good of the other.

CONSENT
Generally used in reference to marriage, the act whereby a man and a woman give themselves to each other, either verbally or through other signs, for the purpose of establishing their union.

CONSUMMATED MARRIAGE
A marriage in which the spouses have engaged together in the conjugal act that is apt for the generation of offspring.

COVENANT
A solemn promise or contract regarding future action binding on the participants and fortified by an oath, expressed either in words or in symbolic action.

DIVORCE
A civil dissolution of marriage. A civil divorce does not free people before God (they are still bound in a valid marriage); thus, an attempted remarriage would be adultery. In addition, divorce introduces disorder into the family and into society. It brings grave harm to the spouses and the children.

DOMESTIC CHURCH
An ancient expression for the family, recognizing the parents as the first heralds of the Faith to their children in both word and example.

FAMILY—The domestic church; a man and a woman united in marriage, together with their children; a community of faith, hope, and charity. Each member, in accord with his or her own role, exercises the baptismal priesthood and contributes toward making a community of grace and prayer, a school of human and Christian virtue, and the place where the Faith is first proclaimed to children.

VOCABULARY Continued

FAMILY
The domestic church; a man and a woman united in marriage, together with their children; a community of faith, hope, and charity. Each member, in accord with his or her own role, exercises the baptismal priesthood and contributes toward making a community of grace and prayer, a school of human and Christian virtue, and the place where the Faith is first proclaimed to children.

HUMANÆ VITÆ
The Latin title of Pope Paul VI's encyclical meaning, "Of Human Life," reaffirming that the use of artificial birth control is intrinsically wrong. This document has sometimes been called prophetic for its accurate prediction of the decline in morality which would occur if the use of artificial birth control became widespread.

IMPEDIMENT
A barrier that arises out of a person's condition or something he has done preventing the valid reception of the Sacraments of Matrimony or Holy Orders.

INDISSOLUBLE
The quality of an entity that cannot be divided into its constituent parts. This quality of the Sacrament of Matrimony means the union of marriage cannot be broken except by the death of a spouse.

MARRIAGE PREPARATION COURSE (Pre-Cana)
A course or series of conferences sponsored by the Church to assist engaged couples in preparing for sacramental marriage. It takes its name from the location of the wedding at which Our Lord performed his first miracle.

MATRIMONIAL CONSENT
An act of the will by which a man and a woman, through an irrevocable covenant, mutually give and accept each other, declaring their willingness to accept children.

MATRIMONY (Sacrament of)
The sacrament by which a baptized man and a baptized woman, in accordance with God's design from the beginning, are joined in an intimate union of life and love, "so they are no longer two but one." (Mt 19: 6). This union is ordered to the mutual benefit of the spouses and the procreation and education of children ("Be fruitful and multiply." [Gn 1: 28]).

NATURAL FAMILY PLANNING
The practice of engaging in sexual intercourse based on the woman's natural cycles of fertility and infertility. Intended for use to postpone a new birth only for serious reasons, it can also be used to conceive.

NUPTIAL MASS
The liturgical service consisting of a special Mass and blessing at which a couple exchange marital consent.

POLYGAMY
Attempted marriage between more than two people (one man and one woman) at the same time. Polygamy refers to a man attempting marriage with more than one wife; polyandry refers to a woman attempting marriage with more than one husband. This is a sin against the unity of marriage and forbidden by the Sixth Commandment.

PREMARITAL SEX
Also known as fornication, engaging in sexual intercourse outside the bond of marriage and condemned by St. Paul as a grave sin.

PROCREATION
The formation of new life through a married couple's cooperation with God and in response to their vocation.

UNITIVE
That dimension of the marital act which expresses love and intimacy.

VOW
A solemn promise before God to perform some act or make a gift or sacrifice; a solemn engagement to devote oneself to religious life.

WITNESS
A person who gives testimony concerning something of which he has direct knowledge. Every Christian is called to be a witness of Jesus Christ.

STUDY QUESTIONS

1. Describe the nature of the relationship that God intended for our first parents in creation.

2. In what way is the marital union an image of God?

3. How does sin affect the marital relationship?

4. Why did Moses permit divorce?

5. What was the intention of Jesus Christ in his teachings on marriage and in making marriage a sacrament?

6. What transformation takes place when a couple receives the Sacrament of Matrimony? What graces do they receive?

7. How can the marital act be viewed as a supernatural act?

8. What are the two purposes or aspects of marital love that are expressed in the marital act? Briefly explain the meaning of each.

9. Explain how the use of artificial birth control contradicts the total gift of self, which is an inherent characteristic of the unitive aspect of marriage. How does it contradict the procreative aspect of marriage?

10. Must Catholics have as many children as possible? Explain.

11. What is the difference between artificial birth control and natural family planning? Why does NFP preserve the unitive or the procreative aspects of the marital act?

12. Under what conditions can Catholics use NFP in good conscience?

13. Who are the ministers of the Sacrament of Matrimony?

14. What is a vow? What do the parties vow in the Sacrament of Matrimony?

15. Why is it appropriate for Catholics to celebrate their marriage within the context of Mass?

16. What is the purpose of the questions that the priest asks the couple before the exchanging of vows?

17. What does the word vocation mean? What is a vocation to the priesthood? What is the vocation of each of the baptized? Explain.

18. How is marriage a vocation of service?

19. Why is the family called the "domestic church"?

20. What are some of the things that children will learn in a Christian home?

21. Select three of the sins against marriage. Explain why each violates the meaning of the marital relationship.

22. Explain why Catholics who obtain a civil divorce but do not have a declaration of nullity are not permitted to remarry in the Church.

23. List the three requirements of a valid marriage.

24. Define an annulment.

25. What is the difference between an annulment and a divorce?

26. Can a person who gets an annulment get married in the Church? Explain.

PRACTICAL EXERCISES

1. Some people argue that if a person is unhappy in a marriage, he or she has the right to end the marriage. List two things that are wrong with this opinion. Consider what the marriage promises say about how long the couple will be together. Think about what a promise is, and who is involved in every union.

2. Explain the meaning of self-sacrificing love. Give three examples. John 3:16 may be of some help.

3. Read the Song of Songs in the Old Testament. What type of love is expressed?

4. The First Letter of John is often called the "Book of Love." Read Chapter 4:7-21 and see what kind of love is expressed there. Describe what the world would be like if everyone lived with this kind of love.

5. In *Humanæ Vitæ*, Pope Paul VI warned of the consequences for modern society if the use of artificial contraceptives became widespread. Analyze these warnings. Have they come true? What is their connection with artificial birth control?

Prayer for Married Couples

Almighty and eternal God, You blessed the union of married couples so that they might reflect the union of Christ with his Church: look with kindness on them. Renew their marriage covenant, increase your love in them, and strengthen their bond of peace so that, with their children, they may always rejoice in the gift of your blessing. We ask this through Christ our Lord. Amen.

"…To experience the gift of married love while respecting the laws of conception is to acknowledge that one is not the master of the sources of life but rather the minister of the design established by the Creator. Just as man does not have unlimited dominion over his body in general, so also, and with more particular reason, he has no such dominion over his specifically sexual faculties, for these are concerned by their very nature with the generation of life, of which God is the source." —Pope Paul VI, *Humanæ Vitæ,* 13.

FROM THE CATECHISM

1659 St. Paul said: "Husbands, love your wives, as Christ loved the Church....This is a great mystery, and I mean in reference to Christ and the Church."[33]

1661 The sacrament of Matrimony signifies the union of Christ and the Church. It gives spouses the grace to love each other with the love with which Christ has loved his Church; the grace of the sacrament thus perfects the human love of the spouses, strengthens their indissoluble unity, and sanctifies them on the way to eternal life.[34]

1662 Marriage is based on the consent of the contracting parties, that is, on their will to give themselves, each to the other, mutually and definitively, in order to live a covenant of faithful and fruitful love.

1663 Since marriage establishes the couple in a public state of life in the Church, it is fitting that its celebration be public, in the framework of a liturgical celebration, before the priest (or a witness authorized by the Church), the witnesses, and the assembly of the faithful.

1664 Unity, indissolubility, and openness to fertility are essential to marriage. Polygamy is incompatible with the unity of marriage; divorce separates what God has joined together; the refusal of fertility turns married life away from its "supreme gift," the child.[35]

1665 The remarriage of persons divorced from a living, lawful spouse contravenes the plan and law of God as taught by Christ. They are not separated from the Church, but they cannot receive Eucharistic communion. They will lead Christian lives especially by educating their children in the faith.

1666 The Christian home is the place where children receive the first proclamation of the faith. For this reason the family home is rightly called "the domestic church," a community of grace and prayer, a school of human virtues and of Christian charity.

ENDNOTES – CHAPTER SEVEN

1. Tertullian (b. 160), *Ad Uxorem*, II, VIII, 6-8: CCL, I, 393; FS,13.
2. Cf. Council of Trent: DS 1799.
3. Cf. Gn 1:27.
4. Cf. Gn 3:21.
5. Cf. CIC, can. 1055 § 1; cf. *GS* 48 § 1.
6. CCC 1660.
7. Ibid.
8. 1 Cor 7:4.
9. *FC* 13.
10. Gn 2:18.
11. Mt 19:4.
12. Gn 1:28.
13. *GS* 50.
14. *GS* 50.
15. *One in Christ Jesus: Toward a Pastoral Response to the Concerns of Women for Church and Society*, N.C.C.B. *Ad Hoc Committee* for a Pastoral Response to Women's Concerns, Origins Vol. 22, no. 29, 1993, p. 83.
16. CIC,1063 § 2.
17. CIC,1083.
18. CCC 1625-1632.
19. CIC,1095.
20. CIC,1065.
21. Cf. CIC, 88, 90,1066,1078,1083-1098.
22. Cf. CIC,1124; CCC 1633,1637 and Statement on the Implementation of the Apostolic Letter on Mixed Marriages, no. 14-15., N.C.C.B., November 16,1970.
23. Cf. CCC 1635.
24. Cf. CCC 1635,1637; CIC,1125.
25. Cf. 1 Cor 10:17.
26. *Ordo celebrandi matrimonium intra missam*, March 19,1969, (1970 Missal).
27. *LG* 40.
28. Cf. Eph 5:22-33.
29. St. Josemaria Escriva, *Christ Is Passing By*, 23.
30. Cf. Gn 1:27; 1 Jn 4:8,16.
31. Gn 1:28; cf. 1:31.
32. Exhortation Before Marriage, *Rituale Romanum*, (1962).
33. Eph 5:25, 32.
34. Cf. Council of Trent: DS 1799.
35. *GS* 50 § 1.

Liturgy
The Church at Worship and Prayer

The Sacraments

CHAPTER 8

Liturgy
The Church at Worship and Prayer

When he had taken the scroll, the four living creatures and the twenty-four elders fell down before the Lamb, each holding a harp, and with golden bowls full of incense, which are the prayers of the saints; and they sang a new song, saying,

"Worthy art thou to take the scroll and to open its seals, for thou wast slain and by thy blood didst ransom men for God from every tribe and tongue and people and nation, and hast made them a kingdom and priests to our God, and they shall reign on earth."

Then I looked, and I heard around the throne and the living creatures and the elders the voice of many angels, numbering myriads of myriads and thousands of thousands, saying with a loud voice,

"Worthy is the Lamb who was slain, to receive power and wealth and wisdom and might and honor and glory and blessing!"

And I heard every creature in heaven and on earth and under the earth and in the sea, and all therein, saying,

"To him who sits upon the throne and to the Lamb be blessing and honor and glory and might for ever and ever!"

And the four living creatures said, "Amen!" and the elders fell down and worshiped. (Rev 5: 8-14)

In the Book of Revelation, St. John describes the dramatic scene of the heavenly liturgy. In his vision, all of the angels and saints, indeed all of creation, participate in a continual worship of God. At the center of the image is Christ, whose Death and Resurrection has won salvation for the world. It is here at this heavenly liturgy that Jesus Christ, the Lamb who was slain, intercedes for mankind, offering his salvation to all who respond to his call, and it is here that our prayers ascend into Heaven like incense before the throne of God.

In the liturgy of the Mass, Heaven and earth unite. Christ, the Lamb who has been slain, becomes present on our altar. The eternal sacrifice, which he offered on Calvary, is re-presented and renewed, becoming our sacrifice, which we can offer with Christ to the Father. The graces earned for us by Jesus Christ are made available to those who wish to receive them. United in Christ through his Mystical Body the Church, we share in the communion of the angels and saints in Heaven. We, who approach his sacraments on earth, encounter Christ himself and are enabled to participate in the liturgy in Heaven.

In the previous chapters, we saw how Christ instituted the sacraments as the means of continuing his saving ministry, making it possible for us to receive God's grace through his Death and Resurrection into new life. At the center of each sacrament is the figure of Christ, who intercedes for us, touching our lives and pouring out the grace of God.

We encounter this great mystery of Christ's salvation in the celebration of the liturgy, especially in the Most Holy Sacrifice of the Mass. Thus, the liturgy of the Church is the very heart and center of the Catholic life. United to all of the angels and saints in Heaven, we join our prayers to theirs and sing:

We encounter this great mystery of Christ's salvation in the celebration of the liturgy, especially in the Most Holy Sacrifice of the Mass.

"Holy, holy, holy Lord, God of power and might, heaven and earth are full of your glory. Hosanna in the highest. Blessed is he who comes in the name of the Lord. Hosanna in the highest."

IN THIS CHAPTER, WE WILL ADDRESS SEVERAL QUESTIONS:

+ What is the purpose of worship?

+ How did Christ intend that we pray and worship him as a community?

+ What is liturgy? What is a rite?

+ How is the liturgy an action of Christ?

+ What are sacramentals and what are their purposes?

ORIGINS OF THE LITURGY

Throughout this book, the word liturgy has been used in conjunction with the celebration of the sacraments. For example, the Liturgy of the Mass is divided into two parts, the Liturgy of the Word and the Liturgy of the Eucharist. We have also referred to the liturgy of the Latin Rite of the Catholic Church and the liturgy of the Eastern Rites of the Catholic Church.

While most often referring to the Liturgy of the Mass, the word liturgy can refer to all of the rituals and ceremonies celebrated in the Church. For example, when a priest celebrates a Baptism, he does not compose an impromptu ceremony but follows the rite of Baptism in accordance with the approved liturgy of the Church. In this manner, each Baptism, Eucharist, Confirmation, etc., throughout the world is celebrated in the manner that the Church prescribes.

The majority of Catholics living in the West are most familiar with the liturgies of the Latin Rite of the Catholic Church. However, the Catholic Church has been blessed with a multitude of liturgical rites arising in different places and times, all of which contribute to the richness of the Catholic Church as a whole. Some examples of these different rites include the Antiochen, Alexandrian, Roman, Milanese, Gallican, Maronite, and Mozarabic Rites, to mention only a few. Although these liturgies contain many different customs and rituals, at their core, they all contain the same essential elements of worship that have a common origin in Jesus Christ and in the practices of the apostolic Church in Jerusalem.

St. Ansanus Baptizing by Giovanni di Paolo. St. Ansanus, called The Baptizer and Apostle of Siena, was martyred in AD 304 by order of Emperor Diocletian. As a missionary, he converted many to Christianity in Bagnorea and Siena, Italy, during the Roman persecutions. He was scourged, but survived; he was placed in boiling oil, but survived; he was finally decapitated.

The word liturgy itself comes from the Greek words *ergos* (work) and *leiton* (of the people). *Leitourgos*, or liturgy, originally referred to the public service that was performed by Greek citizens for the good of the state. When the Hebrew Scriptures were translated into Greek, the word liturgy was used to describe the public worship in the Jewish Temple, which was performed according to the Law of Moses. It was in this context that Christians used the word liturgy to describe their common worship.

Following the instructions left by Jesus, the first Christians in Jerusalem celebrated the sacraments. They met for communal prayer and adopted particular modes of worship. Later, when the Apostles and other followers of Christ left Jerusalem on their missionary journeys, they took with them these forms of worship.

As Christianity began to take root throughout the many regions that comprised the Roman Empire, liturgical practices began to absorb some of the traditions and customs of local believers. For example, by the third century, Greek, which had been the language used in Scripture and worship by the early Christians, was replaced by Latin by the Christians in Rome. By the fourth century, these liturgical practices, especially those found in the three great centers of Christianity—Antioch, Alexandria, and Rome—began to be written down in sacramentaries and liturgical books. All of the liturgies celebrated in the Church today have been handed down, largely unchanged, from one of these ancient communities.

Throughout the history of the Church, many practices and religious customs have evolved in different Christian cultures. They have influenced where and how we worship God, and they have influenced the objects, art, and architecture that help direct our worship. Together, these expressions of faith help the individual believer center his or her daily life on living the Faith.

EASTERN RITE ICONOSTASIS

The iconostasis of St. Joseph the Betrothed Ukrainian Greek Catholic Church in Chicago, IL.

An iconostasis is a screen of icons used in Eastern Rite churches which separates the nave, where the people meet for worship, from the sanctuary and the altar, where the Eucharist is celebrated. In the Eastern tradition, the sanctuary represents Heaven and the spiritual, while the nave represents the world and the material. The iconostasis, with its representation of Christ, the saints, and the angels in Heaven, represents the meeting of these two worlds, while at the same time emphasizing the division that exists between them. It is in the celebration of the Eucharist that the two worlds are united, allowing the faithful to approach the door of Heaven and participate in the heavenly liturgy.

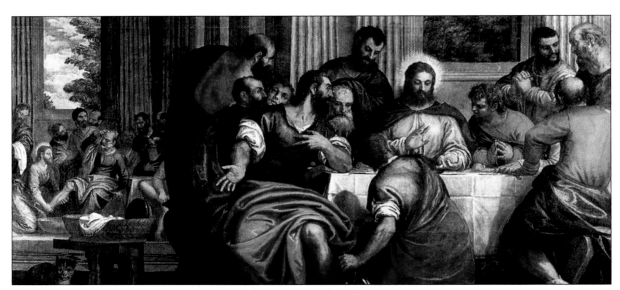

The Last Supper by Caliari.
The communal nature of the liturgy is seen most clearly in the Eucharist, in which the people of God are united together in Christ.

ACTIONS OF JESUS CHRIST

The sacraments are actions of Jesus Christ. Therefore, the liturgy is not a private act of worship but a public celebration of the Church. The communal nature of the liturgy is seen most clearly in the Eucharist, in which the People of God are united together in Christ. In fact, the entire life of the Church is directed toward the celebration of the sacraments, which are the source from which all her power flows and through which the Catholic enters into the mysteries of Christ.

While the liturgy of the Mass is fundamentally a public expression of worship, it is also a profoundly interior act as well. Liturgical worship demands that our hearts and minds be turned towards God. Each person is called to give himself or herself completely to Christ, so that through him the heavenly Father might be worshiped and glorified. In preparing ourselves for worship, we turn to the Holy Spirit, for it is his mission in the celebration of the Church's liturgies "to prepare the assembly to encounter Christ; to recall and manifest Christ to the faith of the assembly; to make the saving work of Christ present and active by his transforming power; and to make the gift of communion bear fruit in the Church."[1]

> The assembly should *prepare* itself to encounter its Lord and to become "a people well disposed." The preparation of hearts is the joint work of the Holy Spirit and the assembly, especially of its ministers. The grace of the Holy Spirit seeks to awaken faith, conversion of heart, and adherence to the Father's will. These dispositions are the precondition both for the reception of other graces conferred in the celebration itself and the fruits of new life which the celebration is intended to produce afterward. (CCC 1098)

> The liturgy is also a participation in Christ's own prayer addressed to the Father in the Holy Spirit. In the liturgy, all Christian prayer finds its source and goal. Through the liturgy the inner man is rooted and grounded in "the great love with which [the Father] loved us" in his beloved Son (Eph 2: 4; 3: 16-17). It is the same "marvelous work of God" that is lived and internalized by all prayer, "at all times in the Spirit" (Eph 6: 18). (CCC 1073)

When we seek union with God, the adoration offered to him in the liturgy becomes an effective means of our sanctification. In this way, the attention of believers to the liturgy—understanding, following, and meditating on its actions and meanings, and participating in prayer and song—is an active participation in the sacred mysteries of Christ's Redemption.

While the sacramental liturgy is celebrated by the Church, it is ultimately God who gives it meaning and makes it effective. Christ is at work in the liturgy of the Church, and therefore it is here where a person can have an intimate encounter with the Person of Jesus Christ. Through signs perceptible to the human senses, Christ touches our lives in the liturgy, giving us the sanctifying grace won by him on Calvary. Through the Church, the Mystical Body of Christ, Jesus communicates God's salvation, and in its liturgy, the sacrifice of Christ is made present and its benefits applied to our lives.

We can say that Christ is present in the celebration of the liturgy in several ways,

- ✠ **IN THE SACRAMENTS:** The sacraments are the continuation of Christ's saving actions in our lives. "If you forgive the sins of any, they are forgiven."[2] "This is my body…This cup is the new covenant in my blood."[3]

- ✠ **IN THE PROCLAMATION OF THE WORD:** "In the beginning was the Word, and the Word was with God, and the Word was God."[4]

- ✠ **IN THE PRAYER OF THE CHURCH:** "Where two or three are gathered together in my name, I am there in the midst of them."[5] As our high priest, he intercedes for us when we pray.

- ✠ **IN ACTS OF CHARITY (LOVE):** "As you did it to one of the least of these my brethren, you did it to me."[6]

THE LORD'S DAY

The Third Commandment instructs us to "Remember the Sabbath day, to keep it holy,"[7] because it was on this day that God rested from his work of creation, thereby blessing and sanctifying the seventh day.[8] The first Christians kept the Sabbath in accordance with their Jewish heritage. This would have involved attending the synagogue. However, as indicated in the New Testament, they also met for the Breaking of Bread (the Eucharist) on the Day of the Lord in celebration his Resurrection.[9] In time, the early Christians combined these two liturgies—the Liturgy of the Word and the Liturgy of the Eucharist—into a single act of worship celebrated on Sunday.

For Christians, Sunday is the Lord's Day on which we celebrate the Resurrection of Jesus Christ. Just as the original act of creation was finished on the seventh day, God's act of re-creation was accomplished on the eighth day. It was on this day that mankind was re-created as children of God in the order of grace.

In obedience to the will of God, as found in the First and Third Commandments and in the first Precept of the Church, and as a proper sanctification of the Lord's Day, Catholics are required to attend Mass on Sundays and Holy Days of Obligation and to refrain from work or activities that hinder the worship of God.[10]

> The first precept ("You shall attend Mass on Sundays and holy days of obligation and rest from servile labor") requires the faithful to sanctify the day commemorating the Resurrection of the Lord as well as the principal liturgical feasts honoring the mysteries of the Lord, the Blessed Virgin Mary, and the saints; in the first place, by participating in the Eucharistic celebration, in which the Christian community is gathered, and by resting from those works and activities which could impede such a sanctification of these days.[11] (CCC 2042)

As the principal day of worship, Catholics should plan their Sunday activities around the celebration of the Holy Mass.

> By a tradition handed down from the apostles which took its origin from the very day of Christ's resurrection, the Church celebrates the paschal mystery every eighth day; with good reason this, then, bears the name of the Lord's Day or Sunday. For on this day Christ's faithful are bound to come together into one place so that; by hearing the word of God and taking part in the Eucharist, they may call to mind the passion, the resurrection and the glorification of the Lord Jesus, and may thank God who "has begotten them again, through the resurrection of Jesus Christ from the dead, unto a living hope."[12] (*Sacrosanctum Concilium*, 106)

While the Lord's Day is a celebration of the Resurrection of Jesus Christ, Holy Days of Obligation commemorate important saints, events in salvation history, and mysteries of the Faith. Many of these feasts developed in response to particular historical circumstances and have since been retained by the

Church because of their importance in reminding the faithful of certain truths that the Church proclaims. An example is the Immaculate Conception, which was instituted to celebrate the fact that Mary was conceived free from all stain of Original Sin.[13]

Canon Law lists ten days as Holy Days of Obligation for the universal Church: The Nativity of our Lord Jesus Christ; Epiphany; the Body and Blood of Christ; the Ascension; Holy Mary, the Mother of God; the Immaculate Conception; the Assumption; St. Joseph; St. Peter and St. Paul the Apostles; and All Saints. However, the Code of Canon Law permits the bishops' conferences of individual countries, with the prior approval of the Holy See, to suppress certain holy days or to transfer their observance to a Sunday.[14] In the United States, there are six solemnities that are Holy Days of Obligation:

✚ **Mary, the Mother of God** (January 1)

✚ **The Ascension of Jesus** (40 days after Easter)

✚ **The Assumption of Mary** (August 15)

✚ **The Feast of All Saints** (November 1)

✚ **The Immaculate Conception** (December 8)

✚ **Nativity of Our Lord Jesus Christ** (December 25)

The Church's precept to attend Mass on Sundays and Holy Days of Obligation emphasizes the most fundamental way that Catholics live the Faith. By attending the liturgy of the Mass, Catholics are enabled to center their minds and hearts on the sacred mysteries of Christ's Redemption achieved by his Passion, Death, and Resurrection. By striving each week to actively participate in the Mass, the Christian makes Jesus the focal point of his or her life.

> The precepts of the Church are set in the context of a moral life bound to and nourished by liturgical life. The obligatory character of these positive laws decreed by the pastoral authorities is meant to guarantee to the faithful the very necessary minimum in the spirit of prayer and moral effort, in the growth in love of God and neighbor. (CCC 2041)

WHERE WE WORSHIP

St. Louis Cathedral, first established in 1718, is the oldest continuously operating cathedral in the United States and the seat of the Archdiocese of New Orleans, Louisiana.

Unlike the prescriptions found in the Law of Moses, the worship of God in the New Covenant is not associated with a particular place. In fact, the liturgy has been celebrated in homes and catacombs, mountain tops and battle fields, as well as in magnificent cathedrals. All the earth is holy and has been entrusted to men. Wherever the faithful are gathered, Christ is present in their midst, and they become the "living stones" that "build a spiritual house."[15]

Although the liturgy may be celebrated in almost any dignified place, Christians, from the earliest times, have constructed buildings dedicated to the worship of God. A church is a house of prayer in which the Holy Eucharist is celebrated and reserved. It is where the faithful gather to worship the Savior of the world. The visible church building becomes a sign of the Church and, therefore, of Christ himself. It is a sacred space, which should invite the faithful to recollection and prayer, and should be suitable for the celebration of the Sacred Liturgy.[16]

Additionally, a church is a sign of the sacred and, therefore, has an otherworldly significance. By entering the house of God, one symbolically passes from a world of creation, wounded by sin, to the world of new and eternal life. One stands in the presence of God at the doorway to Heaven. The visible church symbolizes Our Father's house, towards which the People of God direct their journey.[17]

TYPICAL PARISH CHURCH

ALTAR – A table of sacrifice where the Liturgy of the Eucharist is celebrated.

ALTAR CANDLES – These are two candles on each end of the altar, which are used throughout the Mass.

CONFESSIONAL – The confessional is a closet-like box (sometimes with two or three sections) or a confessional room where the priest hears confessions.

> "Provision must be made in each church or oratory for a sufficient number of places for sacramental confessions which are clearly visible, truly accessible, and which provide a fixed grille between the penitent and the confessor. Provision should also be made for penitents who wish to confess face-to-face, with due regard for the Authentic Interpretation of canon 964 § 2 by the Pontifical Council for the Interpretation of Legislative Texts, 7 July 1998 (AAS 90 [1998] 711),"[18] which states that "the minister of the sacrament, for a just cause and excluding the case of necessity, may legitimately decide—even if the penitent strongly demands otherwise—that sacramental confession should be heard in a confessional constructed with a fixed grille."

CRUCIFIX – Each Catholic church will have a crucifix near the altar. It is a reminder of the sacrifice of Christ, which brings us our salvation.

EASTER CANDLE – Representing the light of Christ, it is lit for the first time at the Easter vigil. It is used in all Masses throughout the Easter season and on other occasions, such as at Baptism.

KNEELERS – A short, sometimes padded bench, slightly elevated from the floor, which allows the faithful to kneel more comfortably at Mass.

MISSALETTES – These are small booklets that contain the prayers, songs, and Scripture readings that will be used at Mass.

NARTHEX – A porch-like room between the front entrance and the main body of the church.

PEWS – Pews are benches where the people sit during various parts of the Mass. In earlier times (and in some Eastern churches today), the people stood throughout the Mass.

PULPIT OR AMBO – The ambo is a raised stand used for reading the Scriptures. Some churches have an elevated pulpit, which may be used for reading the Gospel and for the homily.

SACRISTY – This is a small room off of the sanctuary where the vestments and sacred objects used in Mass are kept.

SANCTUARY – A part of the Church, often elevated, where the altar is situated. Because the priest celebrates Mass in the sanctuary, it is considered the most holy part of the church building. In the Eastern churches, the sanctuary is separated from the rest of the church by an *iconostasis*.

STAINED GLASS WINDOWS – These windows depict scenes from Scripture or from the lives of the saints. Devotional in nature, they were also used as teaching tools during periods of history when few people could read.

STATIONS OF THE CROSS – A devotion popularized by St. Francis of Assisi, these fourteen stations allow one to walk with Christ as he carries his Cross through the streets of Jerusalem from the Roman *praetorium* to Calvary.

STATUES, PICTURES, AND ICONS – These representations of Christ and the saints are used for personal devotion and as an aid in prayer. These sacred objects are respected out of love for the people or events they represent.

TABERNACLE – Of Old Testament origin, the Tabernacle was the dwelling place of God. It is used in a Catholic church as a receptacle to reserve the Blessed Sacrament, the Body and Blood of Our Lord Jesus Christ.

TABERNACLE OR SANCTUARY LAMP – This is a candle, sometimes set in red glass, which signifies that Christ is present in the tabernacle.

Kneeling, bowing one's head, and bowing the body are symbolic gestures of faith and reverence. Through the use of human signs and gestures, we turn our hearts and minds toward God in worship.

HOW WE PRAY AND WORSHIP

As human beings our soul is inseparable from our physical body. Through our physical senses we receive information, form our intellect, learn, and grow, and we express the yearnings of our soul through our bodies. "'Prayer is the raising of one's mind and heart to God or the requesting of good things from God'" (St. John Damascene, *De Fide Orth*. 3, 24: PG 94,1089C; quoted in CCC 2559). "Prayer is *Christian* insofar as it is communion with Christ and extends throughout the Church, which is his Body" (CCC 2565). It is not surprising that God reveals himself through the physical and that our worship of him involves our entire being—body and soul.

Prayer is essential for every believer, the *Catechism* teaches, "so that the life of the faithful may be conformed to Christ in the Holy Spirit to the glory of God the Father" (CCC 2558). Prayer may take on any of four forms: *blessing and adoration*, in which we bless the Father for his gifts and protection and worship him for his goodness; *petition*, in which we request favors and blessings from the Father; *intercession*, which is a petition made on behalf of another person; or *thanksgiving*, in which we show gratitude to the Father for his love and blessings, both material and spiritual (cf. CCC 2626-2643).

Moreover, prayer may take on any of three expressions: *vocal*, in which we use words, whether formal or spontaneous, with others or alone with God; *meditative*, in which we engage the heart and mind to grow in our understanding of Christ or the Faith; or *contemplative*, which is a prayerful habit of focusing our heart and mind on the Lord (cf. CCC 2705-2719).

The liturgical celebrations of the Church include signs and symbols, which refer to creation (light, water, fire, oil, color, and sound) and to human life (washing, anointing, breaking bread, kneeling, bowing, reading, and listening). These human gestures and elements are integrated into the world of faith, becoming instruments of the salvific and sanctifying action of Christ.[19]

In the New Testament, we see how Christ touched those he healed. In the same manner, the sacraments, as encounters with Christ, touch us both physically and spiritually. One example is the Sacrament of Baptism. As the minister of the Sacrament pours water over the body of the recipient, repeating the words of Christ, Christ himself removes the sin from the soul of the recipient, incorporating him or her into his Mystical Body, the Church. This encounter with Christ in the sacraments is expressed through the action of a minister (the person), matter (the sign), and form (the words).

THE SIGN OF THE CROSS

"At every forward step and movement, at every going in and out, when we put on our clothes and shoes, when we bathe, when we sit at table, when we light the lamps, on couch, on seat, in all the ordinary actions of daily life, we trace upon the forehead the sign." (Tertullian, *De Corona*, 4, ca. AD 200)

As indicated by the writings of Tertullian (b. ca. AD 160), the Sign of the Cross dates back to the earliest days of Christianity. In fact, St. John may have been referring to this Christian practice in the Book of Revelation when he speaks of the faithful having the seal on their foreheads.[20] In the Old Testament, moreover, we find a foreshadowing or "type" for the Sign of the Cross when Ezekiel writes of the faithful who mark the Hebrew letter *tav* (x or t), meaning a mark, a sign, or a cross, on their foreheads.[21]

As a sacramental, the Sign of the Cross is used by Christians (Catholics, Orthodox, and some Protestants) to bless themselves when beginning and ending prayers, and at other times throughout the day. It is not only a symbol of faith but a manifestation of belief in the Holy Trinity and in the sacrifice of Jesus on Calvary as the origin of all grace and salvation. Through it, our prayers are offered to God in the name of each Person of the Blessed Trinity—Father, Son, and Holy Spirit.

In the Latin Rite of the Catholic Church, the Sign of the Cross is made with the right hand touching first the forehead and then the chest, forming the vertical beam of the cross, and next the left shoulder and then the right, forming the horizontal beam. (In some of the Eastern Rites of the Catholic Church the last movement is from the right shoulder to the left.) This is done while saying the words, "In the name of the Father, and of the Son, and of the Holy Spirit. Amen."

There are also various Christian traditions regarding the positions of the hand while making the Sign of the Cross.

✣ When used in blessings, the first two fingers are often held upright, while the thumb and ring finger (or remaining fingers) are held together. This symbolizes the two natures of Christ and the Blessed Trinity and also forms the Greek letters IC/XC, which is an abbreviation of Jesus Christ.

✣ All five fingers may be left open (or slightly curved) representing the five wounds of Christ.

✣ The Eastern custom is to join the thumb and first two fingers together, while tucking the last two fingers into the palm. This represents the Blessed Trinity and the two natures of Christ.

  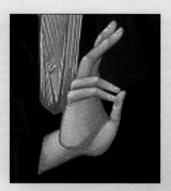

In Christian worship, we respond to Christ both physically and spiritually. Through the use of human signs and gestures (speaking, singing, kneeling, bowing, etc.), we turn our hearts and minds toward God in worship. Just as God comes to us through material creation, we turn to him in the complete unity of our body and soul.

> Making use of its symbolic resources, liturgy should arouse a keen awareness of the truths of faith. Gestures such as the elevation of the host, bows, and genuflections convey the sense of the divine presence more powerfully than does explicit statement. For the dignity and public character of the liturgy, ritual gestures, vestments, sacred song, and periods of silence should be built into the conduct of worship. In the spoken parts of the liturgy, the language, as I have said, should be suggestive and not overly didactic.[22]

The Sign of the Cross goes back to the early Church when people would mark themselves with the sign of Christ.

The following gestures are found in the liturgy:

- ✠ **The Sign of the Cross** is a symbol of our Faith and salvation, which is used in the blessing of persons and things. Its usage goes back to the early Church when people would mark themselves with the sign of Christ.

- ✠ **Striking one's breast** is used in the liturgy (*Confiteor*) as a sign of repentance, contrition, and humility.

- ✠ **Anointing** is a symbol of the Holy Spirit and the grace infused by the Sacraments of Baptism, Anointing of the Sick, Confirmation, and Holy Orders. The word *christ* means the "anointed one"; and in the Old Testament kings, priests, and prophets were anointed. By virtue of their Baptism, the followers of Christ are "anointed ones," having a share in the kingly, priestly, and prophetic mission of Christ.

- ✠ **Ashes** are a sign of humility, repentance, and resurrection. It is the custom to receive ashes on the forehead on Ash Wednesday.

- ✠ The **laying on of hands** signifies Consecration and supernatural action being performed by God. This gesture is used in the Sacraments of Confirmation, Anointing of the Sick, and Holy Orders.

- ✠ **Joining one's hands at the chest** is a gesture of prayer, humility, and submission before the Lord.

- ✠ **Standing** is a sign of joy and of man's adoration of God.

- ✠ **Kneeling** is a sign of repentance or adoration. In some cultures, this sign of respect is performed by bowing in the liturgy.

- ✠ **Sitting** is the attitude of a faithful disciple listening to the teacher.

- ✠ **Bowing one's head** is a sign of reverence often given when hearing the name of Jesus or Mary.

- ✠ **Bowing the body** toward the altar when there is no tabernacle and in the Profession of Faith is a sign of reverence.

- ✠ A **Procession** is symbol of the pilgrim Church. It occurs at several points within the Mass and in some solemn celebrations, in or around the church.

THE DIVINE OFFICE
(LITURGY OF THE HOURS)

The Mystery of Christ's Incarnation and Resurrection, which is celebrated in the Eucharist, is also commemorated through the daily celebration of the *Liturgy of the Hours*. Also called the *Divine Office*, the Liturgy of the Hours is a means by which the Church fulfills Jesus' command to pray constantly. Based primarily on the Psalms, it forms a song written by God, by which he wishes to be praised.[23]

The Liturgy of the Hours is a prayer of the Church, which is composed of readings from Scripture, primarily from the Psalms, and from the Fathers of the Church. This practice of reading Scripture and praying the Psalms throughout the day originated in ancient Judaism more than a millennium before the birth of Christ. The early Christians, many of Hebrew origin, continued this practice of praising God seven times throughout the day.[24] Later, with the rise of the monastic system, the Divine Office became an integral part of Christian piety. The particular times set aside for prayer, and the prayers themselves, became uniform, and it is in this format that the Church has received and continues the liturgy today.

The Church invites each of the faithful to participate in the Liturgy of the Hours according to his or her circumstances in life. For members of religious communities and for the clergy, the daily prayer of the Divine Office is an obligation. However, the Church earnestly invites the laity to join in its prayer, whether in the parish or in community, either as an individual or as a family. As a liturgical prayer, the Liturgy of the Hours, even when celebrated individually, unites a person to the entire Church. Through this constant prayer, rooted in liturgy and based on Scripture, God reveals his sacred mysteries and prepares the hearts of the faithful for an interior life of prayer.

> It is of great advantage for the family, the domestic sanctuary of the Church, not only to pray together to God but also to celebrate some parts of the liturgy of the hours as occasion offers, in order to enter more deeply into the life of the Church. (*General Instruction on the Liturgy of the Hours*, 14, 27)

THE LITURGY OF THE HOURS

Traditionally, the Church has designated six periods throughout the day that are set aside for prayer, plus an Office of Readings, which is usually said in the morning. The Morning Prayer and Evening Prayer are the two pivotal prayers of the day, while the Daytime prayers and Night prayer are somewhat shorter.

The OFFICE OF READINGS is comprised of Psalms, a reading from the Bible, and a reflection from the Fathers of the Church.

MORNING PRAYER (*Lauds*) is prayed early in the morning.

DAYTIME PRAYERS are prayed at midmorning (*Terce*), noon (*Sext*), and midafternoon (*None*).

EVENING PRAYER (*Vespers*) is prayed in the evening.

NIGHT PRAYER (*Compline*) is prayed before going to bed.

A medieval Book of Hours (ca. 1400). The Book of Hours was composed for lay people who wished to incorporate the Liturgy of the Hours into their devotional life. Reciting the Hours could consist of the recitation or singing of a number of Psalms, accompanied by a set of prayers and devotions, and the Litany of Saints.

LITURGICAL VESTMENTS

ALB – The alb is a white liturgical vestment, which comes down to the ankles and is sometimes girded with a cincture. Originally the everyday dress for men in the Mediterranean world, it has come to symbolize baptismal purity.

AMICE – The amice is a rectangular piece of white linen cloth with long tapes on two corners which covers the priest's shoulders. Now an optional vestment, it was originally a hood, which the priest used to cover his head out of respect for God's presence. For this reason, the priest will touch the amice to his head before vesting. It represents the "helmet of salvation" mentioned by St. Paul.

CHASUBLE – The chasuble is an outer garment, and its color corresponds to the liturgical season or particular Church feast which is being celebrated. An outer garment worn in the Roman Empire, it now symbolizes the yoke of Christ.

COPE – The cope is a long mantle, worn over the shoulders. It is worn by the priest at Benediction and processions, especially of the Blessed Sacrament. The cope is also used properly in place of a chasuble in liturgical celebrations outside of Mass.

HUMERAL VEIL – The humeral veil is a large, rectangular piece of cloth, which is worn by the priest over the shoulders. It is used in Benediction and when the Blessed Sacrament is being transferred, as in a procession.

STOLE – The stole is a long band of cloth, which goes over the priest's shoulders and hangs down in the front. It was a sign of authority given to officials in the Roman Empire and now represents the office of the priesthood. The priest will wear a stole when celebrating any of the sacraments.

SACRED VESSELS USED IN THE LITURGY

CHALICE – The chalice is an ornamental cup made from a precious metal or, if permitted by the bishop's conference of that country, other esteemed materials considered precious in that region. The materials must be suitable for sacred use, not easily broken or subject to deterioration, and have bowls of nonabsorbent material. The chalice's design represents the dignity of its use, which is to hold the wine that will become the Blood of Christ.

CIBORIUM – A ciborium is a container, similar to a chalice, with a lid, which is used to hold the consecrated hosts. It is made from precious metal, or, if permitted by the bishop's conference of that country, other esteemed materials considered precious in that region. The materials must be suitable for sacred use and not easily broken or subject to deterioration.

CORPORAL – The corporal is a square piece of white linen. It is placed on the center of the altar. The chalice and paten are placed on the corporal during Mass.

CRUETS – These are small vessels, which contain the water and wine to be used in the Mass.

MONSTRANCE – This is a large, flat, circular container made of precious metal and set on a pedestal. In its center is a round glass door from which the Eucharist can be seen when used at Benediction, Eucharistic adoration, and Eucharistic processions.

PATEN – A small plate on which are laid the hosts that will become the Body of Christ. It is made from precious metal, or, if permitted by the bishop's conference of that country, other esteemed materials considered precious in that region. The materials must be suitable for sacred use and not easily broken or subject to deterioration.

PURIFICATOR – This is a small rectangular piece of linen used to dry the chalice after communion.

THURIBLE OR CENSER – This is a container suspended by a chain, which holds burning charcoal. Incense is then placed on the burning coals. In reference to the Old Testament and the Book of Revelation, the smoking incense represents prayers going up to Heaven, and is used for blessings.

A cope (above left) is worn for Liturgies of Exposition and Benediction of the Blessed Sacrament. A monstrance (right) holds and protects the Eucharist Host.

LITURGICAL SEASONS

ADVENT – Like the calendar year, the Church year is divided into several liturgical seasons. It begins with Advent, which is a preparation for the Birth of Our Lord at Christmas. Advent begins four Sundays before Christmas.

CHRISTMAS – The Christmas Season begins on December 25 and lasts until the Feast of the Baptism of the Lord.

ORDINARY TIME – Ordinary Time begins on the day following the Baptism of the Lord and continues until Ash Wednesday, which marks the beginning of the Season of Lent.

LENT – Ordinary Time ends on Ash Wednesday, the first day of Lent, which is a period of prayer and penitence in remembrance of the suffering, Death, and Resurrection of Jesus Christ. Because it is related to Easter, the date of Ash Wednesday changes from year to year. The last week of Lent, *Holy Week*, begins on *Palm Sunday of the Lord's Passion*, and ends with the *Mass of the Lord's Supper* on the evening of *Holy Thursday*, when the *Triduum* begins. The *Triduum* continues through *Good Friday* and *Holy Saturday*, and concludes with the *Evening Prayer of Easter Sunday*.

EASTER – The Easter Season begins with the proclamation of the Resurrection at the *Easter Vigil*. The Easter Season, which follows, is eight weeks long. Important feasts during this season include the *Ascension*, celebrated forty days after Easter, and *Pentecost*, celebrated fifty days after Easter.

ORDINARY TIME – With the end of the Easter Season, the Church enters again into a period of Ordinary Time, which continues until the cycle starts again next Advent.

LITURGICAL COLORS

Depending on the liturgical season or particular feast that is being celebrated, different colors will be used for the altar and the priestly vestments. Local traditions may vary about what each liturgical color represents.

WHITE represents purity and joy and is used during the Christmas and Easter seasons. It is also worn on feasts of Our Lady, of angels, and of saints who were not martyrs.

RED represents blood and passion and is, therefore, used at *Pentecost* and at feasts commemorating the martyrs. Red is also worn for *Masses of the Holy Spirit* and for celebrating the Sacrament of Confirmation, as well as feasts of Apostles and Evangelists.

GREEN represents hope and growth and is used in Ordinary Time.

PURPLE represents penance and is used in Advent and Lent.

BLACK may be used at funeral masses and at masses for the dead, as well as on November 2, *The Commemoration of All Souls*. White or purple vestments may also be worn at these Masses.

ROSE may be worn on *Gaudete* Sunday, the third Sunday of Advent, and *Lætare* Sunday, the fourth Sunday of Lent.

Chasubles in liturgical colors.

A LIFE OF PRAYER

"Prayer is the raising of one's mind and heart to God or the requesting of good things from God" (St. John Damascene, *De fide orth*. 3, 24: PG 94, 1089C). (CCC 2559)

[It] is the living relationship of the children of God with their Father who is good beyond measure, with his Son Jesus Christ and with the Holy Spirit....Thus, the life of prayer is the habit of being in the presence of the thrice-holy God and in communion with him. This communion of life is always possible because, through Baptism, we have already been united with Christ (cf. Rom 6: 5). Prayer is *Christian* insofar as it is communion with Christ and extends throughout the Church, which is his Body. Its dimensions are those of Christ's love (cf. Eph 3: 18-21). (CCC 2565)

Prayer and Christian life are inseparable, for they concern the same love and the same renunciation, proceeding from love. Christian prayer tries above all to meditate on the mysteries of Christ: to get to know him, to love him, and to be united to him. Thus, prayer is essential in the life of a believer.

We learn what prayer is by reviewing the life of Christ. He taught us how to pray. When Jesus prayed to his Father, he was already teaching us how to pray. Just as Jesus' prayer life was rich and varied, the Church too presents us with many different ways to pray. In fact, it is the Holy Spirit, acting through the living transmission of the faith, that is, the Church's Tradition, that we learn to pray. We generally can speak of prayer taking one or a combination of four main types—petition, adoration, contrition, and thanksgiving. In petition, we humbly ask for God to heal us, to take away our doubts and fears, to help us become more virtuous, and to fill our own needs or those of others; in adoration, we praise God for his infinite goodness and his perfect attributes; in contrition, we sincerely ask forgiveness for our sins; in thanksgiving, we express our gratitude to God for having created us, for blessing us, for sustaining us, for forgiving us, and for redeeming us.

We can categorize prayer in several ways. In form, prayer may be formal, using memorized prayers like the Our Father or the Hail Mary; spontaneous, speaking to God straight from the heart; or a combination of both. It may be mental, spoken, or sung; it may be done alone or with others, in a church or in the privacy of one's home; one may pray sitting or kneeling with eyes closed or while carrying on ordinary tasks, such as working, driving, or performing household chores. Other times, we may simply listen for God to speak to us, usually following a period of prayer or meditation.

The Christian tradition comprises three major expressions of the life of prayer:...

VOCAL PRAYER, founded on the union of body and soul in human nature, associates the body with the interior prayer of the heart, following Christ's example of praying to his Father and teaching the Our Father to his disciples.

MEDITATION is a prayerful quest engaging thought, imagination, emotion, and desire. Its goal is to make our own, in faith, the subject considered, by confronting it with the reality of our own life.

CONTEMPLATIVE PRAYER is the simple expression of the mystery of prayer. It is a gaze of faith fixed on Jesus, an attentiveness to the Word of God, a silent love. It achieves real union with the prayer of Christ to the extent that it makes us share in his mystery. (CCC 2721-2724)

SACRAMENTALS

[Sacramentals] are sacred signs which bear a resemblance to the sacraments. They signify effects, particularly of a spiritual nature, which are obtained through the intercession of the Church. By them men are disposed to receive the chief effect of the sacraments, and various occasions in life are rendered holy.[25] (CCC 1667)

Sacramentals are holy objects, celebrations, and acts of piety that help dispose the faithful towards receiving grace from God. Unlike the sacraments, sacramentals do not confer grace *ex opere operato* (by the very nature of their being celebrated), but they do confer grace through the actions of the recipient. In this regard, their effectiveness is based on the dispositions of the individual. Simply put, sacramentals help direct our minds, hearts, and prayers toward God.

There are many kinds of sacramentals. Some are blessed or consecrated *objects* through which the faithful may receive spiritual benefits. These include crucifixes, holy images, scapulars, blessed candles and palms, and, generally speaking, all blessed objects exclusively used for the worship of God. Sacramentals may also be *actions* that the Church enriches with special graces. The recitation of an act of contrition, the imposition of ashes, exorcisms, processions, pilgrimages, and funeral rites are some examples.

Sacramentals do not confer the grace of the Holy Spirit in the way that the sacraments do, but by the Church's prayer, they prepare us to receive grace and dispose us to cooperate with it. "For well-disposed members of the faithful, the liturgy of the sacraments and sacramentals sanctifies almost every event of their lives with the divine grace which flows from the Paschal mystery of the Passion, Death, and Resurrection of Christ. From this source all sacraments and sacramentals draw their power. There is scarcely any proper use of material things which cannot be thus directed toward the sanctification of men and the praise of God."[26] (CCC 1670)

Holy Water

A large container of holy water allows the faithful to bring holy water to their homes.

One of the most common sacramentals is holy water. The presence of holy water in churches, homes, and in a number of Catholic rituals serves as a reminder of the waters of Baptism through which we were first joined to Christ. When we enter a church and place our hand in the holy water font, making the Sign of the Cross, we are recalling our Baptism and asking God for purity as we approach the celebration of the sacred mysteries. At a funeral, when the priest blesses the coffin with holy water, it is a reminder of the Baptism of the deceased and the hope of new life in Christ.

Most churches have a large container of holy water available for the faithful. This allows them to bring a suitable container to fill with holy water for use in blessing their homes. Many Christian homes will have a small holy water font, which can be hung on the wall. It is a wonderful custom to bless yourself when entering or leaving a home, or before going to bed at night. It is also a custom to ask a priest to bless the home with holy water when he visits. Parents may also do the same, asking God to bless their home and family.

Statues, Icons, and Other Holy Images

To admire the icons and the great masterpieces of Christian art in general, leads us on an inner way, a way of overcoming ourselves; thus in this purification of vision that is a purification of the heart, it reveals the beautiful to us, or at least a ray of it. In this way we are brought into contact with the power of the truth. (Message from Cardinal Joseph Ratzinger, August 2002.)

Most homes have photographs of loved ones displayed on walls and tables throughout the house. These pictures remind us of our loved ones and bring back special memories long after they are gone. Some remind us of our roots and the sacrifices made by our ancestors. In a similar manner, the statues and images found in many Catholic churches form a family history of the Church. These are reminders of our predecessors in the Faith who lived exemplary lives, usually in the face of great difficulty. The presence of these images in our places of worship reminds us that we too are called to the same faithfulness to Jesus, so that we can join him and the saints in Heaven one day.

In the Old Testament, we read how the Law of Moses required images of the cherubim and seraphim to be placed in the Temple.[27] The image of God, on the other hand, was not present in the Temple. It would have been impossible at that time to depict God, because he had not revealed himself in a physical form. When God became man in the Person of Jesus Christ, it became possible to portray the human image of God.

Religious symbols and images of Christ and the saints have been used in Christian places of worship since the beginning of Christianity. The catacombs, where ancient Christians gathered in times of persecution, are filled with religious art and serve as a powerful reminder of the important role that sacred art has always played in the life of the Church. These are visual reminders of the reality of the Communion of Saints and our participation in the heavenly liturgy.

Our Lady (Theotokos) of Vladimir Icon by Andrei Rublev. The *Theotokos* (Mary, the "Bearer of God") is regarded as the holy protectress of Russia.

However, in the eighth century, the Church in the East began to experience resistance to the use of religious images. Some people, known as *iconoclasts* or "image breakers," opposed the use of religious images, claiming that they were a form of idolatry. This movement was influenced by Islam, which prohibited the use of religious art depicting human beings. After much turmoil, the Second Council of Nicaea met to resolve the issue.

The Council firmly restated the ancient Christian belief that worship, called *adoration*, belongs to God and to God alone. However, *veneration*, which is a profound reverence and respect, can be given both to persons and to sacred objects. The iconoclastic debate was settled for nearly 800 years until it was revived again during the Protestant Reformation, when some of the emerging Protestant communities rejected the use of religious images and destroyed many sacred images in churches throughout Europe.

The Rosary

The Rosary is one of the most readily recognized Catholic symbols. The name itself comes from the Latin word *rosarium*, which means a "rose garden." In earlier times, when books were scarce, the possibility of the average person owning a Bible or a prayer book, or even knowing how to read, was remote. For this reason, those charged with teaching religion found many innovative ways to impart the Faith to the average man and woman. The Rosary was one such way.

St. Dominic (1170-1221) and the Dominican friars helped popularize the devotion to the Holy Rosary, encouraging the faithful to pray it often. It had long been the practice of the monks to recite the 150 Psalms in the Divine Office. However, many of the faithful, who could not afford books or could not read, began the practice of reciting 150 Our Fathers as a substitute for the Psalms. As devotion to Our Lady increased, some of the Our Father's were changed to Hail Mary's. Later, a meditation on the life of Christ accompanied the recitation of the prayers. Thus, the Rosary became a wonderful tool of faith and prayer. It provided a simple means for people to pray throughout the day and to meditate on the events of our salvation in the life of Jesus.

THE HOLY ROSARY

THE JOYFUL MYSTERIES (MONDAY AND SATURDAY)

The Annunciation of Gabriel to Mary (Lk 1: 26-38)

The Visitation of Mary to Elizabeth (Lk 1: 39-56)

The Birth of Our Lord (Lk 2: 1-21)

The Presentation of Our Lord in the Temple (Lk 2: 22-38)

The Finding of Our Lord in the Temple (Lk 2: 41-52)

THE LUMINOUS MYSTERIES (THURSDAY)

The Baptism of Our Lord in the River Jordan (Mt 3: 13-16)

The Wedding at Cana, when Christ manifested Himself (Jn 2: 1-11)

The Proclamation of the Kingdom of God, and the Call to Repentance (Mk 1: 14-15)

The Transfiguration of Our Lord (Mt 17: 1-8)

The Last Supper, when Our Lord gave us the Holy Eucharist (Mt 26: 26-29)

THE SORROWFUL MYSTERIES (TUESDAY AND FRIDAY)

The Agony of our Lord in the Garden (Mt 26: 36-56)

Our Lord is Scourged at the Pillar (Mt 27: 26)

Our Lord is Crowned with Thorns (Mt 27: 27-31)

Our Lord Carries the Cross to Calvary (Mt 27: 32)

The Crucifixion of Our Lord (Mt 27: 33-56)

THE GLORIOUS MYSTERIES (WEDNESDAY AND SUNDAY)

The Glorious Resurrection of Our Lord (Jn 20: 1-29)

The Ascension of Our Lord into Heaven (Lk 24: 36-53)

The Descent of the Holy Spirit at Pentecost (Acts 2: 1-41)

The Assumption of Mary into Heaven (See Ps 16: 9-11)

The Coronation of Mary as Queen of Heaven and Earth (See Rev 12: 1)

Pope St. John Paul II

"Announcing each mystery, and perhaps even using a suitable icon to portray it, is as it were *to open up a scenario* on which to focus our attention. The words direct the imagination and the mind towards a particular episode or moment in the life of Christ. In the Church's traditional spirituality, the veneration of icons and the many devotions appealing to the senses, as well as the method of prayer proposed by Saint Ignatius of Loyola in the Spiritual Exercises, make use of visual and imaginative elements (the *compositio loci*), judged to be of great help in concentrating the mind on the particular mystery. This is a methodology, moreover, which *corresponds to the inner logic of the Incarnation*: in Jesus, God wanted to take on human features. It is through his bodily reality that we are led into contact with the mystery of his divinity." (Pope St. John Paul II, Apostolic Letter *Rosarium Virginis Mariæ*, 29)

Station of the Cross, No. 8: Jesus Meets the Women of Jerusalem. Through the sacramental action of walking the Stations of the Cross, Christians retrace the steps of Jesus to Calvary, pray, and meditate on his last hours of life.

Stations of the Cross

For many Catholics, the Stations of the Cross are a regular Lenten devotion. This ancient custom of retracing the steps of Christ to Calvary probably began in the weeks following Jesus' Death and Resurrection. By the fourth century, St. Jerome wrote of the large number of pilgrims coming to visit the holy places.

STATIONS OF THE CROSS

1. Jesus Is Condemned to Death
2. Jesus Carries the Cross
3. Jesus Falls the First Time
4. Jesus Meets His Mother Mary
5. Simon of Cyrene Helps Jesus to Carry the Cross
6. Veronica Wipes the Face of Jesus
7. Jesus Falls the Second Time
8. Jesus Meets the Women of Jerusalem
9. Jesus Falls the Third Time
10. Jesus Is Stripped of His Garments
11. Jesus Is Nailed to the Cross
12. Jesus Dies on the Cross
13. Jesus' Body Is Taken Down from the Cross
14. Jesus' Body Is Placed in the Tomb
15. The Resurrection

At first, there were no set stations or points of meditation. People simply walked the path that Jesus took as he carried his Cross and meditated upon the events that unfolded during those last hours of his life. Later, distinct stations were added, although the number often varied. At one time, for example, some of the Franciscan friars in Jerusalem had set the number of Stations at thirty-one.

Following the Muslim conquest of the Holy Land, Christians found it more difficult to make the pilgrimage there. However, still desiring to retrace the steps of Jesus to Calvary, many began to re-create the Stations of the Cross in their own churches.

In 1219, St. Francis, whose holiness had won a friendship with the reigning sultan, obtained the right of safe passage for himself and his followers to the Holy Land. The Franciscan friars were made the custodians of the Christian holy sites in Jerusalem. Like St. Dominic with the Rosary, St. Francis did not invent the Stations of the Cross, but he did more than anyone else to promote their use in prayer and pious devotion. For this reason, the Stations of the Cross are often associated with the Franciscan Order.

In 1731, Pope Clement XII set the number of the Stations at fourteen and attached a plenary indulgence to their practice. Pope St. John Paul II later added a fifteenth station celebrating the Resurrection of Christ. As they are not an official ritual of the Church, the Stations of the Cross may be celebrated in any number of ways. People, for example, may simply go to a church, stop in front of each station, and meditate for a time on what Jesus endured at that particular point, or they may use one of the many excellent booklets that are available.

Relics and Their Veneration

A relic is the earthly remains of a saint or a personal item associated with him or her. In the early Church, the faithful would celebrate Mass at the tombs of the saints and martyrs. As Christianity became the official religion of the Roman Empire and as Christians began to have their own church buildings, they sometimes transferred the remains of the saints and martyrs for reburial under the altar of the church in a place called a crypt. The church would then be named for that saint. For example, St. Peter's Basilica in Rome is built over the burial place of St. Peter the Apostle. As the Christian Faith grew and spread, the relics of the saints were distributed throughout the Christian world.

Relics have always been seen as a kind of bridge between this world and the next. They might be likened to a valued heirloom, such as a piece of jewelry that belonged to a deceased mother that holds sentimental value. When her daughter wears that ring or brooch, she feels a special attachment to her mother. In like manner, relics connect us with the saints by giving us a concrete reminder of them.

The Tomb of St. Peter under the the Basilica of St. Peter's in Rome. In a radio broadcast on December 23, 1950, Pope Pius XII announced to the world the discovery of St. Peter's tomb.

Medals and Scapulars

The oldest Christian medal found by archeologists is from the fourth century and belonged to a woman named Successa. Along with her name, it is engraved with a representation of St. Lawrence, who was martyred by being roasted alive, and contains the Christian symbols *chi-rho* and *alpha and omega*.

The Miraculous Medal was the result of a number of apparitions of the Blessed Mother to St. Catherine Laboure in the early 1800s.

Today, many Christians continue this ancient practice by wearing a medal depicting their patron saint or another holy person. For example, St. Christopher medals are worn by people who seek his intercession for safety in their travels. One of the best known medals is the Miraculous Medal, which was the result of a number of apparitions of the Blessed Mother to St. Catherine Laboure in the early 1800s. The use of these or any other medal is a reminder of the intercessory power of the prayers of the given saint. People will often buy medals as gifts for graduations, weddings, or other important events, having them blessed first by a priest before they are given. Properly understood, medals can be a means of increasing one's faith.

The origin of the scapular comes from the "habit" worn by men and women in religious orders. It is a long piece of shoulder-wide cloth with a hole in the middle that fits over the head. The habit drapes over the chest, abdomen, and back of the wearer. In time, this symbol of the religious habit was reduced in size and adapted for use by the laity. Today, it is normally made of two small rectangular pieces of cloth connected by strings and worn over the shoulders, hanging down over the chest and back of the wearer.

Besides those taking religious vows, scapulars are worn by laity belonging to third orders (i.e., lay branches of religious orders) and members of confraternities who wish to express devotion to Our Lady. The obligations most often associated with wearing a scapular include: wearing the scapular continually; observing chastity according to one's state in life; and reciting the Little Office of the Blessed Virgin Mary. The obligation of reciting the Little Office may be substituted with the Holy Rosary or some other pious deed.

One of the most popular scapulars in the Church today is the Brown Scapular of Mount Carmel. When Our Lady appeared to St. Simon Stock in the thirteenth century, she gave him a message that those who died in the Carmelite habit (i.e., those who kept the vows or promises made at the time of their investiture) would go to Heaven. Out of devotion to Our Lady and wishing to obtain the promises of her message, many people have joined the Confraternity of Our Lady of Mount Carmel and wear the brown scapular.

(above right) The Brown Scapular of Our Lady of Mount Carmel adapted for use by the laity.

(left) *Our Lady of Mount Carmel* by Novelli. Our Lady appeared to St. Simon Stock in the thirteenth century. In this painting, Our Lady holds the Brown Scapular.

Pilgrims on the road to Santiago de Compostela. Pilgrims walk for months to reach Santiago, the second most visited pilgrimage site in the world after Rome. *(See story on next page.)*

Pilgrimages, Processions, and Visits to Sacred Places

The practice of making a pilgrimage or religious journey to a sacred place is as old as Christianity itself. Throughout Christian history, people of faith have made special trips to shrines, churches, and holy places such as Jerusalem, Rome, and Santiago de Compostela to draw closer to God. Today, pilgrimage sites such as Lourdes, Fatima, or the Basilica of Our Lady of Guadalupe attract millions of pilgrims annually, and pilgrimages to Rome and the Holy Land continue to be very popular.

Processions are also commonplace in the Catholic world. In many places, on the feast day of the patron saint of a given parish, a large community celebration will be held. During this celebration, people process through the streets carrying a statue of their patron saint.

Eucharistic processions are also widespread expressions of faith in the Real Presence of Christ in the Blessed Sacrament. These processions may be held at any time but are most often celebrated on the Feast of Corpus Christi. In such processions, the Blessed Sacrament is carried in a monstrance through the streets, or inside a church, as people sing songs of adoration and pray. Holy Week processions are held in many places to commemorate Jesus' walk to Calvary and his crucifixion. The great variety of processions is a living testament to how the Catholic Faith has been adopted by so many peoples and cultures.

Feast of Corpus Christi procession through the streets of a town in Poland.

SANTIAGO de COMPOSTELA

At the end of the first millennium, Jerusalem and Rome had long been considered the two most important pilgrimage destinations in Christianity. However, as travel to Jerusalem became more difficult, other places of pilgrimage began to arise. One of these, the Cathedral of Santiago de Compostela in

northern Spain, became the most important pilgrimage site for much of Europe, and even today, ten centuries later, Santiago, after Rome, is the second most visited pilgrimage site in the world.

One legend tells how Santiago (*Sant Iago*), or the Apostle St. James the Elder, visited Spain in his missionary journeys. The legend continues that after his death, his remains were brought back to Spain, where they are now kept in the Cathedral of Santiago de Compostela. Devotion to St. James flourished in Spain, and he soon became the Patron of the country.

In time, several pilgrimage routes from France, Portugal, and other parts of Spain were developed. Pilgrims would walk for months to reach Santiago. Along the *camino de Santiago*, monasteries, churches, and

inns were established to serve the flood of pilgrims, who could be identified by their long walking sticks and a scallop-edged conch shell fastened onto their hats or cloaks.

Today, once a pilgrim arrives in the Cathedral at Santiago, he or she will embrace the statue of St. James, which sits behind the altar, and at noon there will be a pilgrim's Mass. One of the distinctive features of this Mass is the use of the *botafumeiro*, a large censer several feet tall, which swings from the ceiling, billowing incense throughout the cathedral.

What makes Santiago unique among pilgrimage sites today is that pilgrims still make the journey on foot. Pilgrims making the journey will carry a passport that is stamped by various designated churches along the *camino* to prove the authenticity of their pilgrimage. In this manner, millions of people walk to Santiago in pilgrimage each and every year.

The *botafumeiro*, a large censer several feet tall, which swings from the ceiling, billowing incense throughout the cathedral.

Using Sacramentals at Home

The home is the "Domestic Church," and as such, there are many sacramentals that can dispose individuals and family members to receive God's grace. These might include such practices as displaying images of Jesus and Our Lady in the home, setting up a Nativity set at Christmas, or using an Advent wreath.

It is an excellent custom to keep holy water at home to bless oneself when entering or leaving and especially before going to bed. Prayers before meals, bedtime prayers, and family devotions such as the Liturgy of the Hours, the Holy Rosary, and Scripture reading are excellent ways to foster spirituality in family life.

Many families also keep certain devotions during the important liturgical seasons in the Church calendar such as Advent, Christmas, Lent, and Easter. Sacramentals are a wonderful way to keep the family focused on Jesus Christ and to inspire a living faith in the home.

The Ascension of Christ by Giotto. "Having united the disciples to himself, Jesus sends them into the world to proclaim his message and carry on his ministry." —Avery Cardinal Dulles, excerpt from *First Things, The Way We Worship*

CONCLUSION

As the expression of public worship established by Christ in the Christian community and the means by which the sacraments are celebrated, the liturgy is an extension of the priestly mission of Jesus Christ. It is the way in which we, as a Church, pray and offer worship to God, entering into the life of the Blessed Trinity. Seated at the right hand of the Father, Christ is our eternal High Priest and spotless Lamb, who intercedes for us and reconciles us with God.

In the celebration of the liturgy of the Church, Jesus reaches out to touch our lives. He gives us the grace to come to him, asking only for our response in faith. Each time that we approach him in the sacraments, whether it is our new birth in Baptism, the reception of our daily bread in the Eucharist, or in the Anointing as we near death, we receive his loving touch, healing our wounded humanity.

> When God acts in history, he does not act alone, but makes use of human agency. Mary, Judas, Pilate, and Jesus in his humanity were involved in very different ways as instruments in bringing about God's supreme redemptive act. Tradition is Christic. Christ goes willingly to his death, surrendering himself for our redemption. Even before his betrayer turned him over to his enemies, Jesus gave himself to his disciples with his own hands. He really hands himself over under the appearances of bread and wine, broken and poured out for our salvation. He instructs the disciples to take, eat, and drink, thus completing the ritual transaction. Having united the disciples to himself, Jesus sends them into the world to proclaim his message and carry on his ministry.[28]

Throughout the history of the Church, the liturgies through which we experience this presence of God have diversified, developed, and matured. However, the significance of the sacraments has remained unchanged since the day they were instituted by Christ. From the crowds present on the day of Pentecost to the newborn baby baptized in the twenty-first century, the sacraments remain a real and actual encounter with Jesus Christ, the Son of God.

SUPPLEMENTARY READING

ST. JUSTIN MARTYR

In the writings of St. Justin Martyr (ca. AD 155), we see a description of the Eucharist celebration as it existed in the early Church:

> On the day we call the day of the sun, all who dwell in the city or country gather in the same place.
>
> The memoirs of the apostles and the writings of the prophets are read, as much as time permits.
>
> When the reader has finished, he who presides over those gathered admonishes and challenges them to imitate these beautiful things.
>
> Then we all rise together and offer prayers for ourselves...and for all others, wherever they may be, so that we may be found righteous by our life and actions, and faithful to the commandments, so as to obtain eternal salvation.
>
> When the prayers are concluded we exchange the kiss.
>
> Then someone brings bread and a cup of water and wine mixed together to him who presides over the brethren.
>
> He takes them and offers praise and glory to the Father of the universe, through the name of the Son and of the Holy Spirit and for a considerable time he gives thanks (in Greek: *eucharistian*) that we have been judged worthy of these gifts.
>
> When he has concluded the prayers and thanksgivings, all present give voice to an acclamation by saying: 'Amen.'
>
> When he who presides has given thanks and the people have responded, those whom we call deacons give those present the "eucharisted" bread, wine, and water and take them to those who are absent. (CCC 1345)

ST. JUSTIN MARTYR
ca. AD 100–165

The Eucharist by Jan Davidszoon de Heem.

VOCABULARY

ADORATION
Worship. This is the humble acknowledgment by human beings that they are creatures of the thrice-holy Creator. By obeying the First Commandment, people acknowledge and respond to the revelation of the glory and power of God.

EASTERN RITES
Practices, traditions, disciplines, and liturgical expressions used in the Catholic Churches in communion with the Pope, but other than the Latin Rite.

GENUFLECT
To kneel down on one knee as a sign of reverence to the Blessed Sacrament when entering or leaving a church or when passing in front of the tabernacle.

HEAVENLY LITURGY
The adoration rendered Almighty God by the angels and saints in Heaven, most especially through the eternal pleading of Christ the High Priest and the perpetual offering of His once-for-all sacrifice of Himself to His heavenly Father.

HOLY WATER
Blessed water; a sacramental whose use is a reminder of Baptism and a means of sanctification.

ICON
A two-dimensional stylized painting or mosaic of Christ, the Virgin Mary, an angel, or one of the saints. This is used as an aid for Christian acts of piety. The artistic style of icons reflects a mystical beauty of Christ the Savior and the saints. An icon, by virtue of what is represented, is an invitation to prayer.

ICONOSTASIS
A screen of icons used in the Eastern Churches which separates the nave from the sanctuary and the altar.

IMAGES
Representations such as statues or pictures.

LATIN RITE
The portion of the Catholic Church that follows the disciplines of the Diocese of Rome, especially regarding the Sacred Liturgy. This rite is called Latin because that has been its official language since the fourth century. Most of the world's Catholics belong to the Latin Rite, but twenty-two other rites also exist in communion with the Bishop of Rome, the Pope.

LITURGY OF THE HOURS (Divine Office)
Also called the Divine Office, or Breviary, it is the official prayer of the Church that allows the faithful to pray throughout the day with Psalms and other biblical readings.

LORD'S DAY (The)
Sunday; the principal day of the week for Christian worship, also known as the Lord's Day. Each Sunday Mass commemorates the Resurrection of Christ on Easter Sunday and is a reminder of the first day of creation for those who have become a "new creation in Christ." Canon Law stipulates that Catholics are to attend Mass on Sunday and to abstain from any labors that impede Sunday worship or detract from the joy proper to the day.

PILGRIMAGE
A journey to a sacred place undertaken as an act of religious devotion. The purpose may be to venerate a certain saint or to ask some spiritual favor, beg for a physical cure, perform an act of penance, express thanks, or fulfill a promise.

RELIC
The earthly remains or personal items of a saint. Usually these are fragments of bone, which are venerated as sacred objects that give us on earth a connection with those who have gone to Heaven.

SABBATH
The Sabbath—or seventh—day on which God rested after the work of the six days of creation was completed. In honor of Christ's Resurrection, Sunday must include rest from labor and the worship of God as required by the Third Commandment.

VOCABULARY Continued

SACRAMENTAL
An action or object that disposes us to God's grace.

SACRAMENTARY
A liturgical book that contains the prayers of the Mass for the use of the priest at the altar, along with instructions for the celebrant of the liturgy. Scripture readings are contained in a book called a Lectionary.

SACRED OBJECTS
Items used to foster the virtue of religion and a life of devotion.

SCAPULAR
Refers either to part of the habit of a man or woman in religious vows, or to the smaller version worn by lay people who strive to follow the holy order of a given religious order or community.

STATIONS OF THE CROSS
The pious practice of meditating upon Jesus' Passion, Death, and Resurrection. This may be done by either walking the *Via Dolorosa* in Jerusalem or passing from one image depicting Jesus' sufferings to the next in a church.

VENERATION
Showing devotion and respect to Our Blessed Mother and the saints who were viewed as faithful witnesses to the Faith, or to things set aside for the worship of God (for example, the Book of Gospels). This is distinct from adoration or worship, which is due to God alone.

Station of the Cross, No. 7: Jesus Falls The Second Time.

STUDY QUESTIONS

1. What is the meaning of the word "liturgy"? What did that word describe in the Old Testament?

2. What is the name of the rite used by most Catholics living in the West? What are the names of other rites celebrated in the Catholic Church?

3. Briefly explain how we received the liturgies that are used in the Church today.

4. Explain the different ways in which Christ is present in the liturgy.

5. What is meant by the term "heavenly liturgy"?

6. In what way can those who participate in the Church's liturgies be said to be participants in the heavenly liturgy?

7. What is an *iconostasis*, and what does it symbolize in the Eastern liturgy?

8. What is the origin of observing the Sabbath as a day of rest and worship?

9. What did the first Christians do on the Sabbath? On Sunday?

10. Explain why the day of worship was changed to Sunday.

11. What is the Liturgy of the Hours, and what is its origin?

12. What is the symbolism of a church building?

13. List ten things found in a typical Catholic church and explain their significance.

14. List three gestures used in worship, and explain their significance. In your own words, explain how worship would be different without these gestures.

15. What is a sacramental?

16. In regard to grace, how is a sacramental different from a sacrament?

17. What does holy water represent, and why is it used when entering a Church?

18. What statues did the Law of Moses require to be placed in the Temple? Why was God not depicted in pictorial form?

19. What enabled Christians to depict the human image of God?

20. What evidence is there that religious images were important to the early Christians?

21. What is the difference between adoration and veneration?

22. What did the Second Council of Nicaea state about the use of religious images?

23. What is the origin of the Rosary? What was the role of St. Dominic in promoting devotion to the Rosary?

24. What is the origin of the Stations of the Cross? How was it practiced in the first centuries of Christianity?

25. Why were the Stations of the Cross eventually erected in parish churches?

26. What is the relationship between the Franciscans and the Stations of the Cross?

27. What was the practice of the early Church in regard to relics?

28. Why are Catholic churches often given the names of saints?

29. What is the significance of relics in the Church today?

30. What is the purpose or value of wearing medals?

31. What is the origin of the scapular? What does it signify when worn by laypersons?

32. What event popularized the wearing of the Brown Scapular of Mount Carmel?

33. Define pilgrimage and procession. What is the purpose of making a pilgrimage? Give one example of a pilgrimage.

34. List three domestic sacramentals and explain how each helps the family to be more centered on Christ.

PRACTICAL EXERCISES

1. Plan to arrive at church five minutes early each Sunday. Before the celebration of Mass begins, read the Sunday readings. When they are read during Mass, ask the Holy Spirit to help you understand how Jesus wants you to apply them in your life this week.

2. List four things that we can do to prepare for receiving the Eucharist. Do at least one of them this Sunday.

3. Either individually or as a class, say a Rosary for your intentions—the Church, your parish, your family, school, friends, souls in purgatory, an end to abortion, peace in our world, etc.

FROM THE CATECHISM

1069 The word "liturgy" originally meant a "public work" or a "service in the name of/on behalf of the people." In Christian tradition it means the participation of the People of God in "the work of God."[29] Through the liturgy Christ, our redeemer and high priest, continues the work of our redemption in, with, and through his Church.

1070 In the New Testament the word "liturgy" refers not only to the celebration of divine worship but also to the proclamation of the Gospel and to active charity.[30] In all of these situations it is a question of the service of God and neighbor. In a liturgical celebration the Church is servant in the image of her Lord, the one *"leitourgos"*;[31] she shares in Christ's priesthood (worship), which is both prophetic (proclamation) and kingly (service of charity):

The liturgy then is rightly seen as an exercise of the priestly office of Jesus Christ. It involves the presentation of man's sanctification under the guise of signs perceptible by the senses and its accomplishment in ways appropriate to each of these signs. In it full public worship is performed by the Mystical Body of Jesus Christ, that is, by the Head and his members. From this it follows that every liturgical celebration, because it is an action of Christ the priest and of his Body which is the Church, is a sacred action surpassing all others. No other action of the Church can equal its efficacy by the same title and to the same degree.[32]

1071 As the work of Christ liturgy is also an action of his *Church*. It makes the Church present and manifests her as the visible sign of the communion in Christ between God and men. It engages the faithful in the new life of the community and involves the "conscious, active, and fruitful participation" of everyone.[33]

1088 "To accomplish so great a work"—the dispensation or communication of his work of salvation—"Christ is always present in his Church, especially in her liturgical celebrations. He is present in the Sacrifice of the Mass not only in the person of his minister, 'the same now offering, through the ministry of priests, who formerly offered himself on the cross,' but especially in the Eucharistic species. By his power he is present in the sacraments so that when anybody baptizes, it is really Christ himself who baptizes. He is present in his word since it is he himself who speaks when the holy Scriptures are read in the Church. Lastly, he is present when the Church prays and sings, for he has promised 'where two or three are gathered together in my name there am I in the midst of them.'"[34]

1090 "In the earthly liturgy we share in a foretaste of that heavenly liturgy which is celebrated in the Holy City of Jerusalem toward which we journey as pilgrims, where Christ is sitting at the right hand of God, Minister of the sanctuary and of the true tabernacle. With all the warriors of the heavenly army we sing

FROM THE CATECHISM Continued

a hymn of glory to the Lord; venerating the memory of the saints, we hope for some part and fellowship with them; we eagerly await the Savior, our Lord Jesus Christ, until he, our life, shall appear and we too will appear with him in glory."[35]

1097 In the *liturgy of the New Covenant* every liturgical action, especially the celebration of the Eucharist and the sacraments, is an encounter between Christ and the Church. The liturgical assembly derives its unity from the "communion of the Holy Spirit" who gathers the children of God into the one Body of Christ. This assembly transcends racial, cultural, social—indeed, all human affinities.

1108 In every liturgical action the Holy Spirit is sent in order to bring us into communion with Christ and so to form his Body. The Holy Spirit is like the sap of the Father's vine which bears fruit on its branches.[36] The most intimate cooperation of the Holy Spirit and the Church is achieved in the liturgy. The Spirit, who is the Spirit of communion, abides indefectibly in the Church. For this reason the Church is the great sacrament of divine communion which gathers God's scattered children together. Communion with the Holy Trinity and fraternal communion are inseparably the fruit of the Spirit in the liturgy.[37]

1670 Sacramentals do not confer the grace of the Holy Spirit in the way that the sacraments do, but by the Church's prayer, they prepare us to receive grace and dispose us to cooperate with it. "For well-disposed members of the faithful, the liturgy of the sacraments and sacramentals sanctifies almost every event of their lives with the divine grace which flows from the Paschal mystery of the Passion, Death, and Resurrection of Christ. From this source all sacraments and sacramentals draw their power. There is scarcely any proper use of material things which cannot be thus directed toward the sanctification of men and the praise of God."[38]

1678 Among the sacramentals blessings occupy an important place. They include both praise of God for his works and gifts, and the Church's intercession for men that they may be able to use God's gifts according to the spirit of the Gospel.

ENDNOTES – CHAPTER EIGHT

1. CCC 1112.
2. Jn 20:23.
3. 1 Cor 11:24-25.
4. Jn 1:1.
5. Mt 18:20.
6. Cf. Mt 25:40.
7. Ex 20:8.
8. Cf. Gn 2:2-3.
9. Cf. Acts 20:7-12.
10. Cf. CIC, 1247.
11. Cf. CIC, cann. 1246-1248; CCEO, can. 880 § 3, 881 §§ 1, 2, 4.
12. 1 Pt 1:3.
13. Cf. CCC 491.
14. CIC, 1246.
15. Cf. CCC 1179; 1 Pt 2:4-5.
16. Cf. CCC 1181.
17. Cf. CCC 1186.
18. USCCB, Canon 964 § 2 – Place of the Celebration of the Sacrament of Reconciliation, October 20, 2000.
19. Cf. CCC 1189.
20. Cf. Rev 7:4, 9:4, 14:1.
21. Cf. Ez 9:4.
22. Avery Dulles, *First Things, The Way We Worship* (1997).
23. CCC 1174.
24. Cf. Ps 119:164.
25. *SC* 60; cf. CIC, can. 1166; CCEO, can. 867.
26. *SC* 61.
27. Cf. Ex 25:18-21.
28. Avery Dulles, *First Things, The Way We Worship* (1997).
29. Cf. Jn 17:4.
30. Cf. Lk 1:23; Acts 13:2; Rom 15:16, 27; 2 Cor 9:12; Phil 2:14-17, 25, 30.
31. Cf. Heb 8:2, 6.
32. *SC* 7 § 2-3.
33. *SC* 11.
34. *SC* 7; Mt 18:20.
35. *SC* 8; cf. *LG* 50.
36. Cf. Jn 15:1-17; Gal 5:22.
37. Cf. 1 Jn 1:3-7.
38. *SC* 61.

ART AND PHOTO CREDITS

Cover

The Crucifixion, Simone Martini; Koninklijk Museum voor Schone Kunsten, Antwerp, Belgium

Front Pages

iii   *See* Cover Credit
iv   *Baptism of Christ*, Piero della Francesca; National Gallery, London
v   bottom left: *The Crucifixion*, Bernardo Daddi; Museo Horne, Florence, Italy; top right: *See* Page 1 Credit
vi   top left: *See* Page 25 Credit; top right: *See* Page 51 Credit
vii   top left: *See* Page 73 Credit; top right: *See* Page 105 Credit
viii top left: *See* Page 131 Credit; top right: *See* Page 149 Credit
ix   top left: *See* Page 179 Credit; top right: *See* Page 207 Credit
xi   *Jesus Christ and the Eucharist*, Juan de Juanes; Museo del Prado, Madrid, Spain; Archivo Oronoz
xii   *World Youth Day, Palm Sunday*, April 5, 2009, St. Peter's Square; ©L'Osservatore Romano

Introduction

1   *The Saviour*, Joos van Cleve; Museo de Santa Cruz, Toledo, Spain; Archivo Oronoz
3   *God Creates Man*, Michelangelo; Sistine Chapel, Vatican
4   *Adam and Eve in the Garden of Eden*, Jan Brueghel the Elder; Royal Collection, Windsor, England
5   *The Three Angels Appearing to Abraham*, Giovanni Battista Tiepolo; Palazzo Patriarcale, Udine, Italy
6   *The Annunciation*, Fra Angelico; Museo del Prado, Madrid, Spain; Archivo Oronoz
8   *Institution of the Eucharist*, Nicolas Poussin; Musee du Louvre, Paris, France
9   *Sacred Chrism Oils Blessed at Holy Week Celebration* (detail); Sts. Simon and Jude Cathedral, Phoenix Diocese; The Catholic Sun, staff photographer
10   *Sacrament of Baptism*, Pietro Longhi; Fondazione Querini Stampalia, Venice, Italy
11   *St. Francis Receiving the Stigmata*, El Greco; Private Collection, Madrid, Spain; Archivo Oronoz
12   *God, the Eternal Father*, Giovanni Francesco Barbieri Guercino; Sabauda Gallery, Turin, Italy
13   *Confirmation*; St. Paul the Apostle Catholic Church; Midwest Theological Forum Archives
14   *Baptism*; Wojciech Dubis, photographer; Midwest Theological Forum Archives
15   *Sacrarium*; Midwest Theological Forum Archives
16   *Confirmation*; Sts. Simon and Jude Cathedral, Phoenix Diocese; The Catholic Sun, staff photographer
17   *Chrism Mass*; Julie Koenig, photographer; Midwest Theological Forum Archives
18   *The Virgin Cardiotissa*, Angelos Akotantos; Byzantine And Christian Museum, Athens, Greece
19   *Bl. Otto Neururer*; Midwest Theological Forum Archives
22   *The Last Communion of St. Joseph of Calasanz*, Goya; Escuelas Pias de San Anton, Madrid, Spain

Chapter 1

25   *The Baptism of Christ*, Juan Fernandez de Navarrete; Museo del Prado, Madrid, Spain
27   *The Great Flood*, Bonaventura Peeters; Private Collection
28   *Moses Drawing Water From the Rock*, Tintoretto; Scuola Grande di San Rocco, Venice, Italy
29   *St. John the Baptist*, El Greco; Fine Arts Museums of San Francisco, San Francisco
30   top right: *The Presentation of Christ*, Melchior Broederlam; Musee des Beaux-Arts, Dijon, France
      bottom left: *Appearance on the Mountain of Galilee*, Duccio di Buoninsegna; Museo dell'Opera del Duomo, Siena, Italy
31   *The Resurrection of Christ*, Paolo Veronese; Gemaldegalerie, Dresden, Germany
32   *The Baptism of Christ*, Annibale Carracci; San Gregorio, Bologna, Italy
33   *Baptism*; St. Thomas the Apostle Church, Naperville, Illinois; Photo courtesy of Debbie Snyder
34   *Expulsion of Adam and Eve*, Aureliano Milani; Private Collection
35   *St. Peter Baptizes the Neophytes*, Masaccio; Cappella Brancacci, Santa Maria del Carmine, Florence, Italy
36   *Pope St. John Paul II Baptizing*; Photo courtesy of Grzegorz Galazka
38   *Baptism*; Wojciech Dubis, photographer; Midwest Theological Forum Archives
39   left: *Center Dome*; St. Joseph the Betrothed Ukrainian Greek Catholic Church, Chicago; ©2008, Jeremy Atherton, photographer
      right: *Eastern Rite Crucifix*; AG Archives
41   *St. Philip Baptizing the Ethiopian*, Rembrandt; Private Collection
43   *St. Francis Xavier*, Elias Salaverra; Javier Castillo Church, Navarra, Spain; Archivo Oronoz
48   *Disputation of the Holy Sacrament* (detail), Raphael; Stanza della Segnatura, Palazzi Pontifici, Vatican
50   *Baptism of Christ*, Giovanni Bellini; Santa Corona, Vicenza, Italy

Chapter 2

51   *The Descent of the Holy Ghost*, Titian; Santa Maria della Salute, Venice, Italy
53   *The Tree of Jesse*; Midwest Theological Forum Archives
54   *Pentecost*, Francisco Zurbaran; Cadiz Museum, Cadiz, Spain; Archivo Oronoz

ART AND PHOTO CREDITS

55 *St. Peter and St. John Laying Their Hands Upon the People*; Book of Hours Illustration, Flanders ca. 1484-1529; MS 7, f. 27r, Syracuse University Library, Department of Special Collections

56 *Christ Carrying the Cross*, Giovanni Battista Tiepolo; Sant'Alvise, Venice, Italy

59 *Bl. Teresa*; India, 1988; Evert Odekerken, photographer

60 *The Holy Trinity*, Hendrick van Balen; Sint-Jacobskerk, Antwerp, Belgium

61 *Sacred Chrism Oils Blessed at Holy Week Celebration*; Sts. Simon and Jude Cathedral, Phoenix Diocese; The Catholic Sun, staff photographer

62 *Confirmation*; St. Paul the Apostle Catholic Church; Midwest Theological Forum Archives

63 *St. Peter Preaching*, Masolino da Panicale; Cappella Brancacci, Santa Maria del Carmine, Florence, Italy

65 *Pentecost*, Taddeo Gaddi; Staatliche Museen, Berlin, Italy

66 *Ascension of Christ*, Garofalo; Galleria Nazionale d'Arte Antica, Rome, Italy

67 left: *St. Therese of Lisieux*, age 15; AG Archives; Public Domain
   right: *St. Therese of Lisieux*, 1895; AG Archives; Public Domain

68 *God Inviting Christ to Sit on the Throne at His Right Hand*, Pieter de Grebber; Museum Catharijneconvent, Utrecht, Netherlands

69 *Pentecost*, Book of Hours Illustration; France ca. 1450; MS 3, f. 50r Syracuse University Library, Department of Special Collections

Chapter 3

73 *The Last Supper*, Juan de Juanes; Museo del Prado, Madrid, Spain

75 *The Last Supper*, Otto van Veen; Academia de San Fernando, Madrid, Spain; Archivo Oronoz

76 *Christ in the Garden of Gethsemane*, Sebastiano Conca; Pinacoteca, Vatican

77 *Jesus on the Cross*, Rembrandt; Parish Church, Le Mas d'Agenais, France

78 *The Miracle of the Loaves and Fishes*, Lambert Lombard; Rockox House, Antwerp, Belgium

80 *The Emmaus Disciples*, Abraham Bloemaert; Musees Royaux des Beaux-Arts, Brussels, Belgium

81 Northridge Preparatory School, Niles, Illinois; Julie Koenig, photographer; Midwest Theological Forum Archives

82 left: *The Second Tabernacle*; High Altar, Church of St. Francis, Lanciano, Italy; Public Domain
   right: *Monstrance and Crystal Chalice* containing the Miracle of Lanciano; Church of St. Francis, Lanciano, Italy; AG Archives; Public Domain

83 *The Ghent Altarpiece: Adoration of the Lamb*, Jan van Eyck; Cathedral of St. Bavo, Ghent, Belgium

84 *The Last Supper*; Midwest Theological Forum Archives

85 *Crucifixion*, Nardo di Cione; Galleria degli Uffizi, Florence, Italy

86 left: *Agate Cup*, Holy Chalice of Valencia; Cathedral of Valencia, Spain; www.catedraldevalencia.es
   right: *Pope Benedict XVI Celebrates the Eucharist*, July 2006, with the Holy Chalice of Valencia; www.catedraldevalencia.es

87 *The Antioch Chalice*; Metropolitan Museum of Art

88 St. Mary of the Angels Church, Chicago, Illinois; Julie Koenig, photographer; Midwest Theological Forum Archives

89 St. Mary of the Angels Church, Chicago, Illinois; Julie Koenig, photographer; Midwest Theological Forum Archives

90 St. Mary of the Angels Church, Chicago, Illinois; Julie Koenig, photographer; Midwest Theological Forum Archives

91 St. Mary of the Angels Church, Chicago, Illinois; Julie Koenig, photographer; Midwest Theological Forum Archives

92 left: *The Trinity*, Russian Icon, Andrei Rublev, ca. 1410; Tretyakov Gallery, Moscow, Russia
   right: *His Excellence Bishop Jan Babjak SJ Celebrating Mass*; St. John the Baptist Cathedral, Presov, Slovakia; AG Archives

93 Willows Academy, Des Plaines, Illinois; Julie Koenig, photographer; Midwest Theological Forum Archives

95 *Eucharistic Procession*; 2005 Southeastern Eucharistic Congress, Charlotte, North Carolina; Public Domain

96 *The Eucharist* (detail), Fra Angelico; Monastery of San Marco, Florence, Italy

97 *St. Paul*, Russian Icon, Andrei Rublev; Tretyakov Gallery, Moscow, Russia

98 *First Communion*; Wojciech Dubis, photographer; Midwest Theological Forum Archives

99 *Pope St. Pius X*; Vatican Embassy, Madrid, Spain; Archivo Oronoz

Chapter 4

105 *The Return of the Prodigal Son*, Rembrandt; The Hermitage, St. Petersburg, Russia

107 *The Return of the Prodigal Son* (detail), Bartolome Esteban Murillo; National Gallery of Art, Washington, D.C.

108 *Original Sin*, Michiel van Coxcie; Kunsthistorisches Museum, Vienna, Austria

109 *Christ Healing the Paralytic*, Giovanni Antonio Pellegrini; Museum of Fine Arts, Budapest, Hungary

110 left: *St. Peter Holding the Key of the Paradise*, Pierre Puget; Parish Church, Grand-Camp, France
    right: *Healing of the Cripple and Raising of Tabatha* (left view), Masolino da Panicale; Cappella Brancacci, Santa Maria del Carmine, Florence, Italy

111 *St. Augustine*, Sandro Botticelli; Ognissanti, Florence, Italy

112 *St. Patrick*, Holy Card (detail); AG Archives

113 *Dome of St. Peter's Basilica*; Corbis Stock Image

114 *The Creation and the Expulsion from the Paradise*, Giovanni di Paolo; Metropolitan Museum of Art, New York

115 *Creation of the Animals*, Raphael; Raphael's Loggia, Palazzi Pontifici, Vatican

116 *Creation of the Sun, Moon, and Planets*; Michelangelo; Sistine Chapel, Vatican

ART AND PHOTO CREDITS

117 *Cain and Abel*, Pietro Novelli; Galleria Nazionale d'Arte Antica, Rome, Italy
118 Willows Academy, Des Plaines, Illinois; Julie Koenig, photographer; Midwest Theological Forum Archives
120 Julie Koenig, photographer; Midwest Theological Forum Archives
121 *St. John Nepomucene*, Stained Glass; St. Stanislaus Catholic Church, Warsaw, North Dakota; Stephanie Walker, photographer; AG Archives
122 top: *Altar Cross*, Gian Lorenzo Bernini; Treasury of San Pietro, Vatican
    bottom: *Rosary*; Julie Koenig, photographer; Midwest Theological Forum Archives
124 *St. John Nepomucene*; Daniel Greef, photographer
126 Julie Koenig, photographer; Midwest Theological Forum Archives
130 *The Expulsion of Adam and Eve*, Domenichino; Musee des Beaux-Arts, Grenoble, France

Chapter 5

131 *St. Paul Healing the Cripple at Lystra*, Karel Dujardin; Rijksmuseum, Amsterdam, Netherlands
133 *Healing the Blind Man*, Carl H. Bloch; Frederiksborg Palace Chapel, Denmark
134 *Healing of the Blind Man*, Duccio di Buoninsegna; National Gallery, London, England
135 *Torchlight Marian Procession*, August 15, 2004; Sanctuary of Our Lady of Lourdes, Pierre Vincent, photographer; AG Archives
136 *The Raising of Lazarus*, Rembrandt; Los Angeles County Museum of Art, Los Angeles
137 *Christ Healing the Leper* (detail from *Sermon on the Mount*), Cosimo Rosselli; Sistine Chapel, Vatican
138 *Anointing the Sick*, Vicente Carducho; Aranjuez Palacio Real, Madrid, Spain; Archivo Oronoz
139 *Apostle James the Greater*, Antonio Veneziano; Staatliche Museen, Berlin, Germany
140 Photo courtesy of Fr. Peter Clark; Lansing, Michigan Diocese; AG Archives
143 left: *Bl. Teresa*; Missionaries of Charity; AG Archives
    right: *Bl. Teresa*; Shishu Bavan 1970; Missionaries of Charity; AG Archives
144 left: *Christ Carrying the Cross*, Sebastiano del Piombo; Museum of Fine Arts, Budapest, Hungary
    right: *Cardinal Joseph Bernadin*; Cincinnati Enquirer, Michael E. Keating, photographer; AG Archives
145 *Jacques Fesch*; www.annball.com/books/look2.shtml
147 *Christ Healing the Blind Man*, Eustache Le Sueur; Schloss Sanssouci, Berlin, Germany

Chapter 6

149 *The Charity of Fra Martin of Vizcaya*; Guadalupe Monastery, Spain; Archivo Oronoz
151 *Celebration of the Sacrament of Holy Orders*; Photo courtesy of Fr. Marty Miller; Midwest Theological Forum Archives
152 *Calling of the Apostles Peter and Andrew*, Lorenzo Veneziano; Staatliche Museen, Berlin, Germany
153 *The Sacrament of Ordination*, Nicolas Poussin; Collection of the Duke of Rutland, Belvoir Castle, England
154 *St. Peter Consecrates Stephen as Deacon* (detail), Fra Angelico; Cappella Niccolina, Palazzi Pontifici, Vatican
155 *Communion of the Apostles*, Luca Signorelli; Museo Diocesano, Cortona, Italy
156 *Madonna and Sts. Clement and Just* (detail), Master of the Castello Nativity; Museum of the Cathedral, Prato, Italy
157 left: *Martyrdom of St. Ignatius*; AG Archives
    right: *St. Polycarp Icon*; Nicholas Papas, iconographer, Greensburg, Pennsylvania; Midwest Theological Forum Archives
158 *Appearance Behind Locked Doors*, Duccio di Buoninsegna; Museo dell'Opera del Duomo, Siena, Italy
160 *2004 Diaconate Ordination Liturgy*, 2004; Cathedral of Our Lady of the Angels, Los Angeles; Photo by Rick Flynn, Photo owned by Eric Stoltz; AG Archives
161 top left: *Book of Gospels*; Midwest Theological Forum Archives
    top right: *Deacon Wearing Dalmatic*; Eric Stoltz, photographer; AG Archives
162 Willows Academy, Des Plaines, Illinois; Julie Koenig, photographer; Midwest Theological Forum Archives
163 left to right: *Chalice and Paten*, Granda Liturgical Arts; *Stole*, Julie Koenig, photographer; Midwest Theological Forum Archives; *Chasuble*, Granda Liturgical Arts
164 *Bishop*; Midwest Theological Forum Archives
165 left: *Bishop Gerhard Ludwig Müller*; Christmas Night Mass at Regensburg Cathedral, Regensburg, Germany, December 24, 2006; Dr. Meierhofer, photographer; AG Archives
    right: *Bishop's Chair*; Basilica of St. John Lateran, Rome, Italy; Ernie Bello, photographer; AG Archives
166 *Celebration of the Sacrament of Holy Orders*; Sts. Simon and Jude Cathedral, Phoenix Diocese; The Catholic Sun, staff photographer
167 left: Willows Academy, Des Plaines, Illinois; right: Andrean High School, Gary, Indiana; Julie Koenig, photographer; Midwest Theological Forum Archives
168 *St. Francis in Prayer Before the Crucifix*, El Greco; Museo de Bellas Artes, Bilbao, Spain
169 *Resurrection of Christ and Women at the Tomb*, Fra Angelico; Convento di San Marco, Florence, Italy
170 *Calling of the Apostles*, Domenico Ghirlandaio; Sistine Chapel, Vatican
171 *Pope St. John Paul II*, Midwest Theological Forum Archives
175 *Celebration of the Sacrament of Holy Orders*; Photo courtesy of Fr. Marty Miller; Midwest Theological Forum Archives
176 *Celebration of the Sacrament of Holy Orders, St. Peter's Basilica*; ©L'Osservatore Romano

ART AND PHOTO CREDITS

Chapter 7

179   *The Marriage of the Virgin*, El Greco; National Museum of Art of Romania, Bucharest, Hungary
181   *Scenes from the Life of the Virgin: 5*, Giotto; Cappella Scrovegni (Arena Chapel), Padua, Italy
182   Wojciech Dubis, photographer; Midwest Theological Forum Archives
183   Comstock Stock Image
184   Comstock Stock Image
185   Comstock Stock Image
186   *Becoming Family*, Fall 2001: 39; Jim Summaria, photographer; Midwest Theological Forum Archives
187   Rubberball Stock Image
188   Stockbyte Stock Image
189   *The Seven Sacraments: Marriage*, Nicolas Poussin; National Gallery of Scotland, Edinburgh, Scotland
191   *Wedding*; St. Mary's Catholic Church, Zach Hetrick, photographer; AG Archives
192   *Wedding*; St. Mary's Catholic Church, Zach Hetrick, photographer; AG Archives
193   Wojciech Dubis, photographer; Midwest Theological Forum Archives
194   Digital Vision Stock Image
195   Comstock Stock Image
196   Rubberball Stock Image
197   Rubberball Stock Image
198   *The Holy Family*, Claudio Coello; Museum of Fine Arts, Budapest, Hungary
199   Comstock Stock Image
200   Comstock Stock Image
201   left and right: *Georges and Pauline Vanier*; National Archives of Canada; AG Archives
202   Photodisc Stock Image
205   Midwest Theological Forum Archives; http://plweb.catholicnews.com/databases/photos/2001/07/24/paul2.jpg

Chapter 8

207   *Easter Mass at the Cathedral*, 2007; Puebla, Mexico; Wojciech Dubis, photographer; Midwest Theological Forum Archives
209   St. Mary of the Angels Church, Chicago, Illinois; Julie Koenig, photographer; Midwest Theological Forum Archives
210   *St. Ansanus Baptizing*, Giovanni di Paolo; Private Collection
211   *Iconostasis*; St. Joseph the Betrothed Ukrainian Greek Catholic Church, Chicago, Illinois; ©2008 Jeremy Atherton, photographer
212   *The Last Supper*, Benedetto Caliari; Basilica dei Santi Giovanni e Paolo, Venice, Italy
214   *St. Louis Cathedral*; Archdiocese of New Orleans, Louisiana, 2004; Rafal Konieczny, photographer; AG Archives
216   *Easter 2007*; Puebla, Mexico, Church East of the Cathedral; Wojciech Dubis, photographer; Midwest Theological Forum Archives
217   *Signs of the Cross*, left to right: Willows Academy, Des Plaines, Illinois, Julie Koenig, photographer; Detail of *Pantocrator Icon*, St. Nicholas of Myra Russian Orthodox Church, Amsterdam, Jim Forest, photographer; Detail of *Pantocrator Icon*, Aidan Hart, iconographer, Jim Forest, photographer; AG Archives
218   St. Mary of the Angels Church, Chicago, Illinois; Julie Koenig, photographer; Midwest Theological Forum Archives
219   *The Last Supper*, Page from the *Très Riches Heures du Duc de Berry* (ca. 1410); MS 65, Musee Conde, Chantilly, France
220-221   *Liturgical Vestments and Monstrance*, Granda Liturgical Arts
223   *Holy Water Vessel*; St. Louis cathedral, New Orleans, Louisiana; AG Archives
224   *Our Lady of Vladimer Icon*, Andrei Rublev; Tretyakov Gallery, Moscow, Russia
225   *Pope St. John Paul II*; Midwest Theological Forum Archives
226   *Station of the Cross, No. 8*; Sts. Peter and Paul Church, Naperville, Illinois; Julie Koenig, photographer; Midwest Theological Forum Archives
227   *The Tomb of St. Peter*; St. Peter's Basilica, Vatican; AG Archives
228   top left: *The Miraculous Medal*; Xhienne, photographer; AG Archives
        middle right: *Brown Scapular of Mount Carmel*; Sarah Sofia, photographer; AG Archives
        bottom left: *Our Lady of Mount Carmel*, Pietro Novelli; Museo Diocesano, Palermo, Italy
229   top: *Road to Santiago de Compostela*, 2005; Oula Lehtinen, photographer; AG Archives
        bottom right: *Feast of Corpus Christi Procession*, 2007; Lowicz, Poland; Magdalena Bryll Cefeida, photographer; AG Archives
230   left: *Cathedral of Santiago de Compostela*, Spain; Luis Miguel Bugallo Sanchez, photographer; AG Archives
        right: *The Botafumeiro* in the Cathedral of Santiago de Compostela, Spain, 2006; Georges Jansoone, photographer; AG Archives
231   *The Ascension of Christ*, Giotto; Cappella Scrovegni (Arena Chapel), Padua, Italy
232   top: *St. Justin Martyr Icon*; Jim Forest, photographer; AG Archives
        bottom: *Eucharist in Fruit Wreath*, Jan Davidszoon de Heem; Kunsthistorisches Museum, Vienna, Austria
234   *Station of the Cross, No. 7*; Sts. Peter and Paul Church, Naperville, Illinois; Julie Koenig, photographer; Midwest Theological Forum Archives

INDEX

INDEX